I BELIEVE IN THE HOLY SPIRIT

II

'He is Lord and Giver of Life'

Principal works by Yves Congar

Chrétiens désunis (1937): *Divided Christendom* (1939)
Esquisses du Mystère de l'Eglise (1941; 2nd ed. 1953): in *The Mystery of the Church* (1960)
Vraie et fausse réforme dans l'Eglise (1950)
Le Christ, Marie et l'Eglise (1952): *Christ, Our Lady and the Church* (1957)
Jalons pour une théologie du laïcat (1953): *Lay People in the Church* (1957)
Le Mystère du Temple (*Lectio divina* series; 1958): *The Mystery of the Temple* (1962)
Vaste monde, ma paroisse (1959): *The Wide World my Parish* (1961)
La Tradition et les traditions (2 vols, 1960, 1963): *Tradition and Traditions* (1966)
Les Voies du Dieu vivant (1962): *The Revelation of God* (1968) and *Faith and Spiritual Life* (1969)
La Foi et la Théologie (*Le mystère chrétien*, 1; 1962)
Sacerdoce et laïcat (1963): *Priest and Layman* (1967)/*A Gospel Priesthood* (1967) and *Christians Active in the World* (1968)
Sainte Eglise (1963)
La Tradition et la vie de l'Eglise (1963): *Tradition and the Life of the Church*/*The Meaning of Tradition* (1964)
Pour une Eglise servante et pauvre (1963): *Power and Poverty in the Church* (1964)
Chrétiens en dialogue (1964): *Dialogue between Christians* (1966)
Jésus-Christ, notre Médiateur, notre Seigneur (1965): *Jesus Christ* (1966)
Situation et tâches présentes de la théologie (1967)
L'Ecclésiologie du haut Moyen Age (1968)
L'Eglise de S. Augustin à l'époque moderne (*Histoire des Dogmes* series; 1970)
L'Eglise une, sainte, catholique, apostolique (*Mysterium Salutis*, 15; 1970)
Ministères et communion ecclésiale (1971)
Un peuple messianique. Salut et libération (1975)
Eglise catholique et France moderne (1978)
Je crois en l'Esprit Saint (3 vols, 1979, 1980): *I Believe in the Holy Spirit* (3 vols, 1983)

YVES M. J. CONGAR

I BELIEVE IN THE HOLY SPIRIT

VOLUME II

'He is Lord and Giver of Life'

TRANSLATED BY
DAVID SMITH

THE SEABURY PRESS
NEW YORK
•
GEOFFREY CHAPMAN
LONDON

To the Abbess
and the Sisters of Pradines

A Geoffrey Chapman book published by
Cassell Ltd.
1 Vincent Square, London SW1P 2PN

The Seabury Press
815 Second Avenue, New York, NY 10017

First published in French as *Je crois en l'Esprit Saint*, II: *Il est Seigneur et Il donne la vie*

English translation first published 1983

Typeset in VIP Times by
D. P. Media Limited, Hitchin, Hertfordshire

Printed and bound in Hungary

Library of Congress Cataloging in Publication Data

Congar, Yves, 1904–
I believe in the Holy Spirit.

Translation of: Je crois en l'Esprit Saint.
Contents: v. 1. The Holy Spirit in the "economy" — v. 2. "He is Lord and giver of life"—v. 3. The river of the water of life (Rev 22:1) flows in the East and in the West.
1. Holy Spirit. I. Title.
BT121.2.C59713 1983 231'.3 82–19420

Geoffrey Chapman:
ISBN 0 225 66354 6 (this volume)
0 225 66352 X (three-volume set)

The Seabury Press:
ISBN 0-8164-0535-2 (this volume)
0-8164-0540-9 (three-volume set)

CONTENTS

CONCLUSION

IN THE UNITY OF THE HOLY SPIRIT, ALL HONOUR AND GLORY

ABBREVIATIONS

AAS *Acta Apostolicae Sedis*
Anal. Greg. *Analecta Gregoriana*
Anal. S. Ord. Cist. *Analecta Sacri Ordinis Cisterciensis*
Arch. hist. doctr. litt. M. A. *Archives d'histoire doctrinale et littéraire du Moyen Age*
ASS *Acta Sanctae Sedis*
Bib *Biblica*
Bibl. Augustin. *Bibliothèque augustinienne*
BullThom *Bulletin thomiste*
CSEL *Corpus Scriptorum Ecclesiasticorum Latinorum*
DB *Dictionnaire de la Bible*
Doc. cath. *La documentation catholique*
DS H. Denzinger, rev. A. Schönmetzer, *Enchiridion Symbolorum*
DTC *Dictionnaire de théologie catholique*
ETL *Ephemerides Theologicae Lovanienses*
GCS *Griechische christliche Schriftsteller*
Greg *Gregorianum*
Jaffé P. Jaffé *et al.* (eds), *Regesta Pontificum Romanorum*
JTS *Journal of Theological Studies*
Mansi J. D. Mansi (ed.), *Sacrorum Conciliorum nova et amplissima Collectio*
M-D *La Maison-Dieu*
MGH *Monumenta Germaniae Historica*
MScRel *Mélanges de science religieuse*
NRT *Nouvelle Revue Théologique*
Or. Chr. Anal. *Orientalia christiana analecta*
Or. Chr. Period. *Orientalia christiana periodica*
PG Migne, *Patrologia Graeca*
PL Migne, *Patrologia Latina*
RAM *Revue d'ascétique et de mystique*
RB *Revue biblique*
RHE *Revue d'histoire ecclésiastique*
RHPR *Revue d'histoire et de philosophie religieuses*
RomQuart *Römische Quartalschrift*
RSPT *Revue des sciences philosophiques et théologiques*
RSR *Recherches de science religieuse*
RSV Revised Standard Version
RThom *Revue thomiste*
SC *Sources chrétiennes*
Schol *Scholastik*
ST *Summa Theologica*

TDNT G. Kittel and G. Friedrich (eds), *Theological Dictionary of the New Testament* (Eng. tr.)
ThSt *Theological Studies*
TQ *Theologische Quartalschrift*
TZ *Theologische Zeitschrift*
VS *La Vie spirituelle*
WA Luther, *Werke,* Weimar edition
ZKT *Zeitschrift für katholische Theologie*
ZNW *Zeitschrift für neutestamentliche Wissenschaft*

PART ONE

THE SPIRIT ANIMATES THE CHURCH

INTRODUCTION

In his first homily on Pentecost, John Chrysostom had this to say about the Holy Spirit. It forms a good introduction to what I have to say in this part of my work and draws attention to its traditional character.

> Where are those who blaspheme against the Spirit now? If he does not remit sins, then our reception of him in baptism is in vain. If, on the other hand, he does remit sins, then the heretics blaspheme against him in vain. If the Holy Spirit did not exist, we would not be able to say that Jesus is Lord, since 'no one can say "Jesus is Lord" except by the Holy Spirit' (1 Cor 12:3). If the Holy Spirit did not exist, we believers would not be able to pray to God, but we say in fact: 'Our Father, who art in heaven' (Mt 6:9). Just as we would not be able to call on our Lord, so too would we not be able to call God our Father. Who proves this? The Apostle, saying: 'Because you are sons God has sent the Spirit of his Son into our hearts, crying "Abba! Father!" '(Gal 4:6). That is why, when you call on the Father, you should remember that the Spirit must have touched your soul so that you would be judged worthy to call God by that name. If the Holy Spirit did not exist, the discourses about wisdom and knowledge would not be in the Church, since 'to one is given through the Spirit the utterance of wisdom and to another the utterance of knowledge according to the same Spirit' (1 Cor 12:8). If the Holy Spirit did not exist, there would not be pastors or teachers in the Church, since 'the Holy Spirit has made you guardians, to feed the Church of the Lord' (Acts 20:28). Do you see that this still takes place by the action of the Spirit? If the Holy Spirit did not exist in the one who is the father and teacher of us all, when he ascended to that holy throne and gave peace to all of you, you would not have been able to reply to him with one voice: 'And with your spirit'. That is why you are able to say these words not only when he ascends to the altar, but also when he converses with you or prays for you; and when he stands at that holy table and is on the point of offering that fearful sacrifice, it is then that you as initiated ones know that he does not touch the offerings before he has implored for you the grace of the Lord or before you have replied: 'And with your spirit'. This response reminds you that the one who is there does nothing by himself and that the gifts that are expected are in no way the works of man, but it is the grace of the Spirit that has descended on all of you that brings about this mystical sacrifice. There is no doubt that a man is present there, but it is God who acts through him. Do not therefore cling to what strikes your eyes, but think of grace which is invisible. There is nothing that comes from man in all the things that take place in the sanctuary. If the Spirit were not present, the Church would not form a consistent whole. The consistency of the Church manifests the presence of the Spirit (*De S. Pent. Hom.* 1, 4 (*PG* 50, 458–459)).

1
THE CHURCH IS MADE BY THE SPIRIT

However far we go back in the sequence of confessions of faith or creeds, we find the article on the Church linked to that on the Holy Spirit: 'I believe in the Holy Spirit, in the Holy Church, for the resurrection of the flesh'.[1] About 200 A.D., this deep unity was expressed in the following way by Tertullian: 'Since both the witness of faith and the guarantee of salvation have the safeguard of the three Persons, the reference to the Church is of necessity added. Where the three, the Father, the Son and the Holy Spirit, are, there too is the Church, which is the body of the three Persons.'[2] It is therefore not surprising to find that the First Council of Constantinople (381) added to the Nicene Creed, after the words 'and in the Holy Spirit': 'Lord and giver of life, who proceeds from the Father, who is co-adored and conglorified with the Father and the Son, who spoke through the prophets' and the article on the Church: 'One, holy, catholic and apostolic'.

Augustine, who did not know the text that was attributed to that Council, always linked the Church with the Holy Spirit, of whom the Church was the temple.[3] This was undoubtedly the meaning of the confession of apostolic and baptismal faith, with its Trinitarian structure. If, in other words, creation is attributed to the Father, then the redemption is the work of the Word made flesh and sanctification is the work of the Holy Spirit.[4] The third article includes the Church, baptism, the remission of sins, the communion of saints (both holy things, *sancta*, and holy people, *sancti-sanctae*), the resurrection and the life of the world to come.

In the West, however, the preposition *eis* or *in* has usually been omitted before *ecclesiam* and this fact has often been accorded a religious or theological significance. It is, in other words, possible to believe *in* God, to accept him as the end of one's life, but it is not possible to believe in the same way *in* the Church.[5] When the great Scholastic theologians, then, came to consider the formula 'Credo in Spiritum Sanctum . . . et in unam . . . Ecclesiam' in the Niceno-Constantinopolitan Creed, they provided the following commentary: I believe in the Holy Spirit, not only in himself, but as the one who makes the Church one, holy, catholic and apostolic. This is fundamentally the teaching of Alexander of Hales,[6] Albert the Great (*In III Sent*. d. 25, q. 2, a. 2, c), Peter of Tarantaise (*ibid*.), Thomas Aquinas,[7] Richard of

Mediavilla (*In III Sent*. d. 25, a. 1, q. 2) and others. This fine passage occurs, for example, in a treatise by Albert the Great:

> There is reference to 'the holy Church', but every article of faith is based on eternal and divine truth and not on created truth, since every creature is vain and no creature has firm truth. This article must therefore be traced back to the work of the Holy Spirit, that is, to 'I believe in the Holy Spirit', not in himself alone, as the previous article states, but I believe in him also as far as his work is concerned, which is to make the Church holy. He communicates that holiness in the sacraments, the virtues and the gifts that he distributes in order to bring holiness about, and finally in the miracles and the graces of a charismatic type (*et donis gratis datis*) such as wisdom, knowledge, faith, the discernment of spirits, healings, prophecy and everything that the Spirit gives in order to make the holiness of the Church manifest.[8]

The Church is undoubtedly an object of faith—we believe that it is one, holy, catholic and apostolic. We trace these attributes, however, back to their cause, which is divine and of the order of grace. The Catechism of the Council of Trent, as it is usually called, a text which does credit to its authors, unites these two aspects of belief and faith:

> It is necessary to believe that there is a Church that is one, holy and catholic. So far as the three Persons of the Trinity are concerned, the Father, the Son and the Holy Spirits, we believe in them in such a way that we place our faith *in* them. But, changing our way of speaking, we profess to believe the holy Church, and not *in* the holy Church. By this difference of expression, then, God, who is the author of all things, is distinguished from all his creatures and, in receiving all the precious good things that he has given to the Church, we refer them back to his divine goodness.[9]

What we *see* of the Church is everything that is made of the material of this world. This is what unbelievers, politicians and sociologists also see. But we *believe* that God acts in that Church according to the plan of his grace. The Church therefore is—as Jesus himself was[10]—both a terrestrial reality and part of history on the one hand, and the work of God, the 'mystery' that is only known to faith, on the other. God, however, works in what is terrestrial and historical in such a way that transcendence is presented in what is visible and offered to rational man's perception. The Church is the sign and at the same time the means of God's intervention in our world and our history. Apologetics has made its own use of this truth, and it is worth what it is worth: no more—but no less either. The four attributes listed in the Creed have been used in apologetics as 'marks' to make the Church known and to enable its truth to be discerned.

This course was followed with varying success for a long time in apologetics,[11] but I would prefer to discuss this question not at this level, but at the level of faith. There is no real opposition or even break between the two: faith in the Holy Spirit who makes the Church one, holy, catholic and apostolic is in fact faith in the fulfilment of God's promise *in the Church*, which, according to the Dogmatic Constitution on the Church, *Lumen Gentium*, promulgated by the Second Vatican Council, consists of 'a divine and a human element'. The same document also has this to say about the Church as a complex and concrete reality:

> Just as the assumed nature inseparably united to the divine Word serves him as a living instrument of salvation, so, in a similar way, does the communal structure of the Church serve Christ's Spirit, who vivifies it by way of building up the body (cf. Eph 4:16). This is the unique Church of Christ, which in the Creed we avow as one, holy, catholic and apostolic. After his resurrection our Saviour handed her over to Peter to be shepherded (Jn 21:17) (*Lumen Gentium*, 8).

The Church, then, is historical and visible and its 'founder' is Jesus, who is always living and active in it and is its lasting foundation. The Spirit gives life to the Church and enables it to grow as the Body of Christ. Both in its life and in its origin, the Church is the fruit of two 'divine missions', in the exact and very profound sense in which Thomas Aquinas uses this phrase. I propose to enlarge on this question in the rest of this chapter.

The 'Two Missions'
The Spirit as the Co-instituting Principle of the Church

'When the time had fully come, God sent forth his Son, born of a woman, born under the law, . . . so that we might receive adoption as sons' (Gal 4:4). There is ample evidence in all the gospels of the theme of the mission of the Son by God, but the gospel of John insists most firmly on this theme and places it in the mouth of Jesus himself (see Mt 10:40; Mk 9:37; 12:6; Lk 9:48; 10:16; Jn 3:17, 34; 5:37; 6:57; 7:28; 8:42; 10:36; 17:18; 20:21). In these texts and in those concerned with the sending of the Spirit, the two verbs *pempein* and *apostellein* are used more or less indiscriminately.[12]

'God has sent the Spirit of his Son into our hearts' (Gal 4:6). Jesus proclaims this sending in the gospel of John as having been brought about by the Father in his name (14:26) or even by him (15:26; 16:7; Lk 24:49). It will later be apparent that the Spirit is the Spirit of the Son, but at present we should note that he descended on Jesus at the time of his baptism—although the verb 'to send' is not used in this context—and that the heavenly voice declared at that time: 'Thou art my beloved Son' (Mk 1:11; Mt 3:17: 'This is my beloved Son'). The mission of the Spirit was also made manifest at Pentecost (Acts) and is seen in Paul's letters to be co-extensive with the life of the Church and of Christians.

The Scholastic theologians interpreted these data at great depth in a theme known as the 'divine missions'. Thomas Aquinas treated this theme as a link between his theology of God in himself and his theology of the activity of God placing a world outside himself and bringing men made in his own image back to himself.[13] I shall here consider two aspects of his working-out of this theme. The first is his idea of mission and the second the connection with the Trinitarian processions.

'Mission' presupposes a connection with the one who sends—the Father, who is the Principle without a beginning, sends, but cannot be sent—and a connection with those to whom the one sent is sent. This is so whether the one sent begins to be near or with those to whom he is sent, not having been there originally, or whether he comes there in an entirely new way, being already there. The Word, then, was already in the world from the beginning (Jn 1:10), but he also came into the world (1:11, 14). The Spirit was also already there (see Gen 1:2) and he also came.

The fact that the Word and the Spirit *come* does not mean that they move. It means that they make a creature exist in a new relationship with them. This means that the procession that situates them in the eternity of the Uni-Trinity culminates freely and effectively in a created effect. The human individuality brought about by the Spirit in Mary's womb was at the same time assumed by the Word, the Son, and began to exist through the Person of that Son.[14] This mission was visible because the Word, the Son, who was an expression of the being of God the Father (Heb 1:3), was a human appearance of God. It was not a mere theophany, but the personal and substantial reality of the Word made flesh: 'I came from the Father and have come into the world' (Jn 16:28).

There are, on the other hand, invisible missions of the Word in the effects of grace through which God expresses himself and makes himself known. In the same way, there are also invisible missions of the Spirit in the effects of grace by which God gives himself in order to make himself loved and to make us love all the things of his love: '*God's* love has been poured into our hearts through the Holy Spirit which has been given to us' (Rom 5:5).

The Church, as an organism of knowledge and love, is entirely dependent on these missions. It is the fruitfulness, outside God, of the Trinitarian processions. We *see* the Church in the manifestations of its ordained ministry, its worship, its assemblies, works and undertakings. We *believe* that the profound life of that great body, which is both scattered and one, is the culmination and the fruit, in the creature, of the very life of God, the Father, the Son and the Holy Spirit. Cyprian's statement on the Church as the 'people whose unity comes from the unity of the Father, the Son and the Holy Spirit',[15] which was taken up again by the Second Vatican Council, expresses the hidden reality that we affirm in faith. From the infinite diversity of mankind and the many different peoples, God, who is three times holy, gathers for himself and unites a people who form his people. This idea can also be extended to the authentic unity, holiness, catholicity and apostolicity that is sought and that exists in the ecumenical movement—insofar as this is God's, it is also dependent on the Trinity and is the fruit or the term, outside God, of the processions of the Word and the Spirit.

What are the visible missions of the Spirit? There are comings of the Spirit accompanied by tangible or visible signs which manifest those missions (or the Spirit himself). These include the wind, the dove, tongues of fire, miracles, speaking in tongues and various tangible or visible phenomena of the mystical life. The Holy Spirit is not substantially or existentially connected with these realities, which are only signs or manifestations of his coming, his activity and therefore his eternal procession. They may even be ambiguous. The manifestations at Pentecost (Acts 2:13) were misunderstood, and mystical phenomena have at least external parallels in the purely 'psychical' or 'carnal' order.

Irenaeus expressed the derivation of the Church from the two missions, that of the Word and that of the Breath, in a poetical manner in the image of the two hands of God. He applied this image especially to the fashioning of man in God's image—one is at once reminded here of the carving on the south portal of Chartres Cathedral—but this was only the beginning of the economy that the Father brought about 'according to his good pleasure' through his Word, the Son, and his Spirit, Wisdom.[16]

> God will be glorified in the work fashioned by him, when he has made it resemble and conform to his Son. For, by the hands of the Father, that is, through the Son and the Spirit, man is made into the image and likeness of God.[17]

> During all this time, man, fashioned in the beginning by the hands of God, I mean by the Son and the Spirit. . . .[18]

Irenaeus, that great and beloved writer, also showed the apostles as instituting and founding the Church by communicating to believers the Spirit that they had received from the Lord: 'That Holy Spirit that they had received from the Lord is shared among and distributed to believers; in this way they instituted and founded the Church'.[19] Towards the end of the fourth century, Didymus the Blind of Alexandria wrote that all progress in the truth was attributable to 'that divine and magnificent Spirit, the author, leader and promoter of the Church'.[20] This must mean that the Spirit did not come simply in order to animate an institution that was already fully determined in all its structures, but that he is really the 'co-instituting' principle. This is clear from countless data and formal declarations.

Suppose we begin with the sacraments. Christ gave to certain actions a signification of grace, but sacramental rites were determined by history. The thirteenth-century Franciscan theologians Alexander of Hales and Bonaventure attributed the definitive institution of the sacraments of confirmation, ordination, marriage and the anointing of the sick to the Holy Spirit, that is, to the active *inspiratio* of the Spirit in the Church and its councils.[21] This question preoccupied those Catholic theologians and apologists who had to reply to Luther's criticisms and who could find scriptural support for baptism, the Eucharist and penance alone. They thought that Christ had determined the communication of sacramental grace, but that the form taken by the sacramental signs was determined and even modified by the Church, subject to the guidance and inspiration of the Spirit.[22]

Is it not possible to say the same about forms of the ministry that comes from the apostles? If it is true that the Twelve were instituted by Jesus—with the co-operation of the Holy Spirit (Acts 1:2)—did the succession in their ministry not begin with the initiative of the Holy Spirit, at least in the historical form of a mono-episcopacy?[23] Neither Trent nor Vatican II attributed the institution of different degrees of the sacramental ministry to Jesus himself. In the actual naming and institution or ordination of ministers, it is clear that the Spirit intervenes. The New Testament bears witness to this in a way that suggests rather than states clearly (see Acts 13:1–3; 20:28; 1 Tim 1:18; 4:14; 2 Tim 1:6ff.). The testimony borne by history, on the other hand, is clear: the Spirit inspires the choice of ministers and enables them to exercise their function by encouraging the qualities required. Ordination is an imploration and a communication of the Holy Spirit. It is an anointing by the Spirit. It is noteworthy that, in the liturgy, the Holy Spirit is invoked especially in connection with the three sacraments conferring 'character', which give structure to the people of God, that is, baptism, confirmation and ordination.[24]

The difference that has sometimes been emphasized between instituted functions and phenomena of a 'charismatic' type is in accordance with certain historical facts. It is in the nature of things that there should be some tension between the two. There are examples of this at almost every period of history. It would be a very questionable undertaking to try to reduce this to a systematic opposition in principle. Such a position was favoured in history by an unavowedly confessional and polemical inspiration—when Catholics insisted emphatically on the substantial rather than on the functional, on the institutional and juridical rather than on the present reality and the freedom of grace, Protestants excluded all trace of 'pre-Catholicism' from the New Testament and set free charisms against the instituted ministry.[25]

This, however, is not biblically, historically or theologically of lasting value. Although not everyone possessing the gifts of the Spirit is instituted as a minister, those who are instituted do in fact possess such gifts. In this context, it is worth comparing Acts 6:3; 16:2 with the texts from Acts and the pastoral epistles cited above and 1 Cor 16:15–16 with 1 Thess 5:12–13. Clement of Alexandria made this comment on the activity of the apostle John: 'After the death of the tyrant, John left Patmos and returned to Ephesus. In response to their request, he visited the neighbouring people, on the one hand in order to appoint bishops among them and, on the other, in order to form and constitute churches and to choose as "clergy" those who had been pointed out by the Spirit.'[26] Those who presided at the Eucharist during the period of the apostles and the martyrs were charismatics, prophets or teachers (Acts 13:1–2; *Didache* IX and X; XIV, 1; XV, 2). There were also many believers who had confessed their faith under torture, and these similarly presided at the Eucharist.[27] Those in whom the qualities of men of God were found continued to be ordained.[28] Scholastic theologians described the episcopate as a 'state of perfection' and the bishops as men who gave themselves totally to God and to their fellow-men.

Theologically, if the false opposition is accepted and a sharp division is made between charism and institution, the unity of the Church as the Body of Christ is destroyed and the claim is made that everything can be regulated and conducted, on the one hand without spirituality and exclusively in the name of power and, on the other, anarchically, in the name of the Spirit. In the first case especially, the theology of ordination would be falsified and the ministry would be seen simply as a transmission of 'power'. The essential element of pneumatology would also be eliminated from ecclesiology, and it is precisely this element that I am attempting at least to suggest in this work.

The opposition between charism and institution is generally speaking not emphasized today. It is widely recognized that there are two types of activity and that, although they are different in the way in which they present themselves and in their style, they lead to the same end, which is the building up of the work of Christ. They are, in other words, complementary.[29] Until quite recently, there has been a tendency to make the charisms subordinate to institutional authority and even to reduce them to that level.[30] Now, however, quite the opposite tendency is making itself felt and some theologians are claiming that the Church should have a charismatic structure, with the institutional element playing a secondary, supplementary part.[31] What is required, however, is to recognize that each type of gift and activity has its place in the building up of the Church.

Some years ago, I suggested a view of these matters that now needs to be revised. My intention was to call attention to the truth and importance of the mission of the Holy Spirit as something more than a simple replacement for Christ. I worked, however, too exclusively in a context of dualism and made too radical a distinction between the institution as derived from Christ and free interventions on the part of the Spirit. I stressed on the one hand the apostolate and the means of grace of which Jesus had established the principles and which were accompanied by the activity of the Spirit and, on the other, a kind of free sector in which the Spirit alone was active.[32] As a result, I was criticized both by Protestant exegetes and by Catholic theologians, each from their own point of view.[33]

I still think that what I called, perhaps rather awkwardly, a free sector is something that really exists. Its existence is, after all, recognized in the encyclical *Mystici Corporis* of Pius XII. After speaking about the powers of the bishops as an institution in succession to the institution of the apostles, that encyclical went on to say: 'But our divine Saviour also governs and directs the Church in a direct manner, either by the enlightenment that he gives to pastors or by raising up men and women saints for the edification of everyone'.[34]

These are, of course, only examples, but this 'invisible and extraordinary' direction has appeared in history in many and infinitely varied forms and manifestations. My mistake was that I followed Acts more closely than the Pauline epistles and I wanted to give the Holy Spirit his full worth. As a result I was not sufficiently conscious of the unity that exists between the activity of the Spirit and that of the *glorified Christ*, since 'the Lord is the Spirit and where the Spirit of the Lord is, there is freedom' (2 Cor 3:17). According to Paul, the glorified Lord and the Spirit may be different in God, but they are functionally so united that we experience them together and are able to accept the one for the other: 'Christ in us', 'the Spirit in our hearts', '(we) in Christ', 'in the Spirit'—all of these are interchangeable. The Lord became a 'life-giving spirit' (1 Cor 15:45). According to John, it is in and through the Spirit (Paraclete) that Jesus comes back and does not leave us orphans (see Jn 14:3, 18).

This activity of the Lord with and through his Spirit[35] cannot be reduced to a mere making present of the structures of the covenant proposed by Christ while he was on earth, that is, before he ceased to be visibly and tangibly present. It is the source of a new element in history. At the same time, however, it is always a question of doing the work *of Christ* and of building up the Body of *Christ*, in such a way that, as P. Bonnard has pointed out, the interventions in question must always be in accordance with the gospel and the apostolic kerygma. As we have already seen and as we shall see in greater detail later, a sound pneumatology always points to the work of Christ and the Word of God.

NOTES

1. This is the title of a little book by P. Nautin: *Je crois à l'Esprit Saint, dans la Sainte Eglise, pour la résurrection de la chair*. It has the sub-title: *Etude sur l'histoire et la théologie du Symbole (Unam Sanctam*, 17) (Paris, 1947).
2. Tertullian, *De bapt.* 6 (*CSEL* 20, p. 206; Fr. tr. F. Refoule, *SC* 35 (1952), p. 75).
3. Augustine, *De fid. et symb*. X (*PL* 40, 193); *De symb. ad cat*. 6, 14 (*PL* 40, 635); *Enchiridion* LVI (*PL* 40, 258–259). The first treatise dates from 393 and the last from 421.
4. J. A. Jungmann, 'Die Gnadenlehre im apostolischen Glaubensbekenntnis', *Gewordene Liturgie* (Innsbruck and Leipzig, 1941), pp. 173–189.
5. This history has been traced by J. P. L. Oulton, 'The Apostles' Creed and Belief concerning the Church', *JTS*, 39 (1938), 239–243; S. Tromp, *Corpus Christi quod est Ecclesia*, I, 2nd ed. (Rome, 1946), pp. 97ff.; H. de Lubac, *La Foi chrétienne. Essai sur la structure du Symbole des Apôtres* (Paris, 1969), chapters IV to VI.
6. Alexander of Hales, *Summa* lib. III, pars III, inq. 2, tract. 2, q. 2, tit. I, No. XVI (Quaracchi ed., IV (1948), p. 1131).
7. Thomas Aquinas, *In III Sent*. d. 25, q. 1, a. 2, ad 5, attributing the statement to Leo and Anselm; *ST* IIa IIae, q. 1, a. 9, ad 5, quoting Leo—actually Rufinus, *In Symb. Apost*. 36 (*PL* 21, 373). See also *Comp*. I, c. 147.

8. Albert the Great, *De sacr. Missae* II, c. 9, art. 9 (ed. A. Borgnet, XXVIII, p. 65); cf. *In III Sent*, d. 21, a. 6ff. See also J. de Ghellink, 'L'explication du Credo par S. Albert', *Studia Albertina (Beiträge Suppl*., Vol. 4) (Münster, 1952), pp. 148ff.
9. Catechism of the Council of Trent, Prima Pars, art. 9, no. 23; tr. based on Fr. tr. by H. de Lubac, *op. cit*. (note 5), p. 169.
10. Hence John's theme of 'he saw and believed'. See O. Cullmann, 'Eiden kai episteusen', *Aux sources de la Tradition chrétienne. Mélanges Maurice Goguel* (Neuchâtel and Paris, 1950), pp. 52–61. For John, believing was a way of seeing and of perceiving the meaning and the deep reality of what was seen corporeally. This profound interpretation was done thanks to the Holy Spirit (p. 58).
11. G. Thils, *Les notes de l'Eglise dans l'apologétique catholique depuis la Réforme* (Gembloux, 1937); see also my *L'Eglise une, sainte, catholique et apostolique (Mysterium Salutis*, 15) (Paris, 1970).
12. See K. H. Rengstorf, '*apostellō* (*pempō*)', *TDNT*, I, pp. 398–406. Rengstorf says that, at the most, *pempein* means simply sending as such, or the fact of sending, whereas *apostellein* points to a precise sending or mission, even a commission, 'bound up with the person of the one sent': see pp. 398 and 404.
13. *ST* Ia, q. 13; *In I Sent*. d. 14, a. 16. See H. Dondaine, *La Trinité*, II (Paris, 1946), pp. 423–454 (bibliography). This theological teaching can be found as early as Augustine: see J.-L. Maier, *Les missions divines selon S. Augustin (Paradosis*, XVI) (Fribourg, 1960). It appeared even earlier, in Origen: see G. Aeby, *Les missions divines. De S. Justin à Origène (Paradosis*, XII) (Fribourg, 1958).
14. The phrase 'he descended from heaven' simply expresses the fact that the (fully human) humanity that the Person of the Word made to exist remains *in* this world and *of* this world. Something very similar (but only similar) is true of the Eucharist.
15. Cyprian, *De orat. dom*. 23 (*PL* 4, 553; *CSEL* 3, p. 285). *Lumen Gentium*, 4 also contains references to Augustine and John Damascene. This *theo*-logy of the Church was also developed in a remarkable way by C. Journet, *L'Eglise du Verbe incarné. Essai de théologie spéculative*, II: *Sa structure interne et son unité catholique* (Paris, 1951).
16. J. Mambrino, 'Les deux mains du Père dans l'œuvre de S. Irénée', *NRT*, 79 (1957), 355–370. For the Holy Spirit as Wisdom, see *Adv. haer*. IV, 20, 1 and 3 (*SC* 100, pp. 627 and 633); *Dem*. 5 and 10 (*SC* 62, p. 36 and la, note 8, p. 46).
17. *Adv. haer*. V, 6, 1 (*SC* 153, p. 73).
18. *Adv. haer*. V, 28, 4 (*SC* 153, p. 361).
19. *Dem*. 41 (*SC* 62, p. 96 and la, note 4).
20. Didymus, *Enarr. in Ep. 2 S. Petri*, 3, 5 (*PG* 39, 1774).
21. J. Bittremieux, 'L'institution des sacrements d'après Alexandre de Halès', *ETL* (1932), 234–251; F. Scholz, *Die Lehre von der Einsetzung der Sakramente nach Alexander von Hales* (Breslau, 1940); J. Bittremieux, 'L'institution des sacrements d'après S. Bonaventure', *Etudes Franciscaines* (1923), 129–152, 337–355; H. Baril, *La doctrine de S. Bonaventure sur l'institution des sacrements* (Montreal, 1954); V. Fagiolo, 'L'istituzione del sacramento del matrimonio nella dottrina di S. Bonaventura', *Antonianum*, 33 (1958), 241–262.
22. A. Poyer, 'Nouveaux propos sur le "salva illorum substantia" ', *Divus Thomas*, 57 (1954), 3–24, who quotes, among others, John Fisher, Clichtove, Pustinger, Contarini, Gropper, Johann Eck, Albert Pighi, as well as Salmeron and others at Trent.
23. At the Council of Constantinople (869–870), the patriarchs Elias of Jerusalem and Nilus of Alexandria attributed the institution of the patriarchate to the Holy Spirit: see Mansi, 16, 35A and 317E; *PG* 132, 1097C. E. Ruckstuhl, 'Einmaligkeit und Nachfolge der Apostel', *Erbe und Auftrag*, 47 (1971), pp. 240–253, says, on p. 247: 'It must be recognized that the monarchical episcopal office is closely associated with the office of the apostle in the New Testament and was in succession to it, although there was a considerable delay in time. May we therefore call the office of the bishop a pneumatic creation that is analogous to that of the apostle?'

24. See F. Vandenbroucke, 'Esprit Saint et structure ecclésiale selon la liturgie', *Questions liturgiques et paroissiales* (1958), pp. 115–131; M. D. Koster, *Ekklesiologie im Werden* (Paderborn, 1940); *idem*, various articles.
25. After the discovery of the *Didache*, A. von Harnack took this stand in *Die Lehre der zwölf Apostel* (Leipzig, 1884). A similar position was taken by R. Sohm, who was, however, in disagreement with Harnack with regard to the place of law in the Church; see his *Kirchenrecht*, I (Leipzig, 1892). More recently, H. von Campenhausen followed this argument in *Kirchliches Amt und geistliche Vollmacht in den ersten drei Jahrhunderten* (Tübingen, 1953). U. Brockhaus provides an excellent historical account and criticism of this phenomenon in *Charisma und Amt. Die paulinische Charismenlehre auf dem Hintergrund der frühchristlichen Gemeindefunktionen* (Wuppertal, 1972). See also H. Legrand, *RSPT*, 59 (1975), 669–671.
26. Clement of Alexandria, *Quis dives salvetur*, verses 208–210 (*PG* 9, 648; ed. O. Stählin, 3, p. 188).
27. C. Vogel, 'Le ministère charismatique de l'Eucharistie: Approche rituelle', *Ministères et célébration de l'Eucharistie* (*Studia Anselmiana*, 61) (Rome, 1973), pp. 181–209; O. Casel, 'Prophetie und Eucharistie', *Jahrbuch für Liturgiewissenschaft*, 9 (1929), pp. 1–19. Recently H. Legrand has contributed to our understanding of this question in 'La présidence de l'Eucharistie selon la tradition ancienne', *Spiritus*, 69 (1977), 409–431.
28. See John Chrysostom's treatise on the priesthood; G. Hocquard, 'L'idéal du pasteur d'âmes selon S. Grégoire le Grand', *La tradition sacerdotal* (Le Puy, 1959). pp. 143–167; see also above, Volume I, p. 69.
29. See, for example, W. Bertrams, 'De constitutione Ecclesiae simul charismatica et institutionali', *Questiones fundamentales Iuris canonici* (Rome, 1961), pp. 260–299; C. García Extremeño, 'Iglesia, Jerarquía y Carisma', *La Ciencia Tomista*, 89 (1959), 3–64; E. O'Connor, 'Charisme et institution', *NRT*, 96 (1974), 3–19; E. Iserloh, *Charisma und Institution im Leben der Kirche dargestellt an Franz von Assisi und die Armutsbewegung seiner Zeit* (Wiesbaden, 1977).
30. I have found signs of this not only in the apologetical treatises *De Ecclesia*, but also, for example, in J. Brosch, *Charismen und Ämter in der Urkirche* (Bonn, 1951); F. Malmberg, *op. cit.* below (note 33).
31. G. Hasenhüttl, *Charisma, Ordnungsprinzip der Kirche* (Freiburg, 1970); H. Küng, *The Church* (London, 1967), pp. 179–191. Küng makes a distinction between temporary and permanent charisms within a structure of the Church that is fundamentally charismatic.
32. Y. Congar, 'The Holy Spirit and the Apostolic Body, Continuators of the Work of Christ', *The Mystery of the Church* (Eng. tr.; London, 1960), pp. 147–186. This can be compared with W. Kasper, *Dogme et Evangile* (Casterman, 1967), pp. 88–90, who speaks of an activity of the Spirit in the Church, first as the 'Spirit of Christ' and then as 'active in the freedom which is peculiar to him'.
33. The Protestant exegetes include P. Bonnard, 'L'Esprit et l'Eglise selon le Nouveau Testament', *RHPR*, 37 (1957), 81–90; M.-A. Chevallier, *Esprit de Dieu et paroles d'homme* (Neuchâtel and Paris, 1966), p. 212, note 3. The Catholic theologians include F. Malmberg, *Ein Leib—ein Geist. Vom Mysterium der Kirche* (Freiburg, 1960), pp. 192ff.
34. *AAS*, 35 (1943), 209–210; no. 38 in Tromp's edition.
35. Thomas Aquinas, *Comm. in Eph*. c. 2, lect. 5: 'Quidquid fit per Sanctum Spiritum etiam fit per Christum'; *ST* Ia, q. 32, a. 1, ad 3: 'Salus generis humani quae perficitur per Filium incarnatum et per donum Spiritus Sancti'.

2
THE HOLY SPIRIT MAKES THE CHURCH ONE
HE IS THE PRINCIPLE OF COMMUNION

The Spirit is given to the Church. He was promised to the apostles, but he was promised to them with the new people of God, of whom they were the first-fruits, in mind.[1] He was given first to the apostles (Jn 20:22) and then to the whole of the early community at Pentecost.[2] There are two significant terms in this context: *epi to auto*, gathered together or in the same place,[3] and *homothumadon*, of one mind or unanimous.[4] Möhler's comment on this expresses something of the deep inspiration of his work:

> When they received the strength and the light from on high, the leaders and members of the new-born Church were not scattered in different places, but gathered together in the same place and in one heart. They formed a single community of brothers. . . . Each disciple therefore was filled with the gifts from on high only because he formed a moral unity with all the other disciples.[5]

The Spirit, the principle of unity, therefore presupposes an initial unity, which he himself is already bringing about, unobserved, and which is a unity of consent to be together and of movement in this direction. Augustine was thinking of this unity when he spoke of *fraterna caritas, caritas unitatis, pacifica mens* and the love of peace, of mutual harmony and unity, the opposite of the partisan, sectarian and schismatic spirit.[6] He was therefore able to say, on the one hand, that it is necessary to be in the Body of Christ in order to have the Spirit of Christ[7] and, on the other, that one has the Spirit of Christ and lives in that Spirit when one is in the Body of Christ.[8] This is of decisive importance, since, if the Spirit is received when believers are *together*, it is not because there is one body that there is only one Spirit—it is rather because there is only one Spirit of Christ that there is only one body, which is the Body of Christ. The Spirit *acts* in order to enable men to enter that Body, but he is *given* to the Body and it is in that Body that we receive the gift of the Spirit. 'By the one Spirit we were all baptized into one body' (1 Cor 12:13; Eph 4:4). 'The Spirit is given to the Church, into which the individual is received by baptism.'[9] The Church Fathers never ceased to affirm, explain and sing of this.[10]

The Holy Spirit is given to the community and individual persons. H. B.

Swete observed how often Christ said, in chapters 14 and 16 of the gospel of John, 'will give *you*', 'will teach *you* all things', 'will guide *you* into all the truth' and so on. This 'you' repeated again and again points both to the community and to individual persons. The Church is in no sense a great system in which, as Arthur Koestler said of another system, the individual is simply the sum of a million divided by a million. It is a communion, a fraternity of persons. This is why a personal principle and a principle of unity are united in the Church. These two principles are brought into harmony by the Holy Spirit.

Persons are the great wealth of the Church. Each one is an original and autonomous principle of sensitivity, experience, relationships and initiatives. What an infinite variety of possibilities is contained in each individual! There are signs of a purely material kind of this individuality—each person's fingerprints are, for example, distinctive. If it is true that no two trees are identical throughout the whole world, what are we to say about mankind in space and time? And how many languages are there in the world? It has been estimated that there are some 5,000. And in each one the possible expressions and combinations are really infinite. This is a sign of man's skill and intelligence and therefore also of the number of initiatives open to him.

In the modern era, excessive emphasis has been given in the Catholic Church to the rôle of authority and there has been a juridical tendency to reduce order to an observance of imposed rules, and unity to uniformity. This has led to a distrust of expressions of the personal principle. It has also led to the development of a system of supervision that has been effective in maintaining an orthodox line and framework, but this has been achieved at the price of marginalizing individuals who have had something to say, and often even reducing them to silence and inactivity. Sometimes those persons have said what they had to say, but they have usually done so in irregular and unfavourable conditions.

Individual persons, however, want to be the subjects of their actions. This demand is felt all the more strongly when the individual leaves a situation of sociologically solid religious practice and enters a situation of personally accepted faith. This situation is especially difficult today. No one would deny that the categories and structures of theology and philosophy within which Christianity has expressed itself since the Middle Ages, including the documents issued by the magisterium, especially during the six pontificates from Pius IX to Pius XII, have become devalued. (This is a question that would be worth examining more closely.) Many Christians, including theologians, however, have been trying to reconstruct and re-express their faith in different categories, which are culturally and philosophically remote from the long Catholic tradition, but in accordance with the modern age. How is it possible not to speak of this as a break-up or a shifting of territory on the part of theology? It has even been called a Protestantization of Catholicism and the establishment of a policy of free inquiry. It is obvious that, in the spirit of the world, the demon, he who is opposed to the kingdom of God, is trying to gain something from this movement in theology, and sometimes comes close to succeeding.

Nothing less than the Spirit *of God* is needed to bring all these different elements to unity, and to do so by respecting and even stimulating their diversity. Not, however, at any price. This activity of the Spirit was something which greatly impressed many of the Church Fathers, as early as Irenaeus and Origen.[11] The Spirit supports the pastoral hierarchy of the Church and through it guides Christian communities, but he does much more than this. He does not bring about unity by using pressure or by reducing the whole of the Church's life to a uniform pattern. He does it by the more delicate way of communion. The Church is not only the enclosure or 'sheepfold' (*aulē*), but also the 'flock' of individual sheep (*poimnē*), each of which the shepherd calls by its own name (Jn 10:1–3, 16).

H. B. Swete had this to say about the communion—or fellowship as he often called it, in the Anglican tradition—of the Holy Spirit:

> The communion of the Holy Spirit is not to be identified with our fellowship with Christ, although the former is inseparable from the latter. The Son was sent into the world, the Spirit into the heart (cf. Gal 4:4–6). The fellowship of the Spirit with the human spirit is immediate and direct. He who searches the deep things of God (1 Cor 2:10ff.) enters also into the depths of our inner man. Our bodies become his shrine (1 Cor 6:19; cf. 3:16); but his presence is out of sight, in the *penetralia* of our spirits, where he throws his searchlight upon our unspoken thoughts and desires. His purpose is to carry forward the work of the divine philanthropy begun in the incarnation, to make it bear on the centre of our being, regenerating and renewing the springs of our life (Tit 3:4–6).[12]

The Spirit, who is both one and transcendent, is able to penetrate all things without violating or doing violence to them. It was with good reason that the book of Wisdom said of the Spirit: 'The Spirit of the Lord has filled the world and that which holds all things together knows what is said' (1:7) and of wisdom itself, which has the same part to play: 'In her there is a spirit that is intelligent, holy, unique, manifold, subtle, mobile, . . . all-powerful, overseeing all and penetrating through all spirits' (7:22–23).

The Spirit, then, is unique and present everywhere, transcendent and inside all things, subtle and sovereign, able to respect freedom and to inspire it. That Spirit can further God's plan, which can be expressed in the words 'communion', 'many in one' and 'uniplurality'. At the end, there will be a state in which God will be 'everything to everyone' (1 Cor 15:28), in other words, there will be one life animating many without doing violence to the inner experience of anyone, just as, on Mount Sinai, Yahweh set fire to the bush and it was not consumed.[13] The Spirit is therefore an eschatological reality. He is the Promised One, of whom we here below have only the *arrha* or earnest-money (see Rom 8:23; 2 Cor 1:22; 5:5; Eph 1:14). He is the extreme communication of God himself, God as grace, God *in us* and, in this sense,

God outside himself. This idea will be further developed in Volume III of the present work. This communication and interiority do not lead to a merging together. It is rather a state of indwelling—God dwells in us and we dwell in him. There is no confusion of persons.

This is the way in which there is a realization of that mutual interiority of the whole in each which constitutes the catholic sense: *kath' holou*, being of a piece with the whole. The Spirit enables all men to be one and unity to be a multitude.[14] He is therefore the principle of the communion of the saints[15]—these terms form part, it should be noted, of the third article of the Creed, that referring to the Holy Spirit—and indeed the principle of communion as such. This communion consists in living and behaving as a conscious member of an organic whole and therefore, to quote Möhler's excellent phrase, 'as thinking and desiring in the spirit and the heart of all' (see note 5 below). The Scholastic formulae are less poetical than Möhler's, but in no sense less profound. Cajetan (†1534), in a commentary on Thomas Aquinas, spoke of 'agere ut pars unius numero populi'—'behaving as part of an undivided people'—and added that the Holy Spirit had provided the only really decisive reason for behaving in this way by having the article on the one holy Church and the communion of saints placed among the other articles of faith (see *Comm. in IIam IIae*, q. 39, a. 1).

This communion of saints (*sancta* as well as *sancti* and *sanctae*) brought about by the Holy Spirit transcends both time and space. This is, after all, in accordance with the nature of the Spirit, already expressed in the texts of the book of Wisdom, and with the condition of the Spirit as an eschatological gift, the supreme and ultimate gift of God as Grace. The Spirit is anticipation (*arrha*: see above), prophecy (see Jn 26:13), and also memory. As memory, he makes the actions and words of the Word made flesh into a present and penetrating reality (see Jn 14:26; 16:13–15). In the Church, then, he is the principle of that presence of the past and the eschatological future in the here and now, of what can be called the 'sacramental era'.[16]

This is also one way in which the Spirit makes the Church *one*, in all the dimensions in which we confess it to be such and which are the dimensions of God's plan of salvation: from Abel the righteous man to the last of the chosen people, the Church of earth and the Church of heaven, the Head and the members, since the same Spirit is in all things. It is the Spirit who, in God, places the seal, in love, on the unity of the Father and the Son from whom he proceeds.[17]

It was the Spirit who sanctified Jesus' humanity from the moment of his conception (Lk 1:35) and at his baptism, with his messianic ministry in view (4:27; Acts 10:37–38), through his resurrection (Rom 1:4: the 'Spirit of holiness') and who, as the Spirit of Christ and by the diversity of his gifts, makes it possible for one Body, which is the Body of *Christ* (1 Cor 12:12–13) to exist.

'There are varieties of gifts, but the same Spirit' (1 Cor 12:4). The Spirit was in Jesus during his life on earth. Since the time of his glorification, the Spirit has been communicated jointly by 'God' and by the Lord in order to form Christ in each believer, and to make all believers, together and with each other, his Body. This is the rôle that the Church Fathers were speaking of in their theme of the Spirit as the soul of the Church or the soul of the Body of Christ. This soul does not form a substantial whole with the body in which it dwells and which it animates. It continues to be transcendent, while at the same time being immanent with regard to that body. In this sense, Hans Küng was right to say that the Spirit is not the 'Spirit of the Church', but always the Spirit of God, and C. Journet and S. Tromp were also right to make a distinction between the uncreated soul, which is the Holy Spirit, and a created soul, consisting of the whole complex of gifts of grace.[18] These positions are quite justified, but the most important affirmation is that which claims that the Holy Spirit himself plays, in the Church, the part played in the body by the soul. Perhaps a better way of expressing this idea is that the identically and personally same Spirit, *idem numero*, is both in the Head, Christ, and in his Body, the Church or its members, that is, us as believers. This idea is quite traditional. It was known to Thomas Aquinas, taken up again by Pius XII and included in the Second Vatican Council's Constitution on the Church.[19] With his habitually strict form of thinking and expressing his thoughts, Thomas Aquinas looked for the principles uniting believers to each other and to God. He recognized that there were some which had only a 'specific' unity—the gifts of grace, of which each person has his own. All these, however, have a common source, however different they may be, and that is charity which is, because of its object, not only one, but also unique, and which has, as its cause and its source of strength, the same Holy Spirit, who is *unus numero in omnibus*, personally identical in all men and in them the transcendent principle of unity. A similar inspiration prompted Gregory of Nyssa to interpret Jesus' statement: 'The glory which thou hast given me I have given to them' (Jn 17:22) as referring to the Holy Spirit.[20]

Is the Church a person?

If this is really the principle of the Church's unity, it is impossible to avoid asking whether the Church is a person. The person 'Church' cannot be reduced to the mere total of the individuals who compose the Church. It has its own reality to which can appropriately be ascribed such specific properties as unity, holiness, catholicity, apostolicity and indefectibility ('Look not on our sins, but on the faith of your Church'). The Holy Spirit, who brings about precisely these properties in the Church, was promised to the Church. Should we therefore say that the Church has a created personality which is peculiar to it, or should we rather say that Christ is the 'I' of the Church[21] or that the Spirit is its supreme personality or its transcendent 'I'?[22] This can be accepted at least in one sense, which we are bound to define more precisely.

If Christ is the 'I' of the Church, how can the Church be his bride? And if the Holy Spirit is the 'I' of the Church, how can it be the Body of Christ?

The unity that is peculiar to the Church has its reality in the Church itself, but it has its foundation in God. In Scripture, the Church is again and again related to the absolute oneness of God, Christ and the Holy Spirit.[23] It is also related to the 'mystery of the will' of God (Eph 1:9ff.; 3:3, 9) and to his 'purpose' or *prothesis* (Rom 8:28; Eph 1:9, 11; 2 Tim 1:9), in other words, his plan of salvation. The person-Church is the one, total reality envisaged by this plan and it is at the same time the term of that plan. That reality and that term are the one 'mystical' Body of Christ and the fruit of the two 'missions' of which I spoke in the previous chapter, that of the Word, the Son, the visible mission of the incarnation and the invisible missions, and that of the Holy Spirit, the visible mission of Pentecost and the invisible missions. In relation to the mystical Body, however, these two missions have a different condition.

By appropriation—and we shall see later on the reality to which this applies—the Holy Spirit is the subject who brings about everything that depends on grace or, as C. Journet said, the supreme and transcendent effective personality of the Church.[24] He is not consubstantial with us. In Christ, on the other hand, the Word, the Son, assumed a humanity that is consubstantial with our humanity—that at least is how the Council of Chalcedon defined it. He united it to himself in a unity that is personal and substantial. Since that time, God has ceased to govern his creation at the natural and the supernatural level exclusively from his heaven and on the basis of his divinity—he governs it also in and through that man, Jesus Christ, assumed in his glory. The humanity of Christ, made entirely holy by the Spirit, has since then been the instrumental cause, not the inert cause, as a thing would be, but the intelligent and free cause, in other words, the voluntary organ of the communication of grace. He gives grace, he gives the Spirit voluntarily, since he is constituted as the Head in this sphere.[25] Since that time, the Lord Jesus and the Holy Spirit have *together* been the authors of the Body, in other words, of the Church in its unity, but Christ is the author as the Head of that Body, homogeneous with its members, in a way that is absolutely his own and strictly personal. That is why the Church is the Body, not of the Holy Spirit and not even of the Word, but of Christ.

In the concrete, everyday life of believers

The communion of which I have spoken in this chapter is an authentic reality, but it is so sublime in the sense in which I have discussed it that, if I were to leave it at that level, it could remain a pure ideal between earth and heaven and have no place in our concrete, everyday life.

The sociologist Jean Séguy asked, in a precise and well-documented study:[26] How is it that the Catholic Church in the United States, which was, in the nineteenth century, the least segregrationist Church in the country, now has so few black members and the latter belong for the most part to the Baptist and Methodist churches? Séguy himself provides the answer to this question. There was, he says, a communion at the level of faith and liturgical practice in the Catholic Church, but there was no trace of what he calls sociological communion—what I would call an effective and concrete *human* communion. Black and white Catholics communicated and received communion at the same altar, but they returned to their places with their hands together and their eyes lowered and left the church without speaking to each other, without shaking hands and even without exchanging a glance. In other words, the mystical communion of which the Holy Spirit is the sovereign principle calls for a concrete, human and personal relationship.

Let us very briefly consider a few examples. An engineer of fifty, who was baptized when he was twenty-three, said: 'The Church is cold and lacking in any kind of brotherliness. Two Scouts, two men from the same school or the same Army unit are more brotherly than two Catholics.' As a second example, there is a statement made by a nun, who was baptized when she was twenty-one: 'In the parish, I suffered a great deal from a lack of welcome on the part of the parishioners. It never seemed to me that the parish was a community.'

There are, however, some much more positive statements, such as this one, made by a married woman, who was also baptized when she was twenty-one: 'Baptism and first communion were for me belonging to Christ and because of that my admission—no, much more than that, my integration into the Church. I really became part of the "family" of the Church and was able to share its happiness, its riches and its aspirations. I began a new life. I can still see myself on the first Sunday after my baptism in the middle of the people in the parish. I was conscious of a very deep joy. I was delighted to belong to the people of God and I don't think that I have ever sung more fervently!' Another married woman with a family, baptized when she was twenty-three, spoke in the same way: 'The Church for me is a family. In the family of the Church, as in a human family, people are at one with each other and dependent on each other. We are all sinners and we have to accept each other as such.' This was the immediately affecting aspect of the solidarity among Christians. One teacher, however, who had been baptized at the age of twenty-five, reviewing the path that he had followed, commented: 'Those who were helping me on my way to the Church in fact helped me most of all in an entirely unconscious way and this made me very sensitive to their *invisible* solidarity'.

If I were to attempt to express this Christian solidarity and to make it visible, I would say on reflection that the charity that the Holy Spirit places in our hearts is not only sublime, but also very concrete. The concrete aspect of Christian love is strikingly expressed in 1 Cor 13:4–5: 'Love is patient and kind; love is not jealous or boastful; it is not arrogant or rude. Love does not insist on its own way; it is not irritable or resentful.' This concrete, practical aspect of love is included in what I have said above about the charity that forms the basis of the communion of saints. And the principle of that charity is the Holy Spirit of God. The most ordinary and concrete aspect of it forms an integral part of the most sublime element.

NOTES

1. See Jn 14:26; 15:26; 16:12–13. For the most part, the Church Fathers applied these promises to the apostles: see *DTC*, I, cols. 2124–2125. Almost all modern exegetes, however, believe that they apply to the Church as a whole as well as to the apostles: see E. Dhanis, *Greg*, 34 (1953), 207.
2. See J. Capmany, 'La communicación del Espíritu Santo a la Iglesia—Cuerpo místico, como principio de su unidad, según S. Cirilo de Alejandría', *Revista Española de Teología*, 17 (1957), 173–204.
3. Acts 1:15; 2:1; 2:47. For the part played by this term in the ideal of unity held by the early Church, see P. S. Zanetti, *Enôsis—epi to auto*. I: *Un 'dossier' preliminare per lo studio dell'unità cristiana all'inizio del 2° secolo* (Bologna, 1969); for *epi to auto*, see pp. 154ff.
4. Acts 1:14; 2:1; 2:46; see also 4:24; 5:12; 15:25; Rom 15:6.
5. J. A. Möhler, *Symbolik*, § 37; see also his *Einheit*, § 63, in which he spoke of the divinity of Christ confessed 'at the Council of Nicaea, where, for the first time, all Christians were visibly assembled in the persons of the representatives of their love': see *Unam Sanctam*, 2 (Paris, 1937), p. 205. A similar idea can also be found in Peter Chrysologus (†c. 450): 'Deo non singularitas, sed accepta est unitas. Spiritus Sanctus apostolis in unum congregatis ubertate tota sui fontis illabitur': *Sermo* 132 (*PL* 52, 653); cf. *Sermo* 139 (*PL* 52, 574).
6. See my note 'Pax chez S. Augustin' in *Œuvres de S. Augustin. Traités antidonatistes*, I (1963), pp. 711ff.; see also S. Tromp, *Corpus Christi quod est Ecclesia*, I, 2nd ed. (Rome, 1946), pp. 135ff.
7. Augustine, *Ep*. 185, 9, 42 and 11, 50 (*PL* 33, 811 and 815); *In Ioan. ev*. XXVI, 6, 13 (*PL* 35, 1612–1613). See also Origen: 'It is only in the community of believers that the Son of God can be found and that is because he only lives in the midst of those who are united': *Comm. in Mat*. XIV, 1 (*PG* 13, 1188).
8. *In Ioan. ev*. XXVII, 6, 6 (*PL* 35, 1618), etc.
9. R. Bultmann, *Theology of the New Testament*, I (Eng. tr.; New York, 1951), p. 160. This theme was developed by L. S. Thornton in *The Common Life in the Body of Christ* (Westminster, 1943), pp. 137–142.
10. J. A. Möhler, *Einheit*; P. Nautin, *Je crois à l'Esprit Saint dans la sainte Eglise* (Paris, 1947); H. J. Jaschke, *Der Heilige Geist im Bekenntnis der Kirche. Eine Studie zur Pneumatologie des Irenäus von Lyon* (Münster, 1976), § 23, pp. 265–277.
11. See Irenaeus, *Adv. haer*. I, 10, 1–5 (*PG* 7, 551ff.); Origen, *De Prin*. I, 4, 3 (*PG* 11, 122–123; ed. P. Koetschau, pp. 18–19); see also Theodoret, *Eranistes* I (*PG* 83, 80C-D).
12. H. B. Swete, *The Holy Catholic Church* (London, 1915), pp. 182–183.
13. See my article, 'Le ciel, buisson ardent du monde', *VS*, 618 (January–February 1976), 69–79.
14. It would be well here to read the little work of Peter Damian, *Dominus vobiscum* (*PL* 145, 231–232; partial Fr. tr. in *M-D*, 21 (1950/1), 174–181).
15. See P. Bernard's excellent texts of the Greek Fathers in 'Communion des saints', *DTC*, III (1908), col. 440. See also Augustine, *Sermo* 142, 7 (*PL* 38, 782); *Sermo* 267, 4 (*PL* 38, 1231); Albert the Great, *In III Sent*. d. 24 B, a. 6 (ed. A. Borgnet, 28, pp. 257–258); Thomas Aquinas, *ST* IIIa, q. 68, a. 9, ad 2; a. 12, ad 1; q. 82, a. 6, ad 3, who is not at all

original in this case, shows that the Spirit brings about in the body the communication of spiritual good things and that it is through him that, in baptism, babies are included in the faith of the Church confessed by their sponsors and their parents.

16. For this, see my *Tradition and Traditions* (Eng. tr.; London and New York, 1966), Part Two, pp. 257–270, esp. p. 260, notes 1 and 2 (with bibliography). In these pages which I wrote in 1960, however, the pneumatological aspect, although it is very important, has been rather overshadowed by the Christological aspect.
17. It is possible and indeed necessary to develop this idea further. See, for example, B. de la Margerie, 'La doctrine de S. Augustin sur l'Esprit Saint comme communion et source de communion', *Augustinianum*, 12 (1972), 107–119. One text can be quoted: 'The Father and the Son wanted us to enter into communion with each other and with them through what is common to them and wanted to join us together as one through that Gift that they both possess together, namely the Holy Spirit, God and the Gift of God. It is in him that we are reconciled with the Deity and that we enjoy the Deity': *Sermo* 71, 12, 18 (*PL* 38, 454). This text can be compared with one by Cyril of Alexandria: 'Since we have all received the same unique spirit, that is, the Holy Spirit, we are all in a certain sense merged together with each other and with God. Although we are many and separate and although Christ has made the Spirit of the Father and his own Spirit dwell in each one of us, that Spirit is still one and indivisible. He thus reduces to unity the different spirits of each one of us through himself and makes them all appear one in him': *Comm. in Ioan*. XI, 11 (*PG* 74, 561).
18. H. Küng, *The Church* (London, 1967), pp. 173ff. See also C. Journet, articles in *Nova et Vetera, VS, RThom* (1936), 651–654, and his final explanation in 'L'âme créée de l'Eglise', *Nova et Vetera* (April 1946), 165–203; *idem*, 'Note sur la distinction de deux âmes de l'Eglise, l'une créée, l'autre incréée', *ibid*. (July 1946), 284–300; *idem, L'Eglise du Verbe incarné*, II (Paris, 1951), pp. 565–579. Journet's position and above all his vocabulary were criticized by E. Mura, *RThom*, 41 (1936), 233–252 and by E. Vauthier, P. Liégé and others. See my *Sainte Eglise. Etudes et approches ecclésiologiques* (Paris, 1963), pp. 503ff., 647ff. See also S. Tromp, *Corpus Christi quod est Ecclesia*, III: *De Spiritu Christi Anima* (Rome, 1960), pp. 36ff., 107ff. and fundamentally the whole of this volume by Tromp, who had previously published two collections of patristic texts: *De Spiritu Sancto Anima Corporis mystici*, 1: *Testimonia selecta e Patribus Graecis*; 2: *Testimonia selecta e Patribus Latinis*, 2nd ed. (Rome, 1948 and 1952).
19. Thomas Aquinas, *In III Sent*. d. 13, q. 2, a. 1, ad 2; q. 2, a. 2; *De ver*. q. 29, a. 4; *Comm. in ev. Ioan*. c. 1, lect. 9 and 10; Pius XII, Encyclical *Mystici Corporis*, 54 and 77 ad sensum (*AAS*, 35 [1943], 219 and 230); Vatican II, Dogmatic Constitution on the Church, *Lumen Gentium*, 7, 7. See also S. Tromp, *Corpus Christi quod est Ecclesia*, *op. cit*., III, pp. 119ff.; G. W. H. Lampe, *Christ, Faith and History* (Cambridge, 1972), pp. 111ff.
20. Gregory of Nyssa, *Hom. 15 in Cant*. (*PG* 44, 1117A).
21. I have listed texts of this kind in my article 'La personne "Eglise" ', *RThom*, 71 (1971), 613–670. To these should be added P. Faynel, *L'Eglise* (Paris, 1971), I, pp. 189ff., 190–191.
22. For E. Klemroth, for example, the Holy Spirit was the 'supra-empirical "I" of the Church': see his *Lutherischer Glaube im Denken der Gegenwart* (Berlin, 1953), p. 137.
23. See Eph 4:4–6; 1 Cor 8:6; 12:6ff.; 10:1ff. (one bread); 2 Cor 11:2 (betrothed to one man); Jn 10:16 (one flock because there is one shepherd). This is also the sequence, although the realities are different, in the Creed: we believe 'eis hena Theon, eis hena Kurion, eis hen hagion Pneuma, eis hen baptisma, eis mian hagian katholikēn Ekklēsian'.
24. C. Journet, *L'Eglise du Verbe incarné, op. cit*. (note 18), II, pp. 96, 232–234, 490, 508. See also Thomas Aquinas, *Comp*. I, 147.
25. Thomas Aquinas, *ST* IIIa, q. 8, a. 1, ad 1; see also Eph 1:23; Col 1:15–20.
26. J. Séguy, 'Constitutions ecclésiastiques, rites liturgiques et attitudes collectives. A propos de la ségrégation religieuse des Noirs aux Etats-Unis', *Archives de Sociologie des Religions*, 6 (No. 11) (1961), pp. 93–128.

3
THE HOLY SPIRIT IS THE PRINCIPLE OF CATHOLICITY

I have not been able to speak about the unity of the Church without mentioning its catholicity. That unity is in fact the unity of many 'according to the whole' and it is this that points to the aspect of catholicity. What is more, unity has, by its very vocation, a universal extension, and this is also incontestably an aspect of the mark of catholicity. It is also not possible to deprive Christ, despite his particular mission in his own time and his own country, of his value as the light of the world and the Lord of all (see Jn 8:12; 12:32, and the whole of Paul). It is quite possible to speak in Christ's case of a concrete universal element, but the reality of Christ as man-God goes far beyond any purely philosophical approach to the question. The same applies to the Church, although the difference between Christ and the Church has to be borne in mind here. The treasure of the Church is contained in an earthly vessel, and the continuity between Christ and the Church is formed on the one hand by what comes to the Church from him institutionally—words, baptism, the Eucharist, the apostolic mission and so on—and, on the other, the Spirit communicated by him to the Church. All that we have of that Spirit who is to renew all things at present, however, is the 'earnest-money'. That earnest-money is quite substantial, since, even though the Spirit does not at present develop the fullness of that activity by which he will enable God to be 'everything to everyone', he is even now the eschatological gift that is substantially present to the Church and active in the Church. He makes the Church catholic, both in space, that is, in the world, and in time, that is, in history.

Mission in Human Space

During the earthly life of Jesus, the Spirit dwelt in him and was active through him. This means that the Easter appearances of the Lord involved a mission (see Mk 16:15–18; Mt 28:18–20; Gal 1:16) and a promise and then the effective gift of the Spirit, whose coming was the beginning of the apostolic mission and testimony (see Lk 24:46–49; Acts 1:6–11; Jn 20:21). As we have already seen, this is an essential theme in the Acts of the Apostles. As soon as the Lord had ascended to the Father, the Spirit was in the Church as a power spreading faith and love.

Everyone who comes to them, friend or foe, must be made welcome.
St. Francis

sphere. It is worth noting that this
postle who had not known Christ
ied by the Lord who was Spirit. Paul
of gentiles into the new people of
ius and his household—but the transi-
nan world. This was the beginning of
ltural level. Many other cultural groups
encountered the apostolic preaching in
of faith! The Graeco-Roman world was,
us. The 'barbarian' Ostrogoths and Vis-
rth and fifth centuries. There followed the
plete process of 'alienation' between the
f the Church, the Greeks and later the Slavs
or Latinized Christians on the other. There
nary activity—the heroic Irish period between
ries, the embassies or missions in Asia in the
voyages of discovery and the conquests of the
nied by missionary settlements about which it is
not poss… nple terms, but which certainly resulted in the
establishment of C… ity in Central and South America. Finally, there was the encounter with Asia, with its great number and variety of men, nations, cultures and religions, and with Africa, where a condescending and even scornful missionary attitude has gradually been replaced by a better knowledge and a more positive appreciation.

What interests us most in all this is the encounter of peoples, languages, cultures and religions. For a very long time, the 'other' was not sufficiently recognized as different and diverse, and the profound values concealed by that diversity were not appreciated. It is in fact only quite recently that we have come to understand this, and sometimes this understanding has been accompanied by doubt about our own values and an overestimation of the 'other' and its exotic aspects—the grass is always greener in the other field. Catholic Christianity has for centuries encountered different cultures and religions, but now the need is to encounter, recognize and welcome them in a new way. This is because men are brought much more closely in contact with each other—by travel, exchanges of various kinds, the press and television, it is possible for every man to be present to every other man. It is also because a much better and more authentic knowledge of other cultures and religions is possible, and there is a greater desire to know them. Finally, it is because we have been cured (although not all of us equally) of a certain haste inspired by imperialism in politics, apologetics and even apostolic zeal. The Church today is called to be the Church of the peoples in a new way.

The Church was established in the world by Pentecost, which gave it a vocation to universality, which was to be achieved not by means of a uniform extension, but by the fact that everyone understood and expressed the marvels of God in his own language (Acts 2:6–11). Through the mission and gift of the Holy Spirit, the Church was born universal by being born manifold and particular. The Church is catholic because it is particular, and it has the fullness of gifts because each has his own gifts. The Church overcame Babel, not by a return to a uniformity that existed before Babel, but by proclaiming an implantation of the same gospel and the same faith in varied and diverse cultural soils and human spaces.[1] This process is marked in the Church of today by the emphasis placed on two different but closely related orders of reality:

1. First are the charisms, that is, the talents of which the Holy Spirit makes use *pros to sumpheron*, 'for the common good', so that the community of the Church will be built up.[2] There is no law in the whole of the New Testament and the Christian tradition that is more strongly affirmed than this law of mutual service and mutual building up.[3] There are many gifts of the Spirit—a multiplicity of gifts—and Paul's list is neither systematic nor exhaustive. They are gifts made to persons, but those persons are not monads with individual autonomy. They belong to a people, a tradition, a culture and a sociological group, to which their gifts are in a sense appropriated. The Church's catholicity calls for these gifts to be gathered together and exchanged, and for the different parties contributing them to be aware of the whole and of its unity. This is illustrated at the level of mutual aid by St Paul's collection, *koinōnia tēs diakonias*, a sharing or service for the benefit of the saints.[4] At the level of mutual contributions of knowledge and of a revelation of the wealth of Christ, as well as of spiritual help and reciprocity, it is illustrated in an exemplary and typical way in the theory and practice of catholicity expressed in the Dogmatic Constitution on the Church, *Lumen Gentium*, 13.

2. The second order of reality is that of the local and particular churches. No firmly established terminology can be found either in the documents of Vatican II or in many other texts. I believe, however, that the following distinction is clear and quite well justified. The *local* Church is the Church of God in a certain place, and the excellent definition of the diocese provided by the Second Vatican Council can be applied perfectly to that Church.[5] The *particular* Church is the Church which presents a particular aspect, for example, in language (Basque, perhaps) or in the recruitment of its members (soldiers, for instance). It may perhaps be a diocese, part of a diocese, a group of dioceses or even a patriarchate (the Armenian Church, for example). This rediscovery and reassessment of local or particular Churches is the work and fruit of the Second Vatican Council and, as Karl Rahner called it, its most novel contribution. The Council is conscious that these Churches have been made by the people called and gathered together in the Holy Spirit—the Spirit is for those Churches the principle both of

unity and of their own gifts or talents. It is the task of the Spirit to contain and resolve this fertile tension between the particular and unity. Unity and pluralism are both necessary—pluralism in unity and unity without uniformity.

In an article on liturgy, S. Monast took as his point of departure a gesture made by Pope Paul VI at the ordination of 172 missionaries of different nationalities and languages at the feast of Pentecost, that of giving each missionary, as a sign of unity, a Latin missal.[6] The gesture was indisputably excellent in itself. Monast, however, who was himself a missionary among the Aymaras in the Andes, asked 'Shall I use this missal with my Aymaras? What meaning would it have for them, even if it were linguistically possible, for me to translate the prayers of the Roman missal into their language?' He expressed his doubts and went on to discuss the related terms 'cult' and 'culture', concluding that, if a liturgy is to live, it has to be the liturgy of a *people*. At the same time, however, it has also to be the liturgy of the Church and therefore to translate and express the faith of the apostles. This, then, is clearly a question of unity with diversity, a problem of communion and a matter concerning the Holy Spirit.

The Holy Spirit makes the Church Catholic in History

It is a frequently asserted theological truth that the Holy Spirit ensures that the Church will be faithful to the faith of the apostles. This affirmation is a consequence of the apostolicity of the Church. It will be discussed in the following chapter and we shall see then that there is a close relationship between apostolicity and catholicity, just as there is between catholicity and unity. Rather like the functions of Christ himself, the marks of the Church exist one within the other. Christ's priesthood is royal and prophetic, his prophetism is priestly and royal, and his royalty is prophetic and priestly. In the same way, the unity of the Church is apostolic, holy and catholic, its catholicity is holy, one and apostolic, its apostolicity is catholic, one and holy, and its holiness is apostolic, catholic and one.

The Church gives its faith to the Word of God, to which the inspired Scriptures bear witness. Throughout the centuries, the Church's life has been a meditation on the Scriptures. The need for the Scriptures to be read in the same spirit and through the same Spirit under whose influence they were written has been stressed again and again in the history of Christianity.[7] The only really adequate way of reading and interpreting Scripture is to do so subject to the movement of the Spirit. Scripture is one of those places where the close connection that exists between the Spirit and the Word, the Paraclete and Christ, is revealed. The whole of Scripture speaks of Christ.[8] This deep meaning of Scripture, however, is only disclosed when we are converted to the Lord, who acts in us as the Spirit (see 2 Cor 3:16–18). Origen was sometimes excessively subtle in his interpretations of Scripture, but he brought to the study of the Bible something more than a perspicacious spirit—with a heart in which the Spirit of Jesus dwelt, he read the whole of the Christian mystery in the sacred books.[9]

I have used the words 'Christian mystery'. Christ is the principle and the centre of that mystery, but he came 'for us men and for our salvation' and he does not operate without Christians, not even without all who are called (see Rom 8:28–30). This is what enables us to read Scripture 'spiritually'. In other words, a 'spiritual' reading of Scripture is what is done in the communion of the Church and the Holy Spirit. By inspiring Scripture and by throwing light on believers' reading of it, the Spirit is simply making sure that the text will be without error and those who read it will be orthodox.

This, of course, is a reduction of the part played by the Spirit in the understanding of Scripture. Such a reduction may have been sufficient at a time when the Church was adopting a tight and rather narrow defensive posture against the Higher Criticism. Progress in the study of biblical and patristic sources has now made it possible for us to have a much wider view. The Christian mystery is God's revelation and communication of himself through his Son, Jesus Christ, in the Holy Spirit, who is undoubtedly, in the words of Irenaeus of Lyons, the *communicatio Christi*—'communion with Christ'.[10] This is the 'spiritual sense' of Origen and the Church Fathers.[11] It is also what the Second Vatican Council meant when it dealt with the question: How to interpret Scripture.[12] The Council fully recognized the historical, cultural and human conditioning of the sacred texts, their literary genres and so on. It also regarded Scripture to some extent as a sacrament, like the Church itself and, by analogy, the incarnation. It then claimed, 'since holy Scripture must be read and interpreted according to the same Spirit by whom it was written', that 'no less serious attention must be given to the content and *unity of the whole of Scripture*' and that '*the living tradition of the whole Church* must be taken into account along with the harmony which exists between elements of the faith'.

If Scripture is, as far as its content is concerned, the communication of the mystery of Christ, which is the work of the Holy Spirit, then it is clear how, given the necessary assumptions, the Church's Tradition, the Eucharist and even the Church itself have become assimilated to it, since, because of the activity of the same Spirit, the content is fundamentally the same. This is not simply the teaching of Origen or St Ambrose.[13] It also forms part of a realistic, yet spiritual view of what is involved. It can also be explained on the basis of Jn 6 or that of the traditional theme, which was taken up again by Vatican II, of the two tables—the table of the Word and that of the sacrament.[14] Both tables are Christ given to us so that we shall live, and this requires the activity of the Holy Spirit. Each of these realities has an external aspect, which it is possible to consider alone—it is possible to see nothing in Scripture but a literary text, nothing in Tradition but a human history, nothing in the Eucharist but a ceremony and nothing in the Church but a sociological phenomenon. Each, however, also has a deep spiritual aspect, to which God is committed through his Spirit.

The Spirit makes the Word present, taking the letter of Scripture as the point of departure. He enables the Word to speak to each generation, in every cultural environment and in all kinds of circumstances. He helps the Christian community at different times and in different places to understand its meaning.[15] Is this not what Jesus promised?[16] Did the first witnesses and the first Christian Churches not experience this?[17] Has the Church not always been aware of this and affirmed this when it has spoken about its Tradition?[18] Is it not a point of wide ecumenical agreement today?[19] At certain periods during the history of the Church, notably during the Counter-Reformation and the Catholic restoration after the French Revolution, theologians have especially stressed the guarantee that the Spirit gives to the Church and have interpreted the Church in terms of authority and the magisterium, a guarantee that it cannot err in its teaching. Although I would not wish to overlook this aspect, I would prefer to stress here the part played by the Spirit in making knowledge present in continuity with what has gone before, and to insist on the fact that the whole Christian community, including its pastors, are helped by the Spirit. 'You are not to be called "rabbi", for you have one teacher and you are all brethren' (Mt 23:8). The teaching of the Second Vatican Council here is very firm:

> The holy people of God shares also in Christ's prophetic office. It spreads abroad a living witness to him, especially by means of a life of faith and charity. . . . The body of the faithful as a whole, anointed as they are by the Holy One (cf. Jn 2:20, 27), cannot err in matters of belief. Thanks to a supernatural sense of faith which characterizes the people as a whole, it manifests this unerring quality when, 'from the bishops down to the last member of the laity' (Augustine), it shows universal agreement in matter of faith and morals. For, by this sense of faith which is aroused and sustained by the Spirit of truth, God's people . . . clings without fail to the faith delivered to the saints (cf. Jude 3), it penetrates it more deeply by accurate insights and applies it more thoroughly to life.[20]

This 'anointing' of faith, which comes from the 'Holy One', in other words, the Holy Spirit, takes place in history. A very common practice among the Fathers of the Church, which continued until the period of the Council of Trent and even later, was to describe the effectiveness of the Spirit in the Church by the words *revelatio (revelare), inspiratio (inspirare), illuminare, suggestio (suggerere)* and related terms. I have provided a documentation on this subject which could be extended almost indefinitely.[21] I also gave Thomas Aquinas the credit for having broken with this practice and limited or reserved the word *revelatio* to what we know now as 'revelation', by giving the word a much more precise meaning. I am still convinced that it is not really possible to place at the same level on the one hand the revelation or inspiration of the Spirit at the apostolic, constitutive period of the Church's foundation and, on the other, the continuing activity of the Spirit in the life of the Church that was founded at that time. The fundamental concern of the theologians who spoke in the older way, however, was to show revelation as an event in the present, occurring in the Church as an act of faith. It is also a constant feature in the liturgical use of biblical texts. In the liturgy, they are taken out of their historical setting and divorced from their strictly exegetical meaning so that they may have a contemporary relevance as God's revelation and communication of himself. St Bernard justified this use of the Bible by insisting that the Bride of Christ enjoyed the Spirit of Christ.[22] The disadvantage of Thomas Aquinas' more precise use of the term 'revelation' was that it came to be seen as a completed event which had simply to be interpreted and elaborated by theologians. This resulted in a tendency to see God's act of revelation, religious truth, dogma and faith notionally, and it is only relatively recently that this conception has been called into question.[23] Nonetheless, theologians and the magisterium state now as in the past that the Holy Spirit is active in the Church, enlightening it and guiding it, in accordance with the Lord's promise. In view of the criticisms expressed by Protestant theologians, who also suffer from a positivism of the inspired text of Scripture, it is necessary both to avoid equating the Church's Tradition with the Word of foundation, and to join with our sister-churches in the East[24] and insist that the Church's Tradition is the very life of the Church as the Body of Christ, animated by the same Spirit who spoke through the prophets.

This brings us at once to the question: Does he still speak through the prophets? Who would dare to say that he does not? But, if he does, who is it who prophesies? One reply to this question is that the proposal of an objective revelation or the communication of the Word implies a corresponding 'spirit of revelation' in the subjects who are to receive it.[25] Because of this, God is constantly active revealing himself in men who are called to believe or who are living by faith. It is, however, necessary to go further than this and ask whether God does not speak today in events and in the lives of men. This is certainly a question that modern man asks again and again.

Inner inspirations and even what John of the Cross called 'substantial words', which, in the course of a fervent spiritual life, bring about what they say, such as 'Walk in my presence' or 'Be at peace', have always been recognized in Christianity. Private revelations have also played a part in the history of the Church.[26] It has long been thought that the lives of the saints form a commentary in action on the Scriptures[27] and Pope Pius XII went so far as to say, in connection with Teresa of Lisieux, that the lives of the saints were God's words.[28] It has also always been believed that, as the Church is guided by the Holy Spirit in its life, the Church's way of acting, the *usus Ecclesiae*, was a very precious 'theological locus', especially sacramentally. Thomas Aquinas often referred to this. The sense of faith or *sensus fidei*—the term *sensus fidelium* is often used, less precisely, to point to the feeling of

Christians themselves—can also be included among the 'theological loci'. God also makes certain aspects of faith known to this *sensus*.

All this is very interesting and even important, but it is confined to the purely Christian sphere, while the questions that we are asked as Christians go beyond that sphere. They are concerned with an experience of the world as such through which Christians may be able to know God in a new way. Is the activity of the Spirit involved in this experience? I would like to point to three aspects of that involvement.

1. The members of Catholic Action, at all levels, but especially the Young Christian Workers, have always reflected, in teams, about aspects of life in the environment in which they live. They see in these God's appeal to them and attempt to understand and respond to that appeal in the light of the gospel. J. Bonduelle said some years ago that, in this 'examination of life', as he called it, it was possible to recognize a 'sign of the Spirit', which he illustrated by quoting the well-known text of Joel applied by Peter to the pouring out of the Spirit at Pentecost (Acts 2:17–21).[29] The very facts of the secular world seem to say something concerning God and they do this thanks to the Holy Spirit.

2. In 1963, John XXIII published his Encyclical *Pacem in terris*, and two-and-a-half years later the last document to be produced by Vatican II appeared—*Gaudium et spes*, the Pastoral Constitution on the Church in the Modern World. Both documents, but especially the second, gave an essential place to the idea of the 'signs of the times' in the Church's understanding of itself in its relationship with the world that is both natural and historical:

> To carry out such a task (that is, the task of continuing, subject to the impulse of the Holy Spirit, the work of Christ himself) the Church has always had the duty of scrutinizing the signs of the times and of interpreting them in the light of the gospel. . . . The people of God believes that it is led by the Spirit of the Lord who fills the earth. Motivated by this faith, it labours to decipher authentic signs of God's presence in the happenings, needs and desires in which this people has a part along with other men of our age.[30]

These 'signs of the times' are not always clearly defined, but they are sufficiently clear. They are to be found in the situation in which the Church, as the people of God, has to carry out its mission. This situation somehow conveys the presence and plan and therefore the activity of God. The changing situation of the world is described, together with a number of facts, in *Gaudium et spes*, 4–10, and all these facts point to change in the world and a change in attitude in the Church. Several of these facts are also mentioned in other conciliar documents.[31] Many of them go back to the movement of Christianity itself, but more generally they are characteristic in a broad sense of the movement of the secular world.

However useful and indeed necessary the work of sociologists may be, these indications should not be interpreted purely sociologically, but rather in the light of the gospel, inspired by faith and led by the Holy Spirit. At the least, these broad facts point to developments in the history of mankind which provide the Church, or, more precisely, its catholicity, with its matter. These developments in the history of the first Adam have to be evangelized and therefore first recognized, and they also give a topicality to the Church's message, matter to its mission, and new ways of proclaiming the gospel.[32] At the most, the events taking place in the world that stimulate the consciousness of Christians, enabling them to hope and to act energetically, can be seen as a genuine 'word' of God. The Word can be identified with the 'economy' of God in action in these events. A reaction in the name of positive revelation as attested in the inspired Scriptures is then met with the response that a 'hermeneutical' approach rather than a purely exegetical one is required; in other words, we have to be conscious of the meaning of God's activity in history for us here and now. I do not deny that God acts in the history of the secular world or that historical events and movements can tell us something of what God wants for us and therefore of what he is. What is difficult, however, is the interpretation of those events. Interpretation is able to go further than mere conjecture and personal conviction only if the meaning of the facts is tied to and illuminated by the positive revelation of God's plan with Jesus Christ at its centre. And here we need to bear in mind that the salvation and the kingdom that God's plan envisages include the whole of creation and are God's response to creation's groaning and its hope (see Rom 8:20–24).

3. Nowadays, priests, catechists and others prefer not to take an established text or confession of faith as their point of departure, but very often base their instruction on facts and on life itself. Let me give three different examples, admittedly taken out of their context:

> The Christian . . . must listen to God actually speaking in his life and in the world. God addresses us through every event.[33]

> The ways in which God is revealed to us are: the world, the individual in his relationships with others, and the community, which safeguards the gospel in history.[34]

> Like all our contemporaries, we have less and less faith in the virtue of institutions and the intangibility of dogmas and we are referring more and more to our immediate experience in our search for the meaning of things and of human relationships.[35]

It is possible that these statements simply point to a new development in teaching the faith, a very valid one as such. They may, however, also indicate a tendency to neglect, at least for a time, the acquired and generally accepted datum of positive revelation or the data of a specific religious space, and to look for God or 'Jesus of Nazareth' in human events and relationships. I would not be able to accept, in such an approach pushed to its logical extreme, that listening to the Word of God as reported in the gospel and handed down in the Tradition of the Church can be entirely replaced by an interest in the world and one's fellow-men. This does not, however, mean that I reject the fact that God also speaks to us through events and other human beings. My task here is to try to define more precisely the part played by the Holy Spirit in that area.

The Holy Spirit as the 'Unknown One beyond the Word'

This description of the Spirit originated with Hans Urs von Balthasar[36] and it indicates admirably the unity that exists between the two realities and the tension that accompanies that unity. It also points to the freedom and the mysterious activity that characterize the Holy Spirit. Finally, it suggests that he acts *forwards*, in a time or space that has been made open by the Word.

All that we know about the Spirit is in accordance with this description. In Scripture, he is always characterized by symbols expressing movement, such as wind and breath, living water, the flying dove, tongues and so on. The New Testament attributes such characteristics to the Spirit as the power of new beginnings, freedom and openness to recognizing the other. Christian Duquoc, who has drawn attention to these New Testament aspects of the Spirit,[37] has shown that the Absolute is not, according to the New Testament, the metaphysical Perfectly Solitary One who is closed in on himself, but a kind of 'ecstatic one'. According to Dionysius, love is 'ecstatic', the Father ex-pressing himself in the Word and constituting him as 'different' and the Spirit breaking the self-sufficiency of the 'face to face' of the first two Figures. In the work that God places outside himself through the two missions of the Word and the Spirit, the Spirit is 'the energy which exorcizes the spell of the past or the origin and projects forwards towards a future, the principal characteristic of which is its newness'.

The theme of the Fourth Assembly of the World Council of Churches at Uppsala in August 1968 was: 'Behold, I make all things new' (Acts 21:5). Mgr Ignatius Hazim, the Orthodox Metropolitan of Latakia, who had been asked to make the opening address, described in a striking way this work of God carried out by his Spirit:[38]

> The newness of creation cannot be explained by the past—it can only be explained by the future. It is clear that the activity of the living God can only be creative. The wonder of God, who reveals himself to Abraham, Isaac and Jacob, is, however, that his creative act comes from the future. It is prophetic. God 'comes' into the world as though he were coming to meet it. He goes ahead and he calls, upsets, sends, causes to grow and sets free. . . .
>
> The paschal event, which came once and for all time, has to become ours today—but how? It can only become ours through the one who brought it about in

the beginning and will bring it about in the fullness of time—the Holy Spirit. He is himself Newness, at work in the world. He is the presence of God-with-us, 'bearing witness with our spirit' (Rom 8:16). Without him, God is distant, Christ is in the past and the gospel is a dead letter, the Church is no more than an organization, authority is domination, our mission is propaganda, worship is mere calling to mind, and Christian action is a slave morality.

In him, however, and in indissoluble combined activity, the cosmos is raised up and groans giving birth to the kingdom, man struggles against the flesh, the risen Christ is present, the gospel is the force of life, the Church is the fellowship of the Trinity, authority is a service that sets free, our mission is a Pentecost, the liturgy is a commemoration and an anticipation, and human activity is deified.

The Holy Spirit . . . gives birth. He speaks through the prophets. . . . He takes us towards the second coming. 'He is Lord and giver of life' (Niceno-Constantinopolitan Creed). It is through him that the Church and the world call out with their whole being: 'Come, Lord Jesus!' (Rev 22:17–20).

It is this energy of the Holy Spirit that introduces a new dynamism into our horizontal world. . . . We need a prophetic theology which is able to detect the coming of the Lord in history. . . . Is the Holy Spirit not urging us to hasten the coming of the creative Word, Christ the Saviour, so that he will 'guide us into all the truth', since it is he who will 'declare to us the things that are to come' (Jn 16:13)?

The Holy Spirit makes the Easter event of Christ present with the eschatological destiny of creation in mind. He also makes Christ's Revelation present. He thrusts the gospel forward into the period of history that has not yet come. After all, if it is true that Christ was only born once, only spoke once, only died once and was only raised from the dead once, then this 'once' should be welcomed and should take root and bear fruit in a humanity which has existed throughout the centuries in so many places and in such an infinite variety of cultures. There must be a link between what has already been given and the unexpected, between what has been acquired once and for all time and what is always new. This link is forged by the Holy Spirit, the Spirit of Jesus, Jesus as Spirit, who is also both the 'Spirit of truth' and 'freedom'.[39]

In the Bible, 'truth' is an eschatological reality. It is, in other words, the end towards which all things are destined by God. In the concrete, this means that, however true and venerable they may be, the forms that we know are not the last word about the ultimate realities that they express. Dogmas are not yet perfect. The Church is, in its structures, an open system. The Word is the form and the Spirit is the breath. Jesus instituted the Eucharist and proclaimed a gospel. The Spirit makes them present here and now in what is new in the history of the world. He joins the first Adam who multiplied and invented to the eschatological Adam, the Omega of the world who is also its Alpha and the Omega and Alpha of the Church. The Spirit does this, both in the truth of the One who only brings all that Christ has said to mind (Jn 14:26) and who takes what is Christ's (16:14) and in the freedom of the One who blows where he wills (3:8). As we have already seen, the Spirit is the 'co-instituting' principle. In a sense, then, God has really told and given us everything in Jesus Christ[40] and yet there is also something new and something takes place in history.

The Spirit, however, is the Spirit of *Jesus Christ*. He does no other work but that *of Jesus Christ*. There is no time of the Paraclete that is not the time of Jesus Christ, contrary to what Joachim of Fiore, who misinterpreted the original and correct idea that he had of history as open to hope and newness, seemed to believe. The catholicity of the Church is the catholicity *of Christ*.[41] The soundness of any pneumatology is its reference to Christ.

In the power of Christ and the Holy Spirit, then, the Church is able to be completely open to accomplish its catholicity, which is also the catholicity of Christ. This task can only be carried out in mystery, because it is not possible to distinguish clearly between what is for God and what is not. We shall see later that only the Spirit knows what word is formed within men's hearts. Throughout history, men have claimed to know and to be able to say who was for God and who was not, and those periods in which they claimed this knowledge most persistently were the least tolerant and often the most cruel. Those were periods of 'Christianity', but not of catholicity. In our own age, we are, as we have seen, called in a new way to an encounter of peoples, cultures and religions. The first words of the Declaration on the Non-Christian Religions of Vatican II are, significantly, *Nostra aetate*—'In our times'. This Declaration, however, goes on, in the second paragraph, to say expressly that Christ is 'the way, the truth and the life' (Jn 14:6). He is the Alpha and the Omega of this new and wider catholicity which the 'Unknown One beyond the Word' enables mysteriously to develop to greater and wider maturity.

NOTES

1. Decree on the Church's Missionary Activity, *Ad Gentes divinitus*, 4. It is possible to amplify what is said in this conciliar statement, within the spirit of the Council: '(At Pentecost) that union (of all peoples in the catholicity of faith) was (prefigured) by the Church of the new covenant, which speaks all tongues, which lovingly understands and accepts all tongues and which thus overcomes the divisiveness of Babel'. See also H. Legrand, 'Inverser Babel, mission de l'Eglise', *Spiritus*, 63 (1970), 323–346; *idem*, 'Parce que l'Eglise est catholique, elle doit être particulière', *Cahiers Saint-Dominique*, 127 (April 1972), 346–354.
2. 1 Cor 12:7; see also K. Weiss, '*sumpherō*', *TDNT*, IX, p. 77. For the meaning of this, see 1 Pet 4:10.
3. For the New Testament, see the articles '*diakoneō*' (II, pp. 81ff.), '*doulos*' (II, pp. 261–279) and '*oikodomē*' (V, pp. 144–147) in *TDNT*; see also L. Deimel, *Leib Christi* (Freiburg, 1940), especially pp. 89ff., but also *passim*; P. V. Dias, *Vielfalt der Kirche in der Vielfalt der Jünger, Zeugen und Diener* (Freiburg, 1968). For the Tradition of the Church, see the theme of *subministratio ad invicem*, which was dear to Thomas Aquinas, but which will also be found in many other theological works, including, for example, J. A. Möhler, *Einheit*, §§ 26, 30, 31 and Appendix XIII.

4. 2 Cor 8:4. See also, for the deep meaning of this collection, L. Cerfaux, 'S. Paul et l'unité de l'Eglise', *NRT*, 53 (1926), 657–673; E. B. Allo, 'La portée de la collecte pour Jérusalem dans les plans de S. Paul', *RB*, 45 (1936), 529–537. G. Dieter has written a study in German (Hamburg, 1965); K. F. Nickle, *The Collection: A Study in Paul's Strategy* (London, 1966).
5. Dogmatic Constitution on the Church, *Lumen Gentium*, 23, 1 and 26; Decree on the Pastoral Office of Bishops, *Christus Dominus*, 11.
6. S. Monast, 'Une liturgie, œuvre du peuple', *Spiritus*, 50 (September 1972), 300–307, with reference to J. Dournes, *L'offrande des peuples* (*Lex Orandi*, 44) (Paris, 1967).
7. It is clear from the many references taken from Christian authors throughout the centuries that this principle has been affirmed again and again: Hippolytus, Methodius and Origen: see H. de Lubac, *Histoire et Esprit. L'intelligence de l'Ecriture d'après Origène* (Paris, 1950), p. 315, note 144 and p. 316, note 148; Origen, *In Num., Hom*. XVI, 9 (ed. W. A. Baehrens, 153; *PG* 12, 702); Gregory Thaumaturgus (*PG* 10, 1093A); Jerome, *In Gal*. 5, 19–21 (*PL* 26, 417A); Augustine, *Contra mend*. 15 and 26–27 (*PL* 40, 506); Isidore of Seville, *Etym*. VIII, 5, 70 (*PL* 82, 305); Abelard, *Sic et Non, Prol*. (*PL* 178, 1339B); Richard of Saint-Victor, *De erud. hom. int*. II, 6 (*PL* 196, 1305A-B); William of Saint-Thierry; Stephen of Tournai, *Epist*. 251 (*PL* 211, 517); Thomas Aquinas, *Comm. in Rom*. c. 1, lect. 6; c. 12, lect. 2; *Quodl*. XII, 26; *ST* IIa IIae, q. 173, a. 1; q. 176, a. 2, ad 4; *Contra Gent*. III, 154, post gradum; John Duns Scotus, *Opus Oxon*. IV, d. 11, q. 3, n. 15 (ed. L. Vives, XVII, 376); Eckhart, *Book of Divine Consolation*, Part Two: *Meister Eckhart* (Eng. tr.; paperback ed., London, 1963), p. 130 (Fr. tr. quoted by de Lubac, *op. cit*., pp. 315, note 144). At the time of the Reformation: Johann Eck, *Apologia de conventu Ratisboni*, art. 9; Ambrosius Catharinus, *Claves duas ad aperiendas Scripturas* (Lyons, 1543), p. 32; Alphonsus de Castro, *Adv. omnes haereses*, lib. I, c. 4. In the present century: Benedict XV, Encyclical *Spiritus Paraclitus* (15 September 1920) (*Enchiridion Biblicum*, 469); Vatican II, Dogmatic Constitution on Revelation, *Dei Verbum*, 12.
8. See Jn 5:39, 46; 12:41; Lk 24:25–27; Acts 10:43. When he was inspired by the Spirit, David spoke of Christ as his Lord: see Mt 22:43; Mk 12:36.
9. See H. de Lubac, *op. cit*. (note 7), pp. 274, 303–304, 316–317, for Origen's texts on understanding the Scriptures by conversion to the Lord. See also *Entretien d'Origène avec Héraclide*, Fr. tr. J. Scherer, *SC* 67 (1960), p. 91. See also my *Tradition and Traditions* (Eng. tr.; London and New York, 1966), Part Two, p. 395 and the relevant note.
10. Irenaeus, *Adv. haer*. III, 24, 1 (*PG* 7, 966; ed. W. W. Harvey, II, 131; Fr. tr. A. Rousseau and L. Doutreleau, *SC* 211, pp. 472 and 473).
11. For Origen, see H. de Lubac, *op. cit*. (note 7), pp. 297ff., 304 and note 58; for the others, *see idem, Exégèse médiévale. Les quatre sens de l'Ecriture* (Paris, 1959).
12. Dogmatic Constitution on Revelation, *Dei Verbum*, 12.
13. For Origen, see H. de Lubac, *op. cit*., pp. 366ff.; Ambrose, *Comm. in Luc*. I, 6, 33 (PL 15, 1763); see also Ephraem Syrus, *Diat*. XXII, 3 (Fr. tr. L. Leloir, *SC* 204 (1966), p. 396).
14. See my study 'The Two Forms of the Bread of Life: in the Gospel and Tradition' (orig. pub. in *Parole de Dieu et Sacerdoce. Etudes présentées à Mgr Weber* (Tournai, 1962), pp. 21–58), Eng. tr. in *Priest and Layman* (London, 1967), pp. 103–138. See also Dogmatic Constitution on Revelation, *Dei Verbum*, 21; Decree on the Religious Life, *Perfectae Caritatis*, 6; Decree on the Ministry and Life of Priests, *Presbyterorum ordinis*, 18.
15. C. Molari, 'The Hermeneutical Role of the Church Community on the Basis of the Judaeo-Christian Experience', *Concilium*, 113 (1978), 93–105. For the function of the Spirit as *memoria* for faith, see R. Pesch, *Freiheit in Gesellschaft* (Freiburg, 1971).
16. See Jn 14:15ff., 26; 15:26; 16:13–15. See also Volume I of this work, p. 58.
17. See Jn 2:22; 12:16; 13:7; 16:12ff. See also F. Mussner, *Le langage de Jean et le Jésus de l'histoire* (Paris and Bruges, 1969); A. M. Hunter, *According to John* (Philadelphia and London, 1968).
18. I have provided details and references, firstly in my book, *op. cit*. (note 9), Part One,

pp. 49. 169ff., 194ff.; Part Two, pp. 338–347; and secondly in Volume I of this work, pp. 151ff.

19. I am reminded here of the Faith and Order Conferences at Edinburgh in 1937: see A. Guimond, *Les exigences doctrinales de l'unité de l'Eglise* (Rome, 1972), pp. 50ff.; and at Montreal in the summer of 1963: see L. Vischer, *Foi et Constitution, 1910–1963* (Neuchâtel and Paris, 1968), pp. 172–185. See also the Malta report on the dialogue between the Catholic Church and the World Lutheran Federation: *Doc. cath.*, 1621, 18–25 (3 December 1972), pp. 1072–1073.

20. Dogmatic Constitution on the Church, *Lumen Gentium*, 12, 1. For the interpretation of 1 Jn 2:20, 26 and similar texts, and a theological interpretation, see M.-E. Boismard, 'La connaissance dans l'alliance nouvelle d'après la première lettre de S. Jean', *RB*, 56 (1949), 365–391; I. de la Potterie, 'L'onction du chrétien par la foi', *Bib*, 40 (1959), 12–69; repr. in *La vie selon l'Esprit, condition du chrétien* (Paris, 1965), pp. 107–167; my *Lay People in the Church* (Eng. tr.; London, 1957), pp. 259ff.

21. See my book, *op. cit.* (note 9), Part One, pp. 119–137, text and notes. For Thomas Aquinas, see *ibid.*, pp. 93, 124; for the situation at the time of the Reformation, Trent and later, see pp. 174–176 and the relevant notes. Since I wrote that book, a monograph dealing with one of the most important theologians of the twelfth century has shown that 'in the theology of Hugh (of Saint-Victor), revelation is not first and foremost a body of teaching to which nothing can be added, nor is it limited to a strictly supernatural sphere. . . . It is an event rather than a doctrine': see L.-J. Bataillon's review, *RSPT*, 62 (1978), 259, of C. Schütz, *Deus absconditus, Deus manifestus. Die Lehre Hugos von St. Viktor über die Offenbarung Gottes* (Rome, 1967).

22. Bernard, *In vig. nat., Sermo* 3, 1 (*PL* 183, 94); see also, for the Church as Bride possessing the Spirit of her Bridegroom, *In Dom. Palm., Sermo* 2, 5 (*PL* 183, 253); *In Cant., Sermo* 73, 6 (*PL* 183, 1136–1137); *In festo Petri et Pauli, Sermo* 2, 5 (*PL* 183, 410). See also C. Bodard, 'La Bible, expression d'une expérience religieuse chez S. Bernard', *Saint Bernard théologien (Anal. S. Ord. Cist.)* (Rome, 1953), pp. 24ff.

23. See, for example, W. Kasper, *Dogme et Evangile* (Paris, 1967) and *Renouveau de la méthode théologique* (Paris, 1968). The Council used a concept of 'truth' which respected the notional value of the term, but to some extent accepted the biblical meaning of faithfulness on God's part to his plan of salvation: see *RSPT*, 54 (1970), 329ff.

24. See my book, *op. cit.* (note 20), Part One, chapter III, esp. pp. 87ff.

25. Eph 1:17; 1 Cor 2:10; for the reality, see 2 Cor 4:3–6; Mt 16:17. See also my books *La Foi et la Théologie* (Paris, 1962), pp. 16ff., and *op. cit.* (note 9), Part Two, pp. 386ff.

26. See my article on 'La crédibilité des révélations privées', *VS* (Suppl) (1 October 1937), 29–48; repr. in *Sainte Eglise* (Paris, 1963), pp. 375–392. For a discussion of mystical visions, see *Nouvelles de l'Institut Catholique de Paris* (February 1977).

27. See Augustine, *Contra mend.* 15, 26–27 (*PL* 40, 506); Gregory the Great, *In Ezech., Hom.* 1, 10, 38 (*PL* 76, 901); Thomas Aquinas, *Comm. in Rom.* c. 1, lect. 5; c. 12, lect. 3; *Comm. in Heb.* c. 12, lect. 1.

28. A. Combes, *Sainte Thérèse de Lisieux et sa mission* (Paris, 1954), p. 212, note 4.

29. See J. Bonduelle, article written in 1960 and repr. in *La révision de vie. Situation actuelle* (Paris, 1964), p. 39. See also J.-P. Jossua, 'Chrétiens au monde. Où en est la théologie de la "révision de vie" et de l'"événement"?', *VS* (Suppl), 71 (November 1964), 455–479. There is an echo of this movement in the Decree on the Ministry and Life of Priests, *Presbyterorum Ordinis*, 6, 2.

30. Dogmatic Constitution, *Gaudium et spes*, 4, 1 and 11, 1. For this idea, see also Paul VI, audience given on 16 April 1969; *Doc. cath.*, 1539 (4 May 1969), pp. 403–405; M.-D. Chenu, 'Les signes des temps', *NRT* (January 1965), 29–39, repr. in *Peuple de Dieu dans le monde* (Paris, 1966), pp. 35–55; *idem*, 'Les signes des temps. Réflexion théologique', *Vatican II. L'Eglise dans le monde de ce temps (Unam Sanctam*, 65b) (Paris, 1967), pp. 205–225; P. Valadier, 'Signes des temps, signes de Dieu?', *Etudes*, 335 (August-

September 1971), 261–279, who criticized or rather rejected Chenu's position; L. Lévesque, 'Les signes des temps', *Science et Esprit* (October-December 1968), 351–362; R. Coste, *Théologie de la liberté religieuse* (Gembloux, 1969), pp. 354ff. It is also important to recognize that the idea of the 'signs of the times' has a history or a pre-history. W. Kahle has shown that the 'signs of the times' were observed by nineteenth-century German Protestants in the 1830 and 1848 revolutions and the wars. In 1855, C. C. J. von Bunsen published *Die Zeichen der Zeit*: see W. Kahle, 'Die Zeichen der Zeit. Ein Beitrag zur Theologie und Geistesgeschichte des 19. Jahrhunderts', *Zeitschrift für Religion und Geistesgeschichte*, 24 (1972), 289–315.

31. The liturgical movement, which is like a passage of the Holy Spirit in his Church: see the Constitution on the Liturgy, *Sacrosanctum Concilium*, 43; the ecumenical movement: see the Decree of Ecumenism, *Unitatis redintegratio*, 4, 1; the solidarity of all peoples and nations: see the Decree on the Apostolate of the Laity, *Apostolicam actuositatem*, 14, 3; the recognition of religious freedom, e.g. in legislation: see the Declaration on Religious Freedom, *Dignitatis personae humanae*, 15, 3. Priests and lay people must be alert to the signs of the times: see the Decree on the Ministry and Life of Priests, *Presbyterorum Ordinis*, 9, 2; 6, 2.
32. This last aspect is developed in *Gaudium et spes*, 44, and in many of M.-D. Chenu's writings.
33. Michel Quoist, *Prayers of Life* (Dublin and Melbourne, 1963), p. v.
34. Nuns quoted by P. Régamey, *Redécouvrir la vie religieuse. La rénovation dans l'esprit* (Paris, 1974), p. 161.
35. From a paper read in November 1973 during the fifteenth Semaine des Intellectuels Catholiques. This did not propose a 'programme', nor did it contain a declaration. It was simply a critical questioning.
36. H. U. von Balthasar, 'Der Unbekannte jenseits des Wortes', *Interpretation der Welt. Festgabe R. Guardini*, ed. H. Kuhn (Würzburg, 1966), pp. 638–645, reprinted in *Spiritus Creator. Skizzen zur Theologie*, III (Einsiedeln, 1967), pp. 97ff.
37. C. Duquoc, *Dieu différent* (Paris, 1977). pp. 106ff.; for what follows, see pp. 120ff.
38. The text will be found in *Irénikon*, 42 (1968), 344–359, or *Foi et Vie* (November-December, 1968), 8–23. See also J.-B. Metz, 'Gott vor uns', *Ernst Bloch zu Ehren* (Frankfurt, 1965), pp. 227–241. Although I would not wish to raise him to the status of a Father of the Church, I would also like to cite André Gide in this context: 'If I had to formulate a creed, I would say: God is not behind us. He is to come. We have to look for him not at the beginning, but at the end of the evolution of all beings. He is terminal, not initial. He is at the supreme and ultimate point towards which the whole of nature is moving in time. And, since time does not exist for him, it is a matter of indifference to him whether this evolutionary process of which he is the summit follows or precedes or whether he guides it by calling it or by driving it forward': *Journal*, 30 January 1916, p. 333.
39. 'Spirit of truth': Jn 14:17; 15:26; 16:13; 1 Jn 4:6; Freedom: 2 Cor 3:17; combination of both: Jn 8:32.
40. John of the Cross, *The Ascent of Mount Carmel*, II, Part 8, chapter 20.
41. See Eph 4:10,13; 1:23. Elsewhere I have quoted Tennyson's fine poem on 'The Christ that is to be' (end of Poem CV in *In Memoriam*).

4
THE SPIRIT KEEPS THE CHURCH 'APOSTOLIC'

'Apostolic' means 'relating to the apostles' or 'in conformity with the apostles'. The word therefore indicates a reference to or a conformity with the origins of Christianity. This idea is quite correct, but it needs to be amplified, since it is only half the truth. The other half is a reference to eschatology. Christ is Alpha and Omega, the beginning and the end, the one who is, who was and who is to come, the Pantocrator (see Rev 1:8; 21:6; 22:13). Apostolicity is the mark that for the Church is both a gift of grace and a task. It makes the Church fill the space between the Alpha and the Omega by ensuring that there is a continuity between the two and a substantial identity between the end and the beginning. It can therefore be conceived by reference to the end as well as by reference to the beginning. This truth is, thank God, the object of profound ecumenical agreement, whilst Protestant, Orthodox and Catholic theologians can all preserve their own distinctive emphases;[1] see also the Appendix to this chapter.

It is a question of combining the Alpha of God's intention with the Omega in such a way that his intention and his gift are identical throughout history, throughout the development and hazards of which it has been, is and will be the place. It is a question of preserving the messianic and eschatological way of living in community that was received from the Lord until he comes again. At the level of individual life, the first generations of Christians called this 'keeping the seal of baptism shining'.[2] It is, however, also a question of the Church as such. The means available to this faithfulness that is based above all in the faithfulness of God are:

1. The essential elements of the Church as an institution as given by Jesus: the Word, the sacraments, the ministry of the Twelve and, at a deeper level, the establishment of the Twelve (Mk 3:14) as the beginning of the new people of God, just as the twelve sons of Jacob-Israel had been the beginning of the old people of God.[3] As they were at the beginning, those Twelve will also be at the end, judging the faithfulness of the tribes of the new Israel to the rules that applied at the beginning (see Mt 19:28; Lk 22:30; cf. 1 Cor 6:2; Rev 20:4). We have, as Newman urged, to watch until he returns. This eschatological aspect of the Church's apostolicity has a clear place in the last judgement. Scripture speaks of it in terms of a distinction between

the sheep and the goats (Mt 25:32) or between what has been built on the foundation with gold, silver or precious stones and what has been built with wood, hay or stubble and will therefore be burnt (1 Cor 3:12–15). The apostles, then, will judge whether what reaches the end or the Omega, the last letter of the alphabet through which history has passed, is in conformity with what was given at the Alpha, that is, at the beginning to which they were, are and finally will be witnesses.

2. The mission which has been given once and which is all-embracing ('all nations') and guaranteed ('I am with you always, to the close of the age) (see Mt 28:19–20). Apostolicity is the identity, almost the oneness, of this apostolic mission throughout the centuries until the end, while the men who carry out this mission die one after the other and are replaced by others.[4] This mission is also the mission of Christ, or at least it is a sharing in the mission of Christ.

3. At an even deeper level than the mission of Christ, there is Christ himself as 'consecrated and sent into the world' (Jn 10:36). This Johannine reference points to the fact that it is not so much Christ in himself or in his constitution as man-God—however much that may be the essential condition for the authenticity of the rest—as Christ as the one who is sent and who is for us: *propter nos et nostram salutem*. That Christ is the one who was anointed and sanctified by the Spirit for his mission as the Messiah and Saviour: at the time of his conception (Lk 1:35), when he was baptized, throughout the whole of his activity and especially during his struggle against the Prince of this world, and finally, in a way that was decisive for what was to follow, in his resurrection, glorification and enthronement as Lord. His humanity as the Servant who was obedient to death and crucifixion was established from that time onwards in the full state of a *humanity of the Son of God*, that is, a humanity that is powerful enough to communicate to us, through the Holy Spirit, the quality of sons of God. He is the eschatological Adam, the one who leads us to the God who is 'everything to everyone' by acting as the 'Spirit who gives life'. All this can be reduced to a system of the kind that is now known as a 'Christology of the Spirit',[5] but this kind of Christology is in no sense Adoptionist. It is firmly based on the classical Christology of the Word made flesh, the Chalcedonian Christology of the two natures and the hypostatic union. The 'life-giving spirit' of 1 Cor 15:45 is the same as the Word made flesh of Jn 1:14, as the one who was conceived in Mary by the Holy Spirit (Lk 1:35) and the one whom 'God anointed with the Holy Spirit and with power' and who 'went about doing good and healing all that were oppressed by the devil, for God was with him' (Acts 10:38).[6]

4. Just as they were sent, the Son and the Spirit were also given, but the title 'Gift' can be more particularly applied to the Holy Spirit, as we shall see in

Volume III of this work. Their mission as a gift is the movement by which the eternal and divine processions freely have a term in the history of the world. The same Spirit who is in God, as a Person proceeding by means of love—the love that is common both to the Father and to the Son—is also in Christ, the incarnate Son, sanctifying him, and in us, in other words, in the Church.[7] The Spirit is therefore the ultimate principle, that is, the supreme and fulfilling principle of the identity of the supernatural and saving work of God.

In the case of the Church as such, I propose now to discuss the part played by the Holy Spirit in bringing about and maintaining the continuity and even the identity between the Alpha and the Omega, in the category of testimony. I will consider this question within an authentically biblical perspective.

1. I have derived a great deal of help here from a posthumous work by Ragnar Asting published in 1939.[8] The Hebrew of the Old Testament is very valuable to our understanding of this question, since the New Testament authors wrote in Greek, but their categories of thought were Hebrew. The verb '*ûdh*, which means 'to bear witness', 'to testify', expresses the idea of repetition and this involves the idea of affirmation and a commitment of the will. The Ark and the Tabernacle of the exodus were called 'of testimony', because they were the places from which Yahweh revealed his will. God's law was also called his 'testimonies' (see Ps 119). This testimony is also, like the Word of God (examined by Asting, *op. cit.* (note 8 below), pp. 6–299), *vorwärtsgerichtet*, 'directed forward' and not 'backwards-looking', *zurückschauend*. The Greek words *marturein, martur*, on the other hand, come from an Indo-European root meaning 'to remember', 'to think' or 'to reflect'. The Latin word *memor* is also derived from the same root. In other words, the witness reports and testifies to what he has already seen.

The New Testament expressed in Greek the content of the Hebrew concept. It does not express the meaning that we attach to the word 'martyr', that is, suffering and even death for a cause. One is not a martyr because one dies. On the contrary, one suffers and dies because one is a witness, testifying to and affirming the reality of God's will and commitment as expressed in his covenant and in Jesus Christ, who was the first faithful witness (see 1 Tim 2:5–7, 6–13; Rev 1:5; 3:14). This Christian witness refers to Christ's death and resurrection and to his status as Lord. It is always 'directed forwards', *vorwärtsgerichtet*, since, beyond the affirmation that these things in fact took place, it also proclaims their saving value and their present and effective reality for the world. That is why God also bears witness himself together with his witnesses. He is active in and through their testimony.

It is true, however, that the idea of the eye-witness, that is, the one who has already seen and who remembers and testifies, is also encountered in the Old Testament.[9] There are also undoubted cases of this in several texts in the

New Testament (see, for example, Lk 16:19ff.; 24:48; Acts 1:21–22; cf. 4:13; 3:15; 10:39, 41; 13:31). To these examples can be added the testimony of John the Baptist in the gospel of John, although he bears witness to a fact by affirming in it the dynamic realization of God's plan. There are also cases, as Asting pointed out (*op. cit.* (note 8 below), p. 626), in Paul's epistles, in 1 Pet 5:1, and so on. All this is, of course, normal, since God's intervention to save man and his revelation came in Jesus Christ. Testimony is not simply prophetic—it is also apostolic and bears witness to what has already come. Asting himself recognized this,[10] even though he stressed what was 'directed forwards', in other words, the dynamic affirmation of contemporary importance that looked ahead to fulfilment. In the messianic and eschatological age which began with the mission and gift of Jesus Christ and the Holy Spirit, both values of 'witness' are to be combined. The first is the recollection and attestation of what has already taken place; the second is a dynamic affirmation of the present effectiveness of those realities and their fulfilment in the apostolic mission brought about by the facts themselves, until they are eschatologically consummated (see, for example, 1 Jn 1:1–2).

2. In the Johannine discourses of Jesus, the latter speaks of two 'missions', in which his work will be carried out after his departure. The first is that of the apostles (Jn 13:16, 20; 17:18, which looks forward to 20:21) and the second is that of the Paraclete, the Spirit of truth (Jn 14:16, 26; 15:26). These two missions together bear the weight of that testimony which is, as we have seen, a recollection and an affirmation of what took place in the past and, at the same time, a looking forward to the future:

> When the Paraclete comes, whom I shall send to you from the Father, even the Spirit of truth who proceeds from the Father, he will bear witness to me; and you are also witnesses, because you have been with me from the beginning (Jn 15:26–27).
>
> You are witnesses of these things. And behold I send the promise of my Father upon you (Lk 24:48–49).
>
> You shall receive power when the Holy Spirit has come upon you; and you shall be my witnesses . . . (Acts 1:8).
>
> And we are witnesses to these things and so is the Holy Spirit whom God has given to those who obey him (Acts 5:32).

The relationship between the Spirit and those who are sent can be seen at work in the Acts of the Apostles and the Pauline epistles. Before sending them, the prophets and teachers of Antioch lay hands on Saul and Barnabas, who are also said to have been sent on their mission by the Holy Spirit (Acts 13:3–4). In the same way, Paul appointed elders in Lystra, Iconium and Antioch (Acts 14:23), but when he addressed the elders of the church of

Ephesus, he told them: 'Take heed to yourselves and to all the flock, in which the Holy Spirit has made you overseers' (Acts 20:28). Again, Ananias and Sapphira thought that they were only deceiving the apostles, whereas they had lied to the Holy Spirit (Acts 5:2, 3, 9). Finally, it is also worth quoting the formula of the synod of Jerusalem in this context, because it has been interpreted as pointing to a decision made by the Holy Spirit and the apostles: 'It has seemed good to the Holy Spirit and to us' (Acts 15:28).[11]

Those sent preached the kerygma 'through the Holy Spirit' (1 Pet 1:12) and their words were powerful 'in the Holy Spirit' (1 Thess 1:5; Acts 4:31, 33; Heb 2:3–4), but they were first strengthened by the Spirit in the truth (Jn 16:8–13; 1 Jn 5:6). The Church was born and increased because of preaching and the help given by the Holy Spirit (see Acts 6:7; 4:33; 9:31) and the apostolic ministry was a 'ministry of the Spirit' (2 Cor 3:4–18).

Some of Paul's activities were concerned with the institution—the word and the sacraments, or the ministry of the two tables of the bread of life. In this, the Holy Spirit acted with him, achieving in the souls of men what he celebrated externally. The Church is also built up, however, by unexpected interventions which are sometimes hidden and at others revealed to the senses. These include various encounters, inspirations and events. The experience is so generalized that it is pointless to give examples. It is, however, possible to point to a few such interventions in the ministry of the apostles. The Spirit, for example, prevents Paul from going to Asia (Acts 16:6–7), but later, at least according to Codex D, he leads him there and then prompts him to head for Macedonia (19:1; 20:3). Then Paul, anxious to reach Jerusalem, stopped in Miletus, where he delivered his farewell address to the elders of Ephesus: 'And now, behold, I am going to Jerusalem, bound in the Spirit . . . the Spirit testifies to me in every city that imprisonment and afflictions await me' (20:22–23). In his freedom as the Lord who gives life, the Spirit is therefore also involved in the apostolate and does the work of the gospel.

3. The Spirit is also given to the Church as its transcendent principle of faithfulness. Paul—if Paul was indeed the author—exhorted Timothy: 'Guard the truth that has been entrusted to you by the Holy Spirit who dwells within us' (2 Tim 1:14). It has become almost a commonplace to denounce an early form of 'catholicization' of apostolic Christianity in the pastoral epistles.[12] *Charisma* is used in those letters only in respect of Timothy (see 1 Tim 4:14; 2 Tim 1:6). Jesus had promised the Spirit to his disciples as an exegete or a living and sovereign master.[13] In the second and third centuries, the Church Fathers were conscious of a 'tradition' or communication of the Holy Spirit which ensured the unity of faith in the scattered churches:

> The barbarians possess salvation, which is written without paper and ink by the

Spirit in their hearts (see 2 Cor 3:3) and they scrupulously preserve the ancient Tradition.[14]

> As disciples of that (Christ) and witnesses of all his good works, his teaching, his passion, death, resurrection and ascension to heaven after his resurrection according to the flesh, the apostles, with the power of the Holy Spirit, sent by him to the whole of the earth, realized the appeal of the gentiles . . . purifying their souls and their bodies by means of the baptism of water and the Holy Spirit, that Holy Spirit that they received from the Lord. It was by sharing him and distributing him to believers that they established and founded that Church.[15]

> No one will refute all that (asserted by the philosophical sects) except the Holy Spirit sent into the Church. Having received him first, the apostles communicated him to those who had right faith. We, who are their successors, who share in the same grace of the priesthood and teaching and who are thought to be the guardians of the Church, do not close our eyes and do not suppress the word.[16]

The 'tradition/transmission' of the Spirit, which enables the Church to be faithful to and united in its faith, is tied to the function of the bishops. There is evidence of the process described in the pastoral epistles at the beginning of[17] and during the second century: 'It is necessary to listen to the presbyters (bishops) who are in the Church. They are the successors of the apostles and, with the succession of the episcopate, they have received the certain charism of truth according to the good pleasure of the Father.'[18] Since Irenaeus wrote these words, there have, throughout the centuries, been dozens of testimonies to the Church's consciousness of having been helped and 'inspired' by the Holy Spirit, who was promised and given to the Church so that it would be unfailingly faithful to the faith received from the apostles. This has been affirmed again and again as applying to the whole Church[19] and especially to the ecumenical councils 'assembled in the Holy Spirit',[20] to the pastoral government of the Church in general[21] and in particular to the magisterium of the Bishop of Rome.[22] All this goes back ultimately to the Church's apostolicity.

The presence of the Holy Spirit inspiring the Church was frequently presented as automatic and occurring as a matter of course in the predominantly juridical ecclesiology that resulted from the Church's conflict with the secular power, the Counter-Reformation and the reaction to the French Revolution. This is one of the most formidable obstacles in the ecumenical debate and I would like to make three comments which, I believe, go to the root of the problem.

1. We profess to believe that it is the Church that is apostolic and to believe in the Holy Spirit as the one who makes the *Church* apostolic. It was to the Church, assembled and unanimous in the company of the apostles, that the Spirit came at Pentecost. The first community of 120 members was extended by the addition of new members, who joined the earliest nucleus.[23] The

apostolicity of the Church is a communion with the apostles, and with and through them a communion with the Father and his Son Jesus Christ (1 Jn 1:3, 7). The Holy Spirit is the principle of that communion (2 Cor 13:13) and 'to each is given the manifestation of the Spirit for the common good' (1 Cor 12:7).

This universal apostolicity is fundamentally an apostolicity of faith, but it is also an apostolicity of service, witness, suffering and struggle. The 'apostolic succession', in the technical sense of this term, has to be placed within the context of this apostolicity, that is, of this communion extended in time. It is, after all, possible to speak of an apostolic succession in the case of all believers, but only in the wider context of the faithful transmission of faith.[24] It is only within this communion that the 'apostolic succession' in the strict sense of the term, in other words, the succession of the bishops, can take place. This is the profound meaning of the episcopal consecration carried out by several bishops in the midst of the people, who bear witness to the fact that the bishop elect is in the catholic and apostolic faith.[25] What is more, since the Church is also 'apostolic' even in heaven (Rev 21:14), the communion of saints in heaven is also involved in the ordination of ministers (in the litany of the saints).

2. There is therefore, in principle, no automatic, juridical formalism in this question, since the 'hierarchical' function exists within the communion of the *ecclesia*. One ultimate thesis that is almost universally maintained—I only know of two exceptions in the whole domain of theology—is the one which claims that a heretical Pope would cease to be Pope, since he would, as a heretic, have left the communion of faith.

In concrete, this means that the Spirit must actively intervene in the case of any activity that is related to the sacramental or 'hierarchical' institution, whether it has to do with the Word, the pastoral government of the Church or the sacraments in the widest sense of the word, that is, those acts which are concerned with the general sacramentality of the Church. In a study written some thirty years ago and therefore in the categories and the vocabulary of that period—it was, after all, hardly possible to do otherwise—J. de Bacchiochi showed that the visible aspect or 'pole' in the sacramental act, which was connected with the 'apostolic succession' and the historical decisions of the incarnate Word, had to be received and therefore complemented inwardly in the theologal life of the subject at the 'spiritual' or 'prophetic' level or 'pole' at which the influence of the Holy Spirit who was sent by Christ was felt in the soul.[26]

Both poles are necessary. Without the coming of the Spirit, there is only a rite, but the necessity for the act by the ordained minister points to the need for the institution by Christ. In this way, the two 'missions' of the Word and the Breath, the 'Unknown One beyond the Word' or the free Gift according to grace are united and complement one another. That is the function of the epiclesis, of which I shall have more to say in Volume III of this work. Every action performed by the ministry calls for an epiclesis. Orthodox Christians are right when they say that the life of the Church is entirely epicletic. I am therefore in complete agreement with Walter Kasper in his claim that 'the Church is the specific place in which God's saving work in Jesus Christ is made present by the Holy Spirit. Ecclesiology is a function of pneumatology. In modern theology, on the other hand, one often gets the impression that pneumatology has become a function of ecclesiology; the Spirit has become the guarantor of the Church as an institution and pneumatology has become the ideological superstructure on top of ecclesiology.'[27]

We have left behind, or at least are leaving behind, the latter sort of ecclesiology.

3. The Spirit not only keeps the Church faithful to the faith of the apostles and the structures of the covenant, but also helps the Church, so that, when it is called on to confess, affirm and define that faith, it can do so in a confident and even, we have to say, an 'infallible' way. This was the conviction of the Church even before the disturbingly heavy term 'infallible' came to be used.[28] When the Church is called on to declare whether the Holy Spirit is substantially God, whether Jesus Christ had a human will, or whether his body and blood that were offered in sacrifice are really given to us in the Eucharist, it is inevitably helped to confess the truth.

This attribute has, of course, been wrongly used, just as the term 'magisterium' has been misused since the time of Pius IX.[29] 'Infallibility' can only really be applied to certain acts and to judgements made by the Church when it is called on to make a declaration about points concerning the substance of the religious relationship as it has been revealed and offered to us by God in Jesus Christ. The concept which is most suitable to express the whole of the Church's attempt throughout history to profess the saving truth is, however, 'indefectibility'.[30] The Church has, in its pastoral magisterium, approached truth in different ways. It has made mistakes. It has fallen short and has been forgetful of its task. It has been frustrated and has experienced critical moments. These all form part of its historical conditioning—its witness is always conditioned by the historical nature of knowledge, language and expression. The Holy Spirit helps the Church *ne finaliter erret*—so that error will not ultimately prevail (see Mt 16:18).

Protestants may agree with this, and indeed many have stated that they are in agreement with this position.[31] They have constantly stressed that it is not the Church itself that is the primary subject of this indefectibility, or possibly of this infallibility, but the Holy Spirit, and we can gladly accept even this insistence, provided we can also say that grace is *given*. Orthodox Christians also agree within their own theological context, as expressed by the terms *sobornost*' or 'communion' (see section 1 above, pp. 44–45) and epiclesis (see section 2 above), and an apostolicity and a life in the truth which are inseparable from the doxological existence of the Church and from its life in holiness.[32] I shall deal with the latter question in the next chapter. As I have already pointed out, the marks of the Church are not only inseparable from each other—they are also contained within each other. The apostolicity of the Church, in other words, is holy and catholic.

NOTES

1. Certain Protestant theologians, such as W. Pannenberg and K. Barth, have seen apostolicity as identical with mission; with each new generation, believers take their place with the first witnesses and receive authority, power and order to carry out the apostolic mission. J. D. Zizioulas is representative of the Orthodox position. At the end of this chapter, I append a brief survey of the teachings of Pannenberg and Zizioulas on apostolicity.
2. *The Shepherd of Hermas*, Fr. tr. by R. Joly, § 93; Pseudo-Clement, 2 Cor VIII, 6; see also the inscription of Abercius, line 9 of his epitaph. In the classical patristic period, see also John Chrysostom, *Baptismal Catechesis* I, 44 (ed. A. Wenger, SC 50, p. 131); Augustine, *De symb. ad cat.* 7, 15; *Sermo* 352, 2–8 (seal restored by penance).
3. It is possible to compare the canonical exactness of the rules of the 'apostolic succession' with the care taken for the succession and the authenticity of heredity within the tribe of Judah in the course of history: see the explanation that W. Vischer has given for the sharp practices of the patriarchs to prevent their wives from being taken away from them in *Das Christuszeugnis des Alten Testaments*, I, 6th ed. (Zürich), p. 157, or even the episode of Tamar in Gen 38: see Vischer, *ibid*., p. 200.
4. This accounts for the fairly frequent quotation (from Augustine onwards) of Ps 44:77 (Vulgate): 'pro patribus tuis nati sunt tibi filii'. See also the chapter on apostolicity in my *L'Eglise une, sainte, catholique et apostolique (Mysterium Salutis*, 15) (Paris, 1970), especially pp. 216ff.
5. W. Kasper, *Jesus the Christ* (Eng. tr.; London and New York, 1976), has, for example, provided a synthesis of this. See also P. J. Rosato, 'Spirit Christology: Ambiguity and Promise', *ThSt* 38 (1977), 423–449.
6. The main texts in the New Testament which form the basis for this section are those relating to the life of Jesus on earth, studied in J. D. G. Dunn, *Jesus and the Spirit. A Study of the Religious and Charismatic Experience of Jesus and the First Christians as Reflected in the New Testament* (London, 1975). For Jesus at Easter and the glorified Jesus, see Rom 1:4; 8:11; 1 Cor 15:45; 1 Pet 3:18; 1 Tim 3:16.
7. For the Spirit as *idem numero* or 'identically the same' in Christ and in us, see above, p. 23, note 19. For the Spirit filling us with love with which God himself loves us, see Volume I, pp. 86–87, for the admirable prayer of William of Saint-Thierry. See also Albert the Great: 'illud autem *unum* quod Pater coelestis habet in Filio naturali (the Word, the Son) et in filio per adoptionem (ourselves) est Spiritus, quia ipse nos diligit Spiritu Sancto et nos eum et nos invicem nos diligimus Spiritu Sancto'; see his *Comm, in Ioan*. 8, 41 (ed. A. Borgnet, XXIV, 360); see also *Comm. in Luc*. q. 35 (Borgnet, XXII, 667).
8. R. Asting, *Die Verkündigung des Wortes im Urchristentum. Dargestellt an den Begriffen 'Wort Gottes', 'Evangelium' und 'Zeugnis'* (Stuttgart, 1939): for 'testimony', see pp. 458–712.
9. See, for example, Gen 31:50 (Asting, *op. cit*., p. 476); Is 43:9ff.; 44:8, although the active meaning is emphasized here; cf. 55:4 (Asting, pp. 490ff.); Job 16:19.
10. See Asting, *op. cit*., pp. 597, 601, 607, 626, 671ff., 685.
11. The French *Traduction Œcuménique* prefers: 'The Holy Spirit and we have decided . . .'.

Some scholars believe that the decision attributed to the Spirit was not the one about the decree borne by the apostles, the elders and the brethren, but the initiative concerning Cornelius (see Acts 10:44–47; 15:8).

12. See J. D. G. Dunn, *op. cit.* (note 6), pp. 347ff., who provides references to earlier studies.
13. Jn 14:16ff., 26; 16:13ff. See J. Michl, 'Der Geist als Garant des rechten Lebens', *Vom Wort des Lebens. Festschrift M. Meinertz*, ed. N. Adler (Münster, 1951), p. 147; J. J. von Allmen, 'L'Esprit de vérité vous conduira dans toute la vérité', O. Rousseau *et al.*, *L'Infaillibilité de l'Eglise. Journées œcuméniques de Chevetogne, 25–29 September 1961* (Chevetogne, 1963), pp. 13–26.
14. Irenaeus, *Adv, haer.* III, 4, 2 (*PG* 7, 855; ed. W. W. Harvey, II, 15; *SC* 211, p. 47).
15. Irenaeus, *Dem.* 41 (*SC* 62, p. 96).
16. Hippolytus, *Philosophoumena* I, praef. 6.
17. Ignatius of Antioch, *Smyrn.* VIII and IX, 1.
18. Irenaeus, *Adv. haer.* IV, 26, 2 (*PG* 7, 1053; Harvey, II, 236; *SC* 100, p. 719). The meaning of this *charisma veritatis certum* has been widely disputed. There have been three main interpretations: (1) a grace of infallibility or at least of orthodoxy, received at ordination with the succession: see L. Ligier, 'Le ch. ver. cer. des évêques. Ses attaches liturgiques, patristiques et bibliques', *L'homme devant Dieu. Mélanges H. de Lubac* (Paris, 1964), I, pp. 247–268. In favour of this interpretation, there are its harmony with a much wider context and the connection that it appears to make between consecration and the grace that is the effect of that consecration. More recently, J. D. Quinn has based a similar interpretation on a study of the Latin text, which is the only one that we have: *ThSt*, 39 (1978), 520–525. There are, however, certain objections to this interpretation: (a) there is no parallel to this formal statement; (b) it presupposes a kind of automatism which is excluded by other texts: see *Adv. haer.* III, 3, 1; IV, 26, 5; (c) Irenaeus' theology of Tradition calls for an objective meaning of *veritas*. (2) Several scholars, such as D. van den Eynde (*Normes de l'enseignement* (1933), p. 187) and H. von Campenhausen, have suggested that *charisma veritatis* indicates the spiritual gift of truth, in other words, Tradition in the objective sense. (3) A study of the ways in which Irenaeus used the word *charisma* and in which it was used after him has led some scholars to understand it as personal spiritual gifts. According to E. Flesseman-van Leer, *Tradition and Scripture in the Early Church* (Assen, 1954), pp. 119–122; R. P. C. Hanson, *Tradition in the Early Church* (London 1962), p. 159, and others, the meaning is: obey the presbyters whom *God* has called to the episcopate, which was and is obvious from the fact that their consecration has been preceded and accompanied by spiritual gifts, and especially the gift of unfailing faithfulness to the Tradition of the apostles: cf. *Adv. haer.* IV, 26, 5.
19. I have already cited the important text of Irenaeus, *Adv. haer.* III, 24, 1 (*SC* 211, p. 473). Thomas Aquinas appealed to Jn 16:13 to support his affirmation that the Church cannot err in matters of faith; see *ST* IIa IIae, q. 1, a. 9; *Quodl.* IX, 16. For this theme in Scholastic theology generally, see my *L'Eglise de S. Augustin à l'époque moderne* (Paris, 1970), pp. 244, 232. Statements by theologians writing during the second half of the sixteenth century on the Holy Spirit dwelling in and animating the Church have been brought together by M. Midali, *Corpus Christi mysticum apud D. Bañez eiusque fontes (Anal. Greg.*, 116) (Rome, 1962), pp. 153–188. See also the Dogmatic Constitution on the Church, *Lumen Gentium*, 12; the Constitution on the Church in the Modern World, *Gaudium et spes*, 11; 43, 6, etc.
20. I quoted a number of statements made at ecumenical councils in my *Tradition and Traditions* (Eng. tr.; London and New York, 1966), Part Two, pp. 346–347; Part One, p. 172, note 3: Trent. See also H. du Manoir, 'Le symbole de Nicée au concile d'Ephèse', *Greg*, 12 (1931), 126–129. For patristic texts, see John Chrysostom, *Adv. Iud.* 3, 3 (*PG* 49, 865); Cyril of Alexandria, *Ep.* 1 (*PG* 77, 16B); 17 (*PG* 77, 108C-D)); 53 (*PG* 77, 292D-293A); Celestine I, letter to the Council of Ephesus (Mansi IV, 1283-84; *PL* 50, 505–506); Leo the Great, letter on Chalcedon, *Ep.* 103 (*PL* 54, 988–989) and on Nicaea,

Ep. 104, 3 (*PL* 54, 995–96) and 106, 2 (*PL* 54, 1003–04); Fulgentius, *Ep*. 6, 3 (*PL* 67, 923); Pope Vigilius, *Ep*. 15 (*PL* 69, 56); *De tribus cap*. (*PL* 69, 72), etc.

21. See Volume I, pp. 151ff. See also the Dogmatic Constitution on the Church, *Lumen Gentium*, 21, 2; 24; Decree on the Bishops' Pastoral Office, *Christus Dominus*, 2, 2; K. Hardt, *Die Unsichtbare Regierung der Kirche* (Würzburg, 1956).
22. L. Merklen, 'La continuité pontificale', *Doc. cath*., 739 (3 March 1935), 515–530. There are many examples given.
23. See Acts 2:41, 47; 5:14; 11:24; 17:4. The Fathers often described the Church as a kind of expansion or enlargement from the apostles; see the texts and references in my book, *op. cit*. (note 4), p. 188.
24. Protestant theologians often speak about a wider apostolic succession applying to all believers: see, for example, the report of the European Section of the Faith and Order Commission of the World Council of Churches in preparation for the Montreal Conference and the report of that Conference, in *Verbum Caro*, 67 (1963), 301; 69 (1964), 1–29. Thomas Aquinas also spoke of oral traditions kept 'in observatione Ecclesiae per successionem fidelium': see *ST* IIIa, q. 25, a. 3, ad 4. Luther wrote 'alia et alia est ecclesia et tamen semper eadem in successionem fidelium': *WA*, 4, 169^{30}. Jean Guitton also recorded these words of Pope Paul VI: 'The layman is, like the bishop, a successor of the Apostles': *The Pope Speaks* (Eng. tr.; London, 1968), p. 253.
25. In the early Church, pastors were appointed 'with the consent of the whole Church': see Clement of Rome, 1 Cor XLIV, 3; *Didache* XV, 1. See also H. Legrand, 'Theology and the Election of Bishops in the Early Church', *Concilium*, 7 (September 1972), 31–42; J. Remmers, 'Apostolic Succession: an Attribute of the Whole Church', *Concilium*, 4, no. 4 (1968), 20–27; my 'Apostolicité de ministère et apostolicité de doctrine' (first pub. 1967; later repr. in *Ministères et Communion ecclésiale* (Paris, 1971), pp. 51–94); H. Küng, *The Church* (London, 1967), pp. 355ff.
26. J. de Bacciochi, 'Les sacrements, actes libres du Seigneur', *NRT*, 73 (1951), 681–706. For the early Church, see my *Ecclésiologie du Haut Moyen Age* (Paris, 1968), pp. 113–116.
27. W. Kasper, *An Introduction to Christian Faith* (London, 1980), pp. 138–139.
28. B.-D. Dupuy, 'Le magistère de l'Eglise, service de la parole', *L'Infaillibilité de l'Eglise*, *op. cit*. (note 13), 53–98.
29. See my two notes, published in *RSPT*, 60 (1976), 85–112.
30. See my articles 'Infaillibilité et indéfectibilité', *ibid*., 54 (1970), 601–618, repr. in *Ministères et Communion ecclésiale* (Paris, 1971), pp. 141–165; and 'Après *Infaillible?* de Hans Küng: bilans et perspectives', *RSPT*, 58 (1974), 243–252. See also Dogmatic Constitution on the Church, *Lumen Gentium*, 39, where the Church is said to be '*indefectibiliter* sancta'.
31. See J. J. von Allmen, *op. cit*. (note 13); J. Bosc, 'L'attitude des Eglises réformées concernant l'Infaillibilité de l'Eglise', *ibid*., pp. 211–222, with quotations: the Scottish Confession of Faith and C. XVI of Calvin's *Institutes*, IV, 8, 13; L. Ott, who was K. Barth's successor at Basle, *Die Lehre des I. Vatikanischen Konzils. Ein evangelischer Kommentar* (Basle, 1963), pp. 161–172; the comments of several American Lutherans, *Irénikon*, 51 (1978), 251.
32. E. Lanne, 'Le Mystère de l'Eglise et de son unité', *ibid*., 46 (1973), 298–342, compared the Vatican declaration *Mysterium Ecclesiae* of 24 June 1973 with the Encyclical of the Orthodox bishops of the United States, published at the end of March 1973. Both documents have a similar content, but the Orthodox text places the Church's magisterium and its charism of truth within a context of doxology and holy life to a far greater extent that the Roman document does.

APPENDIX
TWO THEOLOGIES OF APOSTOLICITY
W. Pannenberg and J. D. Zizioulas

W. Pannenberg, 'Apostolizität und Katholizität der Kirche in der Perspektive der Eschatologie', *Theologische Literaturzeitung*, 94 (1965), 97–112. The text of this article has also been published in R. Groscurth (ed.), *Katholizität und Apostolizität*, supplement to *Kerygma und Dogma*, 2 (Göttingen, 1971); and a French translation in *Istina*, 14 (1969), 154–170.

The apostles are not, Pannenberg stresses, simply witnesses. They are also men who have been sent out on a mission for the unfolding of history until the eschatological era and also with that era in view. Faithfulness to the testimony is therefore not only directed back into the past – it is also orientated towards the future eschatological era and consequently towards a fulfilment in the whole of history. Fundamentally, apostolicity and dynamic catholicity are the same. This is more or less my position. Pannenberg, however, has connected this with his idea of revelation as history (see his *Revelation as History* (Eng. tr.; London, 1979). God, in other words, reveals himself in history. That is, as we have seen in the case of the Church's catholicity, fairly obvious, but it is a significant step forward in Protestant theology, in that Pannenberg has gone beyond *Scriptura sola* and a too narrow positivism of scriptural revelation.

J. D. Zizioulas, 'La continuité avec les origines apostoliques dans la conscience théologique des Eglises orthodoxes', *Istina*, 19 (1974), 65–94.

According to Zizioulas, the task of the Christian mystery and the meaning of apostolicity are to realize the 'one and the many'. This can be conceived in accordance with two patterns – a historical and an eschatological pattern.

According to the historical pattern, the apostles were sent and therefore scattered in the world in order to spread the gospel there. This pattern is found in the texts of Clement of Rome. The apostles are thus taken individually. Their succession is historical and ensures a reference to an event in the distant past. This succession is also conceived juridically.[1]

According to the eschatological pattern, the apostles are gathered around the Lord and call the scattered people together to one place (*epi to auto*). This 'one place' (*epi to auto*) is expressed on earth in the celebration of the Eucharist (1 Cor 11:18), which points to the eschatological assembly (see the *Didache* and Ignatius of Antioch). Continuity is therefore conceived not as a continuity of historical transmission, but as a presence. Zizioulas believes that this presence providing continuity is founded on the Spirit, who is the eschatological Gift, and in a pneumatological constitution of Christ and Christology that enables us to be included in him and therefore united as a body with him.

This continuity of presence takes the historical continuity of transmission and memory to a deeper level, and Zizioulas finds this realized in the eucharistic epiclesis which follows the account or the anamnesis. He therefore speaks of the epicletic nature of the life of the Church, by virtue of which it aspires to be what it is already and has to receive this at the present time from God. This present reception is brought about by the Holy Spirit.

Zizioulas suggests that there is another aspect, referring to ordination and the consecration of bishops. This is, in his opinion, not simply a historical (and juridical) transmission of apostolicity which is individual in nature (the logic of the 'one sent' or *šāliāḥ*), but an insertion into the eschatological and eucharistic community. The same applies to the *charisma veritatis certum* conferred at the consecration of a bishop. That is connected with the entire community. Only those bishops – but all those bishops – who are pastors of an *ecclesia* take part in a council of the Church.

Zizioulas does not think that only one of these patterns should be realized at the expense of the other. In the Eucharist, the epiclesis does not make the historical account unnecessary. How would it be possible for the Spirit to be present if there were not the historical reality of the 'economy'? What would be present, or be being actualized? The Fathers called what related to the consummation or the 'mystery' of Christ 'mystical', but they also stressed the fact that the Christ of the 'economy' was involved, not a heavenly being who had not been given in the economy.[2] The Omega truly comes from the Alpha. I would, however, stress this more than Zizioulas does. To be sure, he follows his own perception, which is very rich and profound, and I am fundamentally in agreement with it. Because of the originality of his approach, I have tried to present it as it stands. I reached my own position, however, before reading his article, which in fact owes a great deal to studies made before my own. I hope to have conveyed an idea of the enrichment, possibly the corrections, that an Orthodox insight can bring to our Western thought, however valuable and convincing this may be.

NOTES

1. This idea is effectively in accordance with the way in which the mediaeval theologians thought of the apostles as scattered and at the head of provinces in which they had founded particular churches. See my study, 'Notes sur le destin de l'idée de collégialité épiscopale en Occident au Moyen Age (VIIe–XVIe siècles)', *La Collégialité épiscopale. Histoire et Théologie (Unam Sanctam*, 52) (Paris, 1965), pp. 99–129, especially pp. 115ff. Since writing that article, I have enlarged my documentation.
2. See L. Bouyer, 'Mystique', *VS* (Suppl) (May 1949), 3–23.

5
THE SPIRIT IS THE PRINCIPLE OF THE CHURCH'S HOLINESS

I was tempted to entitle this chapter 'the principle of holiness *in* the Church', but that would have pointed more to the sanctification of persons and this is a question that I shall consider in Part Two of this volume. In this chapter, I shall deal with the Church as such.

I must begin by repeating that the properties of the Church are not to be seen in isolation. They interpenetrate each other. The Church's oneness is holy. It is different from the phenomenon described by sociologists and is to be found at the level of faith. The Church's apostolicity is also holy. It is the continuity of a mission and a communion which begin in God. Finally, the catholicity of the Church is holy and different from, for example, a multinational or world-wide expansion.

Nothing is said about a holy Church in the New Testament. The texts that come closest to this theme are Eph 5:26 and 27, in which the Church is seen as the Bride of Christ, and the reference to God's holy temple (1 Cor 3:16ff.). The members of the Church are, however, called 'saints' (see, for example, Rom 12:13; 1 Cor 1:2; 6:1, 2; 14:33; Phil 1:1; 4:21, 22; Col 1:1, 4; Eph 4:12; Acts 9:13, 32, 41; 26:10, 18; Rev 13:7), a 'holy priesthood' and a 'holy nation' (1 Pet 2:5, 9) and a 'holy temple' (Eph 2:21). The adjective 'holy' is the first that was attributed to the Church, although it was not used very frequently until Hippolytus expressed the third baptismal question in the following way: 'Do you believe in the Holy Spirit in the holy Church for the resurrection of the flesh?'[1] This takes us back to the turn of the second and third centuries A.D.

The Church, then, is a bride and a temple, but strictly speaking every believing soul is a bride, and every believer is a temple; this is in the New Testament[2] and is proclaimed again and again by the Fathers. At least since Origen, whose influence was very great, but even before him – Hippolytus, for example—the Fathers and other early authors said that 'every soul is the Church'.[3] Every soul is a bride and every soul is a temple. The liturgy passed from one to the other and from the singular to the plural, using the singular first.[4] For the earliest Christian writers, the Church was the 'we' of Christians.[5]

The Church as the Temple

In his commentary on the 'holy catholic Church' in the Creed, Thomas Aquinas said: 'The Church is the same as an assembly (*congregatio*) and "holy Church" must therefore be the same as an "assembly of believers" and each Christian is a member of the Church itself'. He then goes on to explain this attribute of holiness and says:

> The Church of Christ is holy. The temple of God is holy and that temple is you (1 Cor 3:17). Hence the words *sanctam Ecclesiam*. The believers of that assembly (*congregatio*) are made holy in four ways. In the first place, just as a church is, at the time of its consecration, materially washed, so too are the believers washed by the blood of Christ: Rev 1:5: 'he loved us and washed us from our sins in his blood'; and Heb 13:12: 'Jesus, in order to sanctify the people through his own blood'. . . . In the second place, by an anointing: just as the Church is anointed, so too are the believers anointed in order to be consecrated by a spiritual anointing. Otherwise, they would not be 'Christians', since 'Christ' means the 'Anointed One'. This anointing is the grace of the Holy Spirit: 2 Cor 1:21: 'he who has anointed us is God'; 1 Cor 6:11: 'You were sanctified in the name of the Lord Jesus Christ (and by the Spirit of our God)'. In the third place, by the indwelling of the Trinity, since where God dwells, that place is holy: Gen 28:17: 'Truly, this place is holy!'; and Ps 93:5: 'holiness befits thy house, O Lord'. In the fourth place, because God is invoked; Jer 14:9: 'Thou, O Lord, art in the midst of us and thy name is invoked over us'. We must therefore take care, since we are sanctified in this way, that we do not, though sin, defile our soul, which is God's temple; as the Apostle says, 1 Cor 3: 'If anyone destroys God's temple, God will destroy him'.[6]

In connection with the theme of the Church as the holy temple, Thomas is not dealing with this idea as such, but simply quotes 1 Cor 3:16–17. He does not quote other New Testament texts, such as Jn 2:19–22, in which the Body of Christ, the Church, is called the temple or house in which spiritual worship is given to God. Two of the most important texts are:

> Through him (Christ in his suffering) we both have access *in one Spirit* to the Father. So, then, you are no longer strangers and sojourners, but you are *fellow-citizens with the saints* and members of the household of God, built upon the foundation of the apostles and prophets, Christ Jesus himself being the corner-stone in whom the whole structure is joined together and grows into *a holy temple* in the Lord; in whom you are also built up into it for *a dwelling-place of God in the Spirit* (Eph 2:18–22).

> Like living stones be yourselves built into a spiritual house, to be a holy priesthood, to offer spiritual sacrifices acceptable to God through Jesus Christ (1 Pet 2:5).

In these texts, what is stressed is spiritual worship and above all the fact that we have access to the Father: 'Our fellowship with the Father' (1 Jn 1:3). Jesus himself said: 'The hour is coming, and now is, when the true worshippers will worship the Father in spirit and truth. . . . God is spirit and those who worship him must worship in spirit and truth' (Jn 4:23–24). To say that God is spirit is not so much a statement about his nature as about the truth of our religious relationship. The fact that Christian worship must be spiritual does not mean that it cannot be sensible, corporeal: it means that it must proceed from faith and express the theologal reality of faith, hope and charity.[7] That is the work of the Holy Spirit (see Phil 3:3; Jude 20). It is only through the Spirit that it is possible to profess that 'Jesus is Lord' (1 Cor 12:3). The anointing, which is the effect and the mark of the Spirit in us, is an anointing of faith.[8] It is therefore a question of the originality and the truth of *Christian* worship. It is the act in which the Church is most perfectly itself. The Church is the holy temple in which, through the strength of the living water that is the Holy Spirit, faith is celebrated in baptism and love or *agapē* is celebrated in the Eucharist.[9] How beautiful the Church's liturgy is, filling time and space with praise of God the creator and saviour—to the Father through the Son, in the Spirit. When our praise ceases here, it begins a little further to the west, as the sun rises. It goes around the world without interruption, 'uniting all things in him, the Christ, . . . in whom you also, who have heard the word of truth, the gospel of your salvation, and have believed in him, were sealed with the promised Holy Spirit, which is the guarantee of our inheritance until we acquire possession of it, to the praise of his glory' (Eph 1:10, 13).

Temple and house suggest the idea of dwelling or habitation. The New Testament speaks of an indwelling, not simply of 'God', that is, the Father and the Son, but explicitly of the Spirit (Jn 14:15–17; 1 Cor 3:16–17; 6:19; 1 Jn 4:12–13). The Scholastic theologians, and Thomas Aquinas especially, also affirmed this,[10] although certain difficulties are encountered in the way in which Thomists have attempted to explain this indwelling.[11] It is ultimately a question of a substantial indwelling, on the basis of supernatural faith and love, of God in his Tri-unity, as the term or object of knowledge and love. This applies quite well to individual persons,[12] but how can it be applied to the Church as such?

The difficulty does not really exist. In the first place, as Thomas himself was careful to point out, the Church is the assembly of believers. If each soul is the Church, then the latter is even more clearly characterized as the house of God in which the believers are present as 'living stones' (Eph 2:20–22; 1 Pet 2:5). And if it is on the basis of charity that God (the Spirit) dwells fully, then only the Church, as the Body of Christ, is certain always to have a faith that is fashioned by charity,[13] since every individual person is able to fail in this. It was to the Church that the promises were made, and by 'Church' what is meant is not simply the assembled believers or what H. de Lubac called the *ecclesia congregata*, but also the *ecclesia congregans*, the essential elements of the apostolic institution, that is, its function and its teaching ministry together with its sacraments. Is this not the fundamental meaning of the promises contained in Mt 16:18–19; 28:19–20, taken together with

Jn 14:16? The Church, which is the house of the living God, is the sacrament of salvation for mankind. It is not simply liturgy offered to God, but also a sign of God's love for men and of his kingdom. Even the structures that are also known as 'churches' have this part to play in our towns and villages.

The Church as the Bride

Let me begin by quoting the most important New Testament texts that are in some way related to the theme of the Church as the bride. In passing, it should also be pointed out that this theme also occurs in the Old Testament.[14]

> I betrothed you to Christ to present you as a pure bride to her one husband (2 Cor 11:2).
>
> Husbands, love your wives, as Christ loved the Church and gave himself up for her, that he might sanctify her, having cleansed her by the washing of water with the word, that he might present the church to himself in splendour, without spot or wrinkle or any such thing, that she might be holy without blemish. . . . No man ever hates his own flesh, but nourishes it and cherishes it, as Christ does the Church, because we are members of his body. For this reason, a man shall leave his father and mother and be joined to his wife and the two shall become one flesh (Eph 5:25–27, 29–31).
>
> He saved us, not because of deeds done by us in righteousness, but in virtue of his own mercy, by the washing of regeneration and renewal in the Holy Spirit, which he poured out upon us richly through Jesus Christ our Saviour, so that we might be justified by his grace and become heir in hope of eternal life (Tit 3:5–7).

This last text does not refer to a bride or bridegroom, but it completes and explains what Ephesians contains implicitly, namely that the Spirit plays a part in baptismal purification and regeneration, and it also refers explicitly to an eschatological fulfilment.

The Fathers of the Church frequently contemplated the mystery of the wedding between Christ and the Church (mankind), and this theme was often celebrated in the liturgy.[15] Tradition has the task of gathering these data of revelation, harmonizing them and deepening Christian understanding of them. I have studied that Tradition with great love. This is how it sees the mystery of that wedding. In the first place, it sees it as an election of grace, by means of a choice and an appeal and by means of an anticipatory love. The Word, the Son, decided to marry human nature through his incarnation. This aspect of election is stressed by the Fathers together with the aspect of purification.[16] Christ assumed soiled human nature and purified it, by making it his betrothed or bride. He based this purification on his baptism, which is the sacramental foundation of our baptism, and on his death on the cross. Both these realities communicate his Spirit to the Church, the new Eve. On the basis of baptism and the gift of the Spirit in the first place, and secondly on the basis of the Eucharist, in which Jesus nourishes the Church with his own spiritualized body, the Church as the bride becomes the Body of Christ and with him forms, spiritually and mysteriously (or mystically), 'one flesh'. This aspect of mystery, which is also essentially Pauline (see P. Andriessen, note 14 below), was developed by Augustine especially and, some forty years ago, Claude Chavasse gave special attention to it. In the seventeenth century, Bossuet also wrote splendidly about the complementary nature of the two terms—bride and body.[17]

The wedding has been celebrated and the Church is the bride, but she is not yet the perfectly pure bride inaugurated by baptism. She is tempted, in her sinful members, to join other bridegrooms (see 1 Cor 6:15ff.). The union that should be consummated in one spirit (or Spirit) is still imperfect. The Church must also experience an Easter event of death and resurrection in the power of the Spirit. Her wedding will only be perfect eschatologically. She aspires to that perfection. She only possesses the first-fruits of the Spirit, as earnest-money. His groaning in us towards the end of God's plan (Rom 8:26–30) also aspires to that consummation. This ultimate revelation is wonderfully expressed in the Apocalypse:

> The Lord our God the Almighty reigns! Let us rejoice and exult and give him the glory, for the marriage of the Lamb has come and his Bride has made herself ready; it was granted her to be clothed with fine linen, bright and pure, for the linen is the righteous deeds of the saints (Rev 19:6–8).
>
> And I saw the holy city, new Jerusalem, coming down out of heaven from God, prepared as a bride adorned for her husband (Rev 21:2).
>
> The Spirit and the Bride say: 'Come!' (Rev 22:17).

According to the Bible, the truth of all things is found at the end, but it is envisaged at the beginning. What is seen as fulfilled in the last chapters of the last book in this final 'unveiling' or 'Apocalypse' was already in mind in the first chapters of the first book, the book of 'beginnings' or 'Genesis':

> In the beginning . . . the Spirit of God moved over the face of the waters. . . . And God said, 'Let us make man in our image, after our likeness'. . . . So God created man in his own image . . . male and female he created them. . . . God said, 'It is not good that man should be alone; I will make him a helper fit for him'. . . . So the Lord God caused a deep sleep to fall upon the man . . . and the rib which the Lord God had taken from the man he made into a woman and brought her to the man. . . . Therefore a man leaves his father and his mother and cleaves to his wife and they become one flesh (Gen 1:1; 1:26, 27; 2:18, 21–24).

From the time of Tertullian onwards at least, the Fathers of the Church and the early Christian writers have been unanimous in seeing this as a prophetic announcement of the wedding between Christ, the new Adam, and the Church, the new Eve, when, from the pierced side of Jesus, fallen into the deep sleep of death, came water and blood, the sacraments, baptism and the Eucharist, which built up the Church: the marriage of the Cross and the marriage of the Lamb![18]

The Struggles of the Holy Church of Sinners

We are living between Genesis and the Apocalypse, subject to the rule of the Spirit, who is given to us now (only) as *arrha* or earnest-money or as first-fruits. There is always a struggle in our personal lives between the Spirit and the flesh, but the Church as such is also involved in this struggle because it is so carnal. Do I need to stress this? Christians are conscious of the weight of the flesh in the Church, but the Church does not admit it often enough.[19] People's confidence is inhibited by the mass of historical faults and the inadequacies of the Church. The Church, the bride of Christ who is 'gentle and lowly in heart' (Mt 11:29), has often been proud and hard in history. As the disciple of the Son of man who had 'nowhere to lay his head' (Mt 8:20), the Church has often sought a comfortable settled life and wealth. The Church's soul is the Holy Spirit, the 'Unknown One beyond the Word', but it has often misinterpreted the signs of the times and has remained attached to formal practices and to fixed structures of power. Paul stressed that Christians are ministers, not of the letter of the law, but of the Spirit (2 Cor 3:6). That is our task, but we hardly dare to confess it, because we know how many times we have failed in it.

But why should we go on listing these grievances? Surely we should engage, as Jacques Leclercq said, in a 'struggle for the spirit of Christ in the Church',[20] so that the Church, as the messianic people of God, may respond fully to what Bernard called *quod tempus requirit*—the appeals and demands of history, a history that is completed by the kingdom of God. Purity and fullness are the two great themes which call for and give rise, in the Church, to reforms and new creations. They point to a dividing line that is sometimes dramatic, but always open, between ideal and reality, and to what J. B. Metz has called an inexhaustible 'eschatological reserve'.

We possess the Spirit only as *arrha*, earnest-money, or as first-fruits, but he is always the 'Promised One'.[21] He is always ahead of us and calls us, as Mgr Ignatius Hazim so rightly said. He draws us on towards the eschatological inheritance of the kingdom of God. Instead of the words: 'Thy kingdom come' in Lk 11:2, several manuscripts have: 'May thy Spirit come upon us and purify us'. This reading was preferred by some of the Church Fathers.[22] The Spirit thus furthers the cause of the gospel. He encourages great initiatives to renew the Church, missions, the emergence of new religious orders, great works of the mind and heart. He inspires necessary reforms and prevents them from becoming merely external arrangements, so that they are able to lead to a new life according to the spirit of Jesus.

We can 'grieve' the Spirit (Eph 4:30) or 'quench' him (1 Thess 5:19). We can even 'resist' him (Acts 7:51). On the other hand, we can also listen to the

Spirit and co-operate with him so that we can 'reflect the glory of the Lord' and be 'changed into his likeness', by the Lord 'who is the Spirit' (2 Cor 3:18). The Church, then, is a sign of the presence of God. It is a 'hagiophany', revealing the reality and the presence of another world, an anticipation of the kingdom in which God will be 'everything to everyone' (1 Cor 15:28). A few years ago, Malcolm Muggeridge was given the task of preparing a television programme on Mother Teresa of Calcutta for the BBC. He expected it to be a pathetic failure, but it excited world-wide interest. Here is his account of this revelation of the power of God in the Spirit:

> Discussions are endlessly taking place about how to use a mass medium like television for Christian purposes, and all manner of devices are tried, from dialogues with learned atheists and humanists to pop versions of the psalms and psychedelic romps. Here was the answer. Just get on the screen a face shining and overflowing with Christian love; someone for whom the world is nothing and the service of Christ everything; someone reborn out of servitude to the ego and the flesh and into the glorious liberty of the children of God. . . . It might seem surprising, on the face of it, that an obscure nun of Albanian origins, very nervous—as was clearly apparent—in front of the camera, somewhat halting in speech, should reach English viewers on a Sunday evening as no professional Christian apologist, bishop or archbishop, moderator or knockabout progressive dog-collared demonstrator ever has. . . . The message . . . was brought . . . 'in demonstration of the Spirit and of power; that your faith should not stand in the wisdom of men, but in the power of God'.[23]

It is the Holy Spirit who causes this radiation of holiness. Even the most intelligent addresses do not produce a spiritual harvest in the world. Such a crop is produced by souls who are hidden in God, who are totally abandoned and lost to the world and who give themselves unconditionally to God: souls such as Seraphim of Sarov or Charles de Foucauld. The facts are evident: it is lives like these that change the lives of others, because they radiate holiness.

Dare I move on from this brief discussion of the revelation of God's holiness in the lives of Christian believers to mention a hagiophany in and through beauty? According to Irenaeus, Athanasius, Cyril of Alexandria and other Church Fathers, the incarnate Word reveals the invisible Father and the Spirit reveals the Word, Christ. Going further, we can say that the saints reveal the Spirit, that is to say, they reveal God as gift, love, communication and communion. The Christian iconography of the East and the West has frequently expressed this radiation in the apostles and the holy men and women of the Church (see, for example, F. Ostlender's article, cited below, note 24). Many monuments and church buildings reveal the presence of the Spirit—one has only to think of Chartres Cathedral or Le Thoronet, for example. Singing is also an expression of the Spirit in beauty. The Spirit is made audible as sweetness and harmony in the spiritual flight of Gregorian chant, the blending of voices in the intonation of the psalms, the polyphony of the Orthodox liturgies and even in the spontaneous singing at meetings of the Renewal movement. All this is surely 'peace and joy in the Holy Spirit' (Rom 14:17).

The Communion of Saints[24]

This term, which has enjoyed great favour among Catholics, comes from the so-called 'Apostles' Creed', a document of the Western Church. It is not until a little before 400 that the presence of this formula is attested. Contrary to what some scholars believe,[25] it is not in apposition to the formula *sanctam Ecclesiam* and explaining its meaning.[26]

With what or with whom do we claim to be united, when we profess our faith, and in what or in whom are we participating? Does the word *sanctorum* refer to a neuter plural, the *sancta*, or to a masculine, the *sancti* (not forgetting the *sanctae*)? The earliest explanations favour the saints, that is, the community of the blessed anticipated in the Catholic Church. This was the interpretation of Niceta of Remesiana; it was given a more precise definition later in the fifth century by Faustus of Riez, who applied it to the martyrs. Later still, and especially in the Middle Ages, theologians spoke of a participation in holy things (*sancta*), in other words, the sacraments, and above all the Eucharist.[27] In the Niceno-Constantinopolitan Creed, baptism is mentioned at the point where the so-called Apostles' Creed speaks of the communion of saints. In reality, however—and the biblical Greek word *koinōnia*, translated by the Latin *communio*, requires us to see the matter in this light—it means the participation in the good things of the community of salvation together with the other members of that community.

How can this participation be applied and extended? In order to answer this question, we have to ask another: What is the principle of this participation? All those who have written about this matter have replied: charity. This is certainly the divine principle of participation, 'because God's love has been poured into our hearts through the Holy Spirit which has been given to us' (Rom 5:5). All authors agree that this is the love by which God loves himself. John of the Cross said, for example: 'The soul loves God not through itself, but through God himself, because it loves in this way through the Holy Spirit, as the Father and the Son love each other and according to what the Son himself says in the gospel of John: "that the love with which thou hast loved me may be in them, and I in them" (Jn 17:26)'.[28] If this love, which is uncreated grace, is really to be our own, it must produce in us an effect or a created grace, namely charity. It is to that charity that Thomas Aquinas, following a unanimous tradition, attached that unity through which a communication of spiritual good things took place between believers. What is in one member of the community is there for the benefit of another member, just as the health of one member benefits the health of the whole body: 'propter communicantiam in radice operis, quae est charitas'—'by virtue of the communication of everyone with everyone else, through the root of their actions, charity'.[29]

Because the principles of the Church's unity are so real and firmly based, it is possible for us, in Karl Rahner's magnificent phrase, to believe beyond this world and to love as far as God's world, even with and into his heart. That is why the communion of saints extends as far as the blessed in heaven and includes our own dead who have passed beyond the veil that hides them from our sight.

Thomas—although he, like most Scholastic theologians, sometimes gives the impression of concentrating on physical things—can be taken as a sure guide here. His true attitude is clear from the way in which he establishes a foundation for merit in the communion of saints. He takes as his principal text the promise made by Jesus to the Samaritan woman: 'The water that I shall give him will become in him a spring of water welling up to eternal life' (Jn 4:14).[30] Only God, through the Spirit who is what is grace and gift in him, is able to be, in us, the radical principle of that eternal life that is the communication of his own life. By receiving us as his sons, he receives himself, having given himself to us and having dwelt in us. As we have already seen, so that this may really be our own, he brings it about by a gift that we call grace or charity.

This gift, with its radical principle, the Holy Spirit, is present in all the members of the communicational Body of Christ and therefore allows an intercommunication of spiritual energy to take place between them. In this context, Thomas declares: 'Not only are the merits of the passion and the life of Christ communicated to us, but also all the good that the saints have done is communicated to those who live in charity, since all are one: "I am a companion (= participant) of all who fear thee" (Ps 119:63). The one who lives in charity is therefore the participant of all the good that is done in the world.'[31]

As a man of the Middle Ages, Thomas insists on the satisfaction that can be offered for another person, and even stresses the importance of indulgences.[32] Prayer for the departed is based, he claims, on the fact that 'death . . . cannot separate us from the love of God in Christ Jesus our Lord' (Rom 8:38–39), and he bases the effectiveness of that prayer on the unity of charity.[33] That unity makes a bond between the Church on earth and the Church beyond the veil. The liturgy of the Church expresses the conviction that these two parts of the same people of God are united in praise and concelebrate the same mystery, above all in the Eucharist. We enter into the holy action of the Eucharist only in unity with the angels and the blessed who acclaim that God is three times holy. Even more importantly, our sovereign celebrant is Jesus Christ himself, our High Priest (Heb 8:2), and we call on the Spirit to concelebrate with us. 'May the Lord Jesus and the Holy Spirit speak in us and may he sing in hymns through us'—these words are taken from the early anaphora of Serapion.[34] It is the supreme realization here on earth of the communion of the saints, but the holiness of men living in the Spirit also contributes to it.[35] We are, in Christ and as members of his Body, of profit and value to each other (see 1 Pet 4:10). Thomas even applies this pneumatological theology of the communion of saints to the baptism of babies. It is true, he claims, that they do not personally possess faith, but the faith of the whole Church is of profit to them, because that Church lives, through the activity of the Holy Spirit, in the unity and the communion of spiritual good things.[36] What, then, should we not dare to believe and profess if the Holy Spirit, personally and identically the same, is in God, in Christ, in his Body and in all the members of that Body?

NOTES

1. See P. Nautin, *Je crois à l'Esprit Saint dans la sainte Eglise pour la Résurrection de la chair. Etude sur l'histoire et la théologie du Symbole (Unam Sanctam*, 17) (Paris, 1947).
2. The soul as bride: 2 Cor 11:2; the soul as temple: 1 Cor 3:16ff.; 6:19; 2 Cor 6:16. See also 2 Tim 1:14.
3. This was a very common theme; see the texts in H. de Lubac, *Catholicisme (Unam Sanctam*, 3) (Paris, 1938), especially pp. 151ff.; C. Chavasse, *The Bride of Christ* (see below, note 15); E. Dassmann, 'Ecclesia vel anima. Die Kirche und ihre Glieder in der Hoheliederklärung bei Hippolyt, Origenes und Ambrosius von Mailand', *RomQuart*, 61 (1966), 121–144.
4. There are many examples of this in the Hispano-Visigothic liturgy; see R. Schulte, *Die Messe als Opfer der Kirche* (Münster, 1959), pp. 71, 72, 75; see also Peter Damian's small but profound treatise, *Dominus vobiscum*, which appeared in partial Fr. tr. in *M-D*, 21 (1950–51), 174–181.
5. K. Delahaye, *Ecclesia Mater chez les Pères des trois premiers siècles (Unam Sanctam*, 46) (Paris, 1964).
6. Thomas Aquinas, *Collationes de 'Credo in Deum'*, Lent 1273, art. IX (*Opera*, Parma ed., XVI, pp. 147–148).
7. In accordance with the New Testament and in the tradition of Augustine: *Ench*. 3, Thomas defined worship in general as a *protestatio fidei* and saw external worship as the expression of the inward worship of the three theologal virtues: see *ST* Ia IIae, q. 99, a. 3 and 4; IIa IIae, q. 93, a. 2; q. 101, a. 3, ad 2. Also in the Augustinian tradition, Hugh of Saint-Victor and William of Auxerre saw the sacraments as sacraments of faith: see J. Gaillard, *RThom*, 59 (1959), 5–31, 270–309, 664–703; L. Vilette, *Foi et sacrements*, 2 vols (Paris, 1959 and 1964).
8. 2 Cor 1:21–22; 1 Jn 2:20, 27. See I. de la Potterie, 'L'onction du chrétien par la foi', *Bib*, 40 (1959), 12–69, repr. in *La vie selon l'Esprit, condition du chrétien (Unam Sanctam*, 55) (Paris, 1965), pp. 107–167; see also Dogmatic Constitution on the Church, *Lumen Gentium*, 12.
9. This is P. Nautin's interpretation of the texts of the apostolic Fathers and Irenaeus of Lyons: *op. cit.* (note 1), pp. 49–50.
10. See Thomas Aquinas, *In III Sent.* d. 13, q. 2, a. 1, ad 2; q. 2, a. 2; see *Collationes de 'Credo in Deum'*, *op. cit.*, (note 6). E. Vauthier, 'Le Saint-Esprit, principe d'unité de l'Eglise d'après S. Thomas d'Aquin. Corps mystique et inhabitation du Saint-Esprit', *MScRel*, 5 (1948), 175–196; 6 (1949), 57–80, criticized me for having neglected the idea of the

indwelling of the Holy Spirit in the Church in my interpretation of Thomas' ecclesiology. Since that time, however, I have frequently considered these questions and the relevant texts. Thomas in fact rarely deals with the theme of indwelling and even more rarely with that indwelling in the Church as such. The truth of my statement can be seen in his *Comm. in 1 Cor*, c. 3, lect. 3, in which the theme of the indwelling of the Spirit in the Church is simply omitted.

11. See, for example, C. Journet, *L'Eglise du Verbe incarné*, II (Paris, 1951), pp. 510–565.
12. In his *Summa*, Thomas mentions the indwelling of the Spirit (through charity) very briefly five or six times. He always says 'in man' or 'in us': see *ST* Ia, q. 43, a. 3, 5; Ia IIae, q. 68, a. 5; IIa IIae, q. 19, a. 6; q. 24, a. 11; IIIa, q. 7, a. 13.
13. See Thomas Aquinas, *In III Sent*. d. 25, q. 1, a. 2, ad 4; *ST* IIa IIae, q. 1, a. 9, ad 3. There are many texts in which he deals with faith animated by charity as the substance of the mystical Body; see *Comm. in Gal.* c. 6, lect. 4, end; *Comm. in Ioan*. c. 7, lect. 7; *In IV Sent*. d. 9, q. 1, a. 2, sol. 4; *ST* IIa IIae, q. 124, a. 5, ad 1; IIIa, q. 80, a. 2, 4.
14. See, for example, Hos 2:4–20; Ezek 16 and 23; Is 61:10; 62:4–5; Song; Ps 45. For the New Testament, see R. A. Batey, *New Testament Nuptial Imagery* (Leiden, 1971); P. Andriessen, 'La nouvelle Eve, corps du nouvel Adam', *Aux origines de l'Eglise (Recherches Bibliques*, VII), ed. J. Giblet (1965), pp. 87–109.
15. See, for example, S. Tromp, 'Ecclesia sponsa, virgo, mater', *Greg*, 18 (1937), 3–21; *idem*, *Corpus Christi quod est Ecclesia*. I: *Introductio Generalis* (Rome, 1937; 2nd ed. 1946), pp. 26–53; O. Casel, 'Die Taufe als Brautbad der Kirche', *Jahrbuch für Liturgiewissenschaft*, 5 (1925), 144–147; *idem*, 'Die Kirche als Braut Christi nach Schrift, Väterlehre und Liturgie', *Die Kirche des lebendigen Gottes (Theologie der Zeit)* (Vienna, 1936), pp. 91–111; H. Engberding, 'Die Kirche als Braut in der Ostsyrischen Liturgie', *Or. Chr. Period*., 3 (1937), 5–48; F. Graffin, 'Recherches sur le thème de l'Eglise-Epouse dans les liturgies et la littérature de langue syrienne', *L'Orient chrétien,* 3 (1938), 317–336; C. Chavasse, *The Bride of Christ. An Enquiry into the Nuptial Element in Early Christianity* (London, 1940). I have also made a special study of Augustine's and Bernard's writings on this theme; the latter often quotes 1 Cor 6:17.
16. The first marriage rite in the Greek world was the bridal bath: see P. Stergianopoulos, *Die Lutra und ihre Verwendung bei der Hochzeit und im Totenkultus der alten Griechen* (Athens, 1922); O. Casel, *op. cit*. (note 15); J. A. Robilliard, 'Le symbolisme du mariage selon S. Paul', *RSPT*, 21 (1932), 243–247; J. Schmid, 'Brautschaft (Heilige)', *Reallexikon für Antike und Christentum*, II, cols 528–564.
17. Bossuet, 'IVe Lettre à une demoiselle de Metz, XXIX–XXXVI': *Correspondance*, I *(Grands Ecrivains de France)* (Paris, 1909), pp. 68–71.
18. There are hundreds of texts: see S. Tromp, 'De nativitate Ecclesiae ex Corde Iesu in Cruce', *Greg*, 13 (1932), 489–527.
19. See, nonetheless, the Dogmatic Constitution on the Church, *Lumen Gentium*, 8, 3, end; 15; Pastoral Constitution on the Church in the Modern World, *Gaudium et spes*, 43; Decree on Ecumenism, *Unitatis Redintegratio*, 4, 5 and 6; Paul VI, Encyclical *Ecclesiam suam*, 6 July 1964; *AAS*, 56 (1964), 628–630, 649; and Paul VI's addresses to his audiences on 10 August 1966 and 7 May 1969, when he quoted my own book and the *ecclesia semper reformanda*: see *Doc. cath*. (1969), p. 506.
20. This is the title of a chapter in Leclercq's *La vie du Christ dans son Eglise (Unam Sanctam*, 12) (Paris, 1944), pp. 90–111. I would also mention some of my own books and articles in this context: *Vraie et fausse réforme dans l'Eglise (Unam Sanctam*, 20) (Paris, 1950; 2nd ed., 1969); 'Comment l'Eglise sainte doit se renouveler sans cesse', *Irénikon*, 34 (1961), 322–345, reprinted in *Sainte Eglise* (Paris, 1963), pp. 131–154; *Power and Poverty in the Church* (Eng. tr.; London, 1964); 'L'application à l'Eglise comme telle des exigences évangéliques concernant la pauvreté', *Eglise et Pauvreté (Unam Sanctam*, 57) (Paris, 1965), pp. 135–155.
21. For the *arrabōn* or earnest-money, see 2 Cor 1:22; Eph 1:14; 5:5; the first-fruits, see

Rom 8:23; see also Heb 6:4. For the 'Promised One', see Lk 24:49; Acts 1:4; 2:33; Gal 3:14; Eph 1:12.

22. An allusion to this will be found in Tertullian, *Adv. Marc*. IV, 26; it appears formally in Gregory of Nyssa, *De orat. Dom*. 3 (*PG* 44, 1157C); Evagrius, *Traité de l'oraison*, 58, ed. I. Hausherr (Paris, 1960), p. 83; Maximus the Confessor (*PG* 90, 884B).
23. Malcolm Muggeridge, *Something Beautiful for God* (London, 1971), pp. 31–32. The quotation from Scripture at the end of this passage is from 1 Cor 2:4–5.
24. F Kattenbusch, *Das Apostolische Symbol* (Leipzig, 1894 and 1900); P. Bernard in *DTC*, III (1908), pp. 450–454; H. B. Swete, *The Holy Catholic Church* (London, 1915), which has the subtitle *The Communion of Saints. A Study in the Apostles' Creed*; F. J. Badcock, ' "Sanctorum communio" as an Article of the Creed', *JTS*, 21 (1920), 106–126; my own article (Fr. orig. pub. in *VS* (January 1935), 5–17), 'Aspects of the Communion of Saints: some remarks on the way we communicate in holy things' (Eng. tr.), *Faith and Spiritual Life* (London, 1969), pp. 122–131; S. Tromp, *Corpus Christi quod est Ecclesia*, I, *op. cit.* (note 15), pp. 152ff.; F. Ostlender, 'Sanctorum communio. Ihr Wesen, ihre Aufgabe und Bedeutung in der altchristlichen Kunst', *Liturgisches Leben*, 5 (1938), 191–203, with 33 reproductions; *Communion des Saints (Cahiers de la VS)* (Paris, 1945); W. Elert, 'Die Herkunft der Formel Sanctorum communio', *Theologische Literaturzeitung*, 74 (1949), 577–586; J. N. D. Kelly, *Early Christian Creeds* (London, 1950), pp. 388–397; C. Journet, *L'Eglise du Verbe incarné*, II, *op. cit.* (note 11), pp. 554ff., 659ff.; A. Michel, *La Communion des Saints* (*Doctor Communis*, IX) (Rome, 1956); A. Polianti, *Il mistero della Comunione dei Santi nella Rivelazione e nella teologia* (Rome, 1957); R. Foley, 'The Communion of Saints. A Study in St. Augustine', *Bijdragen*, 20 (1959), 267–281; P.-Y. Emery, 'L'unité des croyants au ciel et sur la terre. La communion des saints et son expression dans la prière de l'Eglise,' *Verbum Caro*, 63 (1962); E. Lamirande, *La Communion des Saints (Je sais, Je crois)* (Paris, 1962); S. Benkö, *The Meaning of Sanctorum Communio* (*Studies in Historical Theology*, 3) (Eng. tr.; London, 1964); J. M. R. Tillard, 'La Communion des Saints', *VS*, 113 (No. 519: August-September 1965), 249–274; J. Mühlsteiger, 'Sanctorum communio', *ZKT*, 92 (1970), 113–132, who deals with the question from the historical point of view.
25. Even the Roman Catechism, the so-called Catechism of the Council of Trent, has this: see Part I, art. 9, 4 (Fr. tr. in *Cahiers de la VS, op. cit.* (note 24)), which also provides a good authentic commentary.
26. This is clear from several creeds or explanations of the creed; see J. Mühlsteiger, 'Sanctorum communio', *op. cit.* (note 24), pp. 123ff.
27. See, for example, Ivo of Chartres, Peter Abelard and Thomas Aquinas, who provides a characteristically Scholastic explanation, with a brief account of the seven sacraments: see his *Collationes de 'Credo in Deum', op. cit.* (note 6), art. X, in the edition cited, pp. 148–149.
28. John of the Cross, 'The living flame of love', 3; see Lucien-Marie de Saint-Joseph's Fr. tr. quoted by C. Journet, *op. cit.* (note 11), pp. 532, 551.
29. *In IV Sent*. d. 45, q. 2, a. 1, q^a 1. John Chrysostom's fine text is also worth quoting in this context: 'Charity shows you your neighbour as another you and teaches you to enjoy his good as though it were your own and to endure his sufferings as your own. Charity gathers a great number together into a single body and transforms their souls into as many dwelling-places of the Holy Spirit. It is not in the midst of division, but in the union of hearts that the Spirit of peace dwells. . . . Charity makes each one's good common to all': *De perf. car.* (*PG* 56, 281).
30. *ST* Ia IIae, q, 114, a. 3 and 6; *Comm. in Rom*. c. 8, lect. 4; *Comm. in Ioan*. c. 4, lect. 2; see also *Contra Gent*. IV, 21 and 22; *Comp*. I, 147; see also my article 'Mérite', *Vocabulaire œcuménique* (Paris, 1970), pp. 233–251.
31. Thomas Aquinas, *Collationes de 'Credo in Deum', op. cit.* (note 6), art. X, p. 149.
32. 'Actus unius efficitur alterius charitate mediante, per quam omnes unum sumus in Christo'

(Gal 3:28); *In IV Sent*. d. 20, a. 2, q. 3, ad 1; d. 45, q. 2, a. 1, sol. 1.

33. See *Quodl*. II, 14; VIII, 9.
34. *Sacramentarium Serapionis*, XIII, 7; see F. X. Funk, *Didasc. et Const. Apost*., II (Paderborn, 1905), p. 173. For Christ as the sovereign celebrant—a theme which was taken up again in the Constitution on the Liturgy of Vatican II, see, for the Fathers, J. Lécuyer, *Le sacerdoce dans le mystère du Christ* (Paris, 1957), pp. 289ff.; for the High Middle Ages, my *Ecclésiologie du Haut Moyen Age* (Paris, 1968), p. 109 for the Western Church and p. 330 for the Eastern Church. Bede, *Expos. in Luc.* (*PL* 92, 330), presented the Church as invisibly united by the Holy Spirit around its pontiff.
35. 'Per virtutem Spiritus Sancti, qui per unitatem charitatis communicat invicem bona membrorum Christi, fit quod bonum privatum quod est in missa sacerdotis boni, est fructuosum aliis': *ST* IIIa, q. 82, a. 6, ad 3.
36. 'Fides autem unius, imo totius Ecclesiae, parvulo prodest per operationem Spiritus Sancti qui unit Ecclesiam et bona unius alteri communicat': *ST* IIIa, q. 68, a. 9, ad 2. Thomas does not say that the Holy Spirit unites the child who, in principle, does not yet possess charity, to the Church, but that the faith of the Church is there for the profit of the child. Cajetan commented on this: 'Intellige Ecclesiae merita prodesse infanti et iuxta articulum communionis sanctorum et particulariter tam orando pro infante tam applicando eumdem sacramento ex corde puro et caritate plena'.

PART TWO

THE BREATH OF GOD IN OUR PERSONAL LIVES

In October 1963, at the Second Vatican Council, the schema on the Church was being discussed. I was having lunch with two Orthodox observers, who said: 'If we were to prepare a treatise *De Ecclesia*, we would draft a chapter on the Holy Spirit, to which we would add a second chapter on Christian anthropology, and that would be all'.

Clearly, in the Orthodox tradition, Christian anthropology includes a whole theology of man's image being reshaped not only by an ascesis which corresponds to the activity of the Spirit and which works together with the Spirit, but also by the sacraments in which the Spirit acts to sanctify man. My Orthodox friends were nevertheless making a suggestion full of meaning and very illuminating for Western Christians. The first two divisions in this volume—'The Spirit animates the Church' and 'The Breath of God in our personal lives'—have been made for the sake of clarity. These two aspects should not be confused. The Church, however, at least the *Ecclesia congregata*, is the 'we' of Christians; for this reason the two parts should not be completely separated. There are inevitably some repetitions. Some of the themes in this second part were anticipated in the first, and the substance of Part One is completed in Part Two.

This Part Two forms a single whole, but, because I have wanted to develop certain points, some of them specialized, more fully, and for the sake of the structure of the book, I have divided it into chapters.

1
THE SPIRIT AND MAN IN GOD'S PLAN

God, the Principle and End of our Sanctification

This is not a Platonic, but a biblical concept. God is not the 'eternal celibate of the centuries', but love and goodness.[1] He places beings outside himself in order to bring them back to himself, so that they can participate in what he is in his sovereign existence, in other words, in the beginning and the end of their existence. He places outside himself beings who are similar to himself. Because they are like him, those beings are capable of knowing and loving freely, capable of giving themselves freely and returning to him equally freely. He animates them with a movement and therefore with a desire that is an echo in them of his own desire that he has revealed to us as his Spirit. It is in this context that we can place the idea that was so dear to many spiritual writers of the French school, namely that the Spirit has no intra-divine fruitfulness of his own, because he is the end of the processions from the Father and the Son, and is therefore made fruitful outside God, in the incarnation of the Word and the sanctification of men.[2]

The Spirit is the principle of love and realizes our lives as children of God in the form of a Gift, fulfilling that quality in us. It was he who brought about in Mary the humanity of Jesus and anointed and sanctified him for his messianic activity. Through his resurrection and glorification, Jesus' humanity was made by the Spirit a humanity of (the Son of) God. During his life on earth, Jesus was the temple of the Holy Spirit, containing all men with the intention and the power to accept them as children of God.[3] After the Lord's glorification, the Holy Spirit has that temple in us and in the Church and he is active in the same way in us, enabling us to be born *anōthen* (from above and anew: see Jn 3:3) and to live as a member of the Body of Christ. He himself consummates this quality in our body, in the glory and freedom of children of God (see Rom 8:21–23).

This work of the Spirit in Christ and in us constitutes the mystery which Paul regarded as a plan formed in God 'before the foundation of the world' (Eph 1:4; 3:11; Jn 17:24), in other words, at the level of the intra-divine life, the word 'before' referring to priority not in time, but in the order of God's plan. According to Paul, that plan remained hidden or was kept secret for centuries (see Rom 16:25–26; Col 1:26). It has been revealed to man in his reading or hearing the announcement made by the apostles, the prophets and Paul himself. It is concerned with God as love, in other words, with God in his communication of himself and as grace. This, then, goes back to the mystery of God himself. Before the foundation of the world, the Father conceived his Son, the Word, as having to become human through the Holy Spirit and Mary, the daughter of Zion, and as having to assume a humanity that would begin again and at the same time complete the humanity that had come from Adam, because it would be a humanity of the 'first-born of many brethren' (Rom 8:29).

What is necessary and what is free in God should, it is true, not be confused, but, on the one hand, both are identified in him and, on the other, there is no difference, according to Paul, between Christ and the Son, pre-existing before the incarnation. Finally, the economic Trinity, that is, the revelation and the commitment of the divine Persons in the history of salvation, is the same as the immanent Trinity, that is, God as three and one in his absolute nature. (We shall consider this more fully in Volume III.)

The depths of this mystery are beyond our understanding now; we shall only penetrate as far as them in the world to come, and even then our understanding will never be complete. Here, in this life, all that we can do is to rely on Scripture and stammer a few sentences.[4] Christ is the image of the invisible God[5] and man was—and still is—made in God's image. In Luke's genealogy of Jesus, Jesus is described as the son of . . . , the son of . . . , the son of Adam, the son of God. Both the man who came from this earth and the Christ, the Son of God, come *from God*, as though there was in God a humanity, the expression of which was temporal—in the case of Adam, at the beginning, but in the case of Christ, in the fulfilment of time—but the idea of which is co-eternal with God. The mystery, then, is not simply that Jesus Christ is God. It is first and foremost and even more radically that God is Jesus Christ and that he is expressed in two images, each made for the other, the image of man and that of Jesus Christ. The latter, whose state was divine, became assimilated to and united with men at the lowest point of their destiny and was then raised up to the highest point, taking men with him, since 'only he who has descended from heaven, the Son of man', has ascended to heaven (Jn 3:13) and, to ascend with and in him, we must be born anew in him of (water and) the Spirit (Jn 3:5).

> By one Spirit we were all baptized into one body (1 Cor 12:12).
>
> He has saved us, not because of deeds done by us in righteousness, but in virtue of his own mercy, by the washing of regeneration and renewal in the Holy Spirit, which he poured out upon us richly through Jesus Christ our Saviour, that we might be justified by his grace and become heirs in hope of eternal life (Tit 3:5–7).

The Spirit, then, is the principle realizing the 'Christian mystery', which is the mystery of the Son of God who was made man and who enables us to be born as sons of God. Catholic theologians speak of 'grace'. In so doing, they run the risk of objectivizing it and separating it from the activity of the Spirit, who is uncreated grace and from whom it cannot be separated. Only God is holy, and only he can make us holy, in and through his incarnate Son and in and through his Spirit: 'God chose you from the beginning to be saved, through sanctification by the Spirit and belief in the truth' (2 Thess 2:13); 'You were sanctified, you were justified in the name of the Lord Jesus Christ and the Spirit (spirit) of our God' (1 Cor 6:11; cf. Rom 15:16; Heb 2:11). Yet our co-operation in this process of sanctification is required—it is possible for us neglect the gift and make it in vain (see 1 Thess 4:3, 7–8; Rom 6:22; Heb 10:29).

The Spirit is the Absolute Gift promised in fullness eschatologically, possessed as earnest-money in this present life

In his Pentecost address, quoting Joel, Peter stressed the eschatological character of the gift of the Spirit (Acts 2:16ff.). This eschatological aspect is also implicit in the title of 'Promised One' that is given to the Holy Spirit. It is also clear from the connection made by Paul between Christ's resurrection and glorification and the activity of the Spirit in power (Rom 1:4, 8, 10–11). In his letter to the Ephesians, Paul also said: 'You have believed in him and were sealed with the promised Holy Spirit, which is the guarantee (= earnest-money) of our inheritance until we acquire possession of it, to the praise of his glory' (Eph 1:13–14). Elsewhere, he also says:

> We ourselves, who have the first-fruits of the Spirit, groan inwardly as we wait for adoption as sons, the redemption of our bodies (Rom 8:23).

> While we are still in this tent, we sigh with anxiety; not that we would be unclothed, but that we would be further clothed, so that what is mortal may be swallowed up by life. He who has prepared us for this very thing is God, who has given us the Spirit as a guarantee (= earnest-money) (2 Cor 5:4–5).

As we have already seen (p. 57), several of the Church Fathers retained the reading of Lk 11:2 found in a number of manuscripts: 'May thy Holy Spirit come upon us and purify us' in preference to: 'Thy kingdom come', because they were convinced that the kingdom of God was brought about by the gift of God's Spirit. The East shared this conviction with the West. Nicholas of Flüe wrote on 4 December 1482 from his hermitage to the people of Berne: 'May the Holy Spirit be your last reward'.[6] Much later, Seraphim of Sarov (†1833), who became a *starets* at the age of sixty-six, after many years spent in austere solitude as a hermit, said: 'The real aim of our Christian life is that we should be overcome by the divine Spirit. Prayer, fastening, almsgiving, charity and other good works undertaken in the name of Christ are the means by which we acquire the divine Spirit.'[7] It is worth noting in this context that Seraphim places the Spirit at the end, as the aim of

Christian life, but that he also stresses the place of ascesis and man's co-operation or synergy. Simeon the New Theologian, perhaps the greatest of the Byzantine mystics, taught very much the same:

> Whether he has already received the grace of the Spirit or whether he is waiting to receive it, no one will leave the darkness of the soul and contemplate the light of the most holy Spirit without trials, efforts, sweat, violence and tribulation. 'The kingdom of God has suffered violence and men of violence take it by force' (Mt 11:12), for 'through many tribulations we must enter the kingdom of God' (Acts 14:22). The kingdom of God is, in fact, a participation in the Holy Spirit. It is he of whom it is said: 'The kingdom of God is in the midst of you' (Lk 17:21), so that we are bound to apply ourselves to the task of receiving and possessing the Holy Spirit. . . .
>
> Our father (= Simeon the Elder) worked in such a way that he went far beyond many of the early Fathers. He suffered so many trials and temptations that he may be compared with many of the illustrious martyrs. In this way, having received the gift of the Paraclete, he obtained glory and a constant peace of soul from God. Like a tank filled with water, he received the fullness of Christ our Lord and was filled with the grace of his Spirit, who is living water (Jn 4:10). (Here follow quotations from Jn 4:14 and 7:39a.) The Apostle also said: 'Now we have received not the spirit of the world, but the Spirit who is from God, that we might understand the gifts of God's grace' (1 Cor 2:12).[8]

These texts are typical of the Eastern spiritual tradition, in which a strong sense of God's initiative is combined with an equally powerful conviction of human freedom.[9] It is, however, not possible to claim that the Western Catholic tradition is very different, although an experience of the Spirit as light may certainly have developed more strongly in the East. This idea is quite prominent in the writings of Simeon, and it is difficult to read Seraphim of Sarov's famous dialogue with Motovilov and not be moved. I would like to conclude this chapter by quoting it:

> 'All the same, I do not understand how one can be sure of being in the Spirit of God. How can I recognize for certain his manifestation in me?'
>
> 'I have already told you', said Father Seraphim, 'that it is very simple. I have spoken to you at length about the state in which those who are in the Spirit of God find themselves. I have also explained to you how to recognize his presence in us. . . . What more do you still need, my friend?'
>
> 'I must have a better understanding of all that you have said to me.'
>
> 'My friend, at this moment both of us are in the Spirit of God. . . . Why do you not want to look at me?'
>
> 'I cannot look at you, my Father', I replied. 'Your eyes are flashing lightning; your face has become more dazzling than the sun, and it hurts my eyes to look at you.'
>
> 'Do not be afraid', he said, 'at this moment you have become as bright as I am. You are also now in the fullness of the Spirit of God. Otherwise you would not be able to see me as you see me.'
>
> Then leaning towards me, he whispered in my ear:

'Thank the Lord God for his infinite goodness towards us. As you have observed, I have not even made the sign of the cross. It was enough for me simply to have prayed to God in my thoughts, in my heart, saying within me: "Lord, make him worthy to see clearly with his bodily eyes this descent of your Spirit with which you favour your servants when you deign to appear to them in the magnificent light of your glory". As you see, my friend, the Lord at once granted the prayer of the humble Seraphim. . . . How grateful we should be to God for this inexpressible gift that he has given to both of us! Even the desert Fathers did not always have such manifestations of his goodness! God's grace, like a mother's tender love for her children, deigned to console your bruised heart, through the intercession of the Mother of God herself. . . . Why, then, do you not want to look straight at me, my friend? Look freely and without fear—the Lord is with us.'

Encouraged by his words, I looked and was seized by pious fear. Imagine the centre of the sun in the most dazzling brightness of its noonday rays, and in that centre the face of the man who is speaking to you. You see the movement of his lips, the changing expression of his eyes, you hear his voice and you feel his hands holding you by the shoulders, but you cannot see those hands or the body of your companion—only a great light shining all around in a radius of many feet, illuminating the snow-covered field and the white flakes that are still falling. . . .

'What do you feel?' Father Seraphim asked me.

'An infinite sense of well-being', I replied.

'But what kind of well-being? What exactly?'

'I feel such calm, such peace in my soul', I replied, 'that I cannot find words to express it.'

'My friend, this is the peace of which the Lord was speaking when he said to his disciples: "My peace I give you, the peace that the world cannot give . . . the peace that passes all understanding". What else do you feel?'

'An infinite joy in my heart.'

Father Seraphim continued: 'When the Spirit of God comes down on man and wraps him in the fullness of his presence, the soul overflows with an inexpressible joy, because the Holy Spirit fills everything that he touches with joy. . . . If the first-fruits of future joy already fill our soul with such sweetness, such happiness, what are we to say of the joy that is waiting in the kingdom of heaven for all those who weep here on earth? You have also wept, my friend, in the course of your life on earth, but see the joy that the Lord sends you, to console you here below. At present, we have to work and make constant efforts so that we can "attain to the measure of the stature of the fullness of Christ". . . . Then, that joy that we feel for a little time and in part now will appear in its fullness, overwhelming our being with inexpressible delights that no one will be able to take from us.'[10]

NOTES

1. See Thomas Aquinas, *ST* IIIa, q. 1, a. 1. See also N. Rotenstreich, 'The Notion of Tradition in Judaism', *Journal of Religion*, 28 (1948), 28–36; on p. 33, this author writes: '*Bonum* reveals itself, since the very essence of *bonum* is to pass beyond its limit and to exist for the others'.

2. Bérulle, *Grandeurs de Jésus*, IV, 2 (Migne, p. 208; *Œuvres complètes* of 1644 (1940), p. 212); Louis-Marie Grignion de Montfort, *Traité de la vraie dévotion à la Sainte-Vierge* (Louvain, 1947), Part I, note 17–20. The element of truth contained in this idea can perhaps be found in Thomas Aquinas, *In I Sent*. d. 14, q. 1, a. 1; *De Pot*. q. 9, a. 9, c and ad 14.
3. Jesus described himself several times as the new Temple (see Mt 21:42, par.; Jn 1:50–51; 2:19–22). See also the admirable words of Angelus Silesius: 'When God was lying hidden in the womb of the virgin, the point contained the circle within itself': *Cherubinischer Wandersmann* (1657), III, 28.
4. Basil the Great, *Contra Eunom*. III, 7 (PG 29, 669): 'It is a characteristic of the pious man to say nothing about the Holy Spirit when the Scriptures are silent about him; this is because we are convinced that our experience and understanding of this subject are reserved for the world to come'.
5. See especially 2 Cor 4:4; Col 1:15ff.; Heb 1:3. Before the foundation of the world, because he is the mediator of creation: see 1 Cor 8:6; Col 1:15.
6. See C. Journet, *Saint Nicolas de Flue*, 2nd ed. (Paris, 1947), p. 84.
7. Quoted by R. von Walter, 'Le chrétien russe', *Irénikon*, 6 (1929), 687–720, especially 713.
8. Simeon the New Theologian, *Orat*. VII (*PG* 120, 352 and 354), which I follow here; = *Cat*. VI: Fr. tr. J. Paramelle, *SC* 104 (1964), p. 23 [followed below, p. 121].
9. See Gregory Nazianzen, *Orat*. XX, 12 (*PG* 35, 1080B): 'If you want to become a "theologian" who is worthy of God, keep the commandments and walk in the way of the law'. The greatest teacher of this 'synergy' was Maximus the Confessor (†662): see A. Riou, *Le monde et l'Eglise selon Maxime le Confesseur* (Paris, 1974), pp. 123–135. See also Volume I, p. 102, note 6.
10. This translation follows the Fr. tr. of V. Lossky, *Essai sur la théologie mystique de l'Eglise d'Orient* (Paris, 1944), pp. 225ff. [not precisely the Eng. tr. (London, 1957), pp. 227ff.]. But see Drina Gorianoff, *Séraphin de Sarov* (Bellefontaine, 1974), pp. 210ff. The biblical quotation at the end of this passage is from Eph 4:13.

2
THE GIFT OF THE SPIRIT IN THE MESSIANIC ERA

Under the Old and the New Dispensations

Only God is holy and only God can make men holy. All that belongs to him and all that is attributed to him is holy. The history of revealed holiness therefore clearly began already under the old dispensation. God dwelt among his people Israel. He had his dwelling-place in Zion. His Spirit was active and therefore present in those who carried out his work—in the kings, prophets and pious believers who served him faithfully. It cannot be disputed, however, that the Spirit was neither given nor revealed under the old dispensation in the same way and under the same conditions as he has been under the new, that is, since the incarnation and Pentecost. It has correctly been pointed out that 'In the Old Testament the Holy Spirit is spoken of mainly as a power coming upon individuals at particular times. . . . The New Testament begins by describing how the Holy Spirit descended on Jesus and abode upon him.'[1] The prophets, after all, announced for the messianic era what the New Testament tells us had come in Jesus Christ and at Pentecost. It is not difficult to assemble the texts; I have in fact already quoted many of them in Volume I of this work. The only ones that I shall consider here are those which raise the question of a difference of status or condition between the old and the new dispensations as regards the gift of the Spirit. There is no doubt that there is a difference. Everyone agrees that there is. The question, however, is what the nature is of that difference and how it should be interpreted. It is about this that there is some difference of opinion.[2]

1. 'I tell you, among those born to women, none is greater than John, yet he who is least in the kingdom of God is greater than he' (Lk 7:28; cf. Mt 11:11); 'The law and the prophets were until John; since then the good news of the kingdom of God is preached' (Lk 16:16); 'He who sent me to baptize with water said to me, "He on whom you see the Spirit descend and remain, this is he who baptizes with the Holy Spirit" ' (Jn 1:33; cf. Mt 3:11; Acts 1:5). One economy follows another: preparation gives way to reality, prophecy to a messianic era, when the kingdom is close at hand. Although the Spirit is certainly given, the gift is eschatological and a pledge of the

world to come. The new aspect that is proclaimed concerns both the corporate regime of the gifts of God and the religious state of individuals.

Paul similarly makes a contrast between the evangelical ministry of the Spirit and that of Moses (see especially 2 Cor 3). The people of God exist under new conditions. A text such as: 'By one Spirit we were all baptized into one body' (1 Cor 12:13) would have been inconceivable under the old dispensation. Through the gift of the Spirit, the people of God exist as the Body of Christ and the Temple of the Spirit. This is a radically new element.

Worship is likewise transformed under the new dispensation: 'The hour is coming, and now is, when the true worshippers will worship the Father in spirit and truth' (Jn 4:23). The epistle to the Hebrews is even more instructive here. It shows that the law was unable to obtain access to the Holy of Holies and that man is now, under the new dispensation, able to enter it.[3] Christ leads us to *teleiōsis*, perfection. It is not a question simply of an objective and collective situation as such. It is rather a question of the personal state of believers in their relationship with God and in their blessed state at the end. In Hebrews, the Spirit intervenes as guarantor (2:4) and even more inportantly as an element of Christian life in practice (6:4ff.; 10:29).

The pre-Christian people of Israel were sometimes called 'sons' and Yahweh was known as their 'father'. These names referred to God's special choice of these people and his consequent care of them and interventions to save them. This even led to a special intimacy between God and his people.[4] It was in this sense that Paul attributed adoption to the Israelites (see Rom 9:4). This does not mean that believers had the reality of life as sons of the kind of which Paul and John spoke. That reality presupposed the coming of the Son and the Spirit and was inconceivable without the intervention of the revelation of a Son of God.[5] Paul clearly had a good reason for associating the creation of a 'new' man with the Easter event (2 Cor 5:17).

These different data, which have a remarkable concordance, are explained in one important statement. John Chrysostom and Cyril of Alexandria regarded the affirmation in the fourth gospel: 'As yet the Spirit had not been given, because Jesus was not yet glorified' (Jn 7:39) as decisive. The interpretations of this statement, namely that Christ's glorification at Easter inaugurated a new regime in the communication of the Spirit to men, have, however, differed throughout history and I propose to review them briefly below, in the following section. (But see my study cited in note 2 below.)

2. The Greek Fathers—Irenaeus, John Chrysostom, and Cyril of Alexandria—and several of the Latin Fathers—Tertullian, Ambrosiaster and, much later, Rupert of Deutz—followed the scriptural text quite literally and made a distinction, almost an opposition, not only between the old and the new regimes, but also between the condition of grace before and that

after the coming of Christ. Before Christ, they believed, there were gifts of the Spirit, but the Spirit had not been personally given and he did not dwell substantially in believers.

Almost all the theologians working in the Western, Latin tradition—Augustine, Leo the Great, Thomas Aquinas and Thomists such as Franzelin, Pesch and Galtier—have, however, accepted a difference in regime between the two dispensations, but have insisted that the righteous in the Old Testament were personally, on the basis of their faith in Christ who was to come, subject to the same condition as later Christian believers and that, like them, they had the quality of sons and possessed a substantial indwelling of the Holy Spirit. All that the incarnation and Pentecost brought about was a wider and more abundant dissemination of that grace and that presence of the Spirit. Leo XIII and Pius XII also held this position.[6]

Attempts have been made in modern times to adapt the position of the Eastern Church, which has the merit of being closer to the facts and the biblical texts mentioned above. The Bishop of Bruges, Mgr Waffelaert, took the distinction between created and uncreated grace as his point of departure, the latter being, of course, the Holy Spirit. The righteous men of the Old Testament, he maintained, received created grace and this enabled them to act supernaturally and to acquire merit. They did not, however, possess the quality of sons and heirs of the Father, whose formal cause was the Person of the Holy Spirit as given and dwelling in his temple. Gérard Philips believed that the grace of the righteous in the Old Testament was the grace of Christ with its effect of justification,[7] but, taking up Fr de la Taille's idea of grace as a created effect brought about by an uncreated Act, he regarded that grace as going back to a time of preparation. As a result, it had to be put into effect again, if the full effects of grace were to be obtained, by means of activity connected with the historical missions of the Son and the Spirit. The difference between the righteous men of the Old Testament and Christian believers, then, was not, Philips argued, simply one of individual degree of the kind that exists between one soul and another within the mystical Body. It was a difference of 'economic' degrees and, for that reason, of 'classes'.

My own interpretation, which I have already outlined in some detail (see below, note 2), is very similar. I believe that a distinction must be made, even to the point of total separation, between certain effects of grace and grace itself, and between the supernatural righteousness granted to the patriarchs and the effectiveness of that grace in obtaining its fruits of sonship, the substantial indwelling of the divine Persons and divinization. In fact, inner righteousness was given to men who were moving from a long way off towards the realities that had been promised. We are inclined to see grace only as a created reality within us and therefore as a thing, whereas, before this takes place, it is a divine act of love and what has been created is born of that act, so that its quality, degree and mode follow from this. There is a unique plan of *charis* or grace and of various gifts *kata tēn charin*, that is, according to grace, from the patriarchs to us and from Mary to the most humble believer. Just as God now shows that he is pleased with us as members of the Body of his beloved Son, so that we are 'made to drink' of his Spirit (1 Cor 12:13), so too did he show himself to be pleased with the righteous men of the old dispensation as men who were orientated towards Christ and the promise of his Spirit. Their grace of righteousness can only be attributed to its normal effectiveness if the coming of Christ and his passion are presupposed.

One very important but at the same time mysterious episode can illustrate this: the descent of Christ into 'hell'.[8] It was necessary that the revelation of Christ and contact with him should set free, among the 'spirits in prison' (1 Pet 3:19), the potential of a grace that was otherwise unable to reach its goal. It is at least possible to understand in this light, by giving it this particular place in my interpretation, the verse in the same epistle: 'The gospel was even preached to the dead, that though judged in the flesh like men, they might live in the Spirit like God' (1 Pet 4:6). This point, however, is not a necessary part of my argument in my book published in 1958. My fundamental intention was to distinguish the part played by the decisive moments of the 'economy' and the divine interventions marking and shaping them, which were, in this case, the visible historical missions of the Son and the Spirit of God. On the basis of those missions, God himself has been given together with his gifts and men have reached him through them. These gifts have been made in abundance, but still fall short of their consummation at the end of time. In the eschatological era, there will be a new communication of the Spirit which will provide the grace, the gift and the indwelling, already part of our condition in the present messianic era, with their ultimate and definitive fruit.

3. I submitted my ideas on this subject to my fellow-Dominicans in 1954 and was subjected to quite severe criticism. What, they asked, was a grace that does not make us sons and does not reach the Father? It was simply a title and ineffective. Could justification and the possession of the divine Persons be separated in that way? A radical division of this kind did violence to the substantial unity of grace which was closely related to the unity of faith. It was the great insight of both Augustine and Thomas to recognize this twofold unity. God had pursued the same aim through both dispensations; whatever the understanding and the experience of the righteous men of the old dispensation might have been, their faith in Christ as saviour and their knowledge of the Spirit had been implicit. Thomas had pointed out that the grace received by the righteous men of the Old Testament had not reached its final end, which was spiritual and physical glory, and that it was necessary for the obstacle of the *reatus poenae* which came from the sin of nature to be overcome by the passion of Christ. But could this limitation be extended to

the other immediate and normal effects of sanctifying grace—sonship, God's substantial and objective indwelling, and our effectively reaching that same God?

There was also criticism of my use of biblical texts. It was possible to understand them differently and there were other texts, such as: Our fathers 'all ate the same spiritual food and drank the same spiritual drink, for they drank from the spiritual rock which followed them, and the rock was Christ' (1 Cor 10:3–4).

4. It is not easy to give a satisfactory summary of what is still valuable in my interpretation. Justice must be done, however, to Scripture. We can at least conclude the following: (1) the New Testament contains a revelation and therefore the possibility of a knowledge and a consciousness of what constitutes grace; (2) the economy of salvation is historical. It is punctuated by facts and divine initiatives, which, as soon as they take place, change what comes after them. I am bound, in this context, to quote the words of Gregory of Nyssa about the series of ascents that God places in the hearts of his servants: 'For the one who runs towards the Lord, there is no lack of space. The one who ascends never stops, going from beginning to beginning, by beginnings that never cease.'[9]

It is inconceivable that the incarnation of the Son, Christ's Easter and glorification and the coming of the Spirit who was promised should have changed nothing and should have brought nothing new. Until that time, something was lacking and the gift of the Spirit was not complete. It is still not complete, of course, since in the present era we only have the first-fruits of the Spirit. We have, however, already entered into the condition of sons because of the twofold creative mission of the Church. When we reach the state of glory—spiritual glory in our vision of God and bodily glory through the resurrection—we shall live by the same grace as here on earth, but that grace will be brought about in a different way. It will therefore have new effects or bear new fruit. My position in this question is therefore one which follows Mgr Philips' fairly closely: there is a new putting into effect, however imperfect that may still be, of gifts made *kata tēn charin*, according to grace, according to a unique plan that is historical, an 'economy'.

NOTES

1. Lesslie Newbigin, *The Household of God: Lectures on the Nature of the Church*, 2nd ed. (London, 1964), p. 104. See also my book, cited below (note 2), pp. 269ff. This theme is frequently encountered in patristic texts: see Gregory Nazianzen, *Orat.* XLI, 11 (*PG* 36, 444C); John Chrysostom, *Comm. in 2 Cor. Hom.* 7, 1 (*PG* 61, 443); Cyril of Alexandria, *Comm. in Ioan.* V, c. 2, on Jn 7:39: 'There was an abundant illumination of the Holy Spirit in the holy prophets. . . . In those who believe in Christ, however, there is not simply an illumination. I am not afraid to affirm that it is the Spirit himself who dwells and remains in

us. That is why we are called temples of God. This has never been said of the prophets'; this text is followed by quotations from Mt 11:11; Lk 17:21; Rom 8:11 (*PG* 73, 757A-B). See also Moses Bar Kipko, a ninth-century commentator on the liturgy, quoted by E.-P. Siman, *L'expérience de l'Esprit par l'Eglise d'après la tradition syrienne d'Antioche* (Paris, 1971), pp. 41–42; J. A. Möhler, *Einheit*, Appendix I; J. Lebreton, *Histoire du dogme de la Trinité*, II, pp. 598ff.

2. I have dealt with this question and have provided documentation in Appendix III on my *The Mystery of the Temple, or the Manner of God's Presence to his Creatures from Genesis to the Apocalypse* (Eng. tr.; London, 1962), pp. 262–299, to which reference should be made.
3. The impotence of the law: Heb 7:19; 9:9ff.; 10:1; 11:9–13. Free access: 4:14–16; 6:9, 10–20; 10:19–22; 12:22–24.
4. See M.-J. Lagrange, 'La paternité de Dieu dans l'Ancien Testament', *RB*, New series 5 (1908), 481–499; *Le Judaïsme avant Jésus-Christ* (Paris, 1931), pp. 459ff.; M. W. Schoenberg, 'Huiothesia: The Adoptive Sonship of the Israelites', *The American Ecclesiastical Review*, 143 (1960), 261–273; '*huios, huiothesia*', *TDNT*, VIII, pp. 347–353.
5. Gal 4:5–7; Rom 8:14–17; 1 Jn 3:1. Adoption that is still imperfect: Rom 8:23; 1 Jn 3:2; Eph 1:13–14.
6. Leo XIII, Encyclical *Divinum illud munus, ASS* 29 (1897), 650–651; Pius XII, Encyclical *Mystici Corporis, AAS* 35 (1943), 206–207.
7. G. Philips, 'La grâce des justes de l'Ancien Testament', *ETL*, 23 (1947), 521–556; 24 (1948), 23–58, also published separately as *Bibl. ETL*, 4 (Bruges and Louvain, 1948).
8. See my book, *op. cit.* (note 2), pp. 279f.; to the extensive bibliography provided in that book, the following should be added: E. Biser, 'Abgestiegen zur Hölle. Versuch einer aktuellen Sinndeutung', *Münchener Theologische Zeitschrift*, 9 (1958), 205–212, 283–293; H. J. Schulz, ' "Höllenfahrt" als "Anastasis" ', *ZKT*, 81 (1959), 1–66; M. H. Lelong, 'La descente aux enfers, épiphanie aux morts', *VS*, 100 (1959), 17–28; *Lumière et Vie*, 87 (1968); H. U. von Balthasar, 'Abstieg zur Hölle', *TQ*, 150 (1970), 193–201; H. J. Vogels, *Christi Abstieg ins Totenreich und das Läuterungsgericht an den Toten: eine biblisch-theologisch-dogmatische Untersuchung zum Glaubensartikel 'descendit ad inferos' (Freiburger Theologische Studien*, 102) (Freiburg, 1976).
9. Gregory of Nyssa, *Hom. VIII in Cant.* (*PG* 44, 941C).

3
'GOD HAS SENT THE SPIRIT OF HIS SON INTO OUR HEARTS' (Gal 4:6)

The people of Israel were convinced that God was *with* them. This conviction was expressed in a particularly striking way in the sixth century B.C. by the priest-prophet Ezekiel, who proclaimed a restoration when the people were exiled and in a state of crisis: 'I will set my sanctuary in the midst of them for evermore. My dwelling-place shall be with them and I will be their God and they shall be my people' (37:26–27). This is a theme that recurs quite frequently in the writings of the prophets of the post-exilic restoration (see, for example, Joel 2:27; Hag 2:4–5; Zech 2:10–12) and in the priestly writings, the priestly editors using the terms *miš^{e}kān*, 'dwelling-place', and *miq^{e}dāš*, 'sanctuary':

> And I will make my abode among you and my soul shall not abhor you. And I will walk among you and will be your God and you shall be my people (Lev 26:11–12).

> And I will dwell among the people of Israel and will be their God, . . . who brought them forth out of the land of Egypt that I might dwell among them (Exod 29:45–46).

In order to indicate the transcendence of Yahweh and the tension that this involved even in his presence, his name was neither spoken nor written and one said that God had chosen Zion in order that his Name might dwell there (see Deuteronomy, for example), or one spoke of his Glory.[1] In post-biblical Judaism—the Targums, for instance—this tension and, at the same time, this connection between God's presence and his transcendence were expressed by the excellent term *šekinah*, an Aramaic or Mishnaic Hebrew word derived from the verb *šākan*, to inhabit.[2] It was in this way that the dwelling of a God who remained absolutely transcendent and above the place where he dwelt was described. God himself revealed that he was there, with his own. As G. F. Moore has pointed out, the Old Testament authors spoke of the 'Shekinah' more or less as Christians speak of the 'Holy Spirit' when they do not wish to define with theological precision the activity of the indwelling of God.[3]

When we turn to the New Testament, it is not difficult to be struck, despite the fact that constant repetition may have deadened our senses, by the power of these words:

> Do you not know that you are God's temple (*naos*) and that God's Spirit dwells in you (*oikei en humin*)? (1 Cor 3:16).
>
> Do you not know that your body is a temple of the Holy Spirit within you. . . . You are not your own (1 Cor 6:19).
>
> You are not in the flesh, you are in the Spirit, if the Spirit of God really dwells in you (*oikei en humin*). . . . If the Spirit of him who raised Jesus from the dead dwells in you, he who raised Christ Jesus from the dead will give life to your mortal bodies also through his Spirit which dwells in you (Rom 8:9, 11).
>
> . . . that Christ may dwell [*katoikēsai*] in your hearts through faith (Eph 3:17).
>
> And I will pray the Father and he will give you another Paraclete to be with you for ever (*ē meth' humōn*; subjunctive of 'to be'), even the Spirit of truth . . . ; you know him, for he dwells with you and will be in you (*par' humin menei kai en humin estai*) (Jn 14:16–17).
>
> If a man loves me, he will keep my word and my Father will love him and we will come to him (*pros auton*) and make our home with him (*kai monēn par' autō poiēsometha*) (Jn 14:23; cf. 15:10).[4]
>
> If we love one another, God abides in us (*en hēmin estin*) and his love is perfected in us. By this we know that we abide in him (*en autō menomen*) and he in us (*kai autos en hēmin*), because he has given us his Spirit (1 Jn 4:12–13).
>
> God is love and he who abides in love abides in God and God abides in him (1 Jn 4:16).

As we shall see, this theme of indwelling was developed to such an extent that one is inclined to read a clearly formulated doctrine into these scriptural texts. On their own, however, the terms *oikein* and *menein* do not point so far. In the gospel of John, the word 'to dwell, remain, abide', *menein*, is applied to many different constitutive elements in Christian life.[5] St Paul also speaks of sin in terms of 'dwelling' (*oikein*) (see Rom 7:17–20). The dominant idea is that of stability or indestructible firmness, although the word tends to take its meaning from the context in which it is used. Here, the context is both one of entering into a definitive relationship of covenant with God and of enjoying communion with him on the one hand and, on the other, of being in a state in which one is the true temple in which God dwells and where he is given spiritual worship.[6]

> Through him (the risen Christ) we both have access in the one Spirit to the Father. So, then, you are no longer strangers and sojourners, but you are fellow-citizens with the saints and members of the household of God, built upon the foundation of the apostles and prophets, Christ Jesus himself being the chief corner-stone, in whom the whole structure is joined together and grows into a holy temple in the Lord, in whom you are also built into it for a dwelling-place of God in the Spirit (Eph 2:18–22; cf. 1 Cor 3:10–17).

There are several other terms in the New Testament that are concerned with the theme of indwelling. I have sometimes tried to keep the meaning of *rûaḥ* and *pneuma* by translating them as 'breath', but H. B. Swete pointed out that though such an association with 'wind' is known in the New Testament (see especially Jn 3:8), the comparisons that are characteristic of the Spirit are less with a temporary inspiration than with indwelling and filling.[7] The term *plērēs pneumatos*, 'full of the Spirit', is one that is used in particular by Luke, who applies it in the first place to Jesus (Lk 4:1), and spiritual writers have often regarded Jesus' heart as the first place where the Spirit was received,[8] since, after all, it was from his pierced side that water and blood flowed. However, Luke often also applies this phrase to the disciples (cf. Eph 5:18). M.-A. Chevallier comments: 'In the expression "filled with the divine breath", the gift of breath appears in the form of indwelling, for which Luke shows a great fondness'.[9]

In conformity with Scripture, then, the Fathers and later theologians preferred to stress the indwelling of God rather than simply his presence.[10] In his *Ecclesiastical History* (VI, 2, 11), Eusebius related the following story, which can be dated to about 195: Leonidas, who was later to die as a martyr, came one night to his little son, Origen, who was asleep. He uncovered Origen's breast and kissed it in the conviction that it was a temple in which the Holy Spirit dwelt, since the love of Jesus and of the Scriptures which spoke of him already dwelt in the child, who was to give evidence of that indwelling later.

Which representatives of that 'great cloud of witnesses', the later spiritual writers and mystics, should I choose? Undoubtedly John of the Cross or Jean-Jacques Olier, but also three women religious who are fairly close to us in history and who have written descriptions of their experience: Teresa of Avila (†1582), the Ursuline Marie de l'Incarnation (†1672) and the Carmelite Elizabeth of the Trinity (†1906), whose prayer: 'O my God, Trinity whom I adore' is well known in French'.[11]

These mystics describe a spiritual experience which presupposes an absolute gift, made in faith and love, and a generous and total self-abandonment to God, his activity and his inspiration of the kind that enables Paul's conviction—'It is no longer I who live, but Christ who lives in me' (Gal 2:20)—to become a reality in their lives. In their experience and in the witness that they bear, the spiritual union and the indwelling of the divine Persons are so closely connected that they are almost indistinguishable. This union has often been described as a 'spiritual marriage':

> These souls no longer look for the joys and the tastes of the past; from now onwards they have the Lord himself in them and his Majesty lives in them (Teresa of Avila).

> One day, at prayer in the evening, a sudden attraction seized hold of my soul. The three Persons of the blessed Trinity showed themselves once again to my soul and

> impressed on it the words of the most adorable incarnate Word: 'If a man loves me, my Father will love him and we will come to him and make our home with him'. That impression had the effect of those divine words. . . . And the most blessed Trinity, in its unity, took hold of my soul like a thing that belonged to it and that it had made capable of receiving its divine impression and the effects of its divine interchange. . . . From that time onwards, the effects took root and, as the three divine Persons possessed me, so did I possess them too (Marie de l'Incarnation; March 1631).

St Simeon the New Theologian, whom I could also have cited here, believed, as we have already seen in Volume I, that there has to be an experience of the Holy Spirit, who enables us to act and live. This was also clearly St Paul's conviction. For him, the Spirit acted in man's heart (see Rom 8:16; 9:1).[12] Over and above all critical questions about certainty concerning our state of grace, there is always practical evidence of the presence and activity of God in our lives. As Augustine declared: 'Interroge viscera tua: si plena sunt caritate, habes Spiritum Dei'—'Ask your inward parts; if they are full of charity, you have the Spirit of God!'[13]

If, however, we question ourselves critically or deal with the matter from the dogmatic point of view, we are bound to come to the same conclusion as the Council of Trent, namely that there can be no certainty of an infallible kind concerning man's state of grace.[14] This uncertainty does not, however, impede an experience of the activity of the Spirit in us, or a spontaneous and practical sense of certainty, without which we would never dare to partake of the body and blood of the Lord. The Holy Spirit is rightly called the 'Consoler'!

Our bodies are themselves the temple of the Holy Spirit and they form a substantial unity with our souls or 'hearts'. We must therefore take very seriously those statements which claim that our bodies can be transfigured and are able, in their own way, to reflect God's glory and the peace and joy of the Holy Spirit.[15] This aspect of the *arrha* or earnest-money of the kingdom and its manifestation in light is particularly stressed in the Eastern tradition and in particular by Gregory Palamas and Seraphim of Sarov. Another point also emphasized by Eastern Christians is that God's indwelling in our sanctified bodies is marked by their preservation—even though the body of the *starets* Zosima decomposed—and by the miracles that God works near and through them. The Western Church has, however, not lagged behind the East in this respect, and bodily effects such as transfigured faces, rays or visions of light, are attested in the West as in the East.[16]

Theologians have always considered this great supernatural reality of the indwelling in us of God who is three in one and they have, of course, considered it in their own way, that is, by asking questions and trying to formulate precise definitions. May they be forgiven for this approach! But everyone has to sing with the voice that God has given him. They have in fact asked two great questions: (1) How does this indwelling take place? and (2) Is it a personal indwelling of the Holy Spirit?

1. *How does this indwelling take place?*

There have been various explanations, some of them difficult to follow. For technical information about the different opinions, it is worth consulting specialist works or articles in encyclopaedias.[17] All that I shall do here is to outline in the simplest possible way the most common view encountered among the disciples of Thomas Aquinas. Thomas himself expressed his own view primarily in a work of his youth,[18] thus showing how important a place he gave to the Holy Spirit in his theological synthesis. I propose to discuss it under four headings:

(a) God is everywhere and nowhere. He is nowhere because he is spiritual and neither circumscribed by or settled in any place, but he is present where he is active. This is known as his presence of immensity. His activity does not make him change himself, but brings about a reality outside himself, the word 'outside' meaning simply that that reality is not himself. It is therefore a reality that is placed in a certain relationship with God, and that relationship varies according to the effects that are produced. Is grace involved here? It should not be seen as a thing or a substance, since it is we who are created or transformed according to grace, that is, according to this real relationship and therefore according to the quality of sons and heirs of the Father's goods—eternal life and glory. It is not possible to quote them all here, but it is valuable to read in this context Rom 8:14–17, 21, 29; Gal 4:4–6. The text from Galatians speaks of the two missions of the Son and the Spirit as interpenetrating and completing each other and being directed towards the same end, that of our adoption as sons of God.

(b) Because he brings this about in us and insofar as he brings it about, God becomes firmly present to us as the end of this filial relationship, that is, as the object of knowledge and love. This takes place through faith and charity, which are supernatural gifts of grace. God gives himself to us, in such a way that, although it is purely through grace and we hardly dare to confess it, we really possess him.[19] It is really God himself who is the end of that filial life of knowledge and love. This new, supernatural and deifying presence presupposes a presence of immensity and is grafted on to it.[20] God, who is already present through his activity as creator and is therefore also substantially present—since his action is himself—but only as the cause of being and working, gives himself and becomes substantially present as the object of our love and knowledge, as the end of our return to him as our Father. His presence is also personal. He is not only in us, but also with us, and we are with him.[21] We are with him insofar as it is really him!

Thomas' way of expressing this sublime reality is very similar to Cyril of Alexandria's. The latter spoke of a substantial presence and a union according to a relationship, *enōsis schetikē*, a union that places us in a new and deifying relationship with God and his Holy Spirit (see below, note 33).

(c) For Cyril and indeed for most of the Greek Fathers, this new relationship was attributed to uncreated grace, that is, to the Holy Spirit as given. The Western theologians knew that there is no created grace without uncreated grace, since grace is that gift with which God himself is given or rather, it is what God gives when he gives himself. They spoke, however, above all of the created gift, and debated whether uncreated grace preceded created grace logically and causally (in the very simultaneity of their coming). If this was so, ought it not to be admitted that God dwelt in a man who was (still) a sinner? Would sanctifying grace still be needed? It would be interesting to comment in this context on the episode of Zacchaeus (Lk 19:2–10), in which Jesus stayed with a sinner, but at the same time brought the grace of conversion to his home. However that may be, very many Fathers and later theologians, including Thomas Aquinas (see L. B. Gillon), have been convinced that uncreated grace, that is, the gift of the Holy Spirit, logically and causally precedes created grace which re-creates us according to God. The new presence and indwelling are the fruit of this simultaneous coming.[22] The witness borne by mystics here is very illuminating—they speak above all of God as acting and of coming in sovereign power to the soul in order to become one with it, to take possession of it and to be with it and in it as it is with and in him.

(d) Finally, it is important to remember the eschatological character of our divine sonship, the gift of the Spirit and the reality of God in us. Grace is, theologically, the cell from which glory grows, and we have the Spirit now only as earnest-money or *arrha*. The end will be when God is 'everything to everyone' (1 Cor 15:28) as an intimate, radiant, total and sovereign presence of a kind that does not consume the individual. Moses' burning bush is a clear image of this—it is Yahweh present and it burns, but is not consumed.[23] According to Thomas, the beatific vision does not require the mediation of created concepts. It is God's direct communication of himself, but in it the soul is adapted by him so that what takes place may be an act of its own life. On this view, the beatific vision is the supreme realization of God's indwelling and of man's possessing and enjoying God. In this life, all that we have of that supreme indwelling is a beginning that is mediated by supernatural gifts. It is worth reading Thomas' text from his first book of *Sentences* in this connection (see note 19 below).

2. *Is it a personal indwelling of the Holy Spirit?*

(a) The Eastern and the Western Churches, the Church Fathers, the theologians and the councils of the Church are all unanimous in affirming that what the divinity does outside itself is the work of all three Persons.[24] There is no activity of the nature or essence of the divinity that exists prior to or independent of the Persons. All such activity is performed by those Persons according to and through a divinity that is common to all three, not only because they are consubstantial, but also because they are inside one another. (The latter is known as perichoresis or circumincession, and I shall be discussing this question in Volume III of this work.) It is important, then, to remember that no action can be attributed to the Holy Spirit independently of the Father and the Son. Even in the 'mission' or sending of the Holy Spirit at Pentecost, the Father and the Son 'come' with the Spirit. On the other hand, it is not possible to say that the Father is 'sent'—he sends. Scripture speaks, after all, in a meaningful way!

(b) In the West at least, the fact that every action performed by God is common to all three Persons of the Trinity has given rise to the idea that an activity in creatures can only be *appropriated* to one Person, but is not peculiar to him, or his own. This clearly does not apply to the incarnation insofar as it is a personal union of a humanity with the Person of the Son, within that Person's being. If, however, it is seen as a work that has been actively caused, even the incarnation is common to the three Persons.

Although the idea of appropriation is not peculiar to Thomas Aquinas, it is usual to take his analysis as a point of departure.[25] Appropriation goes back to what Scripture tells us and to what we are able to say in an attempt to express a reality that we are incapable of defining because it has to do with the mystery of the divine Persons in the twofold work of creation and grace. It need not in any way affect what I have already said above in (a).

Certain essential attributes or activities that are really common to the three Persons are appropriated to one of those Persons, even though they may not be peculiar to that Person in a sense that would exclude the other Persons. This is because of their resemblance to the personal property characterizing that Person. This enables us to know, in a mysterious manner, what is peculiar to that Person. There is really something in that Person to justify the appropriation, but we cannot clarify it or say with certainty that there is an attribute peculiar to that one Person that would exclude the other Persons from what is appropriated to the one. This procedure has both strengths and weaknesses: it is suggestive, but at the same time it is open to criticism; it comes near to poetry, it fosters prayer; it is close to Scripture, but is not entirely satisfactory in the rational sense. One can look at it and say either, in disappointment, 'That is all it is' or, with joy, 'That is it exactly!'

It is certainly true that appropriation is used a great deal in Scripture, the liturgy and the patristic texts. The creed attributes creation to the Father, although it is clearly an action performed by the divinity of one in three Persons.[26] The fact that attributes are constantly changing their position points to the non-exclusive nature of appropriations. St Bernard criticized Peter Abelard's appropriation of power to the Father, wisdom to the Word and goodness to the Spirit, yet these are attributes which have remained classical and were upheld not only by Robert of Melun, who defended Abelard,[27] but also by Richard of Saint-Victor[28] and Thomas Aquinas. At the same time, in Scripture, Paul attributed *agapē* to the Father (see 2 Cor 13:13; Rom 15:30–31; 5:5; Gal 5:13, 22; 1 Thess 3:4) and, especially since A. Nygren's writings on this subject, this is not difficult to understand, seeing that *agapē* is love at its source, bringing goodness into being, in short, the principle of all being.[29] We have also seen that Irenaeus attributed wisdom to the Holy Spirit, and that Hermas and Justin identified wisdom with the Spirit. It would be possible to extend these comments into a methodical study of this question of attribution.

What strikes me especially is that whenever the New Testament attributes a work to one Person, it also affirms a communion of activity and describes a sort of concelebration on the part of the three Persons:

Heb 9:14: 'the blood of Christ, who through the eternal Spirit offered himself without blemish to God';

Tit 3:4–6: the 'goodness and loving kindness' of 'God our Saviour', who saved us and poured out his Holy Spirit on us through 'Jesus Christ our Saviour';

Gal 4:4–6: God sent his Son to redeem us and adopt us as sons, then sent 'the Spirit of his Son into our hearts, crying, "Abba! Father!" ';

1 Cor 6:11: we were washed, sanctified and justified 'in the name of the Lord Jesus Christ and in the Spirit of God';

2 Cor 13:14: 'the grace of the Lord Jesus Christ and the love of God and the fellowship of the Holy Spirit';

1 Cor 12:4–6: 'there are varieties of gifts (but the same Spirit); and there are varieties of service (but the same Lord); and there are varieties of working (but . . . the same God)';

2 Cor 1:21–22: God establishes us in Christ and has given us the Spirit as earnest-money;

Mt 28: 'baptizing them (all nations) in the name of the Father and of the Son and of the Holy Spirit'.

(c) Because of these data and the way in which the Greek Fathers spoke about them—a way which is very similar to the way in which Scripture deals with them—there has been a certain dissatisfaction with the category of appropriation, and several twentieth-century theologians have tried to overcome this by suggesting different approaches to the problem.[30] In particular the part played in the process of indwelling by the Holy Spirit has been questioned. As long ago as the seventeenth century, Dionysius Petavius (†1652)[31] expressed this question in terms of a dilemma: either a personal and peculiar property of the Holy Spirit (peculiar in the sense of exclusive), or a common action that is simply appropriated. Petavius believed that sanctification and indwelling were peculiar to the Holy Spirit and that they only went back to the Father and the Son because the latter were inseparable from the Spirit and followed him. In his argument, Petavius relied on the Greek Fathers and especially on Cyril of Alexandria.

P. Galtier resolutely rejected the support of the Greek Fathers.[32] He studied fourteen authors, but found that none of them attributed to the Holy Spirit a rôle of sanctification on the basis of his hypostasis that was not carried out by the Father and the Son. The Fathers were above all anxious to establish the consubstantiality of the Spirit with the first two Persons. None of the Persons did anything on his own. 'The only purpose' of the attributes applied to the individual Persons, Galtier insisted, 'is to make their personality manifest to us. This does not lead to any diversity in their activity, their will or their power' (p. 276). This may be too abrupt a conclusion to draw.[33] The truth is that the Greek Fathers were not conducting such a strictly rational search as the Latin Fathers. They approached the mystery from a different point of departure—from what Scripture had to say about the Persons. This will be elaborated in Volume III.

M. J. Scheeben (†1892) was *par excellence* the theologian of grace, and his ideas about the indwelling of the Holy Spirit in the righteous soul were widely discussed during his lifetime and continue to be discussed.[34] Although his thought is not always clear, he did not fail to recognize on the one hand the inseparability of the divine Persons in their activity outside themselves and, on the other, the part played by created grace as the internal principle of our justification and sanctification. He believed, however, that there was more, and indeed that the New Testament and the patristic texts contained more, in other words, a mission and a gift of the Person of the Holy Spirit realizing our sonship of grace and establishing us in a relationship which terminated in his Person as indwelling in us and taking possession of us:

> Although the substance and the activity are common to all three Persons, the possession of the substance is peculiar to each Person. Each Person possesses the divine nature in a special way and can also possess a created nature in a way that is peculiar to him and thus possess it on his own. The Son alone assumed a created nature in his physical possession. Could the Holy Spirit also not take possession of a creature in a way that is peculiar to his Person, by means of a possession that is less perfect and purely moral . . . so that the other divine Persons may possess that creature in that determined relationship, not directly, but only in him, as is the case with the Son in his humanity? . . . In his hypostatic personality and by virtue of that

personality, the Holy Spirit is the pledge by which we possess the other Persons . . . (*Mysterien des Christentums*, §30 [cf. Eng. tr. (1946) p. 166]).

We have been made similar to the Son of God, not only because we have been conformed to him, but also because we possess the same Spirit personally in us. . . . That is why the Apostle was able to call the Holy Spirit 'the spirit of sonship, in whom we cry "Abba! Father!" ' (Rom 8:15), that is to say, the Spirit brings about our adoption as sons just as he constitutes or rather seals the relationship of sonship that is created by that adoption [cf. *ibid*. p. 169].

This parallelism, which is almost an identification, with the physical union of Jesus' humanity and the Person of the Son is obviously too close to be theologically tenable. It led Scheeben to his unfortunate definition of the Church as 'a kind of incarnation of the Holy Spirit'. His intention, however, was not in any sense unfortunate and I hope to be able to do him justice, since the least that can be said about Scheeben in this context is that he was expressing dissatisfaction with the doctrine of appropriation. Nor was he the only theologian to do this. Others have continued to do so until our own time.[35] Karl Rahner wrote:

It would have to be proved in the strictest possible way that it was impossible for there to be this kind of communication of the divine Persons each in his own personal particularity and hence a non-appropriated relationship to the three Persons. There is no way of producing such a proof. Consequently there can be absolutely no objection to maintaining on the basis of the positive data of Revelation that the attribution of determinate relations of the recipient of grace to the three divine Persons is not merely a matter of appropriation, but is intended to give expression to a proper relationship in each case. In Scripture it is the Father in the Trinity who is our Father, and not the threefold God. The Spirit dwells in us in a particular and proper way. These and like statements of Scripture and Tradition are first of all *in possessione*. It would be necessary to prove that they may be simply appropriated, on the grounds that they can be understood merely as such and that the contrary is impossible; it cannot be presupposed. So long as this has not been achieved, we must take Scripture and the expressions it uses in as exact a sense as we possibly can.[36]

(d) Most theologians are nowadays very open to inspiration from the Greek Fathers, who were the first to fight for the doctrine of the Trinity. It is valuable to quote a few typical texts here:

The Father does all things through the Word and in the Spirit and it is in this way that the unity of the holy Trinity is safeguarded. . . . The grace and the gift granted in the Three are given on behalf of the Father by the Son in the Spirit. Just as the grace granted comes from the Father through the Son, so too can there be no communication of the gift in us if it is not made in the Holy Spirit, since it is by participating in him that we have the charity of the Father and the grace of the Son and the communication of the Spirit himself (2 Cor 13:13).[37]

We have not been taught to say that the Father is active alone and that the Son does not act with him, or that the Son is individually active without the Spirit. But every active power coming from God to enter his creation, whatever concept or name may be used to distinguish it, comes from the Father, goes through the Son and is fulfilled in the Holy Spirit. That is why the active force is not divided among several agents, since the care that each takes of it is neither individual nor separate. Everything that is brought about, either by our providence or by the government of the universe, is brought about by the Three, without thereby being threefold.[38]

Our renewal is in a sense the work of the whole Trinity. . . . We may seem to attribute to each of the Persons something of what happens to us or of what is done with regard to the creature, but we still believe that everything is done by the Father by passing through the Son in the Holy Spirit.[39]

This coming of God to man forms the basis of the return of man in the Spirit through the Son to the Father. In this return, the Three function as one, but, both in the return and in their coming, they also function according to the order and the character of their hypostatic being. The nature, essence or being may be common to the Three, but not in the sense of being a common stock that is somehow prior—even logically prior—to the Persons. Their common essence or existence is situated only in the mutual communication of the processions and being of the Persons (their circumincession or circuminsession). The Three therefore come as one, although this operation is not threefold, but according to the order and characteristics of their hypostatic being. Their action assimilates the soul that they are sanctifying to the divinity by assimilating it to what is peculiar to each hypostasis according to a causality that is quasi-formal or exemplary.

'Quasi-formal' in this context means simply that the form does not become part of the physical composition of the recipient, but remains transcendent. We confess that the Holy Spirit is *Dominum et vivificantem*—he is Lord inasmuch as he is the principle of life. This idea of quasi-formal causality, however, and therefore the idea of assimilation to the hypostatic aspect of each Person can be based on authorities of value.[40] This was the Fathers' aim in regard to the Holy Spirit when they took up Paul's idea of the 'seal' that makes an impression on us (2 Cor 1:22; Eph 1:13–14; 4:30).[41]

Each author has to do what he can with his own insights and the resources at his disposal in considering this very difficult question. I would not like to provide a mixture of every possible element, which would result only in confusion. I would, however, like to point out that substantial agreement has been reached now, at least in certain respects: The three Persons may act together in the descending line of efficient causality, nevertheless (1) they do so according to the order of the procession and the special character of the hypostatic being of each Person.[42] (2) In the order of return established in this way, (a) the image of God as Trinity is realized in the soul in a way that is more profound and more conforming,[43] and (b) the soul thus made holy is placed in a relationship with the three Persons as the term of its knowledge of faith, of supernatural love and often of experience. This is borne out by the evidence of such mystics as Marie de l'Incarnation.[44] In this way, in its relationship of ascent back to God, the soul has a special connection with each of the three Persons, and this relationship will be fulfilled in the beatific vision.[45]

3. *'A Spirit making us adopted sons and making us cry: "Abba! Father!"' (Rom 8:15)*

I do not intend to discuss our life as sons here, even in its aspect of prayer. Continuing the line I have followed in the preceding pages and applying the teaching that I have outlined there, I would like simply to ask the question: To whom is the 'Our Father' addressed?

Most believers would reply, almost without reflecting, that it is addressed to the one whom Jesus called 'my Father and your Father, my God and your God' (Jn 20:17; cf. 2 Cor 1:2–3). This is what Augustine first thought and preached.[46] In his later great work on the Trinity, however, he approached the question after much reflection and wrote:

> The Trinity is called only one God, . . . but we cannot say that the Trinity is the Father, unless we are using a metaphor (*nisi forte translate*) with regard to the creature, because of the adoption as sons. Scripture, after all, says: 'Hear, O Israel, the Lord your God is the only Lord'. It is impossible to understand these words if we do not consider the Son or the Holy Spirit. We quite rightly call that one Lord our Father who regenerates us by his grace. It is, however, in no sense right to give the Trinity the name of Son.[47]

This text, which was quoted by Peter Lombard (*In I Sent*. d. 26, c. 5), impressed the Scholastics, for whom 'God' meant the one who was invoked in the psalms and the whole of the Old Testament and was at the same time the divinity in three Persons. They did not know what Karl Rahner has so clearly pointed out, that *Theos* in the New Testament always refers (with only six exceptions) to the Father.[48] In short, they never failed to respect the universally held principle that all the works brought about in the created world were common to all three Persons of the Trinity. Were they, however, common to all three Persons without distinction? The Greek Fathers thought of this common character on the basis of the consubstantiality and the circumincession of the *Persons*, whereas in the West it was attributed to the essence or nature. This is right, but there is a risk of the direction of thought becoming less personalized. We likewise tend, when we consider our life of grace, to think in a less personalized way of the grace that makes us adopted sons, especially under its aspect of being an 'entitative' and 'accidental' reality produced in us, in other words, as created grace. As such, it is a work of God *ad extra* and therefore a work that is common to the three Persons of the Trinity. It is so even in Christ, and the incarnation, as a work taking place in the creature, is the work of all three Persons together.

As a result of this, a distinction is made in the *Summa Fratris Alexandri* between Christ as the Son of the Father through divine begetting and Christ as the Son of God as a creature and through created grace. Bonaventure wrote: 'Just as the Father and the Son and the Holy Spirit are a single principle of creation by virtue of the production of nature, so too are they a single Father by reason of the gift of grace . . . , Fatherhood is appropriated to the Person of the Father when we speak of his relationship with us.'[49] Albert the Great used nine arguments to prove that the Trinity was our Father, but he also said felicitously that we receive adoption as sons in accordance with the resemblance of the Son of God by nature and that its communication takes place through the Holy Spirit, who produces the image of the Son in us and leads us to call on the Father.[50]

Thomas Aquinas could not deny that, as a reality produced in us, grace went back to all the Persons of the Trinity, that is, to the divinity itself,[51] but at the same time he gave increasing emphasis to personalism. Here are some examples:

> The Holy Spirit makes us children of God because he is the Spirit of the Son. We become adopted sons by assimilation to natural sonship. As Rom 8:29 says, we are 'predestined to be conformed to the image of his Son, in order that he might be the first-born among many brethren' (*Contra Gent.* IV, 21).

> Although it is common to the whole of the Trinity, adoption is appropriated to the Father as its author, to the Son as its exemplar and to the Holy Spirit as the one who impresses in us the resemblance to that exemplar (*ST* IIIa, q. 23, a. 2, ad 3).

> Strictly speaking, sonship is related not to nature, but to the hypostasis or the Person. Adoption as sons is a shared resemblance to natural sonship (*ST* IIIa, q. 23, a. 4).

During the last Lent of his life, in 1273, when he was in Naples, Thomas wrote a commentary on the Our Father. In his explanation of this invocation of the Father, he did not consider the technical question and spoke without further definition as anyone might speak.[52] I do not believe that his point of view had in any way changed here or that he had, as E. Mersch has claimed, 'two series of texts'.[53] Thomas believed that our adoption as sons was a reality that was brought about voluntarily or freely by God as the Trinity of three Persons and that when we used the words 'Our Father' we were addressing the whole Trinity. The reality thus brought about, however, assimilates us to the eternal Son. Again and again he uses the words *similitudo, assimilare, exemplar* ('resemblance', 'assimilate' and 'exemplar' or 'model'). Now, a very positive element is stressed in this use of the idea of assimilation or similarity. It is that grace makes us resemble, not the Father or the Spirit, but the Son, or possibly the divine nature (see, for example, 2 Pet 1:4) insofar as that is hypostasized in the Son. According to the gospel of John, Jesus gives to those who believe in him what he has received from the Father.

Do the New Testament texts, that Thomas knew well and frequently quoted, call for more? We are Jesus' brothers (see, for example, Mt 18:10; Jn 20:17; Rom 8:29) and this is not a merely juridical or moral title. The title of 'sons' that has been given to us assimilates us to the eternal Son more than by way of exemplarity.[54] Is Paul addressing the three Persons generally or is he only addressing the first Person when, for example, he prays to 'the God of our Lord Jesus Christ, the Father of glory' (Eph 1:17) or 'the Father of our Lord Jesus Christ' (Col 1:3) or when he bows his knees before the Father (Eph 3:14) or gives thanks to God the Father through the Lord Jesus (Col 3:17)? When Jesus cried: 'Abba! Father!', was he addressing himself as the second of the three Persons?

Did Augustine not open up a way for us when he spoke forcefully of our unity with Christ in his Body and claimed that we form a single total Christ, one son with him and in him (see the texts quoted in the following chapter, notes 21 and 22)? A. Dorsaz followed this way earlier this century (see note 30 below). We are not, however, members of the body of Christ as a natural body united hypostatically to the Son. It is not possible to make Christians members of the Son as sons of God by nature. We are sons of God by a free decision of grace. This brings us back to Thomas' point of departure (*ST* IIIa, q. 23, a. 2), in which he quotes Jas 1:18: 'Of his own will he brought us forth by the word of truth'. The Church Fathers insisted that the Son was begotten, whereas the sons by adoption were *made*.

The Greek Fathers preserved the principle that God's works done *ad extra* were common to all three Persons, but at the same time spoke more positively about the connection between our created sonship and the uncreated sonship of Christ. They were able to do this because of two factors that were peculiar to them and also closely related to each other. On the one hand, their teaching was situated within a logical framework of participation and exemplarity and of formal and not of efficient causality.[55] Now it is on the basis of production or efficiency that our sonship should be attributed to the divinity as such. On the other hand, they believed that, when he assumed human nature, the Son of God assumed more than the *individual* humanity of Jesus and in fact assumed 'human nature', not in the sense that the hypostatic union extended to all men, but rather in the sense that the nature that each man hypostasizes individually is assumed as such by the Son of God, and that in him that nature is reconformed to the likeness of the Son, who is himself the perfect image.

This provides us with another, but equally Catholic way of constructing and expressing the mystery of our adoption as sons. The most important aspect is not the manner of explanation, but the reality itself, namely that we are truly sons in the true Son. We cry: 'Abba! Father!' and when we do this we are praying to the Father of our Lord Jesus Christ, whose holiness and grace were, in a humanity that is consubstantial with our own, a holiness and a grace of the eternal Son of 'God'.

NOTES

1. See, for example, Exod 24:16–17; 1 Kings 8:10; Ps 85:10. See also the beginning of A. M. Ramsey's excellent book, *The Glory of God and the Transfiguration of Christ* (London, 1949).
2. For the idea of *šekinah*, see J. Abelson, *The Immanence of God in Rabbinical Literature* (London, 1913), pp. 77–149; G. F. Moore, 'Intermediaries in Jewish Theology. Memra, Shekinah, Metatron', *Harvard Theological Review*, 15 (1922), 41–85; M.-J. Lagrange, *Le Judaïsme avant Jésus-Christ* (Paris, 1931), pp. 446–452; J. Bonsirven, *Le Judaïsme palestinien au temps de Jésus-Christ*, 2 vols (Paris, 1935), especially the tables; L. Bouyer, *La Bible et l'Evangile. Le sens de l'Ecriture: du Dieu qui parle au Dieu fait homme (Lectio divina*, 8) (Paris, 1951), pp. 107ff.; my own *The Mystery of the Temple* (Eng. tr.; London, 1962), pp. 11, 12, 17f., 93f., 132, 133, 297–298 note 5; A. M. Goldberg, *Untersuchungen über die Vorstellung von der Schekinah in der frühen rabbinischen Literatur* (Berlin, 1969).
3. G. F. Moore, *op. cit.*, p. 48. It is, however, very difficult to say exactly what the Talmudists themselves believed the relationship between the *šekinah* and the Holy Spirit was: see Goldberg, *op. cit.*, pp. 465–468.
4. F. Hauck, '*menō, monē*', *TDNT*, IV, p. 578: Jn 14:23 'depicts salvation after the departure of the Saviour as a permanent abiding of Christ and God in believers. (*Para* has much the same meaning as *en*, as verse 17 shows.) God's dwelling among his people is expressed cultically in the O.T. (Exod 25:8; 29:45; Lev 26:11) and is expected by promise in the last time (Ezek 37:26ff.; Zech 2:14; Rev 21:3, 22ff.). In spiritual form it has now come into the community's present.'
5. The word of God (Jn 5:38; 15:7; 1 Jn 2:14), life (1 Jn 3:15); love (1 Jn 3:17); truth (2 Jn 2), anointing (1 Jn 2:27); see F. Hauck, '*menō, monē*', *TDNT*, IV, p. 576.
6. M. Fraeymann, 'La spiritualisation de l'idée de temple dans les épîtres pauliniennes', *ETL*, 23 (1947), 378–412; my book, *op. cit.* (note 2); A.-M. Denis, 'La fonction apostolique et la liturgie nouvelle en esprit', *RSPT*, 42 (1958), 401–436, 617–650.
7. H. B. Swete, *The Holy Spirit in the New Testament* (London, 1909), pp. 328–329.
8. M.-J. Le Guillou, *Les témoins sont parmi nous. L'expérience de Dieu dans l'Esprit Saint* (Paris, 1976), p. 144, cites in particular a fine text by Stefan Fridolin, quoted in C. Richstätter, *Die Herz-Jesu-Verehrung des deutschen Mittelalters* (Munich, 1924), p. 187.
9. M.-A. Chevallier, *Souffle de Dieu. Le Saint-Esprit dans le Nouveau Testament* (*Le point théologique*, 26) (Paris, 1978), p. 124. Chevallier's text continues as follows: '*Plērēs pneumatos* is found in Acts 6:3, 5; 7:55; 11:24, and the same idea, but with a verb, is found in Lk 1:15, 41, 67; Acts 2:4; 4:8, 31; 9:17; 13:9; see also 13:52. Because of the formula of indwelling, the man who is filled with the breath—in this case, Jesus—remains the subject of an action and is not, as in Mk and even in Mt, moved by the breath.'
10. See Epiphanius of Salamis. *Adv. haer.* III, *haer.* 74, n. 13 (*PG* 42, 500C) and the long version of his creed (*DS* 44); Basil the Great, *Ep.* 2, 4 (*PG* 32, 229B); Cyril of Alexandria, *Comm. in Ioan.* V, c. 2 (*PG* 73, 757A-B); Augustine, *Ep.* 187 *ad Dardanum*, c. 13, no. 38 (*PL* 33, 847); Thomas Aquinas, *In I Sent.* d. 14, q. 2, a. 1; *Comm. in 2 Cor.* c. 6, lect. 3; *ST* Ia, q. 8, and q. 43, a. 3.
11. For Teresa of Avila and Marie de l'Incarnation, see G.-M. Bertrand, *Dictionnaire de Spiritualité*, VII (1971), cols 1759–1762 and 1762–1767 respectively; for Elizabeth of the Trinity, see M. M. Philipon, *ibid.*, IV, cols 590–594. There are also good bibliographies given in the dictionary. Elizabeth's prayer 'O mon Dieu, Trinité que j'adore' is reproduced in the anthology by Mme Arsène-Henry, *Les plus beaux textes sur le Saint-Esprit*, 2nd ed. (Paris, 1968), pp. 318–319. See also, in the same collection, pp. 283–288, extracts from the spiritual journal of Lucie-Christine (†1908), which can stand comparison with the texts of Marie de l'Incarnation.
12. References in J. D. G. Dunn, *Jesus and the Spirit* (London, 1975), p. 201.
13. Augustine, *In Ep. Ioan.* VIII, 12 (*PL* 35, 2043).

14. Council of Trent, Session VI, c. 9 and 11 and canons 13 ff. (*DS* 803–805, 823ff.). The most frequently quoted texts are Eccles 9:1; 1 Cor 4:4; 10:12; Phil 2:12; Heb 12:28–29. Many monographs have been written on this subject.
15. See V. Lossky, *The Mystical Theology of the Eastern Church* (Eng. tr.; London, 1957) and *In the Image and Likeness of God* (Eng. tr.; Oxford, 1974); M.-J. Le Guillou, *op. cit.* (note 8), pp. 105–122, including many texts.
16. St Gertrude, quoted by Le Guillou, *op. cit.*, pp. 106–107; Teresa of Avila: 'It is certain that, having received it (= the power) in this union, the soul communicates it to all those who dwell in the castle and to the body itself': *Dictionnaire de spiritualité*, col. 1761.
17. See A. Michel, *DTC*, XV/2 (1950), cols 1841–1855; R. Moretti, *Dictionnaire de spiritualité*, VII (1971), cols 1745–1757, with a full bibliography.
18. *In I Sent*. d. 14–17 (in 1254); *Contra Gent*. IV, c. 20–22 (in 1259–1260); *ST* Ia, q. 43 (in 1267). There is as yet no comprehensive study of Thomas' pneumatology. J. Mahoney of Heythrop has written a number of useful shorter studies.
19. John speaks of 'having' the Father and the Son (1 Jn 2:23; 5:12; 2 Jn 9) or of having life. I know no more than the title of H. Hanse, *'Gott haben' in der Antike und im frühen Christentum. Eine religions- und begriffsgeschichtliche Untersuchung* (Berlin, 1939). The classical theologians believed that 'possessing' God was in the first place being possessed by him: *haberi a Deo*; see Bonaventure, *In I Sent*. d. 14, a. 2, q. 1, ad 3; *Breviloquium* p. 1, c. 5, and p. 5, c. 1. Thomas Aquinas noted that God (the divine Persons) gives himself to us, though we cannot have any power over him (see *In I Sent*. d. 15, q. 3, a. 1 sol.), but he gives himself in such a way that we enjoy him (*ST* Ia, q. 38, a. 1; q. 43, a. 3). He also said: 'In the procession of the Holy Spirit in the perspective that we are discussing here, that is, as including the gift of the Holy Spirit, it is not enough for just any new relationship to exist between the creature and God. The creature must have a relationship with God as with a reality that it possesses, because what is given to someone is, in a sense, possessed by him. But a divine Person can only be possessed by us either in perfect enjoyment—this is what the gift of glory obtains—or in imperfect enjoyment—and this is so in the case of sanctifying grace; or rather the divine Person is given to us in the form of that by which we are united to him in order to enjoy him, in that the divine Persons leave in our souls, by a certain impression of themselves, certain gifts through which we formally enjoy (them), those of love and wisdom. It is because of this that the Holy Spirit is called the pledge of our inheritance': *In I Sent*. d. 14, q. 2, a. 2, ad 2.
20. See Thomas Aquinas, *In I Sent*. d. 37, q. 1, a. 2, ad 3; *Comm. in Col*. c. 2, lect. 2. Thomas distinguishes three modes or orders of union: 'secundum similitudinem' (*per potentiam, essentiam*); 'secundum esse', which is the case with Christ, through a union in hypostasis; 'secundum substantiam' (*per gratiam et operationem supernaturalem cognitionis et amoris*), which is the case with us.
21. On the one hand, then, Thomas interprets charity as friendship, which includes reciprocity, and, on the other, the formula that occurs again and again: 'they will be my people and I shall be their God', becomes in Rev 21:6–7: 'To the thirsty I will give water without price from the fountain on the water of life. He who conquers shall have this heritage and I will be his God and he shall be my son.'
22. Documentation in J. C. Martínez-Gómez, 'Relación entre la inhabitación del Espíritu Santo y los dones criados de la justificación', *Estudios eclesiásticos*, 14 (1935), 20–50; see also K. Rahner, *op. cit.* (note 36 below). For the debate in the fourteenth century, see L. B. Gillon, 'La grâce incréée chez quelques théologiens du XIVe siècle', and P. Vignaux, 'La sanctification par l'Esprit incréé d'après Jean de Ripa, I Sent. d. XIV–XV', *Miscellanea A. Combes* (Rome and Paris, 1967), II, pp. 275–284 and 285–317 respectively. The great Scholastic theologians were undoubtedly embarrassed by having to criticize Peter Lombard's thesis on the Holy Spirit as charity.
23. 'Le ciel, buisson ardent du monde', *VS*, 618 (January-February 1976), 69–79. It is also worth seeing what theology has to say about charity in the state of glory; for the grace

inchoatio gloriae, see *ST* Ia, q. 8, a. 3, ad 10; q. 27, a. 5, ad 6; *In III Sent*. d. 13, q. 1, a. 1, ad 5.

24. Need I give references? Fathers of the Church: Athanasius, *Orat. II adv. Arian*. 41–42 (*PG* 26, 234ff.); *Ep. I ad Serap*. 19ff. (*PG* 26, 573ff.); *Ep. III ad Serap*. 6 (*PG* 26, 633–636); Basil the Great, *De Spir. sanct*. 37, 38, 52, 56–60 (*PG* 32, 133–140, 164–165, 172–180); *Contra Eunom*. III (*PG* 29, 660–661); Gregory Nazianzen, *Orat*. XXXIV, 14 (*PG* 36, 256A); Gregory of Nyssa, *Quod non sunt tres dii* (*PG* 45, 124–129); *Contra Eunom*. II (*PG* 45, 504–508); John Chrysostom, *Comm. in Rom. Hom*. 13, 8 (*PG* 60, 519); *Comm. in 2 Cor. Hom*. 30, 2 (*PG* 61, 608); Augustine, *De Trin*. I, 4, 7 and 5, 8 (*PL* 42, 824); *Comm. in Ioan. ev*. XX (*PL* 35, 1557–1558); *Sermo* 213, 6 (*PL* 38, 1065); Cyril of Alexandria, *Comm. in Ioan*. IV, 3 and X, 2 (*PG* 73, 588 and 74, 336); *De SS. Trin. dial*. III (*PG* 75, 801–804); *Adv. Nest*. (*PG* 76, 172A and 180B-D). Councils: Lateran of 649 (*DS* 501); Sixth and Eleventh of Toledo, 638 and 675 (*DS* 491 and 538); Friuli, 796 (*DS* 618); Florence, 1442 (*DS* 1330). Popes: Professions of faith of Vigilius, 552; Pelagius I, 561; Agatho, 680 (*DS* 415, 441, 542, 545); Leo XIII, Encyclical *Divinum illud munus*, 1897 (*DS* 3326); Pius XII, Encyclical *Mystici Corporis*, 1943 (*AAS* 35 (1943), 231; *DS* 3814).

25. Thomas Aquinas, *De ver*. q. 7, a. 3: 'To appropriate simply means to connect a thing that is common to something particular. It is certain that what is common to the whole Trinity cannot be connected to what is peculiar to one Person, if the intention is to claim that it is more suitably applied to him than to any other Person. That would destroy the equality of the Persons. What is common to all three Persons can, however, be thus connected to the extent that it bears a greater resemblance to what is peculiar to one or another Person than to what is peculiar to another. Goodness, for example, is related to what is peculiar to the Holy Spirit, who proceeds as love (and goodness is the object of love). Power is appropriated to the Father, since power is as such a beginning and it is peculiar to the Father to be the beginning of the whole divinity. And by the same reasoning, wisdom is appropriated to the Son, since it is related to what is peculiar to the Son, who proceeds, as a Word, from the Father': *De ver*. q. 10, a. 13; *ST* Ia, q. 37, a. 2, ad 3; q. 38, a. 1, ad 4; q. 39, a. 7; q. 45, a. 6. The translation above from Thomas' *De ver*. q. 7, a. 3 is based on the Fr. tr. by C. Journet. H. Dondaine has provided a clear explanation: *La Trinité*, II (Paris, 1946), pp. 409ff. A. Patfoort, *BullThom*, VIII (1947–1953), no. 3, pp. 864–877, has discussed, from the technical point of view, C. Sträter, 'Het begrip "appropriatie" bij S. Thomas', *Bijdragen*, 9 (1948), 1–41, 144–186.

26. The creed is constructed on the basis of the classical attributions: see Origen, *De prin*. I, 3, 8 (ed. P. Koetschau, p. 61): 'Cum ergo (omnia) primo ut sint habeant ex Deo Patre, secundo ut rationabiliter sint habeant ex Verbo, tertio ut sancta sint habeant ex Spiritu sancto'.

27. See R. M. Martin, 'Pro Petro Abaelardo. Un plaidoyer de Robert de Melun contre S. Bernard', *RSPT*, 12 (1923), 308–333.

28. See Richard's treatises *De Trinitate* and *De tribus appropriatis*.

29. This accounts for the part played in the Church's missionary work by the Father and the *fontalis amor* within him: see the Decree on Missionary Activity, *Ad Gentes divinitus*, 2.

30. A. Dorsaz, *Notre parenté avec les Personnes divines* (Saint-Etienne, 1921), argued, for example, on the basis of the doctrine of the mystical Body, that our being called Christ's brothers enables us to be, through grace, what Christ is by nature, that is, sons of the Father, and at the same time gives us as our own the first Person as Father and the third as life and holiness. H. Mühlen, 'Person und Appropriation', *Münchener Theologische Zeitschrift*, 16 (1965), 37–57, inferred from certain doubtful hypotheses of Thomas Aquinas that it was possible to introduce a new and equally doubtful category, which he called 'personal causality'; see also C. Sträter, *op. cit*. (note 25). I have included what is valid in Mühlen's suggestion in section (d) above, pp. 88–90.

31. For Dionysius Petavius, see the article 'Pétau' in *DTC*, XII, cols 1334–1336, and XV, cols 1851f.; *Dictionnaire de Spiritualité*, IV, cols 1305f.

32. P. Galtier, 'Temples du Saint-Esprit', *RAM*, 7 (1926), 365–413; 8 (1927), 40–76, 170–179; *idem, Le Saint-Esprit en nous d'après les Pères grecs* (*Anal. Greg*. XXXV) (Rome, 1946).
33. J. Mahé, whose article, together with its many quotations, is still valuable, said: 'The work of sanctification is not so peculiar to the Holy Spirit that it belongs exclusively to him . . . but it can be said that it belongs to him in a special way that does not apply to the other two Persons. There are three reasons for this and all are based on the Greek idea of the Trinity: (a) he is the hyphen that connects our souls to the Son and the Father; (b) he is the image of the Son and, by impressing himself on our souls, he reshapes them in the image of the Son and consequently in that of the Father; (c) he is the sanctifying virtue of the divinity; holiness is as essential to the Holy Spirit as Fatherhood is to the Father and Sonship is to the Son': see his 'La sanctification d'après S. Cyrille d'Alexandrie', *RHE*, 10 (1909), 30–40, 469–492; my quotation will be found on p. 480. See also L. Janssens, 'Notre filiation divine d'après S. Cyrille d'Alexandrie', *ETL*, 15 (1938), 233–278; B. Fraigneau-Julien, 'L'inhabitation de la sainte Trinité dans l'âme selon Cyrille d'Alexandrie', *RSR*, 44 (1956), 135–156.
34. Scheeben discusses this question particularly in his *Mysterien des Christentums*, §30, which was first published in 1865. An account of the nineteenth-century debates (especially T. Granderath) and of discussions in the earlier part of the present century (especially A. Eröss and H. Schauf) in E. Hocedez, *Histoire de la Théologie au XIXe siècle*, III (Tournai, 1947), pp. 254ff.; *DTC*, XIV, col. 1273; XV, cols 1852ff.; P. Galtier, *L'inhabitation en nous des trois Personnes. Le fait. Le mode* (Paris, 1928), pp. 98–112; B. Fraigneau-Julien, 'Grâce créée et grâce increée dans la théologie de Scheeben', *NRT*, 77 (1955), 337–358.
35. See H. Mühlen, *L'Esprit dans l'Eglise*; G. Bavaud, 'Note sur la mission du Saint-Esprit', *Freiburger Zeitschrift für Philosophie und Theologie* (1972), 120–126, according to whom it is a relationship enabling us to participate in the knowledge and the divine love personalized by the third Person.
36. K. Rahner, 'Some Implications of the Scholastic Concept of Uncreated Grace', Eng. tr., *Theological Investigations*, I (London and Baltimore, 1961), pp. 319–346; my quotation will be found on pp. 345–346. The 'kind of communication' in the text is explained in the whole article as an ontological communication of the hypostasis (or uncreated grace) by a quasi-formal causality (which finds its supreme realization in the beatific vision). Thomas Aquinas speaks of a 'causa formalis inhaerens' of our divine sonship: see *In III Sent*. d. 10, q. 2, a. 1, sol. 3.
37. Athanasius, *Ad Ser*. I, 28 and 30; Fr. tr. J. Lebon, *SC* 15, pp. 134, 138–139.
38. Gregory of Nyssa, *Quod non sint tres dii* (*PG* 45, 125C).
39. Cyril of Alexandria, *Comm. in Ioan*. X, 2 (*PG* 74, 337).
40. Basil the Great, *De spir. sanct*. XXVI, 61: 'On reflection, it seems to me that the preposition *en*, "in", has very many meanings. All the different meanings of the word are, moreover, used in the service of the idea that we have of the Spirit. We say, for example, that form is *in* the matter, that power is *in* the recipient, a permanent disposition is *in* the subject affected by it and so on. Well, insofar as the Holy Spirit perfects rational beings by consummating their excellence, he has the nature of form. And in fact the one who no longer lives according to the flesh, but lives subject to the guidance of the Spirit of God, who is called a son of God and who is conformed to the image of the Son of God is given the name of "spiritual"': *SC* 17bis (1968), p. 467, Fr. tr. B. Pruche, who comments, in a note, that it is not possible to 'make the text say that Basil attributed a rôle of formal causality to the Person of the Holy Spirit in the process of Christian deification'. According to Dionysius Petavius, *De Trin*. VIII, 5, 12 (*Opera omnia*, ed. Vivès, III, p. 474) and J. Mahé, 'La sanctification d'après S. Cyrille d'Alexandrie', *op. cit*. (note 33), 474ff., that is exactly the position of Cyril of Alexandria. According to the *Summa Fratris Alexandri* (John of La Rochelle and Alexander of Hales), 'We are bound to recognize all created grace as a likeness and disposition of the created soul making it agreeable and like to God, *quia ibi est*

forma transformans—because there is in it a transforming form—that is, uncreated grace' (Quaracchi ed., IV, p. 609). G. Philips has called this sentence a particularly happy one that is fully in accordance with his own idea of personal union with the living God; see his *L'union personnelle avec le Dieu vivant. Essai sur l'origine et le sens de la grâce créée (Bibl. ETL*, XXXVI) (Gembloux, 1975), pp. 93, 277. At the same time, Philips quotes (p. 268) and praises this text of Bonaventure: 'Grace is an inflowing that comes from the supreme Light and always preserves contact with its origin, as light does with the sun': *In II Sent.* d. 26, a. 1, q. 6, end. Thomas Aquinas makes the same comparison in *ST* IIIa, q. 7, a. 13 c, and on at least one occasion calls the Holy Spirit the 'causa formalis inhaerens' of our divine sonship; *In III Sent.* d. 10, q. 2, a. 1. sol. 3. He also says: 'per dona eius ipsi Spiritui Sancto coniungimur': *In I Sent.* d. 14, q. 2, a. 1, q. 1. See also K. Rahner, *op. cit.* (note 36).

41. See Cyril of Alexandria, *Thes. assert.* 34 (*PG* 75, 689D), Fr. tr. J. Mahé, *op. cit.* p. 475: 'How is it possible to call *made* the one by whom the image of the divine essence is imprinted in us and thanks to whom the seal of uncreated nature is impressed in our souls? It is not in the manner of a painter that the Holy Spirit draws the divine essence in us, since that would make the essence separate from him. It is not in that way that he makes us in the likeness of God. God himself and proceeding from God, he impresses himself as though in wax in the hearts of those who receive him, in the manner of a seal, invisibly. By this communication and assimilation with himself, he gives his primordial beauty to human nature and remakes man in the image of God.' See also *De Trin.* VII (*PG* 75, 1088B), quoted by Mahé, pp. 483–484. For Thomas Aquinas, see his *Comm. in 2 Cor.* c. 1, lect. 5; *in Eph.* c. 1, lect. 5 and c. 4, lect. 10; *In I Sent.* d. 14, q. 2, a. 3, ad 2. It would be interesting to investigate the theme of the *sigillatio* in a pneumatological perspective. See, for example, Athanasius, *Ad Ser.* I, 23 and III, 3 (*PG* 26, 584C–585A and 629A-B); Basil the Great, *De spir. sanct.* XXVI, 64 (*SC* 17bis, p. 476). The patristic and Scholastic use of the Pauline texts obviously goes beyond the exegetical meaning of the same texts: see G. Fitzer, '*sphragis, sphragizō*', *TDNT*, VII, pp. 939–953.
42. For Thomas Aquinas, see *ST* Ia, q. 34, a. 3; q. 45, q. 6 c and ad 2 (creation); *In I Sent.* d. 15, q. 4, a. 1 (return to God). See also E. Bailleux, 'Le personnalisme de S. Thomas en théologie trinitaire' and 'La création, œuvre de la Trinité selon S. Thomas', *RThom*, 61 (1961), 25–42; 62 (1962), 27–60.
43. This is a very important theme, but it would take me too far from the present subject if I were to discuss it here. There are many monographs available. I will do no more here than simply indicate the place that it occupies in Thomas' synthesis and point to the coherent nature of his approach. The anthropology of the image (Ia, q. 93), which is taken up again at the beginning of Ia IIae (Prol.) refers to the Trinity. The profound unity that exists between the two treatises is found in Thomas' philosophy and theology of spiritual being, with the two activities that characterize it—the word and love. God's image in man is realized in dependence on the missions of the Word and the Spirit and by the intensity of the acts that are in accordance with them. See S. de Beaurecueil, *L'homme image de Dieu selon S. Thomas d'Aquin. Etudes et Recherches*, VIII and IX (Ottawa, 1952 and 1955); G. Lafont, *Structures et méthodes dans la Somme théologique de S. Thomas d'Aquin* (Tournai, 1961), pp. 265–298. See also H. de Lubac, *Le mystère du surnaturel* (Paris, 1965), pp. 129ff., 240, who insisted that we are made in God's image because he destined us to that similarity (through the Holy Spirit).
44. G.-M. Oury, *Ce que croyait Marie de l'Incarnation* (Brussels, 1972), p. 149: 'The mystery of the divine life is reflected in the sanctified soul, because the mode of the relationship that the soul has with the Father, the Son and the Spirit is determined by the activities that are peculiar to the life of the Trinity'. Thomas Aquinas gives an account of this experience, for example, in his treatises *In I Sent.* d. 14, q. 2, a. 2, sol. and ad 2 (see above, note 19); *In III Sent.* d. 35, q. 2, a. 1, sol. 1 and 3; see G. Philips, *L'union personnelle, op. cit.* (note 40), pp. 170ff.; A. Gardeil, 'L'expérience mystique dans le cadre des "missions divines" ', *VS* (Suppl.), 31 (1932), 129–146; 32 (1932), 1–21, 65–76; 33 (1932), 1–28.

45. The following have explained this question in this way: John of St Thomas, *Cursus theologicus*, IV, ed. Vivès, q. XLIII, dist. 17. ad 2; A. Gardeil, *La structure de l'âme et l'expérience mystique*, II (Paris, 2nd ed., 1927), pp. 135–139; C. Journet, *L'Eglise du Verbe incarné*, II (Paris, 1951), p. 512; S. Dockx, *Fils de Dieu par grâce* (Tournai, 1948); A. Bundervoet, 'Wat behoort tot het wezen van Gods heiligende genade en inwoning volgens Sint Thomas' I Sent. d. XIV–XVII en XXXVII?', *Bijdragen* (1948), 42–58; K. Rahner, *op. cit.* (note 36); G. Philips, 'Le Saint-Esprit en nous. A propos d'un livre récent', *ETL*, 24 (1948), 127–135 (the book in question was by P. Galtier); C. Vagaggini, *Theological Dimensions of the Liturgy* (Eng. tr.; Collegeville, Minn., 1976), pp. 191–192; S. Tromp, *Corpus Christi quod est Ecclesia*, III: *De Spiritu Christi anima* (Rome, 1960), pp. 12ff. It is also possible to mention Thomas Aquinas in this context; in *In I Sent.* d. 30, q. 1, a. 2, he distinguishes the relationship between the creature and God as either 'ut ad principium' or 'ut ad terminum' and, in that case, 'secundum exemplaritatem'; he concludes: 'in infusione caritatis est terminatio in similitudinem processionis personalis Spiritus Sancti'.
46. *Sermo* 57, 11 (*PL* 38, 387), which Philips, *op. cit.* (note 40), p. 33, dates to before 410.
47. *De Trin.* V, 11, 12 (*PL* 42, 918ff.); Fr. tr. Philips, *op. cit.*, p. 34.
48. K. Rahner, 'Theos in the New Testament', Eng. tr., *Theological Investigations*, I (London and Baltimore, 1961), pp. 79–148.
49. Bonaventure, *In III Sent.* d. 10, a. 2, q. 3 concl. and ad 2 (Quaracchi ed., III, p. 238). I have quoted directly or indirectly from Alexander of Hales, Bonaventure and Albert the Great as they appear in G. Philips. *op. cit.* (note 40), pp. 89ff., 115 and 130ff. respectively.
50. Albert the Great, *Comm. in Ioan.* 3, 9 and 13 (ed. A, Borgnet, XXIV, pp. 122ff., 125ff.; see also G. Philips, *op. cit.*, p. 131: Philips clearly does not much like Albert the Great, although he credits him with a 'decisive step forward'). He vehemently refuses to grant Christ the title of Son of the Trinity or Son of the Holy Spirit, even if the words 'son of the Spirit according to grace' were added. His reason for this is irrefutable: sonship is a relation between persons. How, he argues, would it be possible to maintain that Christ is a son of himself? Anyone imagining that sonship could be attributed to 'nature' would be making himself 'ridiculous'. Albert concludes by calling Brother Alexander's opinion 'erroneous': see *In III Sent.* d. 4, a. 4, sed contra: *ridiculum*; ad 6: *erronea*.
51. Thomas Aquinas, *In III Sent.* d. 10, q. 2, a. 2, sol. 2; *ST* IIIa, q. 23, a. 2; 'Pater noster' is addressed to the whole Trinity: see *ST* Ia, q. 33, a. 3, obj. 1.
52. *Coll. in Orat. Dom.* (see *Opera*, Parma ed., XVI, p. 124; ed. L. Vivès, XXVII, p. 183).
53. E. Mersch, *La théologie du Corps mystique* (Paris and Brussels, 1944), II, p. 44.
54. E. Mersch, *ibid*, p. 25, after noting the difference in the terms used in this context by Paul (*huios*) and John (generally *teknon*) and calling attention to the well-known passages in which John indicates the difference between Jesus and ourselves (Jn 20:17; cf. 17:1–2, 26), said: 'he (John) insists even more emphatically than Paul on the union and the similarity that exists between the only Son and those who receive in him the power to become children. As he is of God (8:42, 47; 16:25), so too are they of God (1 Jn 4:4, 6; 5:19; 3 Jn 11) and just as he was begotten by the Father, so are they also begotten by the Father (see Mersch's note 9 for references and the use of the same word, *gennan*). As he dwells in the Father and the Father in him, so too do they dwell in the Father and the Father in them' (see Mersch's references, p. 26, note 1). As the world cannot know him, it cannot know them (references on p. 26, note 2). In a word, they are children only because they are connected with his sonship and by being reborn in him they are born in God (cf. 1 Jn 5:20 with 5:18; 1 Jn 5:1 with Jn 3:1–21)'. On the other hand, an anonymous author (in fact A. Michel) in *L'Ami du Clergé*, 49 (1932), 294–300, elaborated the idea that Christian grace, that is, participation in the grace of Christ, was the grace of sons, since, in Christ, it was the grace that was in accordance with a humanity united hypostatically to the eternal Son of God. I am certainly in favour of this idea, although I would wish to avoid any suggestion of continuity between the Church and the incarnation as such (see H. Mühlen) and I have

certain reservations about the correctness of what the author says about John of the Cross's statement that we breathe the Holy Spirit.

55. See my article (Fr. orig. pub. in *VS* (Suppl) (May 1935), 91–107) 'Deification in the Spiritual Tradition of the East' (Eng. tr.), *Dialogue Between Christians* (London, 1966), pp. 217–231, with a supplementary note (pp. 229ff.) on the agreement reached by many authors; Athanasius spoke, for example, of 'participation' in the Son: see his *Orat. I contra Arianos*, 16 and 56 (*PG* 26, 45 and 129). See also E. Mersch, *op. cit.* (note 53), p. 34, note 1.

4
LIFE IN THE SPIRIT AND ACCORDING TO THE SPIRIT

Although I clearly cannot, in this context, deal in any way fully with the spiritual life, I can and must, because the spiritual life is above all a life in the Spirit and according to the Spirit, touch, in a very over-simplified way, on the main aspects of the life of a Christian.[1]

1. THE HOLY SPIRIT MAKES LIFE 'IN CHRIST' REAL, PERSONAL AND INWARD

Being a Christian is being in Christ, making Christ the principle of life and living on Christ's account. This is expressed in the letters of Paul by such well-known terms as 'Christ in us', 'Christ in you, the hope of glory' (Col 1:27) and 'we are in Christ'. Paul rejoices and is sad, he is strong and he exhorts 'in Christ' or 'in the Lord'. He also expresses the same idea in different terms, especially by using verbs with the prefix *sun-*, often created by himself—'associated (with Christ) in suffering, in death, in resurrection or in glory'—or by using genitives: having the charity *of Christ*, the patience *of Christ* or being a prisoner *of Christ*.[2]

It is the same Spirit that made Mary fruitful that makes the Church fruitful. The beginnings of the Church in the Acts of the Apostles correspond to the infancy gospel in the first two chapters of Luke. Going perhaps too far with the verbal realism of Scripture, the Fathers and others, including Thomas Aquinas and Jean Gerson, identified the *semen Dei, sperma tou Theou* or 'seed' of which we are 'born of God' (1 Jn 3:9) with the Holy Spirit.[3] R. Spitz took up the same idea recently and, in an attempt to illustrate it, used what we know today of the maintenance, despite the continuous changes that take place in our cells, of our genetic code or programme, supported biologically by the nucleic acids DNA or RNA. From the spiritual point of view, it is the Spirit of Jesus who is given to us as the principle of Christian identity until the eschatological fulfilment.[4] This 'seed of God' is also, or is rather, the word received through faith, but this only goes to show once again how intimately related the two are. They are in fact as closely united as Christ and the Spirit are when they come to us and enter us. Paul speaks of our being both 'in the Spirit' and 'in Christ' and of our knowing 'in' the Spirit and 'in' Christ, the preposition *en* here meaning the same as 'through' and indicating not a place, but a principle of life and action.[5] We have already seen in Volume I that there are many different activities and situations which, Paul believed, had their cause or their reason in both the Spirit and Christ. Cyril of Alexandria, whom I have already quoted many times in this work, had this to say about this unity of the Spirit and Christ:

> Jesus called the Spirit 'another Paraclete', because he wanted to reveal him in this way in his own person and show us that the Spirit was so similar to himself and that he worked as well and achieved as effectively, without any difference, what he himself achieved that he seemed to be the Son himself. He is in fact his Spirit. Jesus therefore called him the 'Spirit of truth', describing himself as the truth.
>
> In order to show that the word 'other' should not be understood as meaning a difference, but that it was used because of the personal subsistence (for the Spirit is Spirit and not Son, just as the Son is Son and not Father) at the moment when he said that the Spirit would be sent, Jesus promised that he would come himself.[6]

There are, however, things that Paul says of Christ that he does not say of the Spirit. These things include not only everything that Jesus did in his humanity, but also situations in the lives of Christians. Paul would not, for example, have said that we are the 'temple of Christ', even though Christ dwells in us through faith (Eph 3:17), nor would he have said that we are 'members of the Holy Spirit'. As F.-X. Durrwell has observed, 'It is no longer possible to interchange the formulae *in Spiritu* and *in Christo* as soon as it is recognized that the first applies to the personal Spirit and that the second points to our identification with Christ. We are identified only with Christ and not with the Holy Spirit. . . . According to Paul, there is no "body" of the Holy Spirit. The sacred host carries on a mysterious work of incarnation in us, but on the account of the Son of God, by integrating us into Christ and assimilating us to him.'[7]

This spiritual identification or 'mystical' assimilation to Christ, and this absolute credit that we give him so that he will fill our lives, are brought about by the Holy Spirit as an intimate and transcendent cause and take place, as we have seen, as the indwelling of the Spirit in us. They are also realized by faith as an attitude in us. Through his Spirit, God the Father makes Christ dwell in our hearts, that is, in the depths of our being where our lives are orientated (see Eph 3:14–17).[8] Faith is a gift of God, which he makes through pure love (Eph 2:8). It is on the basis of this (*ex*) or by means of this (*dia*) that the Spirit is given. There can be no doubt that what is involved here is living faith. There are many texts in Paul, Luke and John:

> Did you receive the Spirit by works of the law or by hearing with faith? (Gal 3:2, 5) . . . that we might receive the promise of the Spirit through faith (Gal 3:14; cf. 5:5).
>
> In him (Christ) you have heard the word of truth, the gospel of your salvation and have believed in him and were sealed with the promised Holy Spirit, the guarantee of our inheritance (Eph 1:13).

And God gave them the Holy Spirit just as he did to us and cleansed their hearts by faith (Acts 15:8–9). Did you receive the Holy Spirit when you believed? (19:2).

'If anyone thirst, let him come to me and let him drink who believes in me. As Scripture has said, Out of his heart shall flow rivers of living water.' Now this he said about the Spirit, which those who believed in him were to receive (Jn 7:37–39) [for this punctuation see Volume I, p. 50].

The gift and the activity of the Spirit cannot be limited to a single aspect in the development of faith. The Spirit is active in the word (1 Thess 1:5; 4:8; 1 Pet 1:12) and in listening (Acts 16:14). He is also active in bearing witness to Jesus, both internally and externally (Jn 15:26; Acts 1:8; Rev 19:10). The anointing to which 2 Cor 1:21 and 1 Jn 2:20, 27 refer is an anointing of faith, as I. de la Potterie has, I believe, satisfactorily established.[9] It is, however, obviously connected with the action of the Spirit: 'It is God who establishes us in Christ and who has anointed us; he has put his seal upon us and given us his Spirit in our hearts as a guarantee' (2 Cor 1:21–22). The same scholar has also shown that the seed of God (*sperma Theou*) in 1 Jn 3:9 is the word of God which enables us to be born through the faith with which it is received.[10] This is also the case with 1 Pet 1:23, where the Spirit cannot be separated from our rebirth through the seed or word of God. Indeed, this anointing of faith is so much the work of the Spirit that it is an extension and a communication to believers of the prophetic and messianic anointing that Jesus received from the Spirit at his baptism.[11] This anointing is active in the whole life of faith of the one who is baptized and who bears witness, whether he be personally inspired or officially commissioned. The Spirit deepens the faith of the disciples and strengthens it. He is essentially the Spirit of truth (Jn 14:17; 15:26; 16:13).[12]

The Spirit-Paraclete plays a very important part in nourishing our faith through our reading of the Scriptures. Paul bears witness to this in a very poignant way in the contrast that he makes between the Mosaic ministry and that of the new covenant: 'To this day, when they read the old covenant, that same veil (that covered the face of Moses) remains unlifted, because it is only through Christ that it is taken away. . . . When a man turns to the Lord the veil is removed; for the Lord is the Spirit and where the Spirit of the Lord is, there is freedom' (2 Cor 3:14ff.). This was the charter for the 'spiritual' reading of the Scriptures that was practised by the Fathers. Their reading of Scripture can also be of great help to us, not perhaps in its allegorical flights, but in its sober typological interpretation of the Old Testament. We have to add the word 'sober', because not all of it is authentically typological. Both aspects of the patristic interpretation, the typological and the allegorical reading, are present, for example, in Origen's writing, but it is worth quoting from it here mainly because of the love of Christ with which he examined Scripture:

It is for Jesus alone to remove the veil, so that we can contemplate what was written and fully understand what was said in veiled terms.[13]

Only the Church can understand Scripture; the Church, that is, that part of mankind that has been converted to the Lord.[14]

The Church Fathers affirmed again and again that, just as the Son revealed the Father, the Spirit reveals the Son.[15] In their own vocabulary, the mediaeval theologians said the same.[16] This conviction is absolutely biblical and has a long perspective. In Scripture, the testimony of the Paraclete, which is borne together with that of the apostles but in sovereign freedom, is always related to Christ (see Jn 14:16; 15:13–16). A confession of the truth concerning Christ is a criterion of the authenticity of the action of the Spirit (see 1 Cor 12:3; 1 Jn 4:2). Only the Spirit knows what is of God (1 Cor 2:11) and only he can enable us to reach the depths of the theandric truth of Christ. As G. Martelet said, 'The Spirit has been present with Christ from the eternal beginning of his begetting as the Son and has therefore been with the Son always. He is therefore also the privileged and irreplaceable one who bears witness to him. The apostles, who were only with Christ from the time that he was baptized by John the Baptist, are *also* witnesses, but the absolute witness, if he can be called this, the one without whom the testimony of the apostles would be no more than a testimony of flesh and the letter, of the mouth and the ear, but not of the spirit, is the Holy Spirit himself. He alone, as Paul pointed out, has looked into the depths of God and is able to say what is the radical identity of Christ.'[17]

The theandric truth of Christ impels us to recognize Christ in his humanity and therefore in his socio-cultural and historical conditioning. The Christian will therefore use all available scholarly means to understand that background, but, as a believer, he will inevitably go deeper than this, bearing in mind the words of St Paul: 'Now we have received not the spirit of the world, but the Spirit which is from God, that we understand the gifts bestowed on us by God. And we impart this in words not taught by human wisdom, but taught by the Spirit, interpreting spiritual truths to those who possess the Spirit. The natural man does not receive the gifts of the Spirit of God' (1 Cor 2:12–14).

Although one hardly dares to compare oneself to Paul or to apply such a text to oneself, it is certainly possible to take one's place humbly among the 'we' of whom he speaks and in the school of the cloud of witnesses who have as human beings carried the Tradition and in this way, 'being rooted and grounded in love, . . . have power to comprehend with all the saints what is the breadth and length and height and depth . . . that (we) may be filled with all the fullness of God' (Eph 3:17–19). If we keep to this school, the fruitless ways of 'hetero-interpretation', that is, an interpretation based on ideas and norms that are alien to the divine-human reality of Christ as the centre of God's plan, will be closed to us.

Augustine brought to this Catholic Tradition the excellent theme of the inner Master, without whose secret instruction the external words and the sacred text would not yield the whole truth that they contained:

> The sound of our words strikes your ears and the Master is in them . . . , Have not all of you heard this sermon? How many of you will leave here without having learnt anything? Insofar as it depends on me, I have spoken to all of you, but those to whom this anointing has nothing to say inwardly, those whom the Holy Spirit has not instructed inwardly, will leave without learning anything. External teaching is a help and an invitation to listen. But the throne of the one who instructs our hearts is in heaven. . . . (Here follows a quotation from Mt 8–9.) . . . If the one who has created, redeemed and called you, the one who, through the faith of his Holy Spirit, dwells in you, does not speak inwardly to you, our words will sound in vain.[18]

Life 'in Christ' and subject to the action of the Spirit is a filial life

Christ is the centre and indeed the culmination of our life as Christians, but he is not the end. As the 'Son of man', the type of man, he goes beyond himself and leads us beyond himself. He is everything *ad Patrem, pros ton Patera*—towards the Father and for him. If this were not so, he would not enable us to go beyond ourselves. 'The Spirit leads us to the Son, who leads us to the Father', as the classical theologians said.[19] As we have already seen, our sonship is based on that of Jesus himself. I shall now attempt to outline the way in which this is worked out, beginning with Jesus himself.

His soul as Son, that is, his human attitude and behaviour as the Son of God,[20] can be discerned in many scriptural texts. For example, 'when Christ came into the world, he said: "Sacrifices and offerings thou hast not desired, but a body thou hast prepared for me . . . Then I said: 'Lo, I have come to do thy will, O God' " ' (Heb 10:5, 7; Ps 40:7–9). At his baptism, Jesus became conscious of these words: 'Thou art my beloved Son; with thee I am well pleased' (Mk 1:11). From then onwards, he spoke throughout his adult life about his relationship to his father in a way that had been prepared by his obedience to his earthly father (Lk 2:51). The synoptic gospels already testify to this relationship, but it is expressed in words reported by John:

> 'The Son can do nothing of his own, but only what he sees the Father doing' (5:19).
>
> 'My food is to do the will of him who sent me and to accomplish his work' (4:34; 6:38; cf. 10:18).
>
> 'I can do nothing on my own authority; . . . I seek not my own will, but the will of him who sent me' (5:30).
>
> 'My teaching is not mine, but his who sent me' (7:16).
>
> 'I can do nothing on my own authority, but speak as the Father taught me. . . . I always do what is pleasing to him' (8:28, 29).

'I have not spoken on my own authority; the Father who sent me has himself given me commandment what to say and what to speak. And I know that his commandment is eternal life. What I say therefore I say as the Father has bidden me' (12:49–50).

'I do as the Father has commanded me, so that the world may know that I love the Father' (leaving to go to the garden and to his passion) (14:31).

'Father, the hour has come' (17:1).

This, according to the fourth evangelist, was Jesus. God's plan, however, was to go from the one to the one by way of the many. 'No one has ascended into heaven but he who descended from heaven, the Son of man' (Jn 3:13)—we can only come to the Father in him. That is why God constituted, in Jesus, a unique relationship of perfect sonship with him as Father and why he calls us to enter into communion with his Son (1 Cor 1:9) 'in order that he might be the first-born among many brethren' (Rom 8:29), in a history that is co-extensive with our own, until the time when 'the Son himself will be subjected to him who put all things under him, that God may be everything to every one' (1 Cor 15:28).

Commenting on this 'the Son himself will be subjected', Augustine said that this Son is not simply our head, the Christ, but his body, of which we are the members.[21] As sons of God, we are the body of the only Son.[22] Cyril of Alexandria, who had so much to teach us about our divine sonship, said:

Christ is both the only Son and the first-born son. He is the only Son as God, but he is the first-born son by the saving union that he has constituted between us and him in becoming man. In that, we, in and through him, have become sons of God, both by nature and by grace. We are those sons by nature in him and only in him. We are also those sons by participation and by grace through him in the Spirit.[23]

Our filial life, then, is found in our obedience and our search for a loving and faithful conformity to God's will, without at the same time renouncing our intelligence and our dignity as men. It may sound old-fashioned, but it is solidly and firmly traditional, and it is also true, that God's will is made incarnate in, among other things, the responsibilities of our state of life. This is also a common denominator in Paul's exhortations.[24] The culminating point and the heart of our filial life, however, is reached when we join Jesus in his prayer to the Father: 'I thank thee, Father' (Lk 10:21; prayer subject to the 'action of the Holy Spirit'); 'Father, . . . glorify thy Son' (Jn 17:1); 'Abba! Father!' (in the garden of Gethsemane: Mk 14:36; Lk 22:42); 'Father, into thy hands I commit my spirit!' (Lk 23:46) and finally, the prayer that we all know so well: 'When you pray, say: "Father . . ." ' (Lk 11:2; Mt 6:9). As a result of J. Jeremias' excellent studies, we now know that this invocation of the Father was peculiar to Jesus and that, especially in the form of 'Abba', it had a familiar note of trust and affection.[25] We also know that it is the Holy Spirit who enables us to say it and who even says it in us (Gal 4:6; Rom 8:15).

We may therefore conclude by saying that we need all this—an understanding of the mystery of Christ, a daily life of obedience and a prayer to the Father as sons—if we are to be transfigured into the image of the Son by the Lord who is the Spirit (2 Cor 3:18).

2. TODAY AND IN THE ULTIMATE FULFILMENT 'ALREADY AND NOT YET'

The best expression of the unity and tension that characterizes the status of 'already' and 'not yet', either in the kingdom of God or in 'eternal life', is found in the well-known passage in the first epistle of John: 'See what love the Father has given us, that we should be called children of God (*tekna Theou*); and so we are. . . . We are God's children now; it does not yet appear what we shall be, but we know that when he appears we shall be like him, for we shall see him as he is' (1 Jn 3:1–2).[26]

Whereas Paul speaks at the level of the 'not yet', John prefers to speak at the level of the 'already'. For Paul, our state as adopted sons is a promise and an assurance that we shall inherit the patrimony of God our Father.[27] John, on the other hand, is convinced that we already have eternal life on condition that we believe in the one whom God has sent to us.[28] Paul, however, speaks again and again of Christ in us and of the earnest-money or *arrha* of the Spirit, while John knows that we are looking forward to glory.

In the perspective of the Bible, the truth of a thing is its end or term, that towards which it is directed. 'Possessing the first-fruits of the Spirit, we sigh in ourselves, waiting to be truly treated as sons and for our bodies to be redeemed' (Rom 8:23; translation based on L. Cerfaux's French translation[29]). Those first-fruits are the pledge of our inheritance and they can strengthen our confidence (2 Cor 1:21–22; 5:5; Eph 1:13: 'You . . . who have believed in him were sealed with the promised Holy Spirit, which is the guarantee (= earnest-money) of our inheritance until we acquire possession of it'). The Spirit, given to us in fullness, will obtain for us the resurrection of our bodies as he did for Christ (Rom 1:4; 1 Pet 3:18). We shall only be fully sons of God when we are, like Christ, in the state of sons of God. It was his resurrection and glorification that ensured that state for Christ, with the result that Paul, in his sermon to the Jews (Acts 13:33), was able to claim that Jesus' resurrection was the fulfilment of the words: 'Thou art my son, today I have begotten thee' (Ps 2:7). Jesus, speaking of the state of men in the world to come, said: 'They are sons of God, being sons of the resurrection' (Lk 20:36); 'they all live to him (God)' (verse 38) in the same way that the risen Christ was living and 'the life he lives he lives to God' (Rom 6:10). That life has already begun in us, yet it is still the object of hope and expectation:

> But you are not in the flesh, you are in the Spirit, if the Spirit of God really dwells in

you. Anyone who does not have the Spirit of Christ does not belong to him. But if Christ is in you, although your bodies are dead because of sin, your spirits are alive because of righteousness. If the Spirit of him who raised Jesus from the dead dwells in you, he who raised Christ Jesus from the dead will give life to your mortal bodies also through his Spirit which dwells in you (Rom 8:9–11).

It is the Spirit himself bearing witness with our spirit that we are children of God, and if children, then heirs, heirs of God and fellow-heirs with Christ, provided we suffer with him in order that we may also be glorified with him. I consider that the sufferings of this present time are not worth comparing with the glory that is to be revealed to us. For the creation waits with eager longing for the revealing of the sons of God . . . because the creation itself will be set free from its bondage to decay and obtain the glorious liberty of the children of God . . . and not only creation, but we ourselves, who have the first-fruits of the Spirit, groan inwardly as we wait for adoption as sons, the redemption of our bodies (Rom 8:16–23).

The Christian can surely never grow tired of reading and re-reading that text, so rich in content! After all, we are groaning, which is quite different from complaining or whining. It is an expression of our passionate longing for the coming of the kingdom of God. Eschatologically, we shall reign with him: 'If we have died with him, we shall also live with him; if we endure, we shall also reign with him' (2 Tim 2:12). We have already seen that there is a variant of the text usually given as 'Thy kingdom come' (Lk 11:2) and that this variant: 'May thy Spirit come upon us and purify us' was followed by many of the Fathers.[30] It is also a fact that John expresses in terms of 'life' what the synoptics and Paul express in terms of the kingdom of God.[31] These two realities, in accordance with the two aspects of 'already' and 'not yet' that belong to them, can also be translated in terms of the Holy Spirit.[32]

As L. Cerfaux has pointed out, 'Rom 8, which contains Paul's most explicit doctrine of sonship, considers eschatological as a development of present sonship'.[33] Life, kingdom and Spirit have a dynamic existence in our lives here on earth.[34] The Spirit is both an appeal or a demand and the principle of holy life: 'God has not called us for uncleanness, but in holiness . . . God, who gives his Holy Spirit to you' (1 Thess 4:7–8).

Paul speaks here of purity, a theme that is closely related to that of God's indwelling and of the temple, and the personal aspect on the one hand and the communal or ecclesial aspect on the other that are associated with it.[35] I have already spoken about life in the Church in Part One of this volume and shall have to return to it later. In this chapter, it would be possible to speak about the whole *vita in Christo*. I shall deal with the most important aspects of that life in Christ later: prayer, the struggle against the flesh and our participation in Christ's passion, and life subject to the guidance of the Spirit and the 'gifts'. In Volume III I shall deal with the sacraments in their relationship with the Spirit.

The connection between our present sonship and our eschatological sonship is in the first place obviously that of the reality itself: gift of the Spirit and created grace, as we have seen, are closely linked. This connection can also be seen within the special perspective of 'merit', Thomas Aquinas especially believed that the Holy Spirit played an extremely important part in this.[36] If we are to acquire merit, we have to make use of our freedom, since, without freedom, it is difficult to see what truth there could be in a 'judgement' by God. If, however, it is eternal life that we are to merit, that is, if we are to be worthy to enter the family of God himself and be in communion with him, then the good action of our freedom must be borne up by a power of the order of God himself. That power is Christ himself. This theology was developed in the sixteenth century by Cajetan and was taken up again in the present century by E. Mersch and Cardinal Journet. It is also the Holy Spirit.

In this context, Thomas Aquinas quoted Jn 4:14: 'The water that I shall give him will become in him a spring of water welling up to eternal life' and the Council of Trent made use of the same quotation.[37] It means that the only power that can ascend again to God is one that originally comes from him. This is virtually the image of communicating vessels. Merit only exists because of grace and assumes that the Spirit is 'sent' and given in the gift of grace and that it is through his divine dynamism that we are able to return through the Son to the Father.

In the end, it is God who takes the absolute initiative insofar as he is Love and grace. We have to consent to this initiative and co-operate with it ('synergy'), but it is what carries out and carries through to its term the process described by Paul in Rom 8:29–30. Our actions, which may 'merit' eternal life, are elements in a chain of grace in which the Holy Spirit as uncreated grace takes the initiative and provides the dynamism until the ultimate victory is reached in which God is merely crowning his own gifts when he awards us a crown for our 'merits'.

The Holy Spirit and the divine charity which he pours into our hearts (Rom 5:5) are likewise the principle of the communion of saints and that of the communication of spiritual good things in which that communion is expressed. I have, of course, already spoken about this in an earlier chapter.

NOTES

1. It would be possible to quote a great number of references, but I will confine the list to two general works: L. Cerfaux, *The Christian in the Theology of St Paul* (Eng. tr.; London, 1967); I. de la Potterie and S. Lyonnet, *La vie selon l'Esprit, condition du chrétien* (*Unam Sanctam*, 55) (Paris, 1965).
2. See L. Cerfaux, *op. cit.*, pp. 358ff.
3. See Irenaeus, *Adv. Haer.* IV, 31, 2 (*PG* 7, 1069–1070; *SC* 100, pp. 792, 793), who speaks with extreme realism of a typology of Lot sleeping with his two daughters; Ambrose, *Comm. in Luc.* III, 28 (*PL* 15, 1605), brings together the word and the Spirit: 'Cui nupsit Ecclesia, quae Verbi semine et Spiritu Sancto plena, Christi corpus effudit, populum scilicet christianum'; other references will be found in S. Tromp, *Corpus Christi quod est*

Ecclesia, III: *De Spiritu Christi anima* (Rome, 1960), pp. 165ff., 228ff. In an explanation of our divine sonship. Thomas Aquinas said : 'Semen autem spirituale a Patre procedens est Spiritus Sanctus' and quoted 1 Jn 3:9: *Comm. in Rom*. c. 8, lect. 3; also, 'Semen spirituale est gratia Spiritus Sancti ': *Comm. in Gal*. c. 3, lect. 3. See also Jean Gerson's sermon 'Ambulate dum lucem habetis' (*Œuvres*, ed. P. Glorieux, V, p. 44); see also L. B. Pascoe, *Jean Gerson: Principles of Church Reform* (Leiden, 1973), pp. 45–47, 207–208.

4. R. Spitz, *Le Révélation progressive de l'Esprit Saint* (Paris, 1976), pp. 187, 191ff., 202ff.
5. The causal rather than the local meaning of *en* and its relative equivalence to *dia* are so widely recognized that it would be pointless to provide references.
6. Cyril of Alexandria, *Comm. in Ioan.* IX (*PG* 74, 257A–B and 261A; Fr. tr. A. Solignac, *NRT* (1955), 482).
7. F.-X. Durrwell, *La Résurrection de Jésus, mystère de salut*, 2nd ed. (Le Puy and Paris, 1955), pp. 257–258; 10th ed. (Paris, 1976), p. 170.
8. This is a text which St Bernard often quoted. Reacting against any physical identification of the Christian with Christ, Pius XII rejected the idea of a lengthy indwelling of Christ's humanity in us as a result of eucharistic communion: see his encyclicals *Mystici Corporis* (1943) and *Mediator Dei* (1947); see also *L'Ami du Clergé* (27 April 1950), 257ff.; (14 February 1952), 99; S. Schmitt, 'Päpstliche Entscheidung einer theologischen Streitfrage. Keine Dauergegenwart der Menschheit Christi im Christen', *Benediktinische Monatschrift* (1948); G. Söhngen. 'Die Gegenwart Christi durch den Glauben' in A. Fischer, *Die Messe in der Verkündigung* (Freiburg, 1950).
9. For the anointing of the Christian by faith, see I. de la Potterie, *op. cit.* (note 1), pp. 107–167. The text of 1 Jn 2:20, 27 is quoted in the Dogmatic Constitution on the Church, *Lumen Gentium*, 12, in connection with the *sensus fidei* of the whole people of God.
10. I. de la Potterie, *op. cit*., pp. 53ff., 56, note 1 ('Born of water and the Spirit'), 209ff. (the sinlessness of the Christian according to 1 Jn 3:6–9).
11. *Ibid*., pp. 123ff.
12. *Ibid*., pp. 85–105 (the Paraclete).
13. Origen, *Dialogue with Heraclides*, Fr. tr. J. Scherer, *SC* 67 (1960), p. 91.
14. Quoted by H. de Lubac, *Histoire et Esprit. L'intelligence de l'Ecriture d'après Origène* (*Théologie*, 16) (Paris, 1950), pp. 303, 304, 316ff. See also the very instructive little book by H. Urs von Balthasar, *Parole et Mystère chex Origène* (Paris, 1957), which first appeared as articles in *RSR*, 26 (1936), 513–562 and 27 (1937), 38–64.
15. Athanasius, *Ad Ser.* III (Fr. tr. J. Lebon, *SC* 15 (1947), pp. 163–165).
16. This is apparent from a text in one of Albert the Great's commentaries, *Comm. in Luc*. X, 22 (ed. A. Borgnet, XXIII, 45): 'The apostle clearly attributes revelation to the Holy Spirit when he says: "God has revealed to us through the Spirit" (1 Cor 2:10–13). . . . He says this because, just as man's spirit bears the thought which guides the hand of the worker in his task and bears the thought in the language that he speaks, the Holy Spirit is in the same way the one who bears the Father's Word and who therefore reveals the Father. This revelation goes back both to the Father as its origin and its author and to the Word as his form of light and formal knowledge as well as to the Spirit as the one who bears and inspires it.'
17. G. Martelet, *Sainteté de l'Eglise et Vie religieuse* (Toulouse, 1964), pp. 84–85.
18. Augustine, *Comm. in 1 Ioan*. III, 13; IV, 1 (Fr. tr. P. Agaësse, *SC* 73 (1961), pp. 211, 219; *PL* 35, 2004, 2005). For this same theme in Augustine's other writings, see *De Mag*. XI, 36–XIV, 46 (*PL* 32, 1215–1220); *Conf.* IX, 9 (*PL* 32, 773); *Sermo* 179, 1 (*PL* 38, 966); E. Gilson, *Introduction à l'étude de S. Augustin* (Paris, 1920), pp. 88–103, 137–138, 164–165, 256, note 1; J. Rimaud, 'Le maître intérieur', *Saint Augustin* (*Cahiers de la Nouvelle Journée*, 17) (Paris, 1930), pp. 53–69. For the continuation of this theme, see Gregory the Great, *Hom. in Ev*. II, *Hom*. 30 (*PL* 76, 1222); *Moral*. XXVII, 43 (*PL* 78, 424). J. Alfaro, *Greg*, 44 (1963), 180, note 357, has provided references to Prosper of

Aquitaine, Fulgentius of Ruspe, Bede, Alcuin, Rabanus Maurus, Haymo of Auxerre, Paschasius Radbert, Florus of Lyons, Atto of Vercelli, Rupert of Deutz, Hervetus, Peter Lombard, Robert Pullen, Hugh of Saint-Cher, Nicholas of Lyra and Bonaventure. For the last mentioned, see E. Eilers, *Gottes Wort. Eine Theologie der Predigt nach Bonaventura* (Freiburg, 1941), pp. 57ff., 71ff. To the above list, the following should also be added: Thomas Aquinas, *De ver*. q. 11, a. 1; *ST* Ia, q. 117, a. 1, ad 1; *Comm. in ev. Ioan*. c. 14, lect. 6, and, nearer to our own times, Bossuet, *Sermon sur la parole de Dieu* (13 November 1661) (ed. J. Lebarq, III, pp. 579–580); A. Gratry, *Les Sources*.

19. Ignatius of Antioch's 'Come to the Father' in *Ad Rom*. VII, 2 is well known, but see also Irenaeus, *Adv. haer*. V, 36, 2 (*PG* 7, 1225; *SC* 163 (1969), pp. 460, 461); Thomas Aquinas, *Comm. in ev. Ioan*. c. 14, lect. 6: 'Sicut effectus missionis Filii fuit ducere ad Patrem, ita effectus missionis Spiritus est ducere ad Filium'.
20. D. Lallement, 'La personnalité filiale de Jésus', *VS*, 47 (June 1936), 241–248; P. Glorieux, 'Le Christ adorateur du Père', *RSR* (1949), 245–269; W. Koster, 'Der Vatergott im Jesu Leben und Lehre', *Schol*, 16 (1941), 481–495; J. Guillet, 'L'obéissance de Jésus-Christ', *Christus*, 7 (1955), 298–313; W. Grundmann, 'Zur Rede Jesu vom Vater im Johannes-Evangelium (Jo 20, 17)', *ZNW*, 52 (1961), 213–230; J. Jeremias, *op. cit*. (note 25 below).
21. Augustine, *De div. quaest*. LXXXIII, q. 69, 10 (*PL* 40, 79).
22. *Ep. Ioan. ad Parth*. X, 5, 9 (*PL* 35, 2055); see also *Comm. in ev. Ioan*. XX, 5; XLI, 8 (*PL* 35, 1568 and 1696); *Enarr. in Ps*. 122, 5 (*PL* 37, 1634). To this should be added the theme of *Christus integer* and Augustine's commentary on 'Only one ascends to heaven, the Son of man'. The following quotation from his *Sermo* 71, 28 is also interesting in this context: 'Ad ipsum (Spiritum) pertinet societas qua efficimur unum corpus *unici Filii Dei*' (*PL* 38, 461).
23. Cyril of Alexandria, *De recta fide ad Theod*. (*PG* 76, 1177).
24. H. Pinard de la Boullaye, *La dévotion du devoir* (Paris, 1929), with its application, in chapter X, pp. 69ff., to Jesus' life as Son.
25. J. Jeremias, *The Prayers of Jesus* (London, 1967).
26. Col 3:3–4: 'Your life is hid with Christ in God. When Christ who is our life appears, then you will also appear with him in glory.' See also Phil 3:21. See L. Cerfaux, *op. cit*. (note 1), pp. 322–324.
27. Rom 8:19, 23–24; Eph 1:14; 1 Tim 6:12; Tit 3:7. For the theme of our future inheritance of the Kingdom of God, see 1 Cor 6:9–10; 15:50; Gal 5:21; for the theme of incorruptibility, see 1 Cor 15:50; for that of the wealth of glory, see Eph 1:18, and for that of the 'saints in light', see Col 1:12. For the inheritance of the kingdom, see also Eph 5:5; Jas 2:5. The 'already' and the 'not yet' of Paul's teaching has also been well analysed by J. D. G. Dunn in his *Jesus and the Spirit* (London, 1975), pp. 308ff.
28. See Jn 6:29, 40, 47; 1 Jn 3:1; 5:11, 13. Gregory of Nyssa interpreted the statement in Jn 17:22 as a gift of the Spirit: 'The glory which thou hast given me I have given to them': see his *In Cant. Hom*. 15 (*PG* 44, 1117).
29. L. Cerfaux, *Le chrétien dans la théologie paulinienne* (*Lectio divina*, 33) (Paris, 1962), p. 253 [the Eng. tr., *op. cit*. (note 1), p. 276, follows RSV].
30. See above, pp. 57, 63 note 22.
31. See J. B. Frey, 'Le concept de "vie" dans l'Evangile de saint Jean', *Bib*, 1 (1920), 37–58, 211–239; E. Tobac, 'Grâce', *Dictionnaire Apologétique*.
32. J. D. G. Dunn, 'Spirit and Kingdom', *The Expository Times*, 82 (1970), 36–40.
33. L. Cerfaux, *op. cit*. (note 1), p. 323.
34. E. Bardy, *Le Saint-Esprit en nous et dans l'Eglise, d'après le Nouveau Testament* (Albi, 1950).
35. See the chapter above on the holiness of the Church (pp. 52–64) and that on the indwelling of the Spirit (pp. 79–99). See also my *The Mystery of the Temple* (Eng. tr.; London, 1962), pp. 152ff.
36. See my article 'Mérite', in *Vocabulaire œcuménique* (Paris, 1970), pp. 233–251, with

bibliography. In addition to the references to Thomas Aquinas that I give there, this text is of interest: 'Hominis opera qui Spiritu Sancto agitur, magis dicuntur esse opera Spiritus Sancti quam ipsius hominis': *ST* Ia IIae, q. 93, a. 6, ad 1. I also quoted Albert the Great, who emphatically asserted that we can reach infinity only through the action of God; see also G. Philips, *L'union personnelle avec le Dieu vivant* (Gembloux, 1974), pp. 128–129, 271–275.

37. Council of Trent, session VI, c. 16 (*DS* 1546).

5
THE HOLY SPIRIT AND OUR PRAYER

Prayer to the Holy Spirit was relatively uncommon in the early Church. In Volume I, I gave a few historical examples and texts.[1] One characteristic common to almost all these early prayers is that they ask the Spirit to 'come': 'Come, Creator, Spirit', 'Come, Holy Spirit' and so on. In this context, it is interesting to quote the entreaty of Simeon the New Theologian, which is so full of warmth and intensity:

> Come, true light! Come, eternal life! Come, hidden mystery! Come, nameless treasure! Come, inexpressible reality! Come, inconceivable Person! Come, endless happiness! Come, light that never sets! Come, unfailing expectation of all who are to be saved! Come, awakening of those who have fallen asleep! Come, resurrection of the dead! Come, O powerful one, who always makes, remakes and transforms everything by your unique power! Come, invisible, intangible one! Come, you who never move and yet at every moment move and come to us, lying in hell—you who are above the heavens! Come, O beloved name repeated everywhere, whose being and nature we are forbidden to express or to know! Come, eternal joy! Come, imperishable crown! Come, purple of the great king, our God! Come, crystal belt studded with jewels! Come, inaccessible sandal! Come, royal purple! Come, truly sovereign right-hand! Come, you whom my wretched soul has desired and still desires! Come, only one, to one who is alone, since you can see that I am alone! Come, you who have separated me from everything and who have made me alone in this world! Come, you who have yourself become desire in me and have made me long for you—you who are absolutely inaccessible! Come, my breath and my life! Come, consolation of my poor soul! Come, my joy, my glory and my endless delight![2]

This 'Come!' is clearly a spontaneous cry of the soul. From the theological point of view, it is a call for the divine missions and particularly for the sending of the Spirit by the Father and the Son, with a shade of meaning that points to the procession of the Spirit in love. The prayer addresses the Spirit as though he were not sent, as though he were the inclination of God himself towards us moving, as it were, of its own accord.

'PRAY IN THE HOLY SPIRIT' (Jude 20)

The Church's Life of Praise

In the liturgy of the Church, praise and words of faith, hope and love rise continuously up to God. The Church is the holy temple—and indeed every soul is also the Church—the communion of saints, and the family of God built on the foundation of the apostles and prophets, as we are told in Eph 2:11–22. It is worth recalling verses 18–22 of that text here:

> Through him (Christ in his sacrifice) we both (Jews and gentiles) have access in one Spirit to the Father. So then you are no longer strangers and sojourners, but you are fellow-citizens with the saints and members of the household (= family) of God, built upon the foundation of the apostles and prophets, Christ Jesus himself being the chief cornerstone, in whom the whole structure is joined together and grows into a holy temple in the Lord, in whom you also are built into it for a dwelling-place of God in the Spirit.

What we have here is the worship of the new people of God, the Body of Christ and the Temple of the Holy Spirit offered to 'God' the Father. The structure of the entire liturgy of the Church is: to the Father, through the Son, in the Spirit.[3] Through the Son and in the Spirit, we have access to the Father. The word *prosagōgē* is a very strong one; it is found in Eph 3:12; Rom 5:2 and, in the verbal form, in 1 Pet 3:18. In the Epistle to the Hebrews, the verb *proserchesthai* is used for 'approaching' God.[4] We are able to approach him with boldness (*parrēsia*) because Christ, our High Priest, Lord and Head, has already entered the Holy of Holies which, as Charles de Condren pointed out early in the seventeenth century, is the bosom of the Father.[5] Everything has, in the communication of being, goodness and holiness, come from there, and everything returns there in praise that is not simply the 'fruit of lips' (Heb 13:15). That praise is indeed an offering of the whole of our lives (Rom 12:1) and brotherly love that is effective and beneficial (see Heb 13:16ff.).

This holy worship is able to reach God through Christ, the only priest of the new and definitive covenant, because we are the members of his Body—one new man—in the Holy Spirit, 'for by one Spirit we were all baptized into one body, Jews or Greeks . . .' (1 Cor 12:13; Eph 4:4). That Body is a 'holy temple in the Lord'. There is no longer any other true temple, but the one holy temple is truly a 'house of prayer for all people'.[6]

The Church's holy and precious liturgy is the place where the Spirit and the Bride say 'Come!' to the Lord (Rev 22:17). The Lord does in fact come every day to make his Easter event present for us in the Church's holy Eucharist. There is also the divine Office, the Church's hours which make time holy as the sun rises and sets, the night encloses all things in darkness and 'man goes forth to his work and to his labour until the evening' (Ps 104:23; see also verse 30: 'When thou sendest forth thy Spirit, they are created and thou renewest the face of the earth').

It is also a prayer of the seasons and the year, a cycle of mysteries made present in the celebration through which the Holy Spirit is made present for us and makes our own the incarnation, Easter, Pentecost, the Last Supper and so on. This liturgy also takes many forms—Vespers in the peace and harmony of a monastery; Mass in the parish church, where the Word and the Bread of life are shared; family prayer, a proven source of holiness and vocations; spontaneous prayer and the prayer of silence in groups in which Paul's exhortation is carried out in the 'secular city':

> Be filled with the Spirit, addressing one another in psalms and hymns and spiritual songs, singing and making melody to the Lord with all your heart, always and for everything giving thanks in the name of our Lord Jesus Christ to God the Father (Eph 5:18–20).
>
> Sing psalms and hymns and spiritual songs with thankfulness in your hearts to God. And whatever you do, in word or deed, do everything in the name of the Lord Jesus, giving thanks to God the Father through him (Col 3:16–17).
>
> When you come together, each one has a hymn, a lesson, a revelation, a tongue or an interpretation. Let all things be done for edification (1 Cor 14:26).

Individual Prayer

'When you pray, go into your room and shut the door and pray to your Father who is in secret' (Mt 6:6).

The first thing that I ask from God is that he should give me prayer: 'O Lord, open thou my lips and my mouth shall show forth thy praise' (Ps 51:15) and 'If you who are evil know how to give good gifts to your children, how much more will the heavenly Father give the Holy Spirit to those that ask him!' (Lk 11:13). In fact, 'the Spirit helps us in our weakness, for we do not know how to pray as we ought' (Rom 8:26).

We cry 'Abba! Father!' (Rom 8:15), but we say this through the Spirit, so that it is quite true to say that it is he who cries it (Gal 4:6). It is indeed difficult to say whether it is he or us. He is so deeply within us, because he has been sent 'into our hearts'[7] and, as the Holy Spirit, he is so pure, subtle and penetrating (Wis 7:22) that he is able to be in all of us and in each one of us without doing violence to the person, indiscernible in his spontaneous movement. He is above all the Spirit of freedom.[8]

The Spirit in our Prayer

The Spirit helps us to read Scripture and to meditate. *Lectio divina* is something that goes beyond any scholarly study, and meditation transcends philosophical reflection. Prayer, however, is something else again. It is a theologal activity open to every Christian who practises the spiritual life, and is not dependent on the special grace of the mystical life. Bossuet described it in the following way: 'The reading of spiritual books should never be neglected, but they should be read in a spirit of simplicity and prayer and not in a spirit of questing curiosity. When we read in this way, we let the lights and feelings that our reading reveals to us impress themselves on our souls and this impression is made more by the presence of God than by our own hard work.'[9] God's presence is more important, as Bossuet said, than our own effort, this is critical, but our prayer is neither illuminism nor quietism. We think of God—as Charles de Foucauld said, 'praying is thinking of God while loving him'.[10] During this prayer, we express words and feelings, but only for brief periods—as Tauler said, 'the time of an Our Father'.[11] Why no more than this? God himself, the Word and the Holy Spirit impress on our souls an attitude of peaceful and loving clinging which makes us dependent on them. We do not go to them—they draw us towards them and place in us a love, a quiet assent and a joyful and peaceful fullness. This comes much more from them than from us, but at the same time it points to a core within ourselves deeper than our thinking processes.

All the spiritual writers, including Bossuet, have warned that this prayer of simplicity, which is a purely theologal moment that God himself gives,[12] does not do away with the usefulness of meditation, above all not with the practice of the virtues, which such prayer in fact presupposes and requires. There are, however, certain conditions which dispose us for such a gift; they are not really specific, because they have a more general application, but they are nonetheless very valuable.

It may be too commonplace to say so, but it comes down to this: the essential presupposition is that we should really love God, not simply Jesus of Nazareth, but God himself, who has made himself known to us and who remains transcendent and unknowable. Our task is to ensure that God will be a living Person for us and the most important thought in our lives. If this is so, our lives will be offered to God and connected with him. They will form that 'spiritual worship' that was required by Jesus himself (Jn 4:24), Paul (Rom 12:1) and Peter (1 Pet 2:5).

If this is so, we shall avoid what the world offers—superficial excitement, entertainment, futile and wretched hedonism in many different forms, noise, fever, a lack of moral discipline and a thousand attractions that distract, hurt and even disintegrate us. Elijah heard Yahweh in the 'still, small voice' of the wind (1 Kings 19:12). We too need to lead disciplined lives based on a love of God's law and an attitude of strong obedience. Those who have advanced far in prayer can help us how to pray in this way. We have, in a word, to go back to our 'heart' and build up the inner man again.[13] And may God come to us!

The Spirit in our Petitionary Prayer

I do not intend to deal here with every aspect of the prayer of petition. We are promised in Scripture that it will always be heard and answered (Mt 7:7ff. par.; Mk 11:24; Jn 14:13–14; 16:23ff.; see also 1 Jn 5:14), and yet 'the memory of the prayers that have not been answered may prevent me from praying again', as Ernest Hello lamented.[14] I do not seek to justify petitionary prayer, even in the case of prayer for earthly goods, since this question has, I think, been settled. All that I shall attempt to do here is to point to the part played by the Holy Spirit in that movement in which God enables us to build a bridge between ourselves and him. In this, my point of departure will be the nature of prayer itself.

L. Beinaert made a distinction between 'prayed petition' and 'praying prayer'.[15] The first is an expression of my desire or rather, of my need. It calls for a reality of the order of earthly causes, which I have, because of my impotence, to look for in that mysterious being who is thought to be more potent, but in that search I do not really reach transcendence. 'God' is brought back to our level. This is the prayer of La Hire: 'Lord, do now for La Hire what La Hire would do for you if you were La Hire and La Hire were God'. 'Praying prayer', on the other hand, is, because of love, of the order of God and is not a mere petition, but prayer. Prayer is essentially communion with God and with his will. If Jesus had simply asked in the garden of Gethsemane: 'Let this cup pass from me', he would only have been expressing a petition. His appeal was only a prayer because he added: 'Nevertheless, not as I will, but as thou wilt'. In this way, God is recognized as God. True prayer ensures that God is God and not an extension of my arm which is too short.

Jean-Claude Sagne, who is both a theologian and a psychologist, can help us perhaps to go a step further in the direction of the Holy Spirit.[16] He has made a distinction between three aspects or moments of prayer—need, desire and petition. Conscious need leads to desire, which, if it is addressed to another who is recognized as such becomes a petition. This is where the recognition of the presence of the other begins. If I agree, in the light of this recognition, to give up my need, I will come to recognize the other fully and I will know his desire to exist totally in and through himself. I also experience love in recognizing that the other exists, with his own desire, fully in and through himself. Sagne himself goes on to say: 'In prayer, we have first to experience the dissatisfaction of our own desire, confess our own lack and recognize in faith the absent presence of God. This should lead us to desire the desire of God himself, that is, to desire what God desires and to let God desire in us. At this point, prayer appears as the mystery of God in us and an event of the Spirit, because it is the function of the Holy Spirit to be the desire of God in God himself and also the desire of God in us. The Spirit forms, deepens, expands and adjusts our desire to the desire of God by giving it the same object. The Spirit makes our desire live from the life of God himself, to the point where God himself comes to desire at the heart of our desire' (p. 94).

Let us once again look at some of the important texts:

Pray at all times in the Spirit with all prayer and supplication (Eph 6:18).

Come, you who have yourself become desire in me and have made me long for you (Simeon the New Theologian: see p. 112 above and note 2 below).

God's love has been poured into our hearts through the Holy Spirit which has been given to us (Rom 5:5).

The soul loves God with the will of God, which is also the soul's will and it can love him as it is loved by him, because it loves him through the will of God himself, in the same love with which he loves it; that love is, according to the Apostle (Rom 5:5), the Holy Spirit (Commentary on Rom 5:5 by John of the Cross).[17]

The Spirit searches everything, even the depths of God. For what person knows a man's thoughts except the spirit of the man which is in him? So also no one comprehends the thoughts of God except the Spirit of God. Now we have received not the spirit of the world, but the Spirit which is from God (1 Cor 2:10–12; see also Is 40:12–14; 55:8–9; Job 4:3 and *passim*; Rom 11:33–35; 1 Cor 2:16).

The Spirit helps us in our weakness, for we do not know how to pray as we ought; but the Spirit himself intercedes for us with sighs too deep for words. And he who searches the hearts of men knows what is the mind of the Spirit, because the Spirit intercedes for the saints (Rom 8:26–27).

That is the ultimate and definitive answer to our question about prayer—it reveals a new depth to us. I asked whether it is he or us in prayer. It is us, of course, but, looking forward to God who will be 'everything to everyone' (1 Cor 15:28), it is also him in us. Beyond all that we know consciously and all thoughts that we can form or formulate, the Spirit who *dwells in our hearts* is there himself as prayer, supplication and praise. He is our union with God and for that reason he is our prayer. 'We have to believe in God's love and in his saving presence in us in everything that happens in our lives.'[18] *God himself* is present as a gift and he dwells in our innermost depths—*intimior intimo meo*, 'more inward and more secret than my deepest and innermost self'. This means that the heart of the believer is, to the extent that the Spirit dwells in it, a place where God encounters himself and where there is consequently an inexpressible relationship between the divine Persons.[19] It is really the desire or longing of God himself interceding for the saints at a deeper level than their own expressed or expressible prayer. Jesus himself, after all, said: 'O righteous Father, . . . that the love with which thou hast loved me may be in them' (Jn 17:26).

NOTES

1. See Volume I, pp. 94, 108ff.
2. This prayer precedes Simeon's hymns: translation based on Fr. tr. by J. Paramelle, *SC* 156 (1969), pp. 151, 153. It is also interesting to quote this prayer by John of Fécamp, written

in 1060 (until recently attributed first to Augustine and then to Anselm; A. Wilmart has shown that it was the work of John of Fécamp): 'Come, then, O come, excellent consoler of the suffering soul. . . . Come, you who cleanse blemishes and who heal wounds. Come, strength of the weak and support of all who fall. Come, doctor of the humble and conqueror of the proud. Come, O tender father of orphans. . . . Come, hope of the poor. . . . Come, O star of sailors, port for the shipwrecked. Come, O glory of the living. . . . Come, most holy of Spirits and take me in your mercy. Let me be conformed to you': Mme Arsène-Henry, *Les plus beaux textes sur le Saint-Esprit* (Paris, 1968), pp. 204, 363, note 33.

3. I have already referred to C. Vagaggini, *Theological Dimensions of the Liturgy* (Eng. tr.; Collegeville, Minn., 1976), chapter 7, for this theme.
4. Heb 4:16; 7:25; 10:1; 11:6; 12:18; see also 10:19, where the word used is *eisodos*, entrance.
5. Charles de Condren, *L'idée du sacerdoce et du sacrifice de Jésus-Christ*, Part 3, chapter 4.
6. The important episode of the purification of the Temple, containing the quotation from Is 56:7, will be found in Mt 21:10–17; Mk 11:15–17; Lk 19:45–48; and especially Jn 2:13–16. See also my *The Mystery of the Temple* (Eng. tr.; London, 1962), pp. 120ff.
7. Gal 4:6; 2 Cor 1:22; Rom 5:5; 2:29; Eph 5:19; 3:17; Col 3:16. See also L. Cerfaux, *The Christian in the Theology of St Paul* (Eng. tr.; London, 1967), p. 296.
8. See Chapter 6 below. For another example, referring not only to him, but also to us, see Lk 21:15; cf. 12:12; Mt 10:20; Mk 13:11. Data illustrating this will be found in Acts 4:8; 5:32; 6:10; 7:55. Simeon the New Theologian, *op. cit.* (note 2), p. 153, says: 'I thank you for having become one spirit with me, without confusion, change or transformation, you who are God transcending everything, and for having become all in all for me'.
9. This quotation will be found in No. XIII of Bossuet's 'Méthode pour passer la journée dans l'oraison, en esprit de foi et de simplicité devant Dieu': *Œuvres*, ed. Lachat, VII (Paris, 1862), pp. 504–509.
10. Charles de Foucauld, *Lettre à Madame de Bondy*, 7 April 1890.
11. Johannes Tauler, Sermon 15, No. 7.
12. According to Thomas' theology, the theologal virtues call for an act of God as their 'formal object'. The object of faith is simply first, uncreated Truth and, in hope, what is expected of God is no less than God himself. In the case of charity, the text of Rom 5:5 is quite categorical. For John of the Cross and his understanding of this, see below, note 17.
13. See P.-R. Régamey's excellent account in 'Dieu parle au cœur', *Cahiers Saint-Dominique* (November 1960), 9–17 (425–433) and *Redécouvrir la Vie religieuse. La rénovation dans l'Esprit* (Paris, 1974).
14. Ernest Hello, in P. Guilloux, *Les plus belles pages d'Ernest Hello* (Paris, 1924), p. 17.
15. L. Beinaert, 'La prière de demande dans nos vies d'homme' (written in 1941), *Expérience chrétienne et Psychologie* (Paris, 1966), 333–351; *idem*, 'Prière et demande à l'Autre', *Lumen Vitae*, 22 (Brussels, 1967), 217–224.
16. J.-C. Sagne, 'Du besoin à la demande, ou la conversion du désir dans la prière', *M-D*, 109 (1972), 87–97; *idem*, 'L'Esprit-Saint ou le désir de Dieu', *Concilium* (Fr. ed. only), 99 (1974), 85–95.
17. John of the Cross, *Spiritual Canticle*, 37.
18. A. C. Rzewuski, *A travers l'invisible cristal. Confessions d'un Dominicain* (Paris, 1976), p. 368.
19. See K. Niederwimmer, 'Das Gebet des Geistes. Röm. 8. 26f', *TZ*, 20 (Basle, 1964), 252–265.

6
THE SPIRIT AND THE STRUGGLE AGAINST THE FLESH THE SPIRIT AND FREEDOM

The word 'flesh' can have several different meanings in Scripture.[1] It can, for example, simply point to man's state on earth—'the Word became flesh' (Jn 1:14)—and that condition is characterized by fragility and finiteness. This flesh is good in itself, but even as such it reveals the weakness and insufficiency that is present in everything that belongs to this world in comparison with the divine order. This revelation becomes dramatic when the flesh is seen in a state of tension with the Spirit, as it is in Paul's letters to the Romans and the Galatians, both of which particularly interested Luther. In that case, we are conscious of the opposition between two existential attitudes in our relationship with God (Luther's *coram Deo*), with our brothers, with ourselves and with the world. The flesh is the principle or the seat of opposition to the will of the Spirit. It is a principle of action dwelling in us, just as the Holy Spirit also dwells in us, but it does more than dwell in us, since it is our very dwelling-place, both in the neutral sense of being our simple state here on earth and in its pernicious existential sense as a propensity that goes counter to our calling as sons of God, members of the Body of Christ and temples of the Holy Spirit.

In Gal 3:1–4:12; Rom 3:21ff., this opposition is above all between the law and the promise of faith, the flesh being the Mosaic law. In Gal 5:13–6:18; Rom 7:1–8:30, the opposition is in the Christian himself, whose life is based both on the flesh and the Spirit.[2] Like J. D. G. Dunn, I believe that this tension is the result of our condition of 'already' and 'not yet'. Here we have the truth of the Christian condition, unlike that of the Jews, who were living in the 'not yet', and of the Gnostics, who influenced the Christian community at Corinth and who believed that they were 'already' in a state that went beyond the limitations and demands of the 'not yet'. The Christian, on the other hand, (already) has the Spirit. He is already a son of God. He is, however, still in the flesh, in the sense that this resists the Spirit, and he is still looking forward to the fullness of the quality of a son and to the redemption and spiritualization of his body. This, he believes, will follow in accordance with Christ, who was crucified and was dead according to the flesh, but who was raised from the dead and glorified according to the

Holy Spirit.[3] There are many Pauline texts pointing to this and I will only quote the most important passages:

> Walk by the Spirit and do not gratify the desires of the flesh. For the desires of the flesh are against the Spirit and the desires of the Spirit are against the flesh; for these are opposed to each other, to prevent you from doing what you would (Gal 5:16–18).
>
> Whatever a man sows, that he will also reap. For he who sows to his own flesh will from the flesh reap corruption; but he that sows to the Spirit will from the Spirit reap eternal life (Gal 6:7–8).
>
> Those who live according to the flesh set their minds on the things of the flesh, but those who live according to the Spirit set their minds on the things of the Spirit. To set the mind on the flesh is death, but to set the mind on the Spirit is life and peace. For the mind that is set on the flesh is hostile to God; it does not submit to God's law, indeed it cannot; and those who are in the flesh cannot please God. But you are not in the flesh, if the Spirit of God really dwells in you. Any one who does not have the Spirit of Christ does not belong to him. But if Christ is in you, although your bodies are dead because of sin, your spirits are alive because of righteousness. If the Spirit of him who raised Jesus from the dead dwells in you, he who raised Christ Jesus from the dead will give life to your mortal bodies through his Spirit which dwells in you (Rom 8:5–11).

The Christian should therefore set about living 'in the new life of the Spirit' (Rom 7:6). This involves him in a whole journey. And 'if we live by the Spirit, let us also walk by the Spirit' (Gal 5:25), which leads to an inner struggle. Let us consider this struggle now.

(1) It is a struggle within us between our inner propensities or the two spirits that dwell in us. The theme of the two ways was one with which the Jews were familiar. It can be found in the gospels and in the *Didache*. We know what it means in the concrete: 'Not everyone who says to me, "Lord, Lord" shall enter the kingdom of heaven' (Mt 7:21; Lk 6:46). When Paul said: 'No one can say "Jesus is Lord" except by the Holy Spirit' (1 Cor 12:3), he was undoubtedly thinking of a confession of faith and of praise of the Lord. He also spoke, however, of 'faith working through love' (Gal 5:6; cf. Rom 2:6, 10, 15–16; 2 Cor 13:4; Eph 2:8–10; Col 1:10; 1 Thess 1:3; 2 Thess 1:11) and of love fulfilling the law.[4] James was no different from Paul in urging believers to be 'doers of the word and not hearers only' (Jas 1:22).

The Spirit is also a spirit of sons, making us cry: 'Abba! Father!' This means that we cannot call on the Father of all men if we refuse to behave as brothers towards all men who are created in God's image. Relationships between man and God the Father are so closely connected with relationships between man and his human brothers that Scripture insists: 'He who does not love does not know God' (1 Jn 4:8).[5]

J. Wolinski has forcibly expressed similar ideas, especially in his commentary on a text of Origen:[6] 'The inauguration of our life as sons which begins with baptism should continue as an entire existence as sons, in the course of which the quality of sonship should be made present and should grow gradually as we perform good actions'. Origen himself claimed that 'the more one hears the word of God, the more one becomes a son of God' and goes on to say: 'provided, however, that those words fall on someone who has received the Spirit of adoption'.[7] He also insisted that one becomes the son of the one whose works one does:

> All those who commit sin are born of the devil (1 Jn 3:8). We are therefore born of the devil as many times as we have sinned. How wretched is the one who is always born of the devil, but how blessed is he who is always born of God! For I say: the righteous man is not simply born once of God. He is born again and again. He is born according to each good action through which God begets him. . . . In the same way, if you possess the Spirit of adoption, God will again and again beget you in the Son. He begets you from work to work and from thought to thought. That is the nativity that you receive and through it you become a son of God, begotten again and again in Christ Jesus.[8]

It is easy to express in terms of 'divine missions' this continuous begetting into the filial life in the actions that form the fabric of it. According to the principle of 'synergy', we make ourselves through our actions, and it is the work of God (see Gal 4:7). We know too that the greatest mystics were very remote from any kind of Quietism. In this context, it is worth recalling what Simeon the New Theologian said:

> Whether we have not yet received the grace of the Spirit or whether we have received it, we can only pass through the darkness of the soul and contemplate the light of the Holy Spirit if we suffer pain and hardship, violence, tribulation and distress (Rom 8:35). 'For the kingdom of heaven has suffered violence and men of violence take it by force' (Mt 11:12), because it is 'through many tribulations' that 'we must enter the kingdom of God' (Acts 14:22). The kingdom of heaven is a participation in the Holy Spirit—that is what is meant by the saying that the 'kingdom of God is in the midst of you' (Lk 17:21). We must therefore do all that we can to receive and to keep the Holy Spirit within us. May those who do not have continuously to suffer hardship, violence, tribulation and distress in their hearts not tell us: 'We have the Holy Spirit within us', because no one will obtain that reward without the works, the pain, the hardship and the suffering of virtue.[9]

We know from the New Testament and especially Paul, and from the experience of the saints and the spiritual writers that grace is only gained at the expense of sharing in the sufferings and the cross of Jesus, which are inseparable from his resurrection.[10] The Spirit is not often mentioned explicitly in Paul's many texts on the sufferings and tribulations of the Christian, but such sufferings form part of the tension between the 'not yet' and the 'already' and between the flesh and the Spirit. Life takes place in the weakness of the flesh and in the process of death which is the fate of the flesh (see Gal 3:1–5; Rom 15:18–19; 1 Cor 1:4–9; 2:1–5; 2 Cor 4:7–5:5; 12:9).

Paul points above all to the eschatological significance of these sufferings in the wake of what was for Jesus the conditioning of his glory by his crucifixion (see Rom 5:2ff.; 8:17; 2 Cor 4:17ff. and especially verse 10; 2 Thess 1:4ff.; 1 Pet 4:12–15, which contains an explicit reference to the Spirit). This logic, which began with Jesus' baptism, is the logic of the whole Christian life and of the action of the apostle, who, on this basis, insists that the power of God (as Spirit) is affirmed in man's distress.[11] 'God's' consolation always accompanies an experience of weakness and suffering (2 Cor 1:3–7), Paul assures us, and there is often a true *spiritual* joy (Rom 11:17; Gal 5:22). A charismatic experience occurs in the midst of all this; this is clear from what Paul says to the Thessalonians: 'Our gospel came to you not only in word, but also in power and in the Holy Spirit and with full conviction. You know what kind of men we proved to be among you for your sake. And you became imitators of us and of the Lord, for you received the word in much affliction, with joy inspired by the Holy Spirit' (1 Thess 1:5–6).

(2) Jesus was anointed by the Spirit when he was baptized with his messianic ministry in mind and was at once led by the Spirit to confront the demon in a series of temptations which referred to the two values revealed in his baptism—his quality as the beloved Son which had to prove itself in his destiny as Servant. The Christian is similarly confronted not only with flesh and blood, but also with the spirits of evil who reign between heaven and earth and with the spirit who acts among the 'sons of disobedience' (Eph 2:2; 6:11ff.). Once again, Paul does not name the Holy Spirit explicitly—the Spirit is only named in the exorcisms practised by Jesus[12]—but what can that 'strength of might' be with which the Christian should arm himself in the Lord, if not the strength of the Holy Spirit?[13]

The part played by the Spirit in the conversion of the sinner

The Paraclete whom Jesus was to send would 'confound the world with regard to sin' or 'convince the world of [RSV: concerning] sin' (Jn 16:8). All exegetes agree that this text has a universal significance. M. F. Berrouard has pointed out that 'the framework is that of a trial with the task of reviewing Jesus' historical trial and his condemnation by the world. The need is to discover on what side sin is and on what side justice, and how the first judgement should be assessed. The action of the Paraclete consists in urging the world to recognize its fault and to confess its guilt.'[14] This is all in accordance with the whole thesis of the fourth gospel, which is: Will Jesus, the Son of God and the light of the world, be received, or will he be rejected by the world, the Jews and every individual personally?

Although exegetes are in agreement about this all-embracing meaning of the text, they are divided in their interpretation. Some believe that this conviction of sin, which is the work of the Paraclete, is brought about in the consciousness of the world, while others think that it occurs in the minds of Jesus' disciples. Those who prefer the second interpretation have good arguments to support it, but why should it necessarily exclude the first? Does the Spirit not play a part in the conversion of the world? What the New Testament has to say about his function as a witness together with the apostles (see above, pp. 42–43) clearly points to the *metanoia* or conversion of the world and it is in the context of Pentecost that Luke speaks of it in his Acts of the Apostles (2:37–38).

The Holy Spirit acts within us or he penetrates into us like an anointing. He makes us, at a level that is deeper than that of mere regret for some fault, conscious of the sovereign attraction of the Absolute, the Pure and the True, and of a new life offered to us by the Lord, and he also gives us a clear consciousness of our own wretchedness and of the untruth and selfishness that fills our lives. We are conscious of being judged, but at the same time we are forestalled by forgiveness and grace, with the result that our false excuses, our self-justifying mechanisms and the selfish structure of our lives break down.[15]

Something of this kind happened to Zacchaeus. Grace came into his home, forestalling him, and at once he knew that he was a sinner. It is worth noting the boldness and at the same time the depth of understanding on the part of the Church in using this passage in Scripture (Lk 19:1–10) in the liturgy of the dedication of a church. The Church itself is a sinner forestalled by free forgiveness and is converted when the Lord comes and takes up residence in it. The Church is and always will be the coming of salvation to a house where the Lord comes to dwell, and this process begins with a conviction of injustice or sin.

Religious revivals—and it would be a pity if the 'sects' or the 'evangelistic' movements of the Billy Graham type were regarded as enjoying a monopoly in this field—have almost always begun by a call to conversion from a state of sinfulness. This was the case, for example, in Ireland in the fifth and sixth centuries.[16] It is also the case, it would appear, with the present-day movements concerned with renewal in the Spirit.

The article on the Holy Spirit in the creed is made explicit in terms of a list of the works of the Spirit—the Church, baptism and the remission of sins. It is true that the confessions of faith that were formulated in the fourth century linked the remission of sins with baptism[17] and even Peter made this connection on the day of Pentecost, according to the Acts of the Apostles (2:38). This statement was certainly in accordance with the Christological conviction that 'everyone who believes in him (Christ) receives forgiveness of sins through his name' (Acts 10:43; 13:38–39; Lk 24:47). The glorified Lord, however, acts through his Spirit and, in what is sometimes called the 'Johannine Pentecost', the 'power' to remit sins is attributed, in a view of the

Trinitarian economy, to the virtue of the Holy Spirit: 'As the Father has sent me, even so I send you' and, breathing on them (the Twelve, of whom only ten were present), Jesus goes on to say: 'Receive the Holy Spirit. If you forgive the sins of any, they are forgiven; if you retain the sins of any, they are retained' (Jn 20:21–23). It is, in other words, because the Spirit dwells in the Church that the Church is able to remit sins.[18]

In the Church's Tradition, the coming of the Spirit at Pentecost, fifty days after Easter, has been linked to the jubilee, which occurs every fifty years, after a 'week of weeks of years', as a transcendence or consummation of fullness (Exod 34:22; Lev 23:15). The year of jubilee was a year of setting free and of return to the ancestral property (Lev 25:8ff.). In the Church's liturgy, this is linked to the words of Jesus, and the gift of the Spirit is celebrated as the forgiveness of sins, because Jesus himself is the forgiveness of sins (*quia ipse est remissio peccatorum*).[19] Pentecost is also celebrated as a jubilee of remission in this hymn at Vespers:[20]

Patrata sunt haec mystice Paschae peracto tempore Sacro dierum numero Quo lege fit remissio.	All these things took place mystically, when the time of Easter had passed, on the holy day that had been fixed for remission to be legally enacted.
Dudum sacrata pectora Tua replesti gratia. Dimitte nunc peccamina Et da quieta tempora.	You have just filled the dedicated hearts with your grace; now remit their sins and grant peaceful days.

The Spirit makes us truly free[21]

The prophet Jeremiah described a new covenant in terms of fullness and warmth: 'I will put my law within them and I will write it upon their hearts' (31:31–34), and barely a generation later Ezekiel proclaimed a similar promise in the name of God: 'A new heart I will give you and a new spirit I will put within you; I will take out of your flesh the heart of stone and give you a heart of flesh. And I will put my spirit within you and cause you to walk in my statutes and be careful to observe my ordinances' (36:26ff.; 37:14).

Christians have always believed and still believe that these promises have been fulfilled in the event of Jesus Christ and the gift of the Holy Spirit, but according to the status of the 'already' and the 'not yet' that we have discussed above, that is, as earnest-money or first-fruits, and therefore in such a way that we are still waiting for their fulfilment in the literal sense of the word. As Paul said:

> Where the Spirit of the Lord is, there is freedom (2 Cor 3:17)
>
> You were called to freedom, brethren. . . . If you are led by the Spirit you are not under the law (Gal 5:13, 18).

> The law of the Spirit of life in Christ Jesus has set me free from the law of sin and death. . . . All who are led by the Spirit of God are sons of God (Rom 8:2, 14).

The Spirit is the Spirit of Jesus Christ and a Spirit of adoption. He gives us not a status, but also a condition—that of sons. Adoption as sons is not simply a legal status—it is a real state, since we have in us (in our 'hearts') the Spirit of the Son who became our first-born brother. Nicholas Cabasilas expressed this idea in Trinitarian categories that were fully in accordance with the Eastern tradition when he said that 'the Father sets us free, the Son is the ransom and the Holy Spirit is our freedom'.[22] Christ, however, is more than the ransom—he is the Son. The declarations of Paul which I have quoted above and his allegory of Sarah and Hagar, Ishmael and Isaac (Gal 4:21–31) go together with Jesus' statements: 'The sons are free' (Mt 17:25–26); 'If you continue in my word (proclaiming my quality as the Son of God and letting you share in it through faith), the truth will make you free' (Jn 8:31–32); 'If the Son makes you free, you will be free indeed' (verse 36).

This freedom is not a licence dependent on whim, which is an illusory freedom or a caricature of freedom that in fact destroys true freedom if it is taken too far. According to Augustine, the Christian into whom the Holy Spirit has poured the love of God will spontaneously observe a law which can be summed up in love: 'He is not subject to the law, but he is not without a law' (*non est sub lege, sed cum lege*).[23] The content of the law is the norm for his action, but he is not subjected to the restraints of a law because he has interiorized the law. That is why it is he who determines himself from within himself and that is the very definition of freedom. Thomas Aquinas speaks about this in a strictly theological language that is nonetheless very close to that of the gospel and Paul:

> The free man is the one who belongs to himself; the slave, however, belongs to his master. Whoever acts spontaneously therefore acts freely, but whoever receives his impulse from another does not act freely. The man who avoids evil, not because it is an evil, but because of a law of the Lord's, is therefore not free. On the other hand, the man who avoids evil because it is an evil is free. It is here that the Holy Spirit works, inwardly perfecting our spirit by communicating to it a new dynamism, and this functions so well that man refrains from evil through love, as though divine law were ordering him to do this. He is therefore free not because he is not subject to divine law, but because his inner dynamism leads him to do what divine law prescribes.[24]

In his treatise on the law, Thomas says that the new law is simply the Holy Spirit himself or the proper effect of that Spirit, which is faith working through love.[25] That Spirit is so much within us—in the cry 'Father!', for example, it is the Spirit and us as well—and he is so much the weight or inclination of our love that he is our spontaneity intimately related to what is good. The decision to do the opposite is only an imperfection of a freedom insufficiently illuminated and filled with good. Christ, who could not sin, was entirely free.[26] The Holy Spirit, who is Good and Love, compels us not only by leaving us free, but also by making us free, because he compels us from within and through *our very own* movement. James, for example, was able to speak of the 'perfect law, the law of liberty' (1:25; 2:12), just as Paul spoke of the 'law of Christ' (Gal 6:2) and of our being 'slaves of righteousness . . . for sanctification' (Rom 6:18–19). Many Christian mystics have also spoken of this. At the summit of the ascent of Mount Carmel, John of the Cross wrote: 'There is no longer a path here, because there is no law for the righteous man' and Marie de l'Incarnation, seized by the action of divine Goodness, declared: 'My spirit was free and abandoned, without being able to desire or choose anything'.[27]

As Paul pointed out: 'Now we are discharged from the law, dead to that which held us captive, so that we serve not under the old written code, but in the new life of the Spirit' (Rom 7:6)[28] and 'If we live by the Spirit, let us also walk by the Spirit' (Gal 5:25). Christianity is not a law, although it contains one, and it is not a morality, although it contains one. By the gift of the Spirit of Christ, it is an ontology of grace which involves, as its fruit or product, certain attitudes that are called for and even demanded by what we are.[29] This is both extremely strong and at the same time terribly fragile. A materially defined law that is imposed as such on man produces effective results. Many of us have experienced this in the company of religious Jews, who have had no doubts about their own identity or their duty. The Spirit, on the other hand, is a law imposed not by pressure, but by appeal, as Bergson commented in his book *Les deux sources de la morale et de la religion* (1932). Paul was clearly right when he said: 'You were *called* to freedom, brethren; only do not use your freedom as an opportunity for the flesh, but through love be servants of one another. For the whole law is fulfilled in one word, "You shall love your neighbour as yourself" ' (Gal 5:13–14). In this context, Luther's words of 1520 come to mind: 'The Christian is a free man and the master of all things. He is subject to no one. The Christian is a servant and full of obedience. He is subject to all men.'

Let me, however, cite a witness who is closer to us in time. Just as Savonarola wrote his excellent commentary on the *Miserere* when he was in prison and waiting to die, so too Alfred Delp, a Catholic priest arrested by the Gestapo in August 1944 and hanged on 2 February 1945 with Goerdeler and von Moltke, wrote a meditation on the *Veni Sancte Spiritus* while he was in prison, from 11 January 1945 until the eve of his execution. With his chained hands, he wrote as a free man—liberated by the power of the Holy Spirit. His meditation is interrupted just before the final sentence: *In te confidentibus*:[30]

> The eternal hills are there, from where salvation comes. Their rescue is ready; it is waiting and it is coming. God shows it to me every day and now my whole life is bearing witness to it. All the assurance, cleverness and skill that I had in me burst

under the weight of the violence and the forces that opposed me. My months in captivity have broken my physical resistance and many other things in me and yet I have experienced wonderful times. God has taken everything in hand and I can now pray and wait for the rescue and the power that comes from the eternal hills. . . .

The man who knows how poor he is and who rejects all pride and self-sufficiency, even the pride of his rags, the man who stands before God in his nakedness and his need—that man knows the miracles of love and mercy, from the consolation of the heart and the illumination of the spirit to the allaying of hunger and thirst. . . .

Very often, during the suffering and disturbance of these last few months and bent down under the weight of violence, I have been conscious of peace and joy invading my soul with the victorious power of the rising sun. . . .

The Holy Spirit is the passion with which God loves himself. Man has to correspond to that passion. He has to ratify it and accomplish it. If he learns how to do this, the world will once again become capable of true love. We cannot know and love God unless God himself seizes hold of us and tears us away from our selfishness. God has to love himself in and through us and we shall then live in God's truth and love will once more become the living heart of the world.

There have been many men in our age who have been made strong and free in the Spirit! To mention only those who have died: Dietrich Bonhoeffer,[31] whom I did not know; Emmanuel Mounier, Father Maydieu, Paul Couturier—'Freedom has entered my life and it has the face of love'—and Edmond Michelet, whom I did know personally.

Alfred Delp had outlined a way in which a reference to the Spirit as the principle of freedom could be applied to the Church as the people of God or the messianic people. Vatican II gave special emphasis to this: 'The heritage of this people is the dignity and freedom of the sons of God in whose hearts the Holy Spirit dwells as in his temple. Its law is the new commandment of love as Christ loved us (cf. Jn 13:34).'[32] What, then, is our position with regard to this ideal? It is obvious that there is and always will be a great deal for us to do if we are to fulfil its demands at the level of the Church as an institution and as a way of life.

It is clear, for example, that Paul had a great respect for the legitimate freedom of believers. He did not try to exercise his authority by establishing a relationship between himself and his communities in which he was firmly in control and they were in a subordinate position: 'You were called to freedom, brethren' (Gal 5:13); 'Do not become slaves of men' (1 Cor 7:23); 'Not that we lord it over your faith; we work with you for your joy' (2 Cor 1:24); 'I preferred to do nothing without your consent in order that your goodness might not be by compulsion, but of your own free will' (Philem 14). This, surely, is a long way from the clerical pressure that has weighed so heavily on our pastoral attitudes in the Church—and may still be felt even now.

It is surely with nostalgia that we read what Augustine wrote around 390 in his treatise *De vera religione*, and again about ten years later in his reply to his friend Januarius, a text that was taken up again tranquilly by Thomas Aquinas:

> Piety begins with fear and ends in charity. That is why, when they were slaves subject to the old law, the people were held by fear and subjected to many sacred signs. They needed this so that they should long for the grace of God, the coming of which was proclaimed in the canticles of the prophets. After their coming, however, when divine Wisdom had become the man who called us to freedom, there were only very few sacred signs conveying salvation and these were set up as a social bond between Christians, that is to say, the great number of those subjected to the one God. . . .
>
> I cannot approve of the new practices that have been set up outside the common habits and are imposed as obligatory, as though they were sacraments. . . . Even though nothing can be found in them that is contrary to the law, they must be rejected, because they fill religion with slavery when God in his mercy wanted to establish and settle freedom on a very small number of sacraments, the purpose of which is very clear. The condition of the Jews would be much more tolerable. Although they failed to recognize the time of freedom, they were at least subjected to things established by the law of God and not to things established by human opinions.[33]

This text was frequently quoted by Catholics in the sixteenth century in an attempt to strip their religion of excrescences in which the gospel played only a minimal part.[34] Protestant Christians used the category *adiaphora* or matters of indifference which could be left to the discretion of local communities. Augustine was certainly not preaching anarchy, and Thomas Aquinas was even more certainly not.[35] Both were warning us not to make absolute what is relative, even though it is to be respected.

As Vatican II pointed out, 'the beginning, the subject and the goal of all social institutions is and must be the human person, which for its part and by its very nature stands completely in need of social life'.[36] There are facts on both sides. On the one hand, the freedom with which women and men have, under the influence of the Holy Spirit, created groups and religious communities in the Church is quite admirable. On the other hand, however, we are still a long way from opening the life of the Church, its parishes and its organizations to the free contribution of the charisms. It is true that 'God is not a God of confusion, but of peace' (1 Cor 14:33) and that the gift of manifesting the Spirit is made for the common good (1 Cor 12:7), but do we not suffer too much even now from what Alfred Delp called ecclesiastical functionalism, in which he saw the impression in the Church of the spirit of security and rigidity?

> This has given birth to a type of man who is not open to the Holy Spirit. He is a fortress that is so carefully constructed and guarded that the Spirit is so to speak

impotent and looks in vain for a breach. . . . If appeals to personal responsibility and commitment are to be heard in the life of the Church, the Lord will probably have to test by fire and steel the external apparatus and security of his Church. No one can, after all, pass through fire and not be transformed by it. The life-giving Spirit will help us to be reborn from the ashes with fresh courage and with a wider and more audacious vision. If we are to gain everything, we shall once again have to forget and give up many things. Above all, we shall have to give ourselves up. The soil will have to be ploughed again and sowed with new seed. Let us therefore love the freedom of God, do his truth and give ourselves to life.[37]

If the charisms are simply talents which we are called to place at the service of the building up of the Body of Christ, then there are personal talents, and there are also original collective gifts and resources—those of the different peoples and cultures and of historical experiences and traditions. The Holy Spirit is also at work in all of these. In the greater Church, there are countless local and particular Churches, faithful to the Spirit and respectful of Christian freedom. In this pluralism, the Church must recognize the 'signs of the times'.

There is also the freedom of the Church itself—its apostolic freedom. As Paul himself proudly claimed: 'Am I not free? Am I not an apostle? . . . For though I am free from all men, I have made myself a slave to all, that I might win the more' (1 Cor 9:1, 19). That meant becoming a Greek with the Greeks, and such openness and availability formed an essential part of the apostolic freedom. Another important aspect of that freedom is the confidence with which Paul spoke in public, the *parrēsia* which was a characteristic of Jesus himself (especially in the gospel of John) and became a characteristic of the disciples.[38] Quite frequently in the New Testament, when the courage to preach and confess Jesus Christ is discussed, this *parrēsia* or freedom is related to the Holy Spirit (see Phil 1:19ff.; 2 Cor 3:7ff., 12ff., which deals with the ministry of the Spirit; Acts 4:8, 31; 18:25ff., that is, the passage dealing with Apollos). The same boldness of language in confessing faith in Christ characterized later generations of Christians and notably the early martyrs. In the account of the persecution of Christians at Lyons and Vienne in 177, the believers there praised the courage that the Spirit gave them and, speaking of Alexander, 'a Phrygian by race and a physician by profession', they said that he was 'known to all because of his love of God and the boldness of his language (*parrēsian tou logou*), because he was no stranger to the apostolic charism'.[39]

This is all splendid evidence of apostolic freedom experienced at the level of personal commitment. The same freedom can also be considered at the level of history and therefore seen as the freedom of the Church itself, that freedom which the Church always claimed as a hierarchical and institutional authority over and against the secular power or powers. At certain periods of the Church's history, the struggle was continuous and bitter. It reached a peak during the pontificate of Gregory VII (†1085).

In the changing historical situation of the second half of the twentieth century and especially since Vatican II, this freedom of the Church has taken the form of social criticism directed at the Church's own history, certain important aspects of that history, the historical forms that Christianity has assumed and the cultural and ideological expressions based on a post-mediaeval middle-class and Western European model that have in the more recent history of the Church constituted a norm. This social criticism has also resulted in a movement to go beyond the existing model so that the gospel message can once again 'go over to the barbarians' and penetrate other areas of society where it may be welcomed. These other areas, whose authentic humanity has at last been fully recognized, have hitherto been largely prevented from receiving the gospel because of the predominantly Western bourgeois model of traditional Christianity. They include, for example, the working classes of the developed world, the poor of Latin America, Black societies and, even in Europe, many basic communities and active, creative movements and ways of community life of different kinds.

The *libertas Ecclesiae* is becoming the freedom of the Church in relation to itself in its historical and cultural forms. This freedom exists in the name of the Church's evangelical nature that is a direct result of the two missions of the Word and the Spirit. The Spirit is compelling the Church to go beyond itself. (The words of Ignatius Hazim, the Metropolitan of Latakia, are relevant in this context.) At this level, freedom presupposes an exercise of personal charisms and commitment on the part of all Christians, both pastors and lay people, who have themselves been set free by the Spirit. Thus, the second part of this volume completes the first part—the Church is an institution, but it is also and even primarily the 'we' of Christians.

NOTES

1. See L. Cerfaux, *The Christian in the Theology of St Paul* (Eng. tr.; London, 1967), pp. 446–452; E. Schweizer, '*sarx*', *TDNT*, VII, pp. 98–151; X. Léon-Dufour, 'Flesh', *Dictionary of Biblical Theology*, 2nd Eng. ed. (London, 1973), pp. 185–188; J. D. G. Dunn, *Jesus and the Spirit* (London, 1975), pp. 308ff.
2. Together with Augustine, Thomas Aquinas, Luther and many modern exegetes, I believe that Rom 7:7–25 refers to baptized Christians and to Paul himself. For a history of the exegesis of this passage, see O. Kuss, 'Zur Geschichte der Auslegung von Römer 7, 7–25', *Der Römerbrief* (Regensburg, 1957), pp. 462–485. For Augustine, see A. de Veer, 'L'exégèse de Rom. VII et ses variations', *Bibl. August*. 33 (Paris, 1974), pp. 770–778.

In opposition to W. G. Kümmel, *Römer 7 und die Bekehrung des Paulus* (Leipzig, 1929), J. D. G. Dunn, 'Rom 7, 14–25 in the Theology of Paul', *TZ*, 31 (1975), 257–273, and *op. cit.* (note 1), pp. 312ff., 444, notes, has shown that the passage deals with Paul as a Christian and the state of the Christian on earth as an inner struggle between the *pneuma* ('already') and the *sarx* ('not yet') in him and has pointed out that the struggle does not necessarily end with the coming of the Spirit, but that, on the contrary, it is then that it really begins.

3. See Rom 1:3–4; 6:4–11; 7:4; 8:3, 10–11; Gal 4:4–5; 2 Cor 4:10–14; Col 1:21; 2:12; 1 Tim 3:16a; 1 Pet 3:18. The Fathers regarded the baptism of Jesus as the type of the baptism of all believers and therefore applied to him the theme of Jesus descending into the water to submerge the old man entirely in the depths of the water; see Gregory Nazianzen, *Orat.* 39 (*PG* 36, 302).
4. Rom 13:8ff.: 'Owe no one anything, except to love one another, for he who loves his neighbour has fulfilled the law'.
5. Declaration on Non-Christian Religions, *Nostra aetate*, 5.
6. J. Wolinski, 'Le mystère de l'Esprit Saint', *L'Esprit Saint* (Brussels, 1978), pp. 131–164, especially pp. 141ff.
7. Origen, *Comm. in Ioan. ev.* XX, 293 (*PG* 14, 649B).
8. *Hom. Jer.* IX, 4 (*PG* 13, 356C–357A; Fr. tr. P. Nemeshegyi, *La Paternité de Dieu chez Origène* (Paris, 1960), p. 199; see also *SC* 232, pp. 393–395).
9. Simeon the New Theologian, *Cat.* II (*Cat.* VI; Fr. tr. J. Paramelle, *SC* 104 (1964), p. 23 [another version above, p. 70]). See also note 8 above. Others in the Eastern tradition who could be mentioned here are Mark the Hermit and Gregory of Sinai.
10. See L. Cerfaux, *op. cit.* (note 1), pp. 336–341; Dunn, *op. cit.* (note 1), pp. 326–342. For the Lutheran tradition, see the second part of R. Prenter, *Le Saint-Esprit et le renouveau de l'Eglise* (*Cahiers théologiques de l'actualité protestante*, 23–24) (Neuchâtel, 1949).
11. See 2 Cor 4:7; 12:9ff.; 13:3. See also J. Cambier, 'Le critère paulinien de l'apostolat en II Cor 12, 6ss', *Bib* 43 (1962), 481–518; S. Lyonnet, 'La loi fondamentale de l'apostolat formulée et vécue par S. Paul (2 Cor 13, 9)', *La vie selon l'Esprit* (*Unam Sanctam*, 55) (Paris, 1965), pp. 263–282.
12. Mt 12:28. See also my article 'Le blasphème contre l'Esprit', *L'expérience de l'Esprit, Mélanges Schillebeeckx* (Paris, 1976), pp. 17–29; this article also appeared as 'Blasphemy against the Holy Spirit' in *Concilium* 99 (1974/6), 47–57.
13. Eph 6:10. The word *dunamis*, which is so closely associated with the Holy Spirit, is only found here in the verb *endunamousthe*.
14. M. F. Berrouard, 'Le Paraclet défenseur du Christ devant la conscience du croyant', *RSPT*, 33 (1949), 361–389, especially 364. See also T. Preuss, 'La justification dans la pensée johannique', *La vie en Christ* (Neuchâtel and Paris, 1951), pp. 46–64 (in the 1946 text).
15. It is worth reading, in this context, A. Rabut, 'Accueillir Dieu', *VS* (August 1949), 168–177.
16. J. Chevallier, *Essai sur la formation de la nationalité et les réveils religieux au Pays de Galles des origines à la fin du VIe siècle* (Lyons and Paris, 1923), pp. 392ff, 419ff.
17. O. Cullmann, 'Les premières confessions de foi chrétiennes', *La foi et le culte de l'Eglise primitive* (Neuchâtel, 1963), pp. 73–74, quotes Cyril of Jerusalem, Epiphanius of Salamis and Nestorius. The Apostolic Constitutions and the Epistle of the Apostles, on the other hand, linked the remission of sins with faith in the Church.
18. Ambrose, *De poen.* I, 8 (*PL* 16, 468).
19. Postcommunion of the Tuesday after Pentecost in the Roman rite.
20. By an unknown author living before the tenth century (*PL* 86, 693). It used to appear in the Dominican rite, but was not included in Dom Guéranger's *Année liturgique*, although it has been restored to the new *Liturgia horarum*.
21. See H. Schlier, '*eleutheros, eleutheria*', *TDNT*, II, pp. 487–502; L. Cerfaux, *op. cit.* (note

1), pp. 452–460; S. Lyonnet, 'Liberté chrétienne et loi de l'Esprit selon S. Paul', *La vie selon L'Esprit, op. cit.* (note 11), pp. 169–195; J.-P. Jossua, 'Liberté', *Vocabulaire œcuménique* (Paris, 1970), pp. 283–297; *Lumière et Vie*, 61 (1963), 69 (1964); C. Duquoc, *Jésus, homme libre. Esquisse d'une Christologie* (Paris, 1973). Apart from Lyonnet, the following have written about Thomas Aquinas' theological systematization of this theme: J. Lécuyer, 'Pentecôte et loi nouvelle', *VS* (May 1953), 471–490; my own 'Variations sur le thème "Loi-Grâce" ', *RThom*, 71 (1971), 420–438; 'Le Saint-Esprit dans la théologie thomiste de l'agir moral', *Atti del Congresso Internazionale 1974*, 5: *L'Agire morale* (Naples, 1976), pp. 9–19 (with bibliography); Rémi Parent, *L'Esprit Saint et la liberté chrétienne* (Paris, 1976), which is a personal reflection with a philosophical slant on the part played by our human freedom in a context of a theology of the Holy Spirit.

22. Nicholas Cabasilas, *La vie en Jésus-Christ*, Fr. tr. S. Broussaleux (Amay sur Meuse, 1932), p. 54.
23. Augustine, *In Ioan. ev.* III, 2 (*PL* 35, 1397); cf. *De spir. et litt.* IX, 15: 'ut . . . sancta voluntas impleat legem, non constituta sub lege' (*PL* 44, 209).
24. Thomas Aquinas, *In 2 Cor.* c. 3, lect. 3 (ed. R. Cai, No. 112); translated by Lyonnet, who quotes *In Rom.* c. 2, lect. 3 (Cai No. 217); *Contra Gent.* IV, 22; *ST* Ia IIae, q. 108, a. 1, ad 2, as pointing in the same direction. See also J. Maritain, *Du régime temporel et de la liberté* (1933), pp. 44ff. In his treatise *Contra Gent.*, Thomas follows the theme of charity-friendship. The Spirit communicates his secrets to us through friendship, regarding us as an extension of himself (c. 21). He moves us and leads us to God by means of that contemplation which is peculiar to friendship, by the effects of his presence, which are joy and consolation, and by gentle consent to his will, which constitutes true Christian freedom (c. 22).
25. *ST* Ia IIae, q. 106, a. 1 and 2; *In Rom.* c. 8, lect. 1 (Cai Nos 602–603); *In Heb.* c. 8, lect. 2 (Cai No. 404).
26. R. Garrigou-Lagrange, 'La liberté impeccable du Christ et celle des enfants de Dieu', *VS* (April 1924), 5–20; A. Durand, 'La liberté du Christ dans son rapport à l'impeccabilité', *NRT* (September-October 1948), 811–822.
27. Marie de l'Incarnation, Relation of 1654, XXIX, *Ecrits spirituels et historiques*, ed. Albert Jamet (Paris and Québec, 1930), II, p. 271.
28. See also 2 Cor 3:3. The community of believers is a 'letter from Christ delivered by us, written not with ink but with the Spirit of the living God, not on tablets of stone, but on tablets of human hearts'.
29. See my contribution to *In libertatem vocati estis. Miscellanea Bernhard Häring* (*Studia Moralia*, XV) (Rome, 1977), pp. 31–40, entitled 'Réflexions et Propos sur l'originalité d'une éthique chrétienne'. See also Cerfaux, *op. cit.* (note 1), pp. 460–466, on the theme of the fruits of the Spirit.
30. Fr. tr. in *Alfred Delp, S.J.: Honneur et liberté du Chrétien. Témoignage présenté par le P. M. Rondet, S.J.* (Paris, 1958), pp. 161–200; Eng. tr. [not followed here] in *Facing Death* (London, 1962), pp. 138–179. Delp was handcuffed, but able at times to slip a hand free: *Facing Death*, pp. 11, 15.
31. I cannot resist quoting here Dietrich Bonhoeffer's fragment 'Self-discipline', which can be found at the beginning of his *Ethics* (London, 1968), p. 15 and in his *Letters and Papers from Prison*, p. 15 of paperback ed. (London, 1968):

    'If you set out to seek freedom, you must learn before all things
    Mastery over sense and soul, lest your wayward desirings,
    Lest your undisciplined members lead you now this way, now that way.
    Chaste be your mind and your body, and subject to you and obedient,
    Serving solely to seek their appointed goal and objective.
    None learns the secret of freedom save only by way of control.'

    Thomas Aquinas and Paul would both have agreed with this!

32. Dogmatic Constitution on the Church, *Lumen Gentium*, 9, 2.
33. Augustine, *De vera rel*. 17, 33 (*PL* 33, 136; Fr. tr. J. Pegon, *Œuvres de S. Augustin*, VIII (Paris, 1951), pp. 67, 69); *Ep*. 35 *ad Januarium*, 19, 35 (*PL* 33, 221; Fr. tr. H. Barreau, *Œuvres complètes de S. Augustin*, VI (Paris, 1873), pp. 480–481). See also Thomas Aquinas, *ST* Ia IIae, q. 107, a. 4; *Quodl*. IV, 13.
34. One of these was Erasmus: see A. Humbert, *Les origines de la théologie moderne* (Paris, 1911), pp. 209ff.; another was Raulin: see A. Renaudet, *Préréforme et Humanisme à Paris* (Paris, 1916), p. 170.
35. *ST* IIa IIae, q. 147, a. 3; the two texts of Augustine are quoted in objection 3 as evidence against a commandment to fast. In this text, in *Quodl*. IV, 13 and in *ST* Ia IIae, q. 108, a. 1, Thomas justifies the law, but, with great precision, refers it to its institution by ecclesiastical or temporal authorities. He therefore says: 'Hoc ipsum est de ductu Spiritus Sancti quod homines spirituales legibus humanibus subdantur': see *ST* Ia IIae, q. 96, a. 5, ad 2. See also G. Salet, 'La loi dans nos cœurs', *NRT*, 79 (1957), 449–462, 561–578.
36. Pastoral Constitution on the Church in the Modern World, *Gaudium et Spes*, 25, 1. Two articles written at the end of the last century are worth reading in this context. They are by M. B. Schwalm: 'L'inspiration intérieure et le gouvernement des âmes' and 'Le respect de l'Eglise pour l'action intime de Dieu dans les âmes', *RThom*, 6 (1898), 315–353 and 707–738 respectively. The author considers in these two articles the activity and the indwelling of the Holy Spirit.
37. *Alfred Delp, Honneur et liberté, op. cit*. (note 30), pp. 194–195, 196; *Facing Death, op. cit*., pp. 173, 174–175. See also *Honneur et liberté*, pp. 136–142 for his lecture given in 1943. It is clear that Alfred Delp saw the Church as too firmly settled, and he experienced a terrible coming of the winnowing-fan (Lk 3:17) and the axe (Mt 3:10).
38. See H. Schlier, '*parrēsia*', *TDNT*, V, pp. 871ff.; P. Joüon, 'Divers sens de parrèsia dans le Nouveau Testament', *RSR*, 30 (1940), 239–242. Many studies have been written about *parrēsia* in the New Testament.
39. This account will be found in Eusebius, *Hist. Eccl*. V, 1, 49 (Fr. tr. G. Bardy, *SC* 41 (1955), p. 19). The term has been studied by A. A. R. Bastiensen in *Le sacramentaire de Vérone* (*Graecitas et Latinitas Christianorum Primaeva, Supplementa* III) (Nijmegen, 1970), under the sub-title 'The Church's acquisition of her freedom'. I have already cited Alfred Delp as a contemporary example of the same spirit (and Spirit) made present and would therefore refer back to the collection of his writings in note 30 above and especially to his lecture given in 1943 on trust, both the trust that we should have and that we should inspire.

7
THE GIFTS AND THE FRUITS OF THE SPIRIT

The scriptural source of the theology of the gifts of the Spirit is the messianic text Is 11:1–2 in the translation of the Septuagint—often regarded as 'inspired'—and later in the Latin Vulgate:

> There shall come forth a shoot from the stump of Jesse and a branch shall grow out of his roots. And the Spirit of Yahweh shall rest upon him,
> the spirit of wisdom and understanding,
> the spirit of counsel and might,
> the spirit of knowledge and piety
> and he shall be filled with the spirit of the fear of the Lord.

We know how attached Irenaeus, Origen and many others after them were to this septenarium.[1] These seven gifts were, however, treated as operations of grace and sometimes even as 'charisms', rather than as gifts that were specifically different from the other communications of the Spirit, in the Western Church until the thirteenth century; we can even give a precise date: 1235. According to Hilary of Poitiers and Cyril of Alexandria, the gifts pointed to the Holy Spirit acting in different ways.[2] The history of this theme has been fully traced and I would refer the reader to the numerous studies of this subject.[3]

Between 1235 and 1250, during the time of Philip the Chancellor, a theology of the gifts as specific realities of grace as distinct from the virtues and the charisms was developed. It is the vigorous and profound form given to this theology by Thomas Aquinas that I shall discuss.

It is valuable at this point to delineate the epistemological status of this theology, in other words, to define its authority. It is not a dogma, but simply a theology. Certain theologians, among them Duns Scotus, rejected the specific distinction between the gifts and the virtues. The Council of Trent was careful not to condemn Duns Scotus' position.[4] I am personally all the more inclined to stress the aspect of the theological interpretation and construction in this matter for noting, as we cannot help noting, how the saints and mystics themselves make no distinction in their own experience between the grace of the virtues and that of the gifts of the Spirit. It is their spiritual directors, biographers or interpreters who speak here of the action of the 'gifts' and who even state precisely which gift is active.[5]

We should also give an even more relative value to the many parallels that have been drawn between the seven gifts of the Holy Spirit and the other septenaria found in Scripture or the Church's tradition. Augustine, for example, compared the gifts with the beatitudes and the petitions in the Our Father.[6] A fantastic degree of inventiveness has been shown in the multifarious comparisons that have been made between 'sevens' in the history of Christianity,[7] and this can only serve to re-emphasize the very relative value of these parallels. There is, however, a certain homogeneity in the grace of the Holy Spirit and that of revelation as attested in Scripture, and this justifies a sober attempt to establish a relationship between the virtues, the gifts and the beatitudes. As we shall see, Thomas Aquinas provided a sound justification of the connection that was first made in 1235 by Philip the Chancellor.

Let us therefore consider Thomas' theology of the gifts.[8] It may represent a systematization, but he has, I think, given an authentic interpretation not only of the experience of Christians themselves, but also of the teaching of Paul, whose text: 'All who are led by the Spirit of God are sons of God' (Rom 8:14) he quotes again and again. The dominant idea in his theology is that only God is able to lead us to his own sphere, his own inheritance,[9] his own state of blessedness and his own glory, which is himself. Only God, in other words, can make us act divinely.

It is, however, *we* who act. In this teaching, we are once again confronted with that union between God and ourselves that we have encountered when we discussed Paul's Gal 4:6 and Rom 8:15 and when we considered merit. God is the sovereign Subject and we are really subjects of a life and of actions that are our own. Thomas criticized Augustine here[10] and rejected Augustine's and Bonaventure's theory of illumination and Peter Lombard's thesis on the Holy Spirit as charity. His concern was to ensure supernatural principles of action and a supernatural organism that are really our own, in other words, the theologal virtues and especially charity. He regarded it, however, as necessary that our actions, our virtues and even the theologal virtues of faith, hope and charity should go beyond the purely human mode of experience and our human way of practising them, which is so imperfect and exposed to chance. It is precisely because he had such an extremely lively sense of the theologal nature of the virtues that he was so conscious of the very imperfect use that we could make of them. They were *habitus* or 'haviours' [see Volume I, p. 124, note 18] which came from God, but, so that imperfection should be minimal and the virtues should be practised more fully, God, Thomas believed, had to play a part in man's practice of them and of the other virtues. He did this by creating in the soul a habitual availability—by means of the *habitus* or 'haviours'—to receive from him a movement enabling us to practise the virtues, above all charity, *supra modum humanum* (*Commentary on the Sentences*) or 'beyond the mode of man' by means of an impulse received *ab altiori principio*.[11] Thomas takes pains to stress the significance of the term *spiritus* or 'breath' as a dynamic and motivating reality.[12] The gifts of the Spirit are distinct from the virtues because they make the practice of the latter perfect. They are those permanent dispositions which make the Christian *prompte mobilis ab inspiratione divina* or *a Spiritu Sancto*, that is, at once ready to follow the movement of divine inspiration or of the Holy Spirit.[13]

This is a far cry from purely rational behaviour, or even from a form of regulation governed by a rigidly and permanently established nature, a position sometimes attributed to Thomas. Thomas recognized that human nature and the 'natural law' were to some extent determined by history, but he made room for the event of the Spirit. His ethical cosmos was a cosmos based on the will of God to save and sanctify man, using norms that transcend both human and supernatural reason. We are led by another, who does not act without us and does not use violence,[14] but who nonetheless goes beyond anything that we can see or expect. He goes beyond not only our views and expectations based on human reason, but also those that come from faith. This does not mean that the gifts of the Holy Spirit are superior to the theologal virtues, since these unite us to God himself so that nothing can be above them. No, the gifts of the Spirit are at the service of those virtues, so that they can be practised perfectly.[15] Only God, however, can give his fullness to the practice of the theologal virtues and only he can consummate the action of a child of God. This is true of the whole life of grace and of the presence to God that it establishes as the object of knowledge and love.[16] That is why Thomas attempts to show that the gifts of the Spirit are still given even in the state of blessedness.

All the more reason, therefore, for establishing the part that they play in the practice of the theologal and moral virtues. Since he regarded the beatitudes as the perfect action of the virtues and the gifts, he also tried to make one gift of the Spirit and one of the beatitudes correspond to each of the virtues. He even attempted to attribute to each virtue, with its gift and its corresponding beatitude or beatitudes, one or other of the 'fruits' of the Spirit mentioned by Paul. He devotes an entire question in his *Summa* to these fruits and in it insists on the aspect of spiritual struggle against the 'flesh'.[17]

It is, of course, always possible to find a reason for justifying such parallels. It is thus wrong to give them too much importance or, on the other hand, to attribute no value at all to them, because a great spiritual tradition has found expression in this way.

The action of the Spirit working through the gift of understanding thus perfects faith and makes it capable of a *sanus intellectus* or a certain inner penetration, the peak of which is negative in meaning. It does this by means of a keen appreciation of God's transcendence. The corresponding beatitude is that of the pure in heart (*ST* IIa IIae, q. 8). The activity of faith is also taken to a higher degree of perfection by the gift of knowledge, to which Thomas attributes the benefit of *certum iudicium* or 'sure judgement' which is not discursive, but simple and almost instinctive, *discernendo credenda a non credendis*, in other words, by this judgement it is possible to discern what has to be believed from what should not be believed. Thomas makes this correspond to the beatitude of tears.[18]

To hope, which looks forward to God's salvation, there corresponds the gift of fear, by which man is made *subditus Deo* or 'subjected to God' and the corresponding beatitude is that of the poor in spirit (*ST* IIa IIae, q. 19). To charity, the queen of the virtues, corresponds the gift of wisdom, which guarantees 'correctness of judgement concerning the contemplation or examination of divine realities' (*rectitudo iudicii circa divina conspicienda et consulenda*). The corresponding beatitude is that of the peacemakers (*ST* IIa IIae, q. 45). Prudence is clearly perfected by the gift of counsel, and the beatitude of the merciful corresponds to this (*ST* IIa IIae, q. 52). Justice, which renders to every man his due, is transcended when it is a question of what we owe to those from whom we derive our very being, and it is sustained and completed by the gift of piety, which *exhibet patri (et Deo ut Patro) officium et cultum*—'gives to the father (and to God as Father) duty and respectful attention'. Thomas attributes to this virtue the beatitude of the meek (*ST* IIa IIae, q. 121). The gift of might or power clearly helps the virtue of fortitude and goes together with the beatitude of those who 'hunger and thirst for righteousness' (*ST* IIa IIae, q. 139). Finally, there is the cardinal virtue of temperance, but Thomas seems to have been in difficulty in this case over attributing a gift of the Spirit and a beatitude to this virtue. In the end he settles for 'fear of the Lord' and either *beati pauperes* or *qui esuriunt et sitiunt iustitiam*. We realize how relative these correspondences are, to say nothing of the biblical and exegetical meanings both of the New Testament beatitudes and the Isaian text.

It is, however, interesting to note in this context how Thomas includes the presence of the gifts of the Holy Spirit in the very fabric of his minute analysis of the virtues throughout IIa IIae of his *Summa*. One has the impression, when reading his analysis, in which Aristotle and Cicero act as guides, that moral action is a matter of following the structures of nature, which are set by God, but recognized by human reason. His morality could even be called institutional—although happily we have to say that the institution calls for the event of the Holy Spirit, without which it is difficult to see how holiness of the kind that the Christian saints show in their lives is in fact the most perfect form of Christian life. It consists, as we know, of a continuous series of processes of transcendence of supernatural but human limits based on 'inspirations' that are generously listened to in generously given freedom.

Thomas also devoted a question in his *Summa*, as I have already noted above, to the fruits of the Holy Spirit. He describes them as the ultimate and delightful products of the action of the Spirit in us.[19] The comparison with plant life is interesting. The fruits are what are gathered at the end of branches growing from a vigorous stock and they are delightful to the taste. Alternatively, they are what are reaped from a crop or harvest in a field that has been cultivated and sown. In his commentary on Paul, L. Cerfaux translated the text as the 'harvest of the Spirit'[20] and the word used in Gal 5:22 is in the singular: 'The fruit of the Spirit is love, joy, peace, patience, kindness, goodness, faithfulness, gentleness and self-control'. There are other lists elsewhere in Paul's writings: 'goodness, righteousness and truth' (Eph 5:9); 'righteousness, godliness, faith, love, steadfastness, gentleness' (1 Tim 6:11); 'righteousness and peace and joy in the Holy Spirit' (Rom 14:17; cf. 15:13); and finally '(we commend ourselves . . .) by purity, knowledge, forbearance, kindness, the Holy Spirit, genuine love, truthful speech and the power of God' (2 Cor 6:6–7). These Pauline lists can be compared with the list in Jas 3:17–18.

What emerges from these texts is an ideal portrait of the Christian who is peacefully and joyfully ready to welcome, and calmly and patiently open to love his fellow-man. They are basically manifestations of the love described in 1 Cor 13:4–7, presenting the reader with a fragile imitation of Christ who was 'gentle and lowly in heart' (Mt 11:29), a man given up to God and a man for others, free, truthful, demanding, merciful, recollected and open to all men. The opposite portrait would be one of violence, aggressive self-assertion and a refusal to be available to or to accept others. The fruits of the flesh are listed in Gal 5:19–21; Rom 1:29–31.

Does this mean that the child of God necessarily preserves or acquires an element of infantilism or lacks a spirit of open commitment and combativeness? Does the religion of the Father, that is, of a God who existed before our world and transcends it, imply that the Christian is bound to be unconcerned with the history of that world and to turn away from the world? Christianity's affirmation of an incarnate God serves only to introduce a contradiction which leads to impotence, it has been claimed. This was the critical question asked by the philosopher Merleau-Ponty, whose answer, so frequently repeated, was that, in politics, the Christian was 'a bad conservative and an uncertain revolutionary'.[21]

This criticism can hardly be applied to Paul or the Christian saints, and Merleau-Ponty was too experienced and well-informed to press the question too far—because of the Holy Spirit. He said, for example: 'Pentecost means that the religion of the Father and the religion of the Son have to be consummated in the religion of the Spirit and that God is no longer in heaven, but in society and in communication with men and especially everywhere where men meet in his name. . . . Catholicism has hindered and frozen this development of religion: the Trinity is not a dialectical movement and the three Persons are co-eternal. The Father is not transcended by the Spirit and the fear of God, the law, is not eliminated by love. God is not entirely with us.'

Was Merleau-Ponty not working with a Hegelian concept of the Spirit as immanent in the community of men and above all in history and even identified with them? In Christian teaching, that immanence is real. God, through his Spirit, makes men his sons and places his law in them. That law is summed up in love and his sons are together the brothers of his Son who was made man. There is no fatherhood without brotherhood. God is not paternalistic. Transcendence and immanence go together. The Christian is open and dedicated to God, to his brothers and to the world at the same time. As we can only take hold of part of our life at a time, many of us will inevitably experience transcendence without immanence and others immanence without transcendence.[22] But the truth and the grace of the Holy Spirit unites both aspects.

I have quoted many of Paul's texts and they can seem to be extremely demanding and sublime. They are, however, also very virile and are capable of making us virile and of leading us to adulthood. I have not taken advantage of the opportunity to cite any of the sublime and often poetic formulae and accounts of spiritual writers and those who have written of their life in the Spirit.[23] I would like, however, to end this short chapter on the gifts and the fruits of the Spirit with this beautiful passage from a hymn by Simeon the New Theologian:

> How can you be both a blazing hearth and a cool fountain,
>   a burning, yet a sweetness that cleanses us?
> How can you make man a god, darkness light
>   and draw new life from the pit of death?
> How does night become day? Can you overcome gloom?
> Take the flame to our hearts and change the depths of our being?
> How are you simply one with us? How do you give us the Son of God?
> How do you burn us with love and wound us without a sword?
> How can you bear us and remain so slow to anger,
>   yet from where you are watch our smallest gestures here?
> How do you follow our actions from so high and so far?
> You servant waits for peace and courage in tears.[24]

NOTES

1. Irenaeus, *Adv. haer.* III, 17, 3 (*PG* 7, 929–930); *Dem.* 9 (*SC* 62, p. 45). See also K. Schlurtz, *Isaias 11, 2 (Die sieben Gaben des Hl. Geistes) in den ersten vier christlichen Jahrhunderten* (Münster, 1932), pp. 46–58.
2. Hilary of Poitiers, *Comm. in Mat.* 15, 10 (*PL* 9, 1007A); Cyril of Alexandria, *Comm. in Isa.* XI, 1–3 (*PG* 70, 309ff.).
3. The essential aspects of this history will be found in the articles on the gifts of the Spirit ('Dons du Saint-Esprit') by A. Gardeil, *DTC*, IV (1911), cols 1754–1779; and G. Bardy and F. Vandenbroucke, *Dictionnaire de spiritualité*, III (1954), cols. 1579–1603. More recent research has not made any really substantial additions.

4. The words 'susceptionem gratiae et donorum' occur in the sixth session of the Council of Trent and in the conciliar decree *De justificatione* (c. 7; *DS* 1528). The Council clearly wanted to leave open the question of the distinction between grace on the one hand and charity and the gifts of the Spirit on the other, which Duns Scotus had rejected. What is remarkable here is that most of the Fathers of the Council were inclined towards Duns Scotus' position: see A. Prumbs, *Die Stellung des Trienter Konzils zu der Frage und dem Wesen der heiligmachenden Gnade* (Paderborn, 1909), pp. 114ff. See also, in this connection, P. Dumont, 'Le caractère divin de la grâce d'après la théologie scolastique', *RSR*, 13 (1933), 517–552; 14 (1934), 62–95; J. A. de Aldama, 'Habla el Concilio Tridentino de los dones del Espíritu Santo?', *Estudios eclesiásticos*, 20 (1946), 241–244.
5. This is obvious from the information given in the *Dictionnaire de Spiritualité* for the sixteenth century (cols 1601–1603), the seventeenth century (col. 1605), and individual lives or souls (cols 1635–1641); see also A. Gardeil, *op. cit.* below (note 8).
6. Augustine, *De serm. Dom. in monte*, I, 4, 11; II, 11, 38 (*PL* 34, 1234 and 1236).
7. See *Dictionnaire de Spiritualité*, col. 1592. This enthusiasm for making comparisons reached a peak at the Council of Lavaur in 1368, when parallels were drawn between seven articles on God, seven articles on Christ, seven virtues (three theologal and four cardinal virtues), seven sacraments, seven gifts of the Holy Spirit, seven temporal works of mercy, seven spiritual works of mercy and seven capital vices. It is interesting to note that the beatitudes were not included here! See Mansi, XXVI, 492–493.
8. Thomas Aquinas, *In III Sent.* d. 34 and 35; *ST* Ia IIae, q. 68–70, and, in *ST* IIa IIae, the questions devoted to the gifts. Among the various studies and commentaries, I would mention only the following: A. Gardeil, *op. cit.* (note 3), and *Les dons du Saint-Esprit dans les saints dominicains* (Paris, 1903); R. Garrigou-Lagrange, *Perfection chrétienne et contemplation*, 2 vols (Paris and Tournai, 1923); M.-M. Labourdette, *Dictionnaire de Spiritualité*, III, cols 1610–1635; M.-H. Lavocat, *L'Esprit de vérité et d'amour. Essai de synthèse doctrinale sur le Saint-Esprit* (Paris, 1962); M. Philipon, *Les dons du Saint-Esprit* (1963); A. Guindon, *La pédagogie de la crainte dans l'histoire du salut selon Thomas d'Aquin* (Montréal and Paris, 1975), in which his own articles are cited; my article 'Variations sur le thème Loi-Grâce', *RThom* 71 (1971), 429–438.
9. *ST* Ia IIae, q. 68, a. 2, where Thomas quotes Ps 142:10, 'Spiritus tuus deducet me in terram rectam', and adds: 'quia in haereditatem illius terrae beatorum nullus potest pervenire nisi moveatur et deducatur a Spiritu Sancto'.
10. See E. Gilson, 'Pourquoi S. Thomas a critiqué S. Augustin', *Arch. hist. doctr, litt. M.A.*, 1 (1926), pp. 5–127. This remains a very important study.
11. *ST* Ia IIae, q. 68, a. 2. For the logic of this argument, see P. R. Régamey, 'Esquisse d'un portrait spirituel du chrétien', *VS*, 421 (October 1956), 227–258. The collection *Portrait spirituel du chrétien* (Paris, 1963) only came into my hands when I had already finished the present work, with the result that I could not, unfortunately, take its findings into account.
12. *ST* Ia IIae, q. 68, a. 1.
13. *ST* Ia IIae, q. 68, a. 1 and 8; q. 69, a. 1; IIa IIae, q. 52, a. 1; q. 121, a. 1.
14. We are free to follow or not to follow or to follow generously or reluctantly God's inspiration: see *ST* Ia IIae, q. 9, a. 4 and 6; q. 68, a. 3, ad 2; IIa IIae, q. 23, a. 2; q. 52, a. 1, ad 3. Total and constant generosity leads to heroism—as Teresa of Lisieux said: 'Since the age of three, I have never refused God anything'.
15. *ST* Ia IIae, q. 68, a. 8, c and ad 1; IIa IIae, q. 9, a. 1, ad 3.
16. This point was made by John of St Thomas, *Cursus theologicus*, I, q. 43, d. 17, a. 3, and the Carmelite Joseph of the Holy Spirit. See A. Gardeil, *La structure de l'âme et l'expérience mystique*, II (Paris, 2nd ed., 1927), pp. 232ff.; J. Maritain, *Les degrés du savoir* (Tournai, 4th ed., 1946), chapter VI, §15. John of St Thomas, *The Gifts of the Holy Spirit* (Eng. tr.; London and New York, 1951); also tr. into Fr. by Raïssa Maritain (Paris, 1930).
17. *ST* Ia IIae, q. 70, with reference to Gal 5:22–23. The grace of the Holy Spirit, which is the

main aspect of the new law, brings about in the *affectus* a *contemptus mundi*: see q. 106, a. 1, ad 1. For the connection between virtues, gifts and beatitudes, see P. R. Régamey, *op. cit.* (note 11).

18. *ST* IIa IIae, q. 9; cf. q. 1, a. 4, ad 3; q. 2, a. 3, ad 3; see also *In III Sent*. d. 24, q. 1, a. 3; q. 2, ad 3. There have been many studies; see, for example, G. H. Joyce and S. Harent, 'La foi qui discerne', *RSR*, 6 (1916), 433–467.
19. *ST* Ia IIae, q. 70: 'Ultima et delectabilia quae in nobis proveniunt ex virtute Spiritus Sancti'; cf. *Comm. in Gal*. c. 5, lect. 6.
20. L. Cerfaux, *The Christian in the Theology of St Paul* (Eng. tr.; London, 1967), pp. 461ff., who provides a useful literary analysis; A. Gardeil, *DTC*, VI (1914), cols 944–949; M. Ledrus, 'Fruits du Saint-Esprit', *VS*, 76 (May 1947), 714–733, whose article, with its 145 references, is very full—perhaps too full; C.-A. Bernet, *Dictionnaire de Spiritualité*, V, cols 1569–1575.
21. M. Merleau-Ponty, 'Foi et bonne foi', *Les Temps modernes* (February 1946), 769–782; repr. in *Sens et non-sens* (Paris, 1946).
22. Mgr Matagrin has commented: 'One of the risks of Christianity today is the split between a political Christianity without a sense of God's transcendence and a spiritual renewal without a historical incarnation': *L'Européen*, 160–161 (July-September 1976), 7.
23. Many examples will be found in M.-J. Le Guillou, *Les témoins sont parmi nous. L'expérience de Dieu dans l'Esprit Saint* (Paris, 1976); Mme Arsène-Henry, *Les plus beaux textes sur le Saint-Esprit* (Paris, 1968); Sr Geneviève, *L'Esprit du Seigneur remplit l'univers* (Paris, 1977). See also the journals of the Renewal movement in France such as *Il est vivant* and *Tychique*.
24. Adapted by Brie and Gelineau from Hymn VI (*Hymnes*, II, Fr. tr. J. Paramelle, *SC* 156 (1969), pp. 205, 207). This hymn is frequently sung in this adapted form in monasteries.

PART THREE

THE RENEWAL IN THE SPIRIT
PROMISES AND QUESTIONS

INTRODUCTION

'Do not quench the Spirit, . . . test everything; hold fast to what is good'
(1 Thess 5:19, 21)

The story of the Renewal has been told dozens of times. The reality in question is very well known—it has its own congresses, meetings and gatherings, its own journals and publications. Events are reported in the press. I do not intend to describe its prayer meetings again: as enough has been written about it already to fill a library. Everything has already been said and often by people who have greater authority and ability than I have. Why take up the theme again? By what right? What have I to say on the subject?

I do so because, in a work of the length and breadth that I envisage for this book, it would be impossible not to speak about a religious movement of such significance placed entirely under the sign of the Holy Spirit. It is also the responsibility of theologians, however conscious they may be of their own mediocrity and their duty to be modest, to try to understand the work of God, to fit the different pieces of revelation together into the whole, and to suggest principles of discernment. The theological study of this movement is already well advanced, but some additions have still to be made, and so I venture to enter the field.

The reality involved—it does not matter very much what label we give it, and 'movement' does as well as any other—calls for attentive theological investigation. There can be no doubt that God is active in it—he is transforming lives and often working powerfully in the movement. Has he visited his people? In that case, as Peter exclaimed in similar circumstances, 'Who was I that I could withstand God?' (Acts 11:17).

The movement raises a large number of questions. It asks questions of the Church. It suggests to the Church a way to rejuvenation and renewed vitality. At the same time it also raises questions about itself. Some see it as an enterprise of the devil.[1] Bishops and theologians have warned of the risk of serious errors.[2] The truth is that it is not possible to regard this vast movement, extending over so many different countries, as completely homogeneous. As so many have done before me, I shall ask a number of critical questions. Even if I formulate them in a general way, I ask that generalizations not be made from them. Finally, why should we expect from the members of this movement a perfection not required of any religious order or Church community?

(Text written in October 1978)

NOTES

1. See, for example, F. Hubmer, *Zungenreden, Weissagung, umkämpfte Geistesgaben* (Denkendorf, 1972), who has reproduced in his book the Berlin declaration of the Gnadau Association in 1909. This very severe assessment was made because of certain strange and rather unhealthy phenomena which accompanied the introduction of Pentecostalism into Germany in 1906. See also J. P. Dietle, *op. cit.* in the following bibliography, pp. 230, 234.
2. Almost all Catholic studies have pointed to these risks. I have myself, for example, in 'Renouveau dans l'Esprit et Institution ecclésiale. Mutuelle interrogation', *RHPR*, 55 (1975), 143–156. See also, in the following bibliography, F. A. Sullivan, 'The Pentecostal Movement'; *Pro Mundi Vita*; F. Deleclos, 'Le renouveau charismatique'; the Malines document, etc. Above all, see J.-R. Bouchet and H. Caffarel, *Le renouveau charismatique interpellé. Etudes et documents* (*Collection Renouveau*, 5) (Paris, 1976). Finally—or perhaps first of all—see the declarations of the United States bishops, *Doc. cath*. No. 1670 (16 February 1973), 157–159, and of the Canadian bishops, *Doc. cath*. No. 1678 (15 June 1975), 569–574. H. Caffarel also made a statement in a lecture given in Rome on 5 December 1974: see *Doc. cath*. No. 1670 (16 February 1975), 162ff. There have been many replies to the little book by Bouchet and Caffarel: see especially P. T. Camelot, 'Le Renouveau charismatique', *VS* (November-December 1976), 913–930; J. Mondal, *Tychique*, 7 (January 1977), 64–71.

SELECT BIBLIOGRAPHY

Outlines of the whole movement (mainly Catholic), often with discussion

Walter Hollenweger is the author of the best outline of the whole movement: *The Pentecostals. The Charismatic Movement in the Churches* (Eng. tr.; London, 1972; Minneapolis, 1972, 2nd ed. 1973). Hollenweger, a minister in the Swiss Reformed Church, provides a fully documented account of the very varied forms of the Pentecostal movement in different countries. Because of the date of publication, there is, however, hardly any reference to the movement in the Catholic Church.

F. A. Sullivan, 'The Pentecostal Movement', *Greg*, 53 (1972), 237–266.

W. McCready, 'The Pentecostals. A Social Analysis', *Concilium*, 72 (1972), 112–116.

J. Massingberd Ford, 'Pentecostal Catholicism', *Concilium*, 79 (1972), 85–90.

Cardinal L. J. Suenens, *A New Pentecost?* (London, 1975).

R. Laurentin, *Catholic Pentecostalism* (London, 1977).

Courrier communautaire international, 9 (July-August 1976: 'Ces communautés dites charismatiques'.

VS, 600 (January-February 1974): Le mouvement charismatique'; 609 (July-August 1975): 'Prière et Renouveau'.

E. O'Connor, *The Pentecostal Movement in the Catholic Church* (Notre Dame, Indiana, 1971).

Pro Mundi Vita, 60 (May 1976): 'The Catholic Pentecostal Movement: Creative or Divisive Enthusiasm'; repr. as J. Kerkhofs (ed.), *Catholic Pentecostals Now* (Canfield, Ohio, 1977); American documentation; opinion-sounding and statistics.

F. Deleclos, 'Le renouveau charismatique dans l'Eglise catholique', *NRT*, 99 (1977), 161–170.

Histories and Accounts

K. and D. Ranaghan, *Catholic Pentecostals* (New York, 1969).

J. Randall, *In God's Providence: the Birth of a Catholic Charismatic Parish* (Plainfield, N. J., 1973).

A. Méhat, *Comment peut-on être charismatique?* (Paris, 1976).

Discussions and Studies

'Le Renouveau charismatique. Orientations théologiques et pastorales', *Lumen Vitae* (Brussels), 29 (1974), 367–404. This is the 'Malines document', based on the conference held there and also published separately from this number of *Lumen Vitae*: Eng. tr., *Theological and Pastoral Orientations on the Catholic Charismatic Renewal* (Notre Dame, Indiana, 1974). It is a justification of the reality that it discusses, with numerous references to the New Testament, and at the same time an instrument of theological and pastoral discernment.

J. Gouvernaire, 'Les "Charismatiques" ', *Etudes*, 140 (January 1974), 123–140; a three-cornered dialogue presenting questions and elements of discernment.

A. Godin, 'Moi perdu ou moi retrouvé dans l'expérience charismatique', *Archives de Sciences sociales des Religions*, 40 (July-December 1975), 31–52; a sociological and psychological study with many references to America.

R. Quebedeaux, *The New Charismatics: the Origin, Development and Significance of Neo-Pentecostalism* (New York, 1976).

K. McDonnell, *Charismatic Renewal and the Churches* (New York, 1976).

J.-R. Bouchet and H. Caffarel, *Le Renouveau charismatique interpellé. Etudes et documents* (*Collection Renouveau*, 5) (Paris, 1976).

Protestant Studies

Foi et Vie, 4 and 5 (July-October 1973); see especially the following articles: A. Wohlfahrt, 'Espérance pour l'Eglise: choses vues', 3–20; A. Bittlinger, 'Et ils prient en d'autres langues', 97–108.

J. Dietle, 'Le réveil pentecôtiste dans les Eglises historiques. Problèmes exégétiques et ecclésiologiques', *Positions luthériennes*, 4 (October 1974), 223–287.

Publications of the Movement

Pneumathèque series, 7 bis, rue de la Rosière, 75015 Paris, France.
Il est vivant, 31 rue de l'Abbé-Grégoire, 75006 Paris, France.
Tychique, 49 montée du Chemin-neuf, 69005 Lyons, France.
New Covenant, P.O. Box 8617, Ann Arbor, Michigan 48107, USA.

A. THE POSITIVE CONTRIBUTION OF THE 'CHARISMATIC RENEWAL' TO THE CHARCH

Why has the Renewal in the Spirit revealed itself and spread like wildfire in the traditional churches, since 1956 in the Protestant communions and since 1967 in the Catholic Church? Has this happened because God wanted it to? This may be so, but history has shown that God's grace always acts together with human means and that men prepare the way for it. Did it come about because of John XXIII's calling the bishops to a council 'as for a new Pentecost'?[1] This too is possible, but it should not be forgotten that the Renewal is only one aspect of the immense evangelical flowering which the Church now shows to all who have eyes to see and which is taking pace in the midst of many harmful and disturbing events in the world. Is it a reaction by people at certain levels of the population who are instinctively trying to compensate for a depressed and humiliating way of life, or by believers who are seeking spiritual independence? Sociological studies and explanations point to part of the truth, and elements of these will recur; but, though valuable in certain respects, these are not so in others, and their inadequacy has been recognized. In any case, it is from the ecclesiological point of view that I seek to understand what the Renewal signifies within the changing situation of the contemporary Church, the important questions that it asks of the Church, and the positive contribution that it can make to the Church.

The amazing changes that are taking place in the world and the internal movement in the Church have led to our leaving a situation we can call 'Christendom'. Although it is unequally distributed, this is a world-wide movement. A 'Christendom' is characterized by the fact that the social and legal structures form the socially constraining framework for religious activities that are governed by a clerically dominated authority with great social power. The temporal structures are more or less completely orientated towards and subordinated to that authority. The values and expressions of such a society are part of the conditions imposed by the society itself. Although they are often fine and profound, they are also frequently hindered or shackled by those conditions.

Other conditions are imposed by the changes that are taking place now in society; the secularization (*laïcisation* is also a term used in France) of social structures is gradually modifying those conditions. Social life as such is built up without any reference to spirituality, and religion has become a personal and private affair. Relationships in society are similarly changing. Partly as a reaction against the intolerably impersonal character of urbanization gone mad and excessively rational and programmed organization, men are looking urgently for free groups where it is possible to be together with others without constraint. This search has inevitably led to the formation, at the religious level,[2] of free and spontaneous groups that govern themselves and, in prayer, to a style that is spontaneous, personal, and yet communal, open to free individual initiative and not subject to a leader appointed from outside.[3]

In modern, secularized society, with its fragmented culture, each person is looking for his own way. However weakly conscious many are of their religious need—some indeed seem to have no need at all—it is still felt. Some people find alternative paths—spiritualism, occultism, astrology, for example. Many look outside Christianity or at least outside the Church. Non-Christian Eastern mysticism, often not very authentic, has made considerable progress and many sects have sprung up outside the Church.

In the case of the Renewal, what is remarkable is that it has taken place directly within the Christian and even within the Catholic faith and, what is more, within the framework of a very categorical Trinitarian faith. If we recall that, according to the fourth gospel, Jesus' trial continues throughout history, the Holy Spirit, in the Renewal, greatly strengthens Jesus' disciples by convincing them that the world is wrong (Jn 16:8–11). They are disciples of Jesus *Christ*, of Jesus *the Lord*, and not simply of the 'Jesus of Nazareth' called on by politically orientated and secularized Christians. In addition to this, physical miracles and divine interventions in human history were eliminated from Christianity by the thinkers of the Enlightenment and later by Bultmann and his followers in demythologization, yet the Renewal claims to have experienced the direct intervention of divine power in the lives of its members and insists that God is 'living'.

The Church is not an enclosed monastery, nor is it a ghetto. It exists within the world and is affected by the changes that are taking place in the world. At a very deep level, however, it also has its own distinctive movement. This movement was decisively affirmed and defined at the Second Vatican Council, which had been preceded by decades of liturgical, mystical, pastoral and theological activity. It is not possible to discuss here every aspect of the immensely complex development leading up to the Council. It can, however, be characterized in the following way, at least in its essential tendency and as regards what concerns us here. The movement of thought that prepared the way for the Council can be described as a *re-sourcement* in the sense meant by Péguy, who coined the word—a rising up of vitality from the source into the present, rather than a simple return to the sources of Christian faith, although this also certainly took place. Theology, the official teaching of the Church, preaching and religious instruction had previously imposed a view of the Church defined first of all as a *societas inaequalis hierarchica*—'an unequal, hierarchical society'—with a clear distinction, based on divine right, between clergy and laity, between the hierarchy and ordinary believers. Then it was claimed that the Church was a *societas perfecta* or 'complete society' with all the means necessary for its own life, including its own legislative, judicial and even compulsory power. J. A. Möhler (†1838) summed up this ecclesiology in the formula: 'God created the hierarchy and in this way provided amply for everything that was required until the end of time'. It is not difficult to see the secret affinity between such an ecclesiology and a situation of Christendom. It is likewise surmised that the Renewal will be radically different. It is significant that it has established itself most firmly in countries where an Irish clergy or the ways of old France have kept the lay people very much in a state of tutelage while at the same time giving them a vigorous and forceful Catholicism.[4]

The Second Vatican Council did not deprive the ordained ministry of priests, bishops or the Pope of any of its functions, but it went beyond the hierarchical idea of that ministry and the concept of the Church as a juridical society. The order of chapters in the Dogmatic Constitution *Lumen Gentium* clearly expresses this new priority. In the first chapter of this document, the Church is seen as a mystery, within a Trinitarian perspective, in the second chapter as the people of God (who possess the priesthood of baptism and charism) und it is only in the third chapter that the Church is considered as hierarchically structured by its ordained ministries. What emerges from this is firstly that it is God who made the Church, and secondly that the fundamental aspect is what can be called the ontology of grace, based on the sacraments and the free gifts of God. The ordained ministers are called to the service of this Christian life, but the Church is first and foremost built up by that life.

With regard to that Church, the Renewal has been concerned with maintaining the supernatural quality of the people of God at the base, with giving the charisms a stronger profile, without in any way monopolizing them, and with re-introducing into the ordinary life of the Church activities such as prophecy, in what we shall see later on to be a very modest sense, and healings not only spiritual—the sacrament of reconciliation has always contributed to this—but also physical.[5] The Renewal has, at its own level and in its own way, certainly acted as a response to the pentecostal expectation expressed by John XXIII. Paul VI also declared that 'the Church needs a perpetual Pentecost'.[6] And to say this is not to underestimate what has been coming to life, growing and even flourishing everywhere in the Church.

This is, I believe, a very broad outline of the part played by the Renewal in the present changing situation of the Church and ecclesiology. I now propose to go into certain aspects of this in greater detail. These aspects include both positive contributions that the Renewal can make to the life of the Church, and certain questions that it addresses to the Church.

* * *

I know that it would be wrong to oppose charism and institution and to rewrite the history of the Church as a history of opposition between these two elements. The fact is that each of these two realities is the source of a different kind of order in the Church, with the result that they are often in a state of tension. That tension is normal and can even be beneficial. Grace has frequently gone beyond the fixed institutional forms of the Church. Both are required in the life of the Church. According to *Lumen Gentium*, the Spirit 'furnishes and directs' the Church 'with various gifts, both hierarchical and charismatic'.[7] The Council cannot be criticized for having preserved this duality of gifts, both kinds of which come from the same source and lead to the same end.[8] This view of the matter is theologically sound because it is deeply based on a Trinitarian understanding of God and his activity. This may be regarded as appropriation—I am of the opinion that there is more than one way of speaking in the articles of the creed. It is not possible to separate the work of the Holy Spirit, who is 'Lord and giver of life', from the creative work of the Father and the work accomplished by the Son for our salvation.[9] As I have often stressed, the soundness of a pneumatology consists in its Christology.

The Renewal introduces the vitality of the charisms into the heart of the Church. It is a long way from having a monopoly of charisms, but it bears the label of 'charismatic' and helps to make the 'charismatic' theme more widely known. The movement is not a protest against the institution. Its aim is rather to infuse it with new life. It is neither a rejection nor a criticism of the institution, and the mere fact that it has developed within the institutional Church points to the Church's existence as something other than a great apparatus of grace or a juridical or even a sacramental institution.

It has often been observed that the members of the Renewal movement neither neglect nor despise the sacraments, but, on the contrary, return to the sacrament of penance and the Eucharist with renewed enthusiasm. Their prayer meetings, however, are extra-sacramental and take place without any president, leader or ordained minister. Considered as a sociological phenomenon, the renewal is a 'self-regulating' movement (see below, note 2). It seeks and often finds the fruit of the Spirit without the mediation of a Church other than its own community of brothers and sisters and it does so simply subject to the guidance of the Spirit, for whom the community prays. It is interesting to quote Péguy, who was prevented by his marriage from receiving the Church's sacraments, in this context: 'The clergy should be distrusted. . . . Those fellows are, however, very powerful. Because they administer the sacraments, they let it be known that there is nothing other than the sacraments. They forget to tell us that there is also prayer and that prayer is at least half the reality. The sacraments and prayer, that makes two. And, whereas they hold the first, we always have the second at our disposal.'[10] Surely, then, these free prayer meetings—free because they take place in the sovereign freedom of the Spirit—are an exercise of personal initiative taken not against the Church as an institution, but simply without its mediation? Do they not point to a limitation on the part of the institutional Church in the very sphere which the Church is there to serve?

There is also the question of power. Seen as an institution or an 'establishment', the Church is, compared with, for example, the health service, the educational establishment, the press, the mass media or local or national government structures, obviously incredibly poor both in manpower and in resources. The annual balance sheet of the Catholic Church in France would probably make a pathetic impression compared with that of, say, the cinemas in Paris alone. The Church has to a great extent lost its power and hardly counts any more as a social force. This is undoubtedly good for the Church—as Pascal said, 'the Church is in an excellent state when it is only supported by God'.[11] The Church may, however, be required today to be powerful in a different way. The large-scale activity of the institution is perhaps being replaced by the more subtle action of the Church as leaven. Is it also possible that the Church is required now to be alive and active especially on the basis of its members being spiritual people? It has, of course, always been active in this way, which has long been the best aspect of its life. But perhaps God is now calling it to be like that and simply and solely like that? Is this not what Marcel Légaut has been teaching, in the best of his work, for many years?

I think all this has to be linked with a reassessment in the Church of two elements that certain circumstances in its history have caused to be regarded with great suspicion—the personal principle and spiritual experience.

By the 'personal principle', I mean the place that is accorded to the initiatives of individuals as persons and to what those persons have to say on the basis of personal conscientious conviction and motivation. It is, of course, true that the life of the Church cannot be handed over to 'private judgement' and the anarchy of irresponsible initiatives. On the other hand, however, juridicism,[12] clericalism and an emphasis on protection and safety caused in the first place by the danger of Protestantism and then by fear of rationalism and the revolutionary movements of the nineteenth century have led the Latin Catholic Church to practise—often with fearful efficiency—a pastoral policy of distrust and repression with regard to personal initiative, so that the latter has been restricted and even crushed by the principle of objectivity and by institutional rules.

The principle of objectivity is, of course, very sound and even sacred, and the institutional principle is closely connected with it. But every man is a subject who responds freely and who is always a source of free initiative, self-expression and invention. This need is expressed today in almost every sphere of human activity and in many different ways. It inevitably goes together with an ecclesiology based on the idea of the Church as a communion of persons. At its own level, the Renewal gives scope for expression to this need which, so long as the conditions of soundness which I have discussed often enough in this work are satisfied, is a very positive one.

All experience also has to be checked, tested and proved authentic. In Pentecostalism, experience is the great point of reference, the datum towards which everything is orientated. Discernment is practised in the Renewal, but experience of God plays a decisive part in this. As Cardinal Suenens has pointed out, 'many have attested that their faith was sustained by a personal experience of God and that, as faith grew, God's action became more real to them in their daily existence'.[13] There has often been a tendency to confine this type of experience to a Christian élite, but our life today is characterized by a kind of democratization of talent and knowledge. The word 'democracy' is not really suitable in this context, but it should be clear what is meant by it.

I could hardly speak disparagingly about human reason and understanding, but there are clearly aspects of man, both psychical and physical, which go beyond reason. These are precisely the aspects of man and the values which have been neglected, excluded or misunderstood in the Western Church. Even now, since the best of the aggiornamento of the Second Vatican Council, the Church has, as an institution, continued to share in the general and prevalent climate of rationalism and organization. Its liturgy is still strictly regulated and it is still extremely inclined to indulge in didactic, if not cerebral, explanations. As a result of this, the members of the Renewal tend to say, when they are asked why they belong to the movement and what benefits they derive from it: In a world that is excessively organized and totally dedicated to efficient productivity, we find in the Renewal freedom, simplicity and a certain child-likeness of heart. We find even the liturgy, the preaching and the pastoral care of our Church too external and rational. In the Renewal, we find an inner life and contact with the essence of things in its pure state.

This experience is a source of joy and it gives to the members of the movement a feeling of freedom that they are able to express almost tangibly. Peter Hocken insists that aspects of man that have been neglected in an excessively organized and cerebral religion have been brought back into play in Pentecostalism. He cites here the role of the body in hand-clapping, raised hands, cries and sounds, very rhythmical singing, dancing and the laying-on of hands. Pentecostalists attribute the use of these human resources without hesitation to the Holy Spirit, although it may, of course, be a question of something quite different—in 1 Cor 12:2, for example, Paul refers to the existence of such phenomena in pagan cults. This can also be applied to glossolalia.

A reassessment of these areas of human life that cannot be reduced to mere reason is, of course, to be welcomed. It is, however, impossible not to be to some extent apprehensive of the danger of a rather pietistic anti-intellectualism. Teaching without prophetism can easily degenerate into legalism, but prophetism without teaching can become illusory. There is a clear need for the movement and the institutional Church to question each other continuously, like the hill and the field in Barrès' novel.

This 'experiential' character of the Renewal,[14] its distance from intellectualism, the communicative power it has released, the part played in it by the body, the simplicity of its demands and its overcoming of middle-class inhibitions—all these aspects of the movement open up new and interesting possibilities for the evangelization of those who are normally not reached by the institutional Church. Walter Hollenweger has insisted on the fact that the movement has developed resources and an oral culture that are very well adapted to the twentieth century and particularly well suited to appeal to certain levels of population.[15] He was possibly thinking especially of Africa and Latin America. In Europe and North America, it is above all middle-class Christians who are involved in the Renewal—but so too are gypsies. The 'sects' are to a very great extent successful because of their manner of proselytizing and converting. We do not have to imitate them, of course, but we are bound to recognize that we lack certain forms of communication in evangelization that are in fact used by the Renewal movement. It is an all-embracing and communal form of evangelization making the newcomer an integral part of the group's life. It has a personal, immediate, spontaneous, concrete and non-conceptual character; there is no indoctrination in the charismatic form of evangelization, but a communication of an essentially attractive experience based on a personally deeply felt conviction.

The Renewal can open the way to a different kind of Christian practice which is especially valuable in communicating faith in the Lord Jesus.

This may be of help in our celebration of the sacraments of Christian initiation and especially confirmation, which has been called the 'seal of the Spirit'. Quite apart from the Renewal movement, there is a certain uneasiness with regard to the practice of these sacraments and even, in the case of confirmation, with regard to its precise status. The experience of the Spirit by Christians who have already been baptized and confirmed, often long since, points to a certain insufficiency in the practice of these two sacraments. Is it really possible to say that the Holy Spirit is given when, apparently at least, nothing happens? It has been said that nothing happens in the case of the baptism of infants, either, but here we must believe in the action of God as being deeper and more mysterious than anything of which we have evidence or tangible experience.

I would not deny the truth of this affirmation of faith, but I would like to make three points. The first is that we do find it painful to acknowledge that after confirmation it is as if nothing had happened, apart from a formal religious ceremony. Paul would not have accepted such a situation. Secondly, confirmation is 'given' in the West at an age when the child already has personal conscience and a certain conception of life. Is there, then, not a good reason for taking this seriously into consideration in pastoral practice? I shall attempt to answer this important question when I discuss confirmation in greater detail in Volume III of this work. Thirdly, infant baptism nowadays is not merely avoided by those who have no faith, but it is seriously questioned by convinced Christians for reasons by no means unworthy of consideration. Pascal had some very enlightening things to say about this subject.[16] It is hardly possible to avoid asking such radical questions about infant baptism in our present post-Christian situation. Indeed, they have already been asked again and again and received replies that are theologically and pastorally valuable. We may conclude that the baptism of babies is perfectly justified if the family environment is fully Christian, but this does not solve the problem of conscious reanimation and personal vitalization of what has been given by grace in baptism. The Renewal can make a contribution here.

In the case of the celebration of the sacrament of the 'seal of the Spirit' and the preparation that should precede its reception, the Renewal also offers a number of interesting possibilities. It would, of course, not be enough simply to take one bath of the Holy Spirit in a warm and cordial environment in order to be sure of living according to the Spirit. Life in the Spirit calls for perseverance, a daily recommitment to a generous effort and constant and repeated prayer. But if the practice of renewal in the Spirit formed part of parish life, it might well make a valuable contribution to the reanimation of the pastoral aspect of the sacraments of initiation.

* * *

If it formed part of parish life. . . . Is this possible? Is the Renewal bound to remain simply a movement in the Church, with its own special activities, its meetings, its conferences, its books and other publications, its adherents and its animators and leaders? Or can it perhaps become, in parishes and in the Church as a whole, a means by which the pneumatological aspect, which is an integral part of the life of all Christians individually and collectively, can be displayed and spread? I an afraid that my answer must be a negative one, since I do not believe that the Renewal, in the form in which it appears now, can be extended to the whole of the Church. I have two reasons for thinking this:

(1) The style of its meetings is not acceptable to everyone. J.-L. Leuba has pointed out that 'the gifts of the Spirit are given for the "common good"

(1 Cor 12:7), but there can be no such common good where there is no mutual consent. Every minister who is conscious of his responsibility to the gospel and of the unity of his flock in love will always avoid imposing charismatic manifestations as a *law* on his community.'[17] It is true, of course, that there are 'charismatic parishes'.[18] These are special cases, depending for their continued life on a charismatic minister or on many charismatic members, and they are parishes which Christians choose to join. Their unusual and ideal character is apparent from the very way they are projected. It should also be added that the example of the community at Corinth has often been cited in this contest—though it is not, in every respect, a good model! As far as we can ascertain, the Roman community, the community of Jerusalem and the Johannine churches did not lead the same kind of life.

(2) It would seem that, as we leave a situation of Christendom, as described at the beginning of this chapter, the Church is called upon to provide the world with manifestations of great evangelical value, even though they are very limited in scope—kinds of parables of the love of God and his kingdom. These include the religious communities of the Church, often the smaller ones rather than the larger. Taizé is a manifestation of this kind, with its resolute determination to improvise and to be 'temporary'; its council of youth is another. Yet another such parable of the kingdom of God is the Renewal. These charismatic communities may well have great value as examples, since 'God seems to want to reveal the mystery of the Christian community as he has never done so before'.[19] These communities are not subject to direction by the clergy. They are lay communities. Some have unmarried members, others consist of families. Experience has shown that they have problems, but who does not?

The movement may not be able to claim that the whole Church will eventually become 'charismatic', but it can influence the whole of the Church and, in that sense, win it over. It can point the way. It is, of course, not the only movement in the Church today that aims to renew theology and pastoral care, services and even ministries.[20] There are also, for example, the basic communities of various kinds. Together with those basic groups, the Renewal movement can contribute to a new model of the Church.

All this is of great interest to the theologian, who aims to serve the Church. He will be sufficiently orientated towards God as a *theo*logian to recognize that this new model or vision of the Church is fully in accordance firstly with the movement back to the Bible and the Church Fathers as the sources of Christian faith that has already begun, and secondly with the theological emphasis on the Trinity and on Christology seen in the light of pneumatology.

There are clear indications of the latter development in theology today. Heribert Mühlen has firmly denounced pre-Trinitarian monotheism.[21] Orthodox theologians have more than just fine promptings to offer. In

Christology, Mühlen and Walter Kasper have been following a very fruitful path.[22] They have also provided outlines of a pneumatological ecclesiology.[23] Others have done the same, although I find their attempts less satisfactory.[24]

I shall return to the theology of the Trinity and to Christology in Volume III. In the meantime, I will conclude the present chapter by welcoming the coming of a Church of charisms and ministries, of basic communities and of the sincere prayer of Christians who are dedicated body and soul to the living Lord and to being animated by his Spirit. At the same time I am aware that it is hardly possible to speak of the Renewal as a homogeneous whole that operates in exactly the same way in all its groups and manifestations. For this reason, I am devoting the following section (B) to a number of questions that I feel obliged to ask about the Renewal. However, together with very many bishops and even with the Pope himself, who have greater lights than I do, I think that it is a grace that God has given to the times we are living in.

NOTES

1. John XXIII, address delivered on 17 May 1959; see *Doc. cath.* 56 (1959), p. 770; and the Apostolic Constitution *Humanae salutis* of 25 December 1961; see *Doc. cath.* 59 (1962), p. 104. See also K. and D. Ranaghan, *Catholic Pentecostals* (New York, 1969), p. vi, and E. O'Connor, *The Pentecostal Movement in the Catholic Church* (Notre Dame, Indiana, 1971), p. 287, who quote texts relating to the Renewal. See also the address made at the end of the first session of the Council on 2 December 1962.
2. See J. Séguy, *Les conflits du dialogue* (Paris, 1973), and the very many studies that have been made of the spontaneous, informal 'basic communities'. The bibliographies of CERDIC of Strasbough and the texts of the second colloquium of CERDIC, *Les groupes informels dans l'Eglise* (Strasbourg, 1971), will be found useful in this context.
3. There is a good analysis of this new style of prayer in *Où se manifeste l'Esprit* (*Dossiers libres*) (Paris, 1977), pp. 7ff., a document written by 'A group of Christians in Lyons'.
4. A fellow-Dominican with whom I had been talking about the Renewal in Canada and who knew what it meant, told me that it was a kind of liberation and, to begin with at least, an explosion of freedom. Men—and even more so, women—had previously been living in the first place a life of piety based on fixed, obligatory, closed and very onerous spiritual exercises and in the second place in a state of fear of mortal sin and the punishment of hell. He also emphasized that confessors frequently interfered, in an indiscreet way, in certain spheres. . . . People were breathing a larger Spirit.
5. Peter Hocken in *New Heaven, New Earth? An Encounter with Pentecostalism* (London, 1976), p. 22, has rightly observed: 'I am suggesting then that what distinguishes the charismata described in 1 Corinthians as pneumatika is the particular level or zone of the human that they activate and engage. What is new in pentecostalism is not the occurrence of particular pneumatic phenomena nor the initial opening up of the pneumatic dimension in individual Christians; rather it is the organization, embodiment and expectation of all these gifts within the life of Christian communities, i.e. the articulation and organization in corporate Church life of what has over the centuries been known only spasmodically in isolated instances.'

6. Paul VI, audience on 29 November 1972: see *Doc. cath*. 69 (1972), p. 1105. See also E. O'Connor, *Pope Paul and the Spirit. Charisma and Church Renewal in the Teaching of Paul VI* (Notre Dame, Indiana, 1978).
7. Dogmatic Constitution on the Church, *Lumen Gentium*, 4; cf. 11, 2; see also the Decree on the Apostolate of the Laity, *Apostolicam Actuositatem*, 3; Decree on the Church's Missionary Activity, *Ad Gentes divinitus*, 4, 23, 1.
8. G. Hasenhüttl, *Charisma, Ordnungsprinzip der Kirche* (Freiburg, 1970), criticized the encyclical *Mystici Corporis* and the Dogmatic Constitution *Lumen Gentium* for this. In his view, 'charisms are the structure of the Church and the community is the place of those charisms' (p. 128). He did not deny the usefulness of juridical structures, but believed that they should be secondary and should help or make up for a structure that is in the first place fundamentally charismatic (p. 355; cf. pp. 231–232).
9. This point of view was forcibly expressed by J.-L. Leuba in a lecture given at Salamanca. The French text, 'Charisme et institution', has been published in the Lausanne review *Hokhma*, 5 (1977), 3–20. See also L. Boisset, *Mouvement de Jésus et Renouveau dans l'Esprit* (*Dossiers libres*) (Paris, 1975), 73.
10. Charles Péguy, *Lettres et entretiens, présentés par Marcel Péguy* (Paris, 1954), p. 69.
11. Pascal, *Fragment* 861.
12. See my article, 'La supériorité des pays protestants', *Le Supplément*, 123 (November 1977), 427–442.
13. Cardinal L. J. Suenens, *A New Pentecost?* (London, 1975), p. 54.
14. 'Experiential', as distinct from 'experimental', is the category used by Cardinal Suenens, *op. cit*., p. 53, with reference to Fr Grégoire, 'Note sur les termes "intuition" et "expérience" ', *Revue philosophique de Louvain*, 44 (1946), 411–415.
15. W. Hollenweger, *The Pentecostals. The Charismatic Movement in the Churches* (Philadelphia, 2nd ed. 1973), pp. 468, 501; K. and D. Ranaghan, *op. cit*. (note 1), pp. 259–262; 'There are real possibilities there for discovering a theological methodology in an *oral* culture: one where the medium of communication—as in biblical times—is not definition, but description; not pronouncement, but story; not doctrine, but witness; not the theological *Summa*, but the hymn; not the treatise, but the television programme . . .': quoted by L. Boisset, *op. cit*. (note 9), 75.
16. Pascal, 'Comparaison des chrétiens des premiers temps avec ceux d'aujourd'hui'; pp. 201–208 in the small Brunschvicg edition.
17. J.-L. Leuba, *op. cit*. (note 9), 15.
18. See, for example, J. Randall. *In God's Providence: the Birth of a Catholic Charismatic Parish* (Plainfield, N. J., 1973); Michael Harper, *A New Way of Living* (Plainfield, N.J., and London, 1973), which describes the experience of the Episcopalian Church of the Redeemer at Houston, USA; F. Kohn has also written about this parish in *Il est vivant* (February-March 1976), 30–33.
19. E. O'Connor, *op. cit*. (note 1), pp. 46ff. See also Max Delespesse, *Cette communauté qu'on appelle l'Eglise* (Paris, 1968). Several such communities or groups of communities have been given publicity: Houston (see the previous note) and the most famous of all perhaps, Ann Arbor, Michigan; in France, the community of the Holy Cross at Grenoble; see *Il est vivant*, 12 (April 1977), 20–23; again in the United States, 'People of Praise', South Bend, Indiana.
20. *Tous responsables dans l'Eglise? Le ministère presbytéral dans l'Eglise tout entière "ministérielle"* (Lourdes and Paris, 1973).
21. See H. Mühlen, *Entsakralisierung* (Paderborn, 1971). This prolific author has since that time written frequently about this subject; see especially his *Morgen wird Einheit sein* (Paderborn, 1974) and *Die Erneuerung des christlichen Glaubens. Charisma-Geist-Befreiung* (Munich, 1974).
22. H. Mühlen, *Una mystica Persona* (Paderborn, 1964; 2nd ed., 1967); W. Kasper, *Jesus the Christ* (Eng. tr.; London and New York, 1976), pp. 266–268. See also P. J. Rosato, 'Spirit

Christology. Ambiguity and Promise', *ThSt*, 38 (1977), 423–449; P. J. A. M. Schoonenberg, 'Spirit Christology and Logos Christology', *Bijdragen*, 38 (1977), 350–375.

23. H. Mühlen, *op. cit*. (note 22) and many other publications, which I have reviewed in *RSPT*; W. Kasper, 'Esprit–Christ–Eglise', *L'Expérience de l'Esprit. Mélanges Schillebeeckx* (Paris, 1976), pp. 47–69; *idem*, 'Charismatische Grundstruktur der Kirche', *Glaube und Geschichte* (Mainz, 1970), pp. 356–361; *idem*, 'Die Kirche als Sakrament des Geistes', *Kirche—Ort des Geistes* (Freiburg, 1975), pp. 14–55.
24. G. Hasenhüttl, *op. cit*. (note 8); Donald L. Gelpi, *Charism and Sacrament. A Theology of Christian Conversion* (New York, 1976); the Protestant theologian J. D. G. Dunn, 'Rediscovering the Spirit, II', *Expository Times*, 84 (November 1972), 40–44, is very radical (he is a member of the Presbyterian Church).

B. CRITICAL QUESTIONS

1
WHAT TITLE SHOULD BE USED? 'CHARISMATIC'?

The word 'charism' can be understood in at least two if not three ways. (I would prefer not to use the word 'meanings' in this context, but would rather speak of two or three 'understandings' or 'extensions'.)[1]

(1) Apart from 1 Pet 4:10, the word *charisma* appears only in Paul's writings, and that sixteen times. Its use is fairly constant, even when applied once in a particular way (2 Cor 1:11). The word always goes back to *charis*, 'grace'. Greek words ending in *-ma* usually point to the result of an action. An example of this is *mathēsis*, the act of teaching, and *mathēma*, knowledge.

The term *charisma*, then, has to be understood in connection with the word *charis*, 'grace'.[2] Two or three texts throw light on this. Rom 12:6: *echontes de charismata kata tēn charin tēn dotheisan hēmin diaphora*, 'having gifts that differ according to the grace given to us'; 1 Cor 1:4, 7: 'the grace (*charis*) of God which was given to you in Christ Jesus . . . so that you are not lacking in any spiritual gift (*charisma*)'; 7:7: 'Each has his own special gift (*charisma*) from God, one of one kind and one of another'; 12:4, 11: 'There are varieties of gifts (*charismata*), but the same Spirit. . . . All these are inspired by one and the same Spirit, who apportions to each one individually as he wills'.

Charisms are gifts or talents which Christians owe to the grace of God. That grace aims at the realization of salvation, and Christians are called to put the charisms at the service of the Body of Christ. for its building up (see 1 Cor 12:7). These gifts or talents are as much from 'God' or the Lord as from the Spirit (see 1 Cor 12:4–6). When Paul speaks of 'charism of the Spirit' (*charisma pneumatikon*; Rom 1:11), he is not indulging in pleonasm. The fact that the charisms *are* 'spiritual gifts' or gifts of the Pneuma does not mean that the word 'charism' *means* 'gift of the Pneuma'.

(2) On the basis of 1 Cor 12:7: 'To each is given the manifestation of the Spirit for the common good', the charisms have often been seen as 'tangible manifestations of the presence of the Spirit'.[3] Such a definition fits the

'charismatic' Renewal. This is borne out by the briefing paper given to journalists by the organizers of the 1975 Pentecostal Conference in Rome, who described it as a place where the action of the Holy Spirit is manifested in a perceptible, tangible and visible way.[4] This does make our understanding of the term more precise, but it also narrows it down.

(3) Our understanding is narrowed down even more when the charisms are identified with speaking in tongues, prophecy (what Paul calls the *pneumatika*; see 1 Cor 12:1; 14:1) and healings or miracles, which are all, in fact, the most spectacular 'manifestations' of the gifts. They are often, unfortunately, identified in this way, even by deservedly respected authors.[5] In the same way, the great classical theologians of the Church also identified charisms with graces *gratis datae*, as distinct from sanctifying grace. This unhappy identification[6] marked out a clear and easy path which may have been rather lazily followed.

Paul did not reject the *pneumatika*, but he believed that they could be of use in the task of building up the Church only through the *charismata*, gifts given *kata tēn charin*, that is, according to saving grace, for the common good or the building up of the community.

I am inclined to see the charisms above all from the point of view of ecclesiology. It is, in other words, God who builds up his Church. In order to do this, he instituted, through Jesus Christ his faithful servant, the structures of that Church. At the same time, he continues to build it up, at all periods in history, by the gifts (*charismata*), the services or ministries (*diakoniai*) and the various *energēmata* or 'ways of working' to which Paul refer in 1 Cor 12:4–6. He does this by distributing talents and gifts to all believers. That is why I have been reluctant to accept the term 'charismatic movement' that has been applied to Catholic neo-pentecostalism and have been formally critical of it. Let me reproduce here the terms of that criticism:[7]

> (1) There is a risk of attributing the charisms to a particular group, as though the whole body of believers were deprived of them, whereas, in Paul's teaching, these charisms are gifts of nature and of grace that are distributed and used by the Spirit *kata tēn charin* for the common good and the building up of the community. All believers are therefore charismatic and all are called to use their gifts for the common good. It was in this sense that the Second Vatican Council spoke of the charisms in the people of God (*Lumen Gentium*, 11) and that the conference of French bishops in 1973 had as its theme 'Everyone is responsible in the Church (and for the Church)'.[8] The members of the movement replied to this in the following way: It is true, but, just as all believers are invited to study the Bible and practise the liturgy and yet there are Bible study groups, a biblical and a liturgical movement, so too is it possible for charismatic groups to exist without other Christians being discriminated against, disqualified or excluded from this quality.
>
> (2) Because of the prominent place occupied in public opinion and possibly in the movement itself by 'speaking in tongues', 'prophecy' and healings, there is a risk of

reducing the charisms to the level of extraordinary and even exceptional manifestations. This would be regrettable both for those immediately concerned and for the Church as a whole. When this question was debated at the Second Vatican Council, Cardinal Ruffini, the Archbishop of Palermo, criticized the draft text in the following way: There were charisms at the beginning of the Church's life, but there are no more today. The cardinal was thinking, when he said this, of quasi-miraculous manifestations. The following day, Cardinal Suenens replied to him in an attempt to restore the true idea of charism and to point to the abundant existence of charisms in his own church.[9] Paul in fact 'also mentions less striking charisms, such as exhortation and acts of mercy (Rom 12:8), service (Rom 12:7), teaching (Rom 12:7; 1 Cor 12:28ff.), the utterance of wisdom and knowledge (1 Cor 12:8), faith (1 Cor 12:9), discernment of spirits (1 Cor 12:10), helping and administration (1 Cor 12:28)'. The Catholic members of the movement, in France at least, claim that they do not stress extraordinary manifestations. It is, however, possible that the danger still exists.

I still regard the substance of this criticism and especially the second part of it as valid, despite Kilian McDonnell's reply to it.[10] In making it, I had a view of the whole Church in mind, and my point of departure was not a description or a justification of the movement, but an ecclesiology. The movement, however, exists and makes too many of God's good actions manifest for me not to thank God for it. What name, then, should we give to this 'movement'? This is precisely the question that is asked by the Malines document: What should the Renewal be called? The answer that the document gives is: From the sociological point of view, it would be quite legitimate to describe it as a 'movement', but the word is unsuitable in that it suggests that it is dependent on a human initiative or 'organization'. It would therefore, the document concludes, be better to avoid it.

The document continues: 'The phrase "charismatic renewal" is very widely used. It has the advantage of pointing to one of the concerns of the Renewal—the reintegration of the charisms, in all their dimensions, into the "normal" life of the Church, both at the universal and at the local level' (*op. cit.* (note 2 below), 386–387). My two objections, in an abbreviated form, follow. The document then adds: 'In certain places, the term "charismatic renewal" is avoided and preference is given to "spiritual renewal" or simply to "renewal". This choice of title certainly makes it possible to avoid some of the difficulties mentioned above. It has, however, been pointed out that it may also favour the idea of a monopoly, when there are already several forms of renewal in the Church.'

The terms 'Renewal in the Spirit' or simply 'Renewal' tend to be the most commonly used in France. They seem to me to be preferable, even though this is not the only form of renewal. It is also worth noting, at least in passing, that this term is not the same as 'Revival'. It points to a less abrupt and more continuous process that is more completely fitted into the universal life of the Church. It suggests the joy of the movement. In speaking of 'movement', it is important to add that, although some form of organization exists and is, in fact, inevitable, nothing programmed or highly organized is meant.[11]

It is possible to define the term 'charismatic' more precisely and this has in fact been done by Sr Jeanne d'Arc in her excellent notes on 'charismatic' which form part of her account of the Pentecostal Conference in Rome in 1975. I reproduce them below.

A charismatic group

When a prayer group or a community of believers is flooded with these gifts of the Spirit—prophecies, healings, works of power, striking conversions and so on, we recognize this by saying that it is a 'charismatic group' and we praise the Lord for it.

If, on the other hand, we are tempted to say: 'We want to set up a charismatic group', then the term is unacceptable. To use it would give the impression that we are whistling for the Holy Spirit and that we are able to know his intentions and make him available to us at will. It is not up to us to decide whether a meeting will be charismatic or not. That depends on the Holy Spirit alone.

A charismatic person

The same kind of remarks can be made of the adjective 'charismatic' applied to a person. If we experience the grace of meeting such a person, filled to overflowing with charisms, the gift of consolation and the gift of discernment, and powerful in works and words, we may describe him as 'charismatic'.

I am not sure, however, that it is really possible to say, as it was said, to great applause, at the Conference: 'To be charismatic is to be fully Christian'. We must take care—and we should read Paul again. To be fully Christian—this can only be measured against the fullness of charity. The whole history of the Church and its saints shows that some great saints have had very few charisms, in the sense of visible manifestations of the presence of the Spirit, and that others may have received these gifts, have spoken in the tongues of men and of angels and have had faith so as to remove mountains, but, if they have had less charity, they have inevitably have been less Christian and less holy.

Something very serious is, I think, at stake here. The whole 'charismatic movement' is involved. The danger—and it is a very real one—is not just that we shall become hypnotized, as the Corinthian Christians did, by the more spectacular gifts, but that we shall go even more seriously astray and use the term 'charismatic person' as a superlative, thus making him or her a kind of super-Christian. No, the only valid superlative is that of love.

May it please the Spirit at certain times and in certain places to release a veritable Niagara of charisms! This is a gift that fills us with praise and makes us sing of God's marvels. But all the charisms exist only for charity, which is their summit and their only criterion.

May there be a better climate in our parishes or communities, a better attitude on the part of believers, a better education in faith and a better knowledge of the charisms, so that the Spirit may be more able to fill the people of God! This would be a great blessing for the Church. There would be greater movement of life and a more joyous and powerful witness—but all this would be for charity, on this side of it, not beyond it, since there is nothing beyond love.

> *Charismatic prayer*
> There was an excellent discussion about prayer at the conference. Many attempts were made to define 'charismatic' prayer: 'Prayer that is entirely subject to the activity of the Holy Spirit'—'Prayer that is a gift from God and must be received in a spirit of attentive listening and a silence of poverty, and expressed with the whole of our being'—'Being intensely present and attentive'—'Prayer in which the Spirit reminds us that God is faithful and merciful'—'Prayer that enables us to enter God's plan and makes us conform to his will, and so is always heard and answered'—'Prayer that goes beyond our own abilities'—'Prayer that transforms and soothes us'—'Prayer which glorifies the name of Jesus and hastens his coming'.
>
> All these statements are very fine. They contain a great deal that is spiritually deep and alive. They add up to a description of the flowering of sanctifying grace in us and of the gifts and the action of the Spirit who makes us cry 'Abba! Father!' and attunes us to his sighs that are too deep for words. But I must admit that I cannot exactly determine how this prayer is 'charismatic'. The fact that it is raised up to a high level of intimacy and love does not mean that it is necessarily charismatic.
>
> May this prayer provide in our hearts an environment that is favourable to the emergence of a word of faith, a light for others and a prophecy for a group! May it make us more open to be moved by the Spirit and therefore to receive his charisms! All this would be of enormous benefit, but it would not necessarily transform the prayer itself into 'charismatic' prayer.
>
> May I be forgiven for insisting, but only a very slight adjustment of the points will send the whole train along a different track and its direction is then irreversible.[12]

I personally believe that there is a charism of prayer, which is in itself an excellent gift, even though Paul does not mention it. His lists do not, however, claim to be exhaustive. The series of gifts remains open, in accordance with the abundance of grace and the needs felt in the history of salvation. A place among these gifts has, for example, been claimed for various forms of religious life[13] and for the function of a judge evaluating prudently the merits of the case.[14]

TWO CRITICAL QUESTIONS

Immediacy

The Protestant theologian Gérard Delteil has expressed what is, in my opinion, the most important critical question, at least from the practical point of view. He said: 'The charismatic form of expression seems to be to be linked to a theology of immediacy—an immediacy of the Word grasped via the text, an immediacy of God's presence grasped thorugh experience, an immediacy of relationship expressed by speaking in tongues and an immediacy that by-passes history'.[15] In other words, in the Renewal, Christians look for and find a response or a solution in a quick, immediate and personal relationship that cuts out long and difficult approaches. This emphasis on immediacy applies to the exegesis of Scripture, our understanding of social problems, our analysis of the crisis in the Church and the associated question of the rapid changes in the world, and finally our consideration of the steps to be taken towards ecumenical reunion. I shall return to the question of ecumenism later, but in the meantime would like to stress three points:

(1) I am not a rationalist. I believe that God guides our lives and intervenes in them. I have always trusted and still trust in his conduct and guidance. There is always a danger, however, that we shall fail to use the human means available to us of 'prudence' in the Thomistic sense of the word, and of decision. In the past, I encountered this kind of attitude among members of the Oxford Group which became Moral Rearmament. As J.-Y. Riocreux has said of an experience in the United States:

> God is regarded as the one who is immediately responsible for everything. Secondary causes are connected without the slightest difficulty to primary causes. Let me give an example of this. A young member of the 'charismatic renewal' was on his way to a retreat. He was hitch-hiking, but no cars were stopping. Resorting to a desperate measure, he prayed fervently: 'Lord, if you want me to go to this retreat, let me have a lift in one of the next twenty cars that go past!' This was an ultimatum that paid off! The twentieth car slowed down and stopped—and its driver was a Pentecostalist minister! How can one not see in this incident a sign from heaven?[16]

And indeed, why should we not regard it as a sign from heaven? Trust in God can go as far as that. There is, however, a general problem of balance. It is hardly possible to carry the naivety of a child so far that we make no use of the means of information and reason that God has given to man who has become adult (see 1 Cor 13:11).

(2) This applies especially to our reading of Scripture. It has often been said that there is a tendency in the Renewal towards fundamentalism. The fundamentalist approach consists of interpreting the text of the Bible literally without considering the historical context, without making sound use of criticism and without relating the text to other passages or to Scripture as a whole, and then applying it immediately to the present situation.[17] In saying this, I would not want to take back anything of what I have already written about the spiritual reading of Scripture. Intellectual effort has, however, never been despised in that kind of reading—this is evident in the works of Origen and Augustine, for example. In Pentecostalism generally, experience, above all immediate experience, takes precedence over everything else. This is not entirely true of the Renewal in our own Church, but even there a certain anti-intellectualism has been observed. I have found signs of this in Canada, both in Quebec and in Ontario. Knowledge and intelligence

are not supreme values, of course, and the Renewal fortunately brings with it the warmth of hearts that have been given to Christ. Serious religious formation is also being undertaken within the Renewal. It is, however, important to point to a possible and even real danger.

(3) Olivier Clément correctly observed that 'it is legitimate to ask, in the case of shared experience, whether it is really pneumatic or spiritual or whether it is simply psychical. Greed for psychical experience is in no way a good thing. In the Eastern Christian tradition, there is an attitude of great sobriety and vigilance. It has always been regarded as advisable not to seek the extraordinary experiences that the Spirit is able to provide.'[18] This advice is echoed in the texts that I have cited above from the great Eastern spiritual writers and especially those of Simeon the New Theologian.[19] Very much the same is taught by the saints and spiritual writers of the West.[20] I have also dealt with this question in a previous chapter on 'the struggle against the flesh'. There is no possibility of a total and definitive victory taking place here on earth.

There will, however, always be a danger that people will go looking for a psychical experience of the Spirit with an only too human attitude of greed and therefore 'carnally'. This was undoubtedly the case at Corinth and it may happen even today. It may be that someone will go to a meeting in the hope of seeing or experiencing something sensational, something extraordinary, that will make him rather superior. On the other hand, the meeting itself may be conducted, with the help, for example, of emotional and compelling singing repeated again and again, to the point of conditioning those present to expect *it* to happen—speaking in tongues or 'prophecy'.

Most members and certainly almost all leaders of the Renewal know or will eventually learn that a 'pouring out of the Spirit' implies a response to the demands made by God. Two such leaders have made this declaration:

> Those of us who are engaged in political, family, cultural and other activities can hardly conceive the extent to which prayer in itself demands the total commitment of the whole person. Most of those who move in the ambit of the renewal movement regard a request to the whole community to pray for their conversion as an important step. The words and gestures (laying-on of hands) that accompany this very personal and at the same time very communitary prayer are simple, but this simplicity clothes a very important requirement: if we really commit ourselves to asking the Spirit of the Lord to come upon us, to purify us (Lk 11:13), to send us to our brothers, we will not do so in vain. For many Christians this step is not undertaken without deep fear and the expression 'baptism in the Spirit', even if it can be misunderstood, well expresses this experience of plunging in, drowning, death and resurrection.[21]

* * *

A Lessening of Social Commitment

Is this perhaps a consequence or an application of 'immediacy'? Many criticisms have been made of the Renewal precisely on these grounds—that it deprives its members of their commitment to social and political action. The Renewal, it is claimed, leads to a taste for intimacy. Its eschatological content points exclusively to the hereafter. Although shared prayer and brotherliness form an essential part of the Renewal and it certainly encourages commitment to life in community, it nonetheless favours a sense of personal and vertical relationship with God and therefore turns its adherents away from action in the world. This criticism is sometimes expressed by those who are so exclusively preoccupied with politics and passionate social concerns that they do not even consider the possible hypothesis that God might be able to act in the Renewal.[22] Yet, together with other contemporary realities such as Taizé and the various monastic centres with their great influence, the Renewal bears witness, I believe, to a fact of great importance—the specific character of religion. Faith is not simply a form of commitment to the life of this world, nor does it merely act to motivate that commitment. It has its own distinctive order and activities, and these are first and foremost directed towards the God who has seized hold of the believer's soul. The cry of joy directed towards God is above all a thanksgiving.

In those critical interpretations that are excessively dominated by a social or political concern, the favour shown to the Renewal by responsible ministers of the Church is seen in this light, as typically expressed by J. Chabert (*op. cit.* (note 22 below), p. 27): 'In the final analysis, the members of the hierarchy are only interested in what helps to strengthen the institution which they represent'. Are they then not interested in what may animate or give new life to faith in the Church, or in a re-awakening of the spiritual life of those who belong to the Church? Are they not concerned, in a word, with what is specifically religious? And if they are, would that be wrong? Would that be foreign to their mission?

One genuine question remains, however. It is this. The Renewal may be so firmly situated at the level of the *res* that the *sacramentum* may be underestimated. It may be so orientated towards the vertical dimension of religion, that is, the relationship with the absolute, that the horizontal aspect is neglected, if not in regard to relationships with one's immediate 'neighbour', then at least in the more extended, and in this sense more strictly social, dimension.[23] To be faithful to the gospel as a whole, man must be concerned with the vertical dimension, that is, the transcendental aspect of God, and with the horizontal dimension, man's here and now, in all the particularity of individual callings, situations and destinies.

This question arises above all in those countries which are both fundamentally religious and poor, exploited and subject to domination, for whose liberation from misery and injustice precise analyses and critical commitment are required. At least one representative of Latin American 'liberation theology' has taken up the criticisms and, one might almost say, the accusations of the Renewal that we have already encountered and examined, and done it with greater precision.[24] It is also worth mentioning a simple personal testimony that I received, one of many, in a letter at the end of the 1975 Conference: 'The charismatic movement has flourished in a most remarkable way during the past two years in the Dominican Republic. There have been countless conversions and prayer is abounding. But many people have commented that precisely where the movement has spread most, social work, road-building programmes, and the co-operatives with priests in charge (don't forget that we are in Latin America!) assisted by lay people have been set aside or at least scaled down.'

The fact that this criticism has been made again and again shows that it may be justified. Members of the Renewal have, however, replied, with facts and not simply with theoretical justifications.[25] They may be active in trade unionism and politics and, as much as other people, they have professional work in industry, research, town planning, teaching, and so on.

Although I recognize the dangers pointed out and even condemned by people like J. Chabert (see below, note 22), R. Vidales (see note 24) and others, I would dispute their interpretation of Pentecost at the level of exegesis. Vidales, for example, has said: 'The Spirit was not given to dispense the disciples from their historical responsibility, but precisely to encourage and direct their actions along the same lines as their master's commitment. The presence of the Lord, paradoxically represented as "absence", directs the Church to fulfil its central commitment—to work for the coming of justice.' I am bound to ask: Is that what the New Testament tells us? I do not in any way deny that it forms part of Christian messianism and the Church's mission,[26] but I cannot accept the possible and sinister reduction that it contains. I can no more accept it when I read Vidales' further statement: 'The oppressed *can neither believe in* nor confess *Jesus Christ*, nor can they respond freely to him, *except insofar as* they succeed in freeing themselves from all oppression. They *cannot be witnesses to the Spirit* who liberates and transforms, *except insofar as* they struggle together to win a new order of justice.'[27] The words that I (not the author) have italicized seem to me to be excessive and, as such, open to question.

The Church is not simply the Renewal, nor is it simply liberation theology. The Church is fullness. The members of the Church, however, are not making that fullness a reality and sometimes even betray it!

Three charisms have attracted a great deal of attention because of their unusual, even spectacular nature, and merit special consideration. I shall devote the next chapter to them.

NOTES

1. Among the enormous number of books and articles written about charisms, I would recommend: A. Lemonnyer, 'Charismes', *DB (Suppl)*, I (1928), cols 1233–1243; J. Brosch, *Charismen und Ämter in der Urkirche* (Bonn, 1951); H. Schürmann, 'Les charismes spirituels', *L'Eglise de Vatican II* (*Unam sanctam*, 51b) (Paris, 1966), pp. 541–573; M.-A. Chevallier, *Esprit de Dieu, paroles d'homm. Le rôle de l'Esprit dans les ministères de la parole selon l'apôtre Paul* (Neuchâtel, 1966); H. Conzelmann, '*charisma*', *TDNT*, IX, pp. 402–406; H. Küng, *The Church* (London, 1967), pp. 197ff.; G. Hasenhüttl, *Charisma, Ordnungsprinzip der Kirche* (Freiburg, 1970); J. Hainz, *Ekklesia, Strukturen paulinischer Gemeinde-Theologie und Gemeinde-Ordnung* (Regensburg, 1972); J. D. G. Dunn, *Jesus and the Spirit. A Study of the Religious and Charismatic Experience of Jesus and the First Christians as Reflected in the New Testament* (Philadelphia, 1975), pp. 253ff.; B. N. Wambacq, 'Le mot "charisme" ', *NRT*, 97 (1975), 345–355; Sr Jeanne d'Arc, 'Panorama du charisme. Essai d'une perspective d'ensemble', *VS*, 609 (July-August 1975), 503–521; A. M. de Monléon, 'L'Expérience des charismes. Manifestations de l'Esprit en vue du bien commun', *Istina*, 21 (1976), 340–373.
2. Here I am following almost exactly M.-A. Chevallier, *op. cit.*, pp. 139ff. and J. Hainz, *op. cit.*, pp. 328–335. See also R. Laurentin, who defines charisms as 'freely given . . . diverse gifts bestowed upon various members for the building up of the Church', *Catholic Pentecostalism* (London, 1977), p. 51; see also *Concilium*, 109 (1978), 3–12. The Malines document also says: '. . . charism is understood to be a gift or aptitude which is liberated and empowered by the Spirit of God and is taken into the ministry of building up the body of Christ which is the Church. It is also presupposed that every Christian manifests one or more charisms. The charisms belong to a right ordering of the Church and to ministry' (Eng. tr., *Theological and Pastoral Orientations on the Catholic Charismatic Renewal* (Notre Dame, Indiana, 1974), p. 5); and further on: 'This Spirit, given to the whole Church, comes to visibility in ministries . . .' (*ibid.*, p. 12).
3. See H. Caffarel, *Faut-il parler d'un Pentecôtisme catholique?* (Paris, 1973), p. 30, who recognized that this was the narrow meaning of the word. See also Cardinal L. J. Suenens, *A New Pentecost* (London, 1975), pp. 21f.: 'These manifestations of the Spirit or charisms are . . . gifts of the Spirit recognizable by their visible presence and by their common goal . . . to build anew the kingdom of God'.
4. According to Sr Jeanne d'Arc, VS, 609 (July-August 1975), 569.
5. Leo XIII himself said: 'The charisms are only extraordinary gifts given by the Holy Spirit in exceptional circumstances and with the aim of establishing the divine origin of the Church': see his encyclical *Divinum illud munus* (9 May 1897) and his letter *Testem benevolentiae* (22 January 1899). J. D. G. Dunn quotes numerous authors writing in the Reformed tradition who have been guilty of this identification: see his *Baptism in the Holy Spirit* (London, 4th ed., 1977), p. 225, note 3. See also L. Cerfaux, *The Christian in the Theology of St Paul* (Eng. tr.; London, 1967), esp. pp. 256–261, who speaks of 'ecstatic manifestations and miracles' and thinks that the Corinthian believers were 'fleshly' and children rather than adult Christians. See also Cardinal E. Ruffini's address to the Second Vatican Council on 16 October 1963; A. Bittlinger, 'Die charismatische Erneuerung der Kirchen. Aufbruch urchristlicher Geisteserfahrung', *Erfahrung und Theologie des Heiligen Geistes*, ed. C. Heitmann and H. Mühlen (Hamburg and Munich, 1974), pp. 36–48; P.-R. Régamey, *La Rénovation dans l'Esprit* (Paris, 1974), p. 40, who understands 'charisms . . . in the strict sense of more or less passing favours, such as prophecies, miracles and extraordinary generosity in service, given by the Holy Spirit for the benefit of others, rather than those who receive them. It is possible to recognize the mark of the Spirit in these favours.'
6. I am, in this rather severe statement, criticizing only the use made of this distinction, not the distinction itself as outlined by Thomas Aquinas, for example, in *ST* Ia IIae, q. 111,

a. 1; *Comm. in Rom*. c. 1, lect. 3; *Comp. Theol*. I, c. 114. Especially in connection with the apostles, however, he observed that God generally entrusted missions that were accompanied by signs and miracles to those who were most holy; see *In I Sent*. d. 14, q. 2, a. 2, ad 4; d. 15, a. 1, q^a 2; *ST* Ia, q. 43, a. 1; a. 3, ad 4; a. 4; IIIa, q. 7, a. 10, ad 2.

7. ' "Charismatiques", ou quoi?', *La Croix* (19 January 1974); 'Renouveau dans l'Esprit et Institution ecclésiale. Mutuelle interrogation', *RHPR*, 55 (1975), 143–156, especially pp. 145ff.
8. *Tous responsables dans l'Eglise? Le ministère presbytéral dans l'Eglise tout entière 'ministérielle'* (Paris, 1973).
9. See *Discours au Concile Vatican II*, ed. Y. Congar, D. O'Hanlon and H. Küng (Paris, 1964), pp. 31–36. The quotation that follows in the text is taken from H. Küng, *op. cit*. (note 1), p. 182.
10. K. McDonnell, ed., *The Holy Spirit and Power* (New York, 1975), pp. 63–73. E. O'Connor, *The Pentecostal Movement in the Catholic Church* (Notre Dame, Indiana, 1971), p. 33ff. and note 25, defends the term which provided the title for his book. Just as every believer is liturgical and biblical, he claims, and there is a liturgical and biblical movement in the Church, so too is there a charismatic or Pentecostal movement, although this does not affect the fact that every believer also has his own charism or charisms.
11. H. Caffarel, *Le renouveau charismatique interpellé* (*Collection Renouveau*, 5) (Paris, 1976), p. 71; *Pro mundi vita*, 60 (May 1976), p. 18ff.
12. Sr Jeanne d'Arc, *op. cit*. (note 4), 569ff.
13. J. M. R. Tillard, 'Il y a charisme et charisme. La vie religieuse', *Lumen Vitae* (Brussels, 1977).
14. See W. Bassett, 'To Judge on the Merits of the Case', *Concilium*, 107 (1977), 59–68.
15. G. Delteil, article in *L'Unité des Chrétiens*, 15 (July 1974), 5. A critical question very similar to my own will also be found in A.-M. Besnard, 'Le prisme des opinions', *VS* (January 1974), 18ff.; J.-Y. Riocreux, 'Réflexions d'un Français aux Etats-Unis', *ibid*., 25, 27–28; K. Rahner, in an interview given on the occasion of his seventieth birthday, also said: 'There is an almost naive immediacy to God and an almost naive faith in the rule of the Holy Spirit': *Herder Korrespondenz*, 28 (1974), 91.
16. See J.-Y. Riocreux, *op. cit*., 28. See also H. Caffarel, *op. cit*. (note 11), 75ff., 78; K. and D. Ranaghan, *op. cit*. below (note 21), p. 171.
17. J.-P. Dietle, 'Le réveil pentecôtiste . . .', *Positions luthériennes*, 4 (October 1974), 236.
18. O. Clément, 'La vie dans l'Esprit selon la tradition de l'Orient chrétien', *Cahiers Saint-Dominique*, 138 (May 1973), 370–381, especially 379.
19. I have already quoted two of Simeon's texts above, pp. 70 and 121. Basil of Caesarea showed that the action of the Holy Spirit was not instantaneous, but gradual in his *De spir. sanct*. 18 (*SC* 17bis, pp. 197ff.).
20. Their teaching is so well known that it would be foolish to quote a great number of texts. It is, however, worth mentioning John of the Cross, *The Ascent of Mount Carmel*, III, chapters 29–31; *The Dark Night*, XIII and *Counsels and Maxims*, 38. Marie de l'Incarnation wrote from Quebec to her son: 'The one who is present in the most precious way of all is the Spirit of the incarnate Word when he gives that Spirit in a sublime way, as he has in fact given him to several souls whom I know in this new Church. . . . Normally he only gives him after much suffering in his service and faithful reception of his grace': see Mme Arsène-Henry, *Les plus beaux textes sur le Saint-Esprit* (Paris, 1968), p. 24.
21. G. Combet and L. Fabre, 'The Pentecostal Movement and the Gift of Healing', *Concilium*, 99 (1975), 106–110. See also K. and D. Ranaghan, *Catholic Pentecostals* (New York, 1969), chapter 7, 'Walking in the Spirit', especially pp. 214–216.
22. This is, I think, the case with 'Le mouvement charismatique: nouvelle Pentecôte ou nouvelle aliénation?', *La Lettre*, 211 (March 1976), 7–18, (M. Clévenot) 19–26; and with Arlette Sabiani, 'Non, mille fois non', *Hebdo T.C.*, 1774 (6 July 1978), 19. Many readers

sent in their reactions. It is also similar in the case of J. Chabert, 'La hiérarchie catholique et le renouveau charismatique', *Lumière et Vie*, 125 (November-December 1975), 22–32, especially 29: 'an institution built on the ruins of human hope' and 'care for structures, material and social mediations and their transformation cannot but be absent in this framework (of an almost immediate relationship with the absolute)'.

23. See Paul Ricœur's very illuminating analysis: 'Le socius et le prochain', *Cahiers de la VS* (1954); repr. in *Histoire et Vérité* (Paris, 2nd ed. 1955), pp. 99–111.
24. See Raul Vidales, 'Charisms and Political Action', *Concilium*, 109 (1978), 67–77; Enrique Dussel, 'The Differentiation of Charisms', *ibid.*, 38–55. Vidales says, p. 71: 'Religious practice effectively becomes an alienating factor within the overall framework of dependent capitalist structure, particularly amongst the traditionally exploited working classes, who have little or no historical and political consciousness and hardly any active participation in transforming the ruling system. To the extent that religious practice contributes to the maintenance of a mythical, a-historical and a-political consciousness, it sacralizes the established order and in the end becomes the one element that keeps the establishment in its place.'
25. See John Orme Mills' long note on pp. 116–117 of *New Heaven? New Earth?* (London, 1976), with reference, among others, to W. Hollenweger, *Pentecost and Politics* (Bristol, 1975); see also R. Laurentin, *Catholic Pentecostalism, op. cit.* (note 2), pp. 173–177. See also the personal witness borne in *Unité des chrétiens*, 21 (January 1976), 24–25: J.-M. Fiolet; *Il est vivant*, 11 (n.d. = 1976), 12–17: Jean, Raymonde, Michèle, Jacques and Yves.
26. See my *Un peuple messianique. L'Eglise sacrement du salut. Salut et libération* (Paris, 1975).
27. Raul Vidales, *op. cit.* (note 24), 74, 75. My italics.

2

SPECTACULAR CHARISMS

Speaking and Praying in Tongues
Prophecy · Healings

Cardinal Ruffini, in his address to the Second Vatican Council in 1963, believed, as did John Chrysostom at the end of the fourth century, that tongues had been useful at the beginning of the Church's history, but that the phenomenon had ceased now. On the contrary, however, it has in no way ceased—it is very much with us. In fact, it never ceased completely, but the evidence in the history of Christianity is neither abundant nor always very precise.[1] There is, on the other hand, a great deal of clear evidence in the past of the gift of tears. Often these have been tears of penance or 'compunction'.[2] Often, also, they have been tears of emotion, expressing great love,[3] in which case they have been a language going beyond words. In this respect, then, tears are clearly related to speaking or praying in tongues.

There have been dozens of studies of the evidence of glossolalia in the New Testament, and to date about 400 books or articles have been written about speaking or praying in tongues in the Pentecostalist or Neo-pentecostalist movement.[4] It cannot be established *a priori* that what is reported in the Acts of the Apostles about the first Pentecost, what happened at Corinth, what was personally experienced by Paul, and what is encountered now in the Renewal are identical. There has been considerable discussion about the evidence in Acts. It is certain that something quite striking happened, but did not Luke, it has been asked, reconstruct in a historical form a theology of missionary catholicity on the basis of the instances of glossolalia that were fairly common in the early Christian communities? Was it xenoglossia (speaking in foreign languages), or was it an enthusiastic manifestation of exultant praise that witnesses might have taken either as a language which they seemed to recognize or as a drunken delirium (see Acts 2:6–13)? Luke himself seems to interpreted what happened at the first Pentecost as a replica of what the Jewish tradition affirmed about Sinai, or perhaps as a reversal of Babel.

Glossolalia at Corinth was rather anarchic and at the same time overestimated as a charism. Paul himself believed that it should be controlled; he valued, but did not overvalue it. What are we, then, to say about this phenomenon among our brothers and sisters in the Renewal?

The first thing that has to be said is that it has become famous. Although it plays a relatively small part in Renewal meetings, whether they are large or small, it interests many people and has provided the subject-matter for many studies. It often occupies a considerable amount of space in more general works about the movement as a whole.[5] An extraordinary aspect of the Renewal is thus given a privileged place. In the New Testament, on the other hand, it has a relatively small place. In Acts, it appears each time that the mission which was inaugurated at Pentecost reaches a new human space—it occurs, for example, in Samaria, among the gentiles of Caesarea and among John's disciples at Ephesus. Our knowledge of glossolalia comes essentially from the case of the community at Corinth. There are allusions to it, but no descriptions of it, outside Paul's account in 1 Corinthians, but it is not found anywhere in Romans or Ephesians, which, on the other hand, provide lists of the gifts of the Spirit.[6] There is no reference at all to glossolalia in John.

Should we speak here of glossolalia, or of xenoglossia? Are these phenomena which do not correspond to any real spoken language, or are they sentences or phrases in an existing language or dialect unknown to the subject himself? Some experts claim that there have been no cases to their knowledge in which sentences or phrases of a real language have been heard and properly checked. Other scholars have provided different evidence.[7] I am inclined to agree with Peter Hocken, in his report to the English bishops, that the question is wrongly put. On the one hand, in fact, this 'language' is not a means of communication with men, but an expression of a relationship with God (1 Cor 14:2). On the other hand, it is experienced, as it was in the apostolic Church, as giving, in joy and with a feeling of fullness, a sign of the coming of the Spirit and his gifts and as strengthening the Christian's total commitment to Jesus Christ. The evidence provided by those who have this gift is categorical: they claim to have a deep sense of awakening to a communion which involves their whole person, including their body, at a level that is both below and beyond and concepts and our human words. Here is one such testimony:

> The Holy Spirit purifies and refashions certain very profound elements of the human personality that lie beyond the reach of therapeutic exploration. He reshapes us in the foundations of our personality, that basic structure which precedes even the acquisition of our mother-tongue and the first social control of our feelings and their expressions. This activity can be felt all the more strongly when the Holy Spirit makes use of the prayers that he himself gives us in the form that precedes acquired, controlled language, as in the case of praying in tongues and, by extension, praying with the prayer of the heart.[8]

Another testimony describes the phenomenon known as 'singing in tongues':

> In singing in tongues, words are pronounced expressing unity regained, perfect newness and eager anticipation. It is the language of gratuitous freedom. A deep thankfulness, the desire for which exceeds all possible expression, corresponds to

> the abundant gift of God, who gives himself without counting the cost. It takes place when the heart overflows and can no longer find the words and phrases that it is seeking. Singing in tongues is a stammering of great abundance and thankfulness.[9]

Evidence of this kind, which cannot as such be refuted, is always to be welcomed, but two kinds of criticism have to be made of the glossolalia of Neo-pentecostalism—religious criticism and criticism based on the human sciences. My purely religious criticism of this phenomenon can be grouped under four headings:

(a) It is not possible to go beyond the clear language of Paul in 1 Cor 14:1–33. In this passage, he outlines a criticism and practical norms in accordance with three criteria. The first is the benefit to others: 'he who speaks in a tongue edifies only himself' (1 Cor 14:4). The second is the inalienable place accorded to understanding: 'I will pray with the Spirit and I will pray with the mind also. . . . Nevertheless, in church I would rather speak five words with my mind . . . than ten thousand words in a tongue' (14:15, 19). The third criterion is that the Christian should aim at an adult rather than at a childish level of understanding: 'do not be children in your thinking. . . . In thinking be mature' (14:20).

(b) In Pentecostalism, speaking in tongues is fairly generally regarded as an indispensable sign of having been baptized in the Spirit. It is not quite the same in the Renewal. This difference between the two is accompanied by another difference, which has to do with the wider ecclesiological and theological context. As Simon Tugwell has acutely observed,[10] for Pentecostalists, neither baptism of water nor the Eucharist are what they are for us, namely sacraments in the sense of acts of God, but rather actions of believers. On the other hand, speaking in tongues is brought about in us by God as the sign of baptism in the Spirit and is therefore experienced by Pentecostalists in the sense of a sacrament.

(c) In the renewal, praying in tongues is frequently identified with the inexpressible groanings (*stenagmois alalētois*) which Paul speaks of as being, in us, the prayer of the Spirit (Rom 8:26). I agree with K. Niederwimmer, however, in believing that what Paul is speaking about in this text is something quite different, namely a prayer of the Holy Spirit himself, a prayer that is not pronounced and therefore not audible. This is not so in the case of praying in tongues. The prayer of the Holy Spirit within us is something that does not belong to our conscious spirit, but to the presence or the indwelling of the Holy Spirit in us which I have already discussed.[11] It is, nevertheless, related to speaking, praying or singing in tongues, so long as these latter phenomena are really gifts of God, by the fact that a certain depth in our own 'heart' is involved with both.

(d) I have stated an important condition: 'so long as these phenomena are really gifts of God'. This critical question is certainly important, because similar phenomena have existed and still exist in the pagan world or outside the life of the Spirit. Paul was well aware of this (see 1 Cor 12:2). What is more, many psychologists have stressed the induced character of 'tongues' and the imitative and enthusiastic nature of the activity, despite the fact that a certain number of cases defy explanation. As Pascal commented, charity is what enables true miracles to be discerned. The fact that the same phenomena occur outside the life in the Spirit does not necessarily mean that they do not come from the Spirit or that they do not bear witness to his presence for our consolation and joy where there is life in the Spirit. This is clear from the fruits that are received and especially the gifts of charity, which is for Paul the supreme norm. 1 Cor 13 is in no sense a foreign body between 1 Cor 12 and 1 Cor 14—it is rather the master-light that illuminates what the apostle wants to tell his readers about the use of the gifts of the Spirit. Charity is the supreme charism.

Let us now consider the important contribution made to our understanding of glossolalia by the human sciences. Several authors have summarized the conclusions of experts in this field.[12] I shall do no more here than simply draw attention to the methods used to examine the data and the points of view from which they have been seen.

The Linguistic Sciences: In a few rare and even then doubtful cases, certain sentences or phrases in an existing language or dialect that have been recognized by observers have been uttered by a subject who has claimed ignorance of the language in question. These cases may be regarded as miraculous. Apart from them, a real language is not involved, either at the level of phonemes or at that of lexical combinations. William J. Samarin has made a systematic study of glossolalia from this viewpoint.[13]

Comparative Religion and Ethnography: Glossolalia has existed in shamanism, in pagan antiquity, in ancient Mesopotamia and in Greece (the Pythia of the oracle at Delphi), and also in Judaism during New Testament times.[14]

Sociology and Psychology: The conclusions of specialists working in this sphere have changed in the course of time. Kilian McDonnell has distinguished two periods, from 1910 to 1966 and from 1967 to 1975. The break in 1966/67 corresponds significantly to the transition from Pentecostalism proper to Neo-pentecostalism, that is, to the wider movement of the Renewal in the classical churches. It was first thought that entry into Pentecostal groups was a response to a need to escape from an insecure social situation based on economic and cultural deprivation. It is now believed that, even though this may have been the case for a time and is still the reason here and there, this is no longer strictly true. It was also thought that an important part was played by a pathological element or that the subjects were predisposed to be influenced in this way. Psychological tests have revealed that those who speak in tongues have an inclination to be dependent on a model, a leader or a group. At the same time, however, these tests have not shown in any way that members of the Renewal are, as a whole, less mature, more anxious or less adapted to living than other people.

One positive aspect of glossolalia that has been observed is that it has a 'liberating effect. From the religious point of view, it liberates man from inhibitions in regard to men and to God, that is, from human respect and from fear of approaching the God whom no words can describe. As a result, interior energies, both mystical and apostolic, are released. This is a fact of daily experience.'[15]

'Interpretation' and 'Prophecy'

Just as it is not a question of speaking a foreign language, so too is there no 'translation' in the case of 'interpretation' of tongues. This interpretation is a charism: 'The Spirit gives . . . to another various kinds of tongues, to another the interpretation of tongues' (1 Cor 12:10), although it can happen that the same person has both gifts (14:5, 13). Clearly, this interpretation cannot be checked. I have personally heard too little about it to be able to provide a valuable assessment of it, especially as what I have heard is very trivial. What is certain, however, is that the charism of interpretation is closely related to that of speaking in tongues and, since the latter does not play a large part in Renewal meetings as such, interpretation similarly has hardly any place in those meetings.

Paul attaches much more importance to 'prophecy' (see 1 Cor 14:1, 5, 39; 1 Thess 5:20). Prophets always figure in his lists of gifts and ministries and in his discussions of those matters. It is worth noting, for example, that he names them immediately after the 'apostles'.[16] The Fathers stressed the permanent nature of this gift in the Church. It has a direct bearing on its building up, whether it is seen within the ordinary framework of life in the small communities of the kind that Corinth might well have been or considered within the much wider context of the historical movement of the Church's life.

We are most conscious of this second aspect today, the prophet being seen above all as the one who opens to the Church new ways for and a new understanding of its future, the one who is able to read the 'signs of the times' and the one who goes beyond the established structures and ideas and makes gestures or creates institutions that are very promising.[17] These 'prophetic' men and women are related to the biblical prophets in that they open the way for and throw light on the accomplishment of God's plan in history.

This is not, however, exactly what we have in 1 Cor 12:10; 14:1–33, nor is it what is found in the Renewal. What is involved is the building up of persons and this leads to the building up of the Church. It is also not the habitual gift of understanding and explaining the Word of God or of teaching (*didascalia*). But nor is it, like glossolalia, an irrational form of expression. It is fully intelligible, but above all given or 'inbreathed' by the Spirit. Its effect is to make the recipient open to the truth of God and the truth of what he is himself.

The revelation that is imparted by this prophecy is not usually astonishing. The bishop and martyr Polycarp is described in a letter from his Church as an 'apostolic and prophetic teacher'[18] and we have one of his letters, which contains wise exhortation and very classical morality. In the Renewal, several cases of 'prophecy' have been recorded. These have proclaimed the future,[19] have disclosed the depths of a person's heart or have announced a precise and providential appeal. Most of them, however, have been simple, edifying exhortations: 'Prophecy exhorts, warns, comforts and corrects. . . . Prophecy can be a simple word of encouragement, an admonition, a prophetic act, or a decision for a new line of action.'[20]

Miracles and Healings

The healing of the sick or injured was, in New Testament times, a sign of the coming of the messianic era.[21] Paul listed the gifts of healing and working miracles among the charisms of the Spirit (see 1 Cor 12:9, 28–30). Was the Spirit himself not the messianic gift *par excellence*? The Acts of the Apostles are full of stories of healings and miracles. There are also many accounts of healings and miracles occurring throughout the centuries in the history of the Church, although it has, of course, to be recognized that the reality has often been exaggerated in hagiography and monastic writings as well as in the minds of the people. On the other hand, it has for centuries been maintained by many Christians that miracles, like the gift of tongues, were granted only in the early period of the Church's history.[22] Despite the fact that we are now so proud of our knowledge and our control of the elements, however, there has, in our own period, been a striking contradiction of this interpretation—miracles, appearances and, in the Renewal especially, the gift of tongues and healings.[23] What is taking place in the Renewal is of ecclesiological importance, quite apart from its pneumatological interest. In the Catholic Church, men of God have always been the instruments of healings, and the celebration of the sacrament of the sick has often resulted in noticeable improvements in health.[24] As F. Lovsky has observed, however, healings have frequently been attributed to the saints in heaven and especially to the Virgin Mary.[25] Now, with the Renewal, they have once again become an aspect of the Church here on earth and a normal, everyday feature. Attempts have even been made to avoid the sensational aspect with which they can so easily be associated.

The context of these healings in the Renewal is usually that of a prayer meeting, and the pattern followed is usually as follows: an absolute faith in Jesus who is living and whose Spirit works with power is required;[26] there is brotherly prayer in the community of the group; the one who has the gift of healing does not work alone, although there are exceptions, notably Kathryn Kuhlman;[27] finally there is a laying on of hands, which is a classic, biblical gesture, expressing the powerful action of the Spirit who is invoked; this is accompanied by prayer in faith;[28] thanksgiving, even before any improvement is observed. Basically, it is above all a question of living, with one's brethren, in a fellowship of faith and prayer and in a relationship with the living God, who transforms one's attitude, both in soul and in body, towards oneself. There are physical healings, but there have been many more healings that are spiritual, inner—psychical, if that term is preferred.

This spiritual healing gives us access to our true relationship with God. This latter is what all the Church's pastoral activity, both the Word and the sacraments, tends to secure. As J.-C. Sagne has said: 'Inner healing is . . . a healing of the psyche. It does not immediately concern the relation to God and the God-orientated life but the organization of our intelligence, our will, our memory and our emotional sensitivity.'[29] There may be hiatuses or blockages in our psyche and these may have a spiritual origin. It is important for us to be set free from these impediments. This does not usually happen suddenly, with the speed of lightning. It comes as the result of trusting prayer, in the conviction that God will bestow his gift, a brotherly, persistent prayer made in humble and peaceful practice in the life of the Church. The atmosphere of friendly welcome and joyous praise which so characterizes Renewal meetings, and tends to erase conflicts, and the freedom and power of the Spirit who is invoked in prayer should not by-pass normal human psychological development. As A. Vergote has pointed out, 'The Spirit acts by coming together with the human spirit and not by going against it or acting outside it'. The members of the Renewal and especially those who are responsible for imposing restraint on it have to exercise discernment. There have been cases, in the movement and outside it, of failure or at least of indiscreet intervention.

Physical healings of organic diseases are clearly more striking. There have been accounts that are almost incredible, but which have been supported by witnesses.[30] We should not be inflexibly sceptical or, on the other hand, childishly credulous. 'Who knows where God wants to let down his ladder?' We believe in the Holy Spirit and we believe in his power to give life. We believe in the power of prayer and faith and know that prayer is especially powerful when it is made with ardent brotherly unanimity. A messianic sign of the proximity of the kingdom of God has been given in our present century, which is critical and well provided with therapeutic means. The Church has rediscovered a forgotten form of ministry—that of healing. May God be praised for our recovery of a ministry that has so many different forms!

It should be added that there is a miraculous element in some of the cases that have been reported, but that this is in keeping with what philosophers such as Maurice Blondel and theologians have said about miracles as a manifestation of God's love of man and of the nature of his salvation, which points to the glorious freedom of the children of God and the restoration of their nature, both body and soul, in a fullness of life.

Discernment

Two aspects of discernment can be distinguished in Paul's teaching about this charism: in the first place, the special charism of discernment itself and, in the second, the general exercise of discernment, which every Christian must try to practise. In connection with 1 Cor 12:10, J. D. G. Dunn said that it is important to recognize that this gift of discernment of spirits is on a par with prophecy. It should not be regarded, he insists, as an independent gift. It provides a 'test' for the prophetic statement and a check against its abuses (see 1 Cor 14:29). It is, he concluded, the equivalent of the rôle played by the interpretation of tongues in the case of glossolalia (1 Cor 12:10; 14:27ff.).[31] It therefore clearly has its limitations. An illustration of this can be found in 1 Cor 14:29, in which Paul, having given the rules for the exercise of the *pneumatika*, speaking in tongues and prophecies—to which the Corinthians were strongly attracted (1 Cor 14:12)—invites the brethren to assess (*diakrinein*) the prophecies (1 Cor 14:29), the function of which is not to predict the future, but rather to announce, in a concrete situation, the will of God for an individual or the community. This prophetic function is, moreover, not to take place on the basis of human criteria, that is, human reason, but it must be carried out in a spiritual fashion, using the resources that come from the Spirit (1 Cor 2:13–16; 7:40).

An absolutely sovereign and objective criterion can be found in orthodox Christology (see 1 Cor 12:3; 1 Jn 4:1–3). This is an indispensable condition for authenticity, which can be expressed in the concrete as an ability to build up the Body of Christ. V. Therrien, who has specialized in this question, situated the charism of discernment within the more general framework of Christian discernment as such and then, in his detailed study of spiritual discernment, went on to say:

> It provides a source of dynamic knowledge and revelation for the service of the glory of God within a pastoral service of the people of God. The end in view is his people's freedom from influences which do not come from God and which are replaced by the lordship of Jesus as restored by the Holy Spirit. . . . Like all the charisms, charismatic discernment is an experience of actual grace. It is instantaneous, spontaneous, gratuitous, confusing, unforeseen and accidental. It is, in other words, given to be used in a situation of need. It disappears when that need disappears. . . . Charismatic discernment is a wide-reaching form of perception. . . . The climate and the conditions within which this experience takes place and

> this dynamism is exercised can be defined by the following terms: peace, compassion, gentleness, merciful charity and service of the glory of God and our brethren. It can never take place in an environment of scandalized astonishment, haste, aggression, terrorism, possessiveness and oppression.[32]

Such a description cannot be read without some misgivings. What a fantastic degree of authority for a man (or woman) to have! Is there not also a need for external criteria which enable us to discern whether the Spirit has really intervened? The author, apparently aware of this, adds:

> The first condition for the validity of the experience of charismatic discernment is to have recourse to other forms of discernment in order to confirm and justify charismatic discernment, because it is new and often spontaneous and confusing. . . . The second condition of validity is to go back to the charismatic community and the exercise of this dynamism of service within the community.

These conditions are not, of course, always observed. There have been many recorded cases of abuse, imprudence, indiscretion and, on the other hand, unacceptable and authoritarian control.[33] These cases to some extent bring the Renewal into disrepute, but no more than mistakes and errors of judgement bring other movements or institutions into disrepute. It has, however, to be recognized that some environments are more favourable than others to abuses.

It is important in this context to consider another element mentioned by Therrien, that is, 'freedom from influences which do not come from God'. This clearly refers to the devil. In its early days, Pentecostalism had a rather simplistic, but very full demonology.[34] Even in the most Catholic branches of the Renewal, there is often a similarly simplistic way of speaking about the devil and liberation from his influence.[35] And on the fringe of the movement are an exercise of a 'ministry of deliverance' and certain practices of exorcism which give rise to a certain uneasiness.[36] I would not wish to rule out this hypothesis of demons, since there are data supporting it, but there is good reason, in this particular sphere, for sobriety and a sound demythologization.[37] Just before he died, the great spiritual writer Albert-Marie Besnard wrote to me about his worrying observation that 'members of the Renewal are more and more frequently tending to see the demon at work in everything that is no more than human'.

If 'charismatic discernment' exists, it is rare and, when it occurs, it calls for co-operation. In any case Scripture, and Paul in particular, requires all believers to exercise discernment: 'Do not quench the Spirit, do not despise prophesying, but test everything (*panta de dokimazete*), hold fast to what is good, abstain from every form of evil' (1 Thess 5:19–22; cf. Jn 4:1–6). One of the most perceptive commentators has said: 'Paul's exhortation applies first and foremost to the discernment of charisms and above all to the discernment of prophecies, but it is in itself a universal principle of "spiritual prudence" '. The same author goes on to summarize his study of the act of discernment and define it as 'an act that is both unique and complex, both human and divine and both personal and ecclesial. It is both specific for a particular situation and at the same time fitted into God's one plan of salvation. It points to the building up of the brethren and is orientated towards God's glory. Finally, although it takes place in time, it also shares in the judgement at the end of time.'[38] What a programme! This is in fact the rôle of the 'discernment of spirits', which has been discussed in countless spiritual works, though no author has ever succeeded in exhausting the subject.[39] With the help of Therrien,[40] the author of the above summary, it is possible to group the criteria for the discernment of spirits under three headings:

(1) *Doctrinal or Objective Discernment*: This is basic. The first task of a believer, a brother or a 'spiritual director' is to act as a mirror in which we can see and check whether the movements of our spirit are authentic. This discernment consists of certain objective criteria: the Word of God seen as a whole and not simply certain passages of Scripture; the teaching of the Church and the masters of spirituality; the duties of our state; our observation of the commandments (see 1 Jn 2:3–5); our attitude of obedience (Teresa of Avila is an excellent model of this). All our research leads us to the conclusion that Christology is the most important condition for the soundness of any pneumatology (see below, pp. 210–211).

(2) *Subjective or Personal Discernment*:[41] This consists of an assessment of our inner tendencies on the basis of that renewal of our understanding and value-judgements of which Paul speaks in Rom 12:2 and Eph 4:23. What is the origin of these movements and where do they lead? A knowledge of what the human sciences can tell us is helpful in our attempt to discover their origin. In the last resort, however, it is our quality of life as Christians which provides the real sign of authenticity and the fruit(s) of the Spirit of which Paul speaks in Gal 5:22 play(s) a part here: 'love, joy, peace, patience, kindness, goodness, faithfulness, gentleness, self-control'. The tradition of spirituality in the Church provides an echo of this fundamental programme that has sounded throughout the centuries. There was an emphasis on peace and joy, for example, in the second century, in the writings of the Roman Hermas,[42] and at the end of the fourth century, in the homilies of Macarius the Great.[43] In the sixteenth century another classical author writing about the rules of discernment, Ignatius Loyola, attached great importance to the effects of consolation or sadness. His aim was above all to bring his readers to a mature decision in life that corresponded to God's will for us. For that reason, he is the great model to whom we return again and again.[44]

(3) *Discernment within the Community*: This form of discernment can be divided into two types: (a) 'A search conducted by all the members of a group for a clear consensus of God's will for the group or for one of its members in a particular case or situation. . . . The criteria for the validity of such an exercise in discernment [are] the presence of spiritual guides or competent animators. . . .'[45] The objective criterion will be what builds up the community (see 1 Cor 14:26). What is involved here is a life that forms an integral part of the greater or lesser fabric of history. For this reason, (b) a good criterion will consist in correspondence to the needs of the Church and the general tendency of its life. It is here that the 'signs of the times' have to be discerned.[46] A sense of history, a concern for events, a little prophetic perception and above all a spiritual understanding of God's work are all necessary, especially as the beginnings, in which the Spirit of God is active, are often very ambivalent and ambiguous. Our spontaneous actions have to be tested because not everything that emerges from them is necessarily from the Spirit. The Acts of the Apostles contain a certain number of new situations, through which the Church's mission had to find its way in conformity with the will of God and his plan. The solution to this difficulty was found by applying these three criteria: Experience of the Spirit, the support of scriptural evidence and the approval of the *ecclesia*.[47]

It should be clear, then, that discernment is a very complex act, calling for the exercise of many human means and of many gifts of the Spirit. The gifts which classical theology knows in the form of understanding, knowledge, counsel and wisdom all have to be used so long as the Holy Spirit gives them. He blows where he wills: one of his titles is 'counsellor'. But he does not act like the prompter in a theatre, so that we also have to use our own understanding and out own resources: 'Brethren, . . . in your thinking be mature!' (1 Cor 14:20).

NOTES

1. The following can be mentioned: Catherine de Dormans (*c.* 1110), who, according to Guibert de Nogent, bore witness to a *rotatus sermonum*: see P. Alphandéry, *Revue de l'Histoire des Religions*, 52 (1905), 186; possibly Hildegard of Bingen: see F. Vernet, *DTC*, VI, p. 2470; Elizabeth of Schönau (†1164), *Vita*, Prol. 1 (*PL* 195, 119B); Dorothy of Montau (see Volume I of this work, p. 122); Teresa of Avila, *Life*, chapter 16; Ignatius Loyola and his *loquela, Diary*, 11 and 22 May 1544; Marie de l'Incarnation, Relation of 1654, XXIV: 'I sang to my divine Bridegroom a canticle that his Spirit inspired me to sing'; *The Way of a Pilgrim* (Russian; between 1856 and 1861): '. . . a strong feeling came over me, urging me to withdraw within myself again. The Prayer was surging up in my heart, and I needed peace and silence to give free play to this quickening flame of prayer, as well as to hide from others the outward signs which went with it, such as tears and sighs and unusual movements of the face and lips': paperback ed. (London, 1972), pp. 78–79. I do not intend to speak here about the Cévennes Protestants of the early eighteenth century: see Morton T. Kelsey, *Tongue Speaking* (London, 1973), pp. 52ff. I also omit

any reference to Wesley's or Irving's disciples in the nineteenth century. Following K. Richstaetter, 'Die Glossolalie im Lichte der Mystik', *Schol*, 11 (1936), 321–345, however, it is possible to compare with speaking or singing in tongues what Augustine said about the *jubilus*: *Enarr, in Ps*. 102 (*PL* 37, 1322ff.), or St Bernard about what the ardour of love causes us to 'belch out'; *In Cant. Sermo* 67, 3 (*PL* 183, 1103D–1104A); also the comments of David of Augsburg: *De septem spir. rel.* VII, c. 15; and Jan Ruysbroeck's remarks about the *jubilus: Spiritual Notes*, liv. II, c. 25.

2. I. Hausherr, *Penthos. La doctrine de la componction dans l'Orient chrétien* (*Or. Chr. Anal*., 132) (Rome, 1944); P. R. Régamey, *Portrait spirituel du chrétien* (Paris, 1963), pp. 67–116: 'compunction of the heart'.
3. See P. Adnès, 'Larmes', *Dictionnaire de Spiritualité*, IX, col. 287–303; M. Lot-Borodine, 'Le mystère du don des larmes dans l'Orient chrétien', *VS* (Suppl) (1 September 1936); repr. in *La douloureuse joie* (Bellefontaine, 1974), pp. 131–195; G. Gaucher, 'Le don des larmes aujourd'hui et hier', *Tychique*, 10 (July 1977), 33–40.
4. Cases will be found in K. and D. Ranaghan, *Catholic Pentecostals* (New York, 1969), pp. 195ff.; E. O'Connor, *The Pentecostal Movement in the Catholic Church* (1971) pp. 49–57, 121–131. R. Laurentin, *Catholic Pentecostalism* (London, 1977), pp. 213–221, has compiled a chronological bibliography on glossolalia, to which the following might be added: B. N. Wambacq, 'Het spreken in talen'. *Ons Geloof*, 30 (1948), 389–401: in 1 Cor, it is a question of ecstatic and incomprehensible speech which calls for 'interpretation'; A. Bittlinger, 'Et ils prient en d'autres langues', *Foi et Vie* (July-October 1973), 97–108, which Laurentin mentions (*op. cit.*, p. 221); A. Godin, 'Moi perdu ou moi retrouvé dans l'expérience charismatique', *Archives des Sciences sociales des religions*, 40 (July-December 1975), 31–52; J. D. G. Dunn, *Jesus and the Spirit* (Philadelphia, 1975), pp. 146ff. for Pentecost and pp. 242ff. for Corinth; see also the corresponding notes; F. A. Sullivan, 'Ils parlent en langues', *Lumen Vitae*, 31 (1976), 21–46; S. Tugwell, 'The Speech-Giving Spirit', *New Heaven? New Earth? An Encounter with Pentecostalism* (London, 1976), pp. 119–159; P. Barthel, 'De la glossolalie religieuse en Occident: Soixante-dix ans (1906–1976) de dérivations du sens', *Revue de Théologie et de Philosophie* (1977), 113–135; see also K. McDonnell, *op. cit.* (note 5 below), pp. 187–195, who provides an alphabetically listed bibliography of mainly American studies.
5. See R. Laurentin, *op. cit.*, pp. 58–99; K. McDonnell, *Charismatic Renewal and the Churches* (New York, 1976), devotes almost the whole of his book to this question. It is the most complete account of the reaction of the different churches and the studies made by specialists in the human sciences in the United States.
6. I do not think that glossolalia is implied in Rom 8:26, and Eph 5:19 and 6:18 do not, in my opinion, imply glossolalia any more than Jude 19 does. The same, I believe, applies to 1 Thess 5:19. Mk 16:17 forms part of a conclusion to the gospel; there is general agreement that it is canonical, but neither primitive nor authentic.
7. See R. Laurentin, *op. cit.* (note 4), pp. 67–77. J.-C. Sagne, *Lumière et Vie*, 125 (November-December 1975), 65, note 6, claims to have personal knowledge of at least five cases of an identification of a real language, including two in his presence. Ralph W. Harris, who is himself a Pentecostalist, has examined 60 cases and has concluded that real languages were spoken: see his *Spoken by the Spirit. Documental Accounts of 'Other Tongues' from Arabic to Zulu* (Springfield, 1973).
8. J. C. Sagne, *VS*, 609 (January-February 1975), 547. A.-M. de Monléon, 'L'expérience des charismes', *Istina*, 21, 357, also says: 'It is not a prayer based on reason or intelligence; it is a prayer of the spirit: "If I pray in a tongue, my spirit prays" (1 Cor 14:14). Praying in tongues is a prayer of the heart. . . . All the same, this form of prayer is essentially praise given by the Holy Spirit as a sign of a new invasion of his grace. It plays a very important part, among those who practise it, not only in enabling them to pray continuously with a prayer of the spirit in accordance with the Spirit, but also in enabling them to grow in

personal edification, that is, in that gradual transformation which is often invisible and intangible and in which the whole of life and the whole of their being become prayer as an expression of divine sonship (see Rom 8:26–27, 15; Gal 4:6).'

9. Ephrem Yon, *VS*, 609 (January-February 1975), 530.
10. S. Tugwell, *op. cit.* (note 4), p. 151.
11. K. Niederwimmer, 'Das Gebet des Geistes, Röm. 8, 26', *TZ*, 20 (1964), 252–265.
12. See R. Laurentin, *op. cit.* (note 4), pp. 70–79; A. Godin, *op. cit.* (*ibid.*), 42ff.; *Pro Mundi Vita*, 60 (May 1976), 26ff.; K. McDonnell, *op. cit.* (note 5).
13. W. J. Samarin, *Tongues of Men and Angels. The Religious Language of Pentecostalism* (New York, 1973); see also K. McDonnell, *op. cit.*, pp. 115–119, and bibliography, pp. 193–194.
14. See J. D. G. Dunn, *op. cit.* (note 4), p. 304; references p. 441, note 19, especially to Qumran.
15. R. Laurentin, *op. cit.*, p. 80.
16. See Rom 12:6–8; 1 Cor 12:8–10, 28ff.; 13:1–3, 8ff.; 14:1–5, 25–32; Eph 4:11; 1 Thess 5:19–22. After the apostles: Eph 2:20; 3:5; 4:11; 1 Cor 12:28. See also *Didache* XI. For the charism of prophecy, see W. J. Hollenweger. *The Pentecostals* (London, 1972; Minneapolis, 1972, 2nd ed. 1973), pp. 345ff.; J. D. G. Dunn, *op. cit.*, pp. 227–233; M. Harper, 'La prophétie: un don pour le corps du Christ', *Foi et Vie* (July-October 1973), 84–89; L. Dallière, 'Le charisme prophétique', *ibid.*, 90–96.
17. See my *Vraie et fausse réforme dans l'Eglise* (Paris, 1950), pp. 196–228; 2nd ed. (1969), pp. 179–207. Between these two editions, the following books and articles have been published: R. Grosche, *Das prophetische Element in der Kirche* (1956), repr. in *Et intra et extra* (Düsseldorf, 1958); K. Rahner, *The Dynamic Element in the Church* (Eng. tr.; Freiburg and London, 1964); P. Duployé, *La religion de Péguy* (Paris, 1965), pp. 427ff.; A. Ulryn, *Actualité de la fonction prophétique* (Tournai, 1966); *Concilium* (September 1968): various articles, by M.-D. Chenu and others, on the 'signs of the times'.
18. *Mart. Polycarpi*, XVI, 2.
19. In the Acts of the Apostles, prophetic interventions are often similar to the Old Testament type of prophecies and point to the future. See M.-A. Chevallier, *Souffle de Dieu. Le Saint-Esprit dans le Nouveau Testament*, I (Paris, 1978), pp. 166ff.
20. Malines document, *Theological and Pastoral Orientations on the Catholic Charismatic Renewal* (Eng. tr.: Notre Dame, Indiana, 1974), p. 54, which also says: 'Extreme care is used with both predictive and directive prophecy. Predictive prophecy is not to be acted upon except as tested and confirmed in other ways. . . . Neither the prophet nor his prophecy is self-authenticating. Prophecies are to be submitted to the Christian community. . . . They are also submitted to those who have pastoral responsibilities.'
21. See my *Un peuple messianique. L'Eglise sacrement du salut. Salut et libération* (Paris, 1975), pp. 110ff.; A. Mongillo, 'La guérison', *Concilium* (Fr. ed.), 99 (1974), 13–16.
22. During those very periods when accounts of miracles abounded, one type of text occurred again and again. It was to the effect that it was quite normal for there to be no more miracles; they were necessary at the beginning, as confirmation of the proclamation of the gospel, but, since its establishment, the Church has been the sign of that gospel and the evangelical promises had been transferred to the spiritual level. See, for example, Origen. *Contra Cels.* I, 9, on spiritual healing; John Chrysostom, *In Act. Apost.* (*PG* 51, 81); Augustine, *De vera rel.* XXV, 47; *De util. cred.*; *De Civ. Dei*, XXII, 8; Gregory the Great, *Hom, in Ev.*, lib. II, *Hom.* 29, 4 (*PL* 76, 1215–1216); Isidore of Seville, *In I Sent.* c. 24 (*PL* 83, 591–592); Odo of Cluny, *Collat.* I, 125; Thomas Aquinas, *In I Sent.* d. 16, q. 1, a. 2, ad 2 and 3; *ST* Ia, q. 43, a. 7, ad 6; Ia IIae, q. 106, a. 4. Modern authors could also be quoted in this context, but space forbids this. The diminishing number of miracles is noted from the second century onwards: see Justin Martyr, *Apol.* II, 6; *Contra Tryph.* 39; Irenaeus, *Adv. Haer.* II, 31, 2; 32, 4; Tertullian, *Apol.* 37. Thomas Aquinas thought that tongues had been replaced by the different voices reading the epistle and the gospel at

Mass and the nine lessons of Matins; see *Comm. in 1 Cor*. c. 14, lect. 6. The Protestant author H. E. Alexander writes: 'Signs and miracles were necessary to prove to Israel that Jesus was the Messiah, the Son of God. But as soon as the Jews had definitively rejected the gospel [references], these signs and miracles gradually disappeared. These signs—and especially speaking in tongues—were in fact gifts peculiar to the infancy of the Church (1 Cor 12:31, 11)': *La mission temporaire du Saint-Esprit pendant la disposition de grâce* (n.d., *c*. 1945), p. 12.

23. For healings, see W. J. Hollenweger, *op. cit*. (note 16), pp. 353ff.; Francis MacNutt, *Healing* (Indiana, 1974); M. Scanlon, *Inner Healing* (New York, 1974); O. Melançon, *Guérison et Renouveau charismatique* (Montréal, 1976); R. Laurentin, *op. cit*. (note 4), pp. 100–131.
24. The basis for this is Jas 5:12–20; *insinuatum*, as the Council of Trent said for our sacrament of the sick. See the journal *Présences*, 90 (1965), for the state of sickness, healing and the anointing of the sick; *MD*, 101 (1970), 161ff.; Donald Gelpi, 'The Ministry of Healing' in *Pentecostal Piety* (New York, 1972).
25. F. Lovsky, *L'Eglise et les malades depuis le IIe siècle jusqu'au début du XXe siècle* (Thonon, 1958). For the healing saints, see M. Leproux, *Dévotions et saints guérisseurs* (Paris, 1955); P. Jakez Helias, *Le cheval d'orgueil* (Paris, 1975), chapter III, pp. 111ff. For Lourdes, see R. Laurentin, *op. cit*., pp. 100ff., 123ff.
26. The connection between the Spirit and power is biblical (see Lk 4:14; 24:49; Acts 1:8; 10:38; Rom 15:13–19; 1 Cor 2:4–5; 1 Thess 1:5; see also 2 Tim 1:7; Heb 2:4); see also '*pneuma*', *TDNT*, VI, pp. 397–398. For the connection between healing (miracles) and faith, see Mk 11:23–24 par.
27. What is strange and sensational here goes together with a firm affirmation of faith; see the account in A. Wohlfahrt, *Foi et Vie* (July-October 1973), 6ff.; this account also appears in R. Laurentin, *op. cit*., pp. 107–110.
28. Human hands are a sign and a means of power: see V. E. Fiala, 'L'imposition des mains comme signe de la communication de l'Esprit Saint dans les rites latins', *Le Saint-Esprit dans la liturgie* (*Conférence Saint-Serge 1969*), (Rome, 1977), 87–103.
29. For inner healing, see, in addition to R. Laurentin, *op. cit*. (note 4), H. Kahlefeld, 'Jesus as Therapist', and G. Combet and F. Fabre, 'The Pentecostal Movement and the Gift of Healing', *Concilium*, 99 (1974/6), 111–117 and 106–110 respectively; M. Scanlon, *op. cit*. (note 23); J.-C. Sagne, 'Literature on Charisms and the Charismatic Movement: Inner Healing', *Concilium*, 109 (1978), 110–115; my quotation is on p. 111; A. Vergote, 'L'Esprit, puissance de salut et de santé spirituelle', *L'expérience de l'Esprit. Mélanges Schillebeeckx* (Paris, 1976), pp. 209–223.
30. See R. Laurentin, *op. cit*., pp. 102–105, for the Healing Service of Notre Dame, Indiana, 14 June 1974; the journal *Il est vivant*, 6–7 (February-March 1976), 26–33; *ibid*., 15 (n.d.), 15–18, for the case of Jeanine Bévenot; Dr P. Solignac, in the Appendix to *La névrose chrétienne* (Paris, 1976; the Eng. tr. (London, 1982) lacks this Appendix), reports the apparently miraculous case of George Duc, who was healed in November 1974. See also R. Laurentin, *op. cit*., pp. 119ff., for the charism at work.
31. J. D. G. Dunn, *op. cit*. (note 4), p. 233. The author criticizes, p. 419, note 168, the extended application of 1 Cor 12:10 in Pentecostalism and gives references.
32. V. Therrien, 'Le discernement spirituel', *Il est vivant*, 8 (June-July 1976), 16–19, 23–25, especially 23–24. Therrien is a Redemptorist and is the director of the 'Alliance' Centre in Trois Rivières (Canada). He has also written an extremely detailed study of discernment, *Le discernement dans les écrits pauliniens (Etudes bibliques)* (Paris, 1973).
33. The most serious accusations have been made by one of the pioneers of the movement in the United States, William Storey, in an interview published in *A.D. Correspondence* (24 May 1975). See also Gary McEvin, 'Les méthodes des groupes charismatiques américains vivement critiquées', *Informations Catholiques Internationales* (1 October 1975), 22–24. Kevin Ranaghan replied to William Storey (see R. Ackermann, *La Croix* (13 June 1975)),

easily refuting the accusation that the Renewal was close to schism. Edward O'Connor resigned from the National Service Committee at the end of November 1973 because he disagreed with some of the directions that it had taken and, in the French edition of his book *The Pentecostal Movement* (Paris, 1975; p. 295, note 25), he referred to certain errors made by the directors of the 'True House' community at South Bend. This community (mentioned on pp. 93ff. of the American original), was dissolved in the autumn of 1974. Finally, in *La Croix* (4 October 1978), there is a statement of opposition to the indiscretion on the part of a certain group which maintained that those who did not belong to the Renewal were not Christians. Such data, which I have not assembled for the pleasure of doing so, have to be mentioned for the sake of truth and in order to serve the church and the Renewal itself.

34. See W. Hollenweger, *op. cit.* (note 16), pp. 377ff.
35. See, for example, J. Isaac, 'Le Mal, le Christ et le Bonheur', *Cahiers Saint-Dominique*, 169 (October 1977), 20–49.
36. J.-R. Bouchet, *Le Renouveau charismatique interpellé* (Paris, 1976), pp. 41ff. For the 'ministry of deliverance', he refers to Jules Thobois, 'Possession et exorcisme', *Unité des Chrétiens*, 21 (January 1976), 20–22. A correspondent wrote to me from Canada in 1978: 'In certain charismatic groups, in Quebec at least, what is called "exorcism" is practised without rhyme or reason. Certain people, who claim to have the gift of "discernment", see possessed people everywhere and practise "charismatic" exorcism, which they distinguish from "official" exorcism.'
37. See Donald L. Gelpi, *Charism and Sacrament. A Theology of Christian Conversion* (New York, 1976), pp. 115–121.
38. V. Therrien, *Le discernement*, *op. cit.* (note 32), pp. 76, 292. Among other texts of Paul, see especially Rom 12:2; Phil 1:9–10; Eph 5:10.
39. The following list includes some of the many books and articles that have been written fairly recently about discernment. This list can be completed by the works mentioned in the following notes in this chapter and by those contained in V. Therrien's bibliographies, most of which relate to the Bible. A. Cholet, 'Discernement des esprits', *DTC*, IV, cols 1380–1384; J. Guillet, G. Bardy, F. Vandenbroucke and J. Pegon, 'Discernement des esprits', *Dictionnaire de spiritualité*, III, cols 1222–1291; J. B. Scaramelli, *Le discernement des esprits* (Fr. tr.; Brussels and Paris, 1910); J. Mouroux, *L'expérience chrétienne. Introduction à une théologie* (Paris, 1954), pp. 173–181 (for John), 345–365; L. Beinaert, 'Discernement et psychisme', *Christus*, 4 (1954), 50–61; Michel Rondet, 'La formation au discernement personnel et communautaire', *Forma Gregis* (1972), 175–261, repr. in *Choix et discernements de la vie religieuse* (Paris, 1974), pp. 95–221, for adaptations in the community life of female religious; J. Gouvernaire, 'Le discernement chez S. Paul', *Vie chrétienne* (Suppl), 195 (Paris, 1976); F. Urbina, 'Movements of Religious Awakening and the Christian Discernment of Spirits', *Concilium* (November 1973), 58–71. The November 1978 number (109) of *Concilium* is entirely devoted to discernment ('Charisms in the Church'). There is a bibliography of American works on the subject in Donald L. Gelpi, *op. cit.* (note 37), p. 96, note 26.
40. See V. Therrien, 'Le discernement spirituel', *op. cit.* (note 32).
41. There is a good chapter on this subject in John C. Haughey, *The Conspiracy of God: the Holy Spirit in Men* (Garden City, N.Y., 1973), pp. 118–154.
42. The Shepherd of Hermas, XI, 43, 8ff. (*SC* 39 (1958), pp. 195ff.).
43. *Hom.* 18 in *L'Evangile au désert* (Paris, 1965), pp. 152ff. These texts by Macarius and Hermas can also be found in *L'Esprit du Seigneur remplit l'univers*, texts chosen by Sr Geneviève (Paris, 1977), pp. 74–78.
44. See J. Clémence, 'Le discernement des esprits dans les Exercices spirituels de S. Ignace de Loyola', *RAM*, 27 (1951), 347–375; 28 (1952), 65–81; J. Laplace, 'L'expérience du discernement dans les Exercices spirituels de S. Ignace', *Christus*, 4 (1954), 399–404; H. Rahner, ' "Werdet kundige Geldwechsler!" Zur Geschichte der Lehre des hl. Ignatius

von der Unterscheidung der Geister', *Greg*, 37 (1956), 444–483; Leo Bakker, *Freiheit und Erfahrung. Redaktionsgeschichtliche Untersuchungen über die Unterscheidung der Geister bei Ignatius von Loyola* (Würzburg, 1970); J. C. Haughey, *op. cit.* (note 41).

45. V. Therrien, 'Le discernement spirituel', *op. cit.* (note 32), 19.
46. M.-D. Chenu, 'Les signes des temps', *NRT*, 87 (1965), 29–39, repr. in *Peuple de Dieu dans le monde* (*Foi vivante*, 35) (Paris, 1966), pp. 35–55; J.-P. Jossua, 'Discerner les signes des temps', *VS*, 114 (1966), 546–569.
47. See G. Haya-Prats, *L'Esprit force de l'Eglise. Sa nature et son activité d'après les Actes des Apôtres* (Paris, 1975), pp. 208ff. Scriptural evidence: Is 61 for the baptism of Jesus; Ps 69 and 109 for the replacement of Judas; Joel 3 for Pentecost, a promise of the gift of the Spirit for the episode of Cornelius. Approval of the *ecclesia* for this last event: Acts 11:1–8; chapter 15.

3
BAPTISM IN THE SPIRIT

Baptism in the Spirit clearly plays an important part not only in the Pentecostal movement, but also in the New Testament.[1] I shall look briefly at the way in which it is interpreted by the Pentecostalists, then go on to consider the New Testament evidence—Paul, Q, John and Luke (Acts)—before returning to the (Catholic) Renewal and its understanding of the reality.

In Pentecostalism[2]

Pentecostals generally insist on a distinction between rebirth and baptism of the Spirit. The second is experienced as a state of being filled with the Holy Spirit as the apostles were on the day of Pentecost. The key document is Acts, and the other texts are read in the light of that document, in such a way that they constitute, as it were, a 'canon within the canon'. There are, however, within this general framework, two or even three different Pentecostal positions.

Following in the tradition of the Holiness Movement, which itself began with Wesley, many Pentecostal Christians believe that there are two stages or aspects in this process: conversion, which leads to rebirth (baptism with water), and sanctification, which is tied to the baptism of the Spirit. Some of these Christians, but not all, believe that speaking in tongues is the necessary sign of baptism of the Spirit. Others—particularly the Assemblies of God—distinguish three aspects: conversion, baptism of the Spirit and sanctification, which lasts throughout life. Finally, some Pentecostals, especially those who belong to the Apostolic Church, also accept the authority of the 'apostles'.

Paul

(a) We are made Christians by the gift which is made to us of the Spirit, who is the Spirit of Jesus (see Rom 8:9, 14ff.; Gal 3:26–27;[3] 4:6; 1 Cor 12:13; Tit 3:5ff.).

(b) This life given by the Spirit is life 'in Christ'. We enter that life through faith (Gal 3:2) which is expressed and consummated by water-baptism and integration into the death and resurrection of Christ (Rom 6:3ff.; 8:1; Col 2:12). This is why there are so many Pauline texts in which the Spirit is said to be given with water-baptism. Paul wanted the Corinthians to aspire to the gifts of the Spirit and especially to the gift of prophecy (1 Cor 14:1), yet these same Corinthians had been baptized with this baptism. Writing to the Corinthian Christians, Paul said:

> But you were washed, you were sanctified, you were justified in the name of the Lord Jesus Christ and the spirit (Spirit) of our God (1 Cor 6:11).

> For by one Spirit we were all baptized into one body (1 Cor 12:13).

> It is God who . . . has commissioned (= anointed) us; he has put his seal upon us and given us his Spirit in our hearts as a guarantee (= earnest-money) (2 Cor 1:21–22).[4]

> As Christ loved the church . . . that he might sanctify her, having cleansed her by the washing of water with the word (Eph 5:26).

> He saved us . . . in virtue of his own mercy, by the washing of regeneration and renewal in the Holy Spirit (Tit 3:5).

Paul describes the process by which we become Christians and members of the Body of Christ, that is, of the eschatological community to which the promise has been made that it will inherit the kingdom.[5] This process includes (a) faith in the name of Jesus (see 1 Cor 6:11; Acts 19:1–6); (b) being plunged into water; this is something to which faith in Jesus' death and resurrection leads. It is God who gives the Spirit (see 2 Cor 1:21; Tit 3:5; 1 Pet 3:21). That is why we can also speak of being plunged in the Spirit (1 Cor 12:13). All this constitutes the process of becoming a Christian. The decisive aspects are, on our part, faith and, on God's part, the gift of the Spirit.

In the second century, attention was above all directed towards the action of the *Church*: the administration of water-baptism as a public and visible act. Irenaeus stressed the unity that existed between water-baptism and the gift of the Spirit. Later there was a tendency to speak about the water being sanctified by the Spirit and about receiving the Spirit *through* the baptism by water, because it was by the Spirit that one became a Christian.[6] In Paul's teaching, these two are combined in the same simple process, although the rite of baptism cannot legitimately be regarded as the instrumental cause of reception of the Spirit. A connection between the Spirit and water has been made not only in poetry, but also in Scripture itself (see Gen 1:3; Is 44:3ff.; Jn 4:10–14; 7:37–39; Rev 22:1, 17; cf. Ezek 19:10ff.; 47; Ps 1:3; 46:5).[7] This connection has exerted a powerful influence on the Christian imagination and has had an effect on the liturgy and the theology of baptism.

The Synoptics and Q

John the Baptist protests and bears witness: 'I have baptized you with water, but he will baptize you with the Holy Spirit'. This is the basic textual reference for the Pentecostal movement.[8] In the gospels, including the fourth gospel, these texts have a particular context: the fact that groups faithful to the Baptist existed on the fringe of the Church (see Acts 19:1–6). It was therefore important to affirm the originality of the baptism that was given in the name of Christ. J.-P. Dietle has pointed out correctly that the noun 'baptism in the Spirit' was not used by New Testament authors, who used the verb 'baptize in the Spirit', always precisely in order to mark the difference between this and the baptism of John, because the verb drew attention to *the one who was baptizing*. This was Jesus, inaugurating, especially from the time of his own anointing as the Messiah and the gift of Pentecost onwards, the eschatological régime of the Spirit. Within this régime, 'baptizing' should not be identified with the rite. It points to the whole of Jesus' activity and to his mission, which was declared when he received John the Baptist's water-baptism, following by anointing by the Spirit, and which inaugurates the messianic era, which is characterized by the gift of the Holy Spirit.

In Mt 3:11 and Lk 3:16, John the Baptist says: 'I baptize you with water for repentance, but he who is coming after me . . . will baptize you in (the) Holy Spirit and fire'. This is a version of a text from the common source of both the first and the third gospels: Q. In it, John the Baptist announces, at the same time as the coming of the Messiah, the eschatological judgement, which is described in Lk 3:17 (the fire burning the chaff). In both the Old and the New Testaments and in Judaism, the last judgement and fire are closely associated.[9] Why, however, is the Spirit or Breath mentioned in Matthew and Luke in connection with the last judgement? Together with E. Schweizer and M.-A. Chevallier, I think that what we have here is a judgement by the breath of the Messiah or the Son of man; these elements are often closely associated.[10] I am also in agreement with M.-A. Chevallier's interpretation that there is a connection between baptism with water and the gift of the Spirit (see below, under *Luke: Acts*).

John

The key text in this gospel is that contained in Jesus' dialogue with Nicodemus: 'Unless one is born of water and the Spirit, he cannot enter the kingdom of God' (3:5). There have been several excellent studies to help us to understand this text.[11] Jesus himself probably did not speak of water in this context, since it would at that time only have made Nicodemus think of the baptism of John the Baptist. It is, of course, true that all the texts contain the words *hudatos kai*, 'of water and', but this only shows that the Church practised Christian baptism and has always understood the text as announcing that baptism with water. What, however, did Jesus say and what therefore is the fundamental teaching contained in this text? We can grasp it if we place the two words in question between brackets and read the text simply as: 'Unless one is born of Spirit'.[12]

In any case, even in the text as we have it now, the Spirit is not given as the effect of the water. There are two principles—the Spirit *and* the water—yielding the same, single result, rebirth from above. A long exegetical tradition traces 'being born of the Spirit' back to faith or the practice of the virtues. The whole dialogue with Nicodemus is an instruction with a direct bearing on the real object and the real dimensions of Christian faith. John regards the new birth of the Christian as the effect of faith in Christ and of conversion which is the consequence of faith in the gospel.[13] The text refers to 'Spirit' and not literally to faith, and this is because the author is pointing to the action of God.

There are, then, two supernatural causes—that of the Spirit and that of water-baptism, which the Church practised and still practises. There is a close bond between the two—this was clear to the evangelist, and therefore we, who read his canonical text now, are also conscious of it. John, who was one of the Baptist's disciples (see 1:37ff.), records the words of the Baptist with regard to the one who was greater than he and on whom the Spirit descended and remained as the one 'who baptizes with the Holy Spirit' (1:32, 33; cf. 3:34).

In the course of the dialogue with Nicodemus, John tells us that Jesus also baptized with water (3:22, 26),[14] or rather, that his disciples baptized (4:2). The Jesus who baptizes with water (and who was followed by the Church baptizing with water) is the same Jesus who enables man to be born from above by faith in his name (3:15–18) and baptizes in the Spirit. The fourth evangelist was anxious to make a connection between what was practised in the Church and what was said and done during Jesus' ministry on earth. It is clear that the evangelist was thinking, in 3:5, of Christian baptism, which is a baptism both of water and of Spirit. This does not mean that the rite and the water are the instrumental cause of the gift of the Spirit. This may be a theological interpretation, for which there are good arguments in the Church's tradition.[15] The text does not say this: the *kai*, 'and', points, as it does in Tit 3:5, for example, to two associated and combined causes that is all. But baptism of Spirit and baptism of water are not two distinctly separate realities.

Luke: Acts[16]

We will first look at the Lucan texts and then, after reaching a fairly general conclusion, consider the use to which Pentecostal Christians put these texts.

> They were cut to the heart and said to Peter and the rest of the apostles, 'Brethren, what shall we do?' And Peter said to them, 'Repent and be baptized every one of you in the name of Jesus Christ for the forgiveness of your sins; and you shall receive the gift of the Holy Spirit. For the promise is to you and to your children and to all who are far off, every one whom the Lord our God calls to him' (2:37–39).

This basic text is of the first importance for our understanding of Luke's theology of the gift of the Spirit. It proclaims the extension of that gift beyond Jerusalem, according to the plan of the book itself, which is concerned with the promise (1:8). According to the author of the Acts of the Apostles, a kind of Pentecost was to take place in Jerusalem (4:31), in Samaria (8:14–17) and among the gentiles (10:44–47; 15:1–7). In this first sermon, the essential elements follow in this sequence: conversion, baptism in the name of Jesus, that is, by accepting his power as Lord and saviour,[17] and the gift of the Spirit. This is reminiscent of 1 Cor 6:11, which we considered above.

The Samaritans (8:5–25) would seem to have been a special case. Philip's preaching is more 'prophetic' and 'wild' than 'apostolic' and there is also the question of the magician, Simon. The Samaritans 'believed Philip as he preached good news about the kingdom of God and the name of Jesus Christ' and they were baptized. They did not, however, receive the Spirit. To receive the Spirit, they had to have the Pentecost of Jerusalem. This was brought to them by Peter and John, who laid hands on them. It is not said whether they began to speak in tongues.[18] J. D. G. Dunn's interpretation does not strike me as acceptable. He thinks that the Samaritans and Simon (who, according to Dunn, had a very high standing among the Samaritans) did not, to begin with, have real faith in Christ; they rather believed in Philip because he worked miracles. I would also not agree with Walter Hollenweger, who believes that it is possible to be a Christian without having received the Holy Spirit. Two aspects of the case of the Samaritans are particularly striking. In the first place, it is marginal and uncertain. In the second place, the two leading apostles who came from Jerusalem to lay hands on them made them fully members of the eschatological people that had emerged out of Pentecost by means of a kind of *sanatio*.[19]

The case of Cornelius and the first gentile converts is another 'blow' struck by God in which Peter has once again to intervene (see 10:1–11:18). The connection between the word, faith, conversion, baptism, the gift of the Spirit and even, as at Pentecost, speaking in tongues is quite clear, but the initiative is taken entirely by the Holy Spirit, because it was necessary to open a door that God had until then kept closed. The Holy Spirit 'fell on' the group of gentiles gathered in Cornelius' house even before Peter had finished speaking and the gifts of the Spirit preceded their baptism, which was nevertheless required for them to be made members of the Church. This splendid story has, of course, become very well known and it is particular popular among Pentecostal Christians, partly because it seems to them to make a distinction between the baptism of the Spirit and that of water.

Very much the same applies to the case of the disciples who had been imperfectly instructed by Apollos and whom Paul found at Ephesus. They had only received John's baptism. Paul baptized them 'in the name of the Lord Jesus' and then 'when he had laid his hands on them, the Holy Spirit came on them and they spoke with tongues and prophesied' (19:5–6). It would be as wrong to generalize on the basis of this single case and dissociate baptism of the Spirit from water-baptism as it would be to see in this case, and in that of the Samaritans, our sacrament of confirmation.[20] The important aspect of the story is the bond between the gift of the Spirit and the 'name of the Lord Jesus' professed at baptism. The issue is important, because it shows that pneumatology cannot be separated from Christology and soteriology.

I should like to conclude by referring to the view of J. D. G. Dunn, who is followed, with a rather important change of emphasis, by M.-A. Chevallier. We are made Christians by faith in Jesus as our saviour and by the gift of the Spirit. The Spirit is given to faith, but that faith is professed at baptism and consecrated by baptism. We do not baptize ourselves—baptism presupposes the intervention of a Christian who already belongs to the Church, and it is an act by which we become members of that Church, the Body of Christ, to which the Spirit is promised and given. Because we receive the Spirit together with our baptism with water which consecrates the confession of faith, baptism, which is the 'sacrament of faith', is also the sacrament of the gift of the Spirit.[21] 'Confirmation', as we shall see in Volume III, is only a completion of this. Dunn, however, insists on the fact that the Spirit is given *in response to faith*, to the extent that, even though he recognizes that, in Acts, faith and baptism are generally closely connected[22] and thus that baptism is normally followed by the gift of the Spirit, he maintains that 'baptism in the name of the Lord Jesus expresses commitment to Jesus as Lord, [but] the water-baptism itself does not effect entrance into the new age and Christian experience but only points forward and leads up to the messianic baptism in Spirit which alone effects that entrance' (*op. cit.* (note 1 below), p. 99). He also goes on to say: 'The view which regards [Acts] 2:38 as proof that water-baptism is the vehicle of the Spirit is one which has no foundation except in the theology of later centuries' (*ibid*., p. 100). Kittel (see note 1 below) was even more radical in his criticism of the ecclesiastical (Lutheran) theology of baptism and concluded that, according to the New Testament, baptism was not substantially different from John's baptism of repentance!

Dunn regards the sacrament of baptism simply as a rite. In reality, however, baptism is a reality which includes conversion, the Church, an action carried out by God (by Christ through his Spirit) and a rite which refers back to the baptism of Jesus himself, all in one organic whole (see note 21 below). Many exegetes, however, have been more positive than Dunn.[23] M.-A. Chevallier, for example, has said:

> Access to the eschatological reality that is represented by the breath (the Spirit) is obtained by 'conversion' to the gospel and this conversion is signified by baptism with water. The only way by which we can come to the messianic baptism of the

breath is by the baptism of conversion. Luke's parallel between the outpouring at Pentecost and Jesus' baptism is also a way of establishing and emphasizing this connection between a water-baptism to be given henceforth 'in the name of Jesus' and the gift of the breath. Jesus' baptism, which is a baptism both in water and in the breath, joins together the two periods of the history of salvation that are combined in the time before the end (*op. cit.* (note 1 below), p. 198; cf. p. 207).

I am bound, together with other authors who are favourably disposed towards the charisms, to add at this point a critical reference to the use made by Pentecostals generally of the Acts of the Apostles.[24] This book is often employed by them as a 'canon within the canon', as we have already observed. (The comment was first made by Piet Schoonenberg.) In other words, it is used as a norm against which to measure the normative texts of Scripture. The texts dealing with glossolalia are above all singled out. But, apart from Pentecost itself, which is still subject to dispute, what in fact happened? Was it xenoglossia rather than glossolalia? There are only two examples in Acts: 10:46 and 19:6, the case of Cornelius at Caesarea and that of the disciples of John the Baptist at Ephesus respectively. Both of these are, so to speak, mini-Pentecosts in accordance with the plan for expansion which forms the basic structure of Luke's story. As M.-A. Chevallier has pointed out, however:

> It is clearly a mistake to think that it is possible, on the basis of these data, to construct a theory that the gift of the breath is always manifested in glossolalia. This illusion has perhaps come about because, apart from rehearsing over and over again the model of the pouring out of Pentecost, Luke generally does not describe the first communication of the breath. He is usually satisfied with a reference to conversion, faith and the growth of the Church. When he mentions baptism, he often says nothing about the communication of the divine breath which, he believes, accompanies baptism. This is so in the case of the three thousand converts at Pentecost (2:41), the Ethiopian eunuch (8:38), Lydia and her household (16:15), Philip's jailer (16:33) and the group of Corinthians (18:8). He says nothing of the gift of the breath in these cases, and so he does not mention speaking in tongues. In one case, in which he mentions the gift of the breath, that of the baptism of Paul, there is no question of speaking in tongues (9:17ff.). All things considered, it would seem that, far from having thought of glossolalia as a usual sign of the communication of the breath, Luke believed that normally nothing especially remarkable happened when the breath was first communicated at baptism.[25]

It is clear that Luke was particularly interested in the Holy Spirit. At a time when it may perhaps no longer have followed as a simple matter of course that a Christian would be a missionary, he systematically developed that aspect of faith and he did so in connection with the action and interventions of the Spirit. It was on this basis that he compiled his history of the apostles, in which he made full use of visible and tangible manifestations. Sometimes he simplified things and used material representations, as in his account of the resurrection, his story of the early Church and the sudden 'fall' of the Spirit. He worked with great genius and clearly had great religious feeling. It was, however, Paul rather than Luke who provided the primary testimony and the fundamental theology.

The testimony and the interpretation of the Renewal with regard to the Baptism of the Spirit

What is involved here? Men and women are longing for the fullness of the Spirit to come into their lives and dwell and act in them. They may have read about this indwelling and activity of the Spirit and about lives that have been changed and made joyful by it and have wanted the same experience themselves. Or they may have been drawn in by a friend or have been to a meeting to see for themselves. They may at first have hesitated. They may even have been full of doubts and have resisted for a long time. Eventually, however, they have asked for hands to be laid on them and prayers to be said over them.

There is usually a certain preparation and instruction together with prayer. When the moment has arrived, several members of the group pray over the 'candidate' and lay their hands on his head or shoulders. Although the brethren, the community are mediating, it is only God who is acting. Sometimes nothing may seem to be happening to the 'candidate'. At other times an experience of peace and joy and a deep feeling for prayer ensues in a few days. At yet other times, he is invaded by the power of God, who seizes hold of his whole being—his heart, his mind and his feelings. He is perhaps conscious of a gentle inner pressure which makes tears flow. A desire to give thanks rises from his heart to his lips, and this may be expressed as praying in tongues. The Spirit is making himself manifest. His coming is powerfully experienced. We have only to read the testimonies of some of the men and women who have received the Spirit in this way:

> 'I was invaded by a new power of love.'
>
> 'Before, I was on the bank of a river. Now I am in it.'
>
> 'At the time nothing of which I was aware happened. I got up. I felt a bit put out. But very quickly I found inner peace and was quite sure that I had received the gift of God himself. During the time that followed, I experienced a deep certainty of faith, rather like Mary after she had been visited by the angel. It was as if I had discovered for myself the depths of my own heart, the spiritual centre of my being where God dwells. This intimate presence was like an intense but gentle fire' (*VS* (January-February 1974), 125, 126).
>
> 'A new life, I felt, was beginning for me. It consisted above all of an intense consciousness of the presence of God, but also of a new kind of prayer. At times I could hardly bear to tear myself away from that prayer. I found myself living in a climate of great trust and joy' (*ibid*., p. 127).

'We are drawn along by the Spirit in the wake of Christ. The pouring out of the Spirit has handed us over to him. I am no longer afraid' (*ibid*., p. 109).

'My heart was set free.'

'The whole of my being was tingling.'

'I have now begun to see more and more a vision of what life in the Spirit is like. It is truly a life of miracles, of waiting on God for his guidance and teaching, of relying on the power of the Spirit to radically change the lives of men and of being filled over and over with the creative, life-giving love of the Spirit of God' (K. and D. Ranaghan, *op. cit.* (note 29 below), p. 65).

There is a summary of the testimony of some of those who have had this experience in the Malines document:

> . . . a perception of concrete presence. This sense of concrete, factual presence is the perception of the nearness of Jesus as Lord, the realization at the personal level that Jesus is real and is a person. . . . With great frequency this sense of presence is accompanied with an awareness of power, more specifically, the power of the Holy Spirit. . . . This power is experienced in direct relation to mission. It is a power manifesting itself in a courageous faith animated by a new love which enables one to undertake and accomplish great things beyond one's natural capabilities for the kingdom of God. Another characteristic response to presence and power is an intensification of the whole prayer life, with a special love for the prayer of praise. . . . The experience has a resurrection quality about it that is joyous and triumphant. . . . The experience of the Spirit is also the experience of the cross (cf. 2 Cor 4:10). It expresses itself in a continuing *metanoia*. . . .[26]

In a very impressive testimony, a priest made the following extremely interesting suggestion:

> The Bible speaks of two actions of the Holy Spirit: the Spirit who acts 'in' (*pneuma en* in the Septuagint) and the Spirit who acts 'on' (*pneuma epi*). This distinction can be found above all in a prophetic book such as Ezekiel: The 'Spirit in' comes to cleanse (Ezek 36:25–27) and to give life (37:5–10). The 'Spirit on' seizes hold of someone for a mission, often a prophetic mission, and his coming is accompanied by visible signs. . . . The 'Spirit in' who cleanses and gives life accounts for the action of the Spirit in the initial acts of Christian life (baptism, to which must be added confirmation in the Catholic Church) and in sanctifying the believer throughout his life. The 'Spirit on', on the other hand, accounts for the sudden and visible action of the Spirit who seizes hold of someone for a special mission; Luke calls this 'baptism in the Spirit'.[27]

What is the value of this suggestion in terms of exegesis?[28] Theologically, it is interesting and even contains an element of truth. The members of the Catholic Renewal, however, interpret the term 'baptism in the Spirit' perhaps a little too facilely. Sometimes the terms is used but its content is explained—after all, the monastic life used to be interpreted as a second baptism, and Simon Tugwell has observed (see below, note 1) that it was so called because it was (ideally at least!) a way of experiencing baptism more radically and more fruitfully. At other times—fortunately—the term 'baptism in the Spirit' is avoided and other expressions are used instead: 'pouring out or outpouring of the Spirit' or 'renewal in the Holy Spirit', as the Ranaghans would seem to prefer. Whatever the case may be, it is not disputed that there is only one 'baptism' and that this baptism, given and received in faith, in the name of Jesus, communicated the Spirit. What, then, is involved here? The Ranaghans have provided a clear answer to this question:

> 'Baptism in the Holy Spirit' is not something replacing baptism and confirmation. Rather it may be seen as an adult re-affirmation and renewal of these sacraments. an opening of ourselves to all their sacramental graces. The gesture of 'laying on of hands' which often accompanies 'baptism in the Holy Spirit' is not a new sacramental rite. It is a fraternal gesture of love and concern, a visible sign of human corporeality (K. and D. Ranaghan, *op. cit.*, p. 20).[29]
>
> What this new pentecostal movement seeks to do through faithful prayer and by trusting in the Word of God is to ask the Lord to actualize in a concrete living way what the Christian people have already received (*ibid.*, p. 141).
>
> Prayer for baptism in the Holy Spirit is, most simply, a prayer in expectant faith that an individual's or community's baptismal initiation be existentially renewed and actualized (*ibid.*, p. 147).[30]

The theology of the 'divine missions' that I have discussed earlier in this work enables us to situate this new coming of the Spirit theologically,[31] assuming, of course, that the Spirit does in fact come. It is, however, difficult to doubt this when his presence is so clearly revealed by his fruits.[32]

NOTES

1. The following is a selective bibliography of works on baptism in the Spirit: G. Kittel, 'Die Wirkungen der christlichen Wassertaufe nach dem Neuen Testament', *Theologische Studien und Kritiken*, 87 (1914), 25–53; P. van Imschoot, 'Baptême d'eau et baptême d'Esprit', *ETL*, 13 (1936), 653–666; S. Tugwell, 'Reflections on the Pentecostal Doctrine of "Baptism in the Holy Spirit" ', *The Heythrop Journal*, 13 (1972), 268–281, 402–414; J. D. G. Dunn, *Baptism in the Holy Spirit* (London, 1970; 2nd ed. 1977); P. Schoonenberg, 'Le Baptême d'Esprit Saint', *L'expérience de l'Esprit. Mélanges Schillebeeckx* (*Le Point théologique*, 18) (Paris, 1976), pp. 7–96; R. Schwager, 'Wassertaufe, ein Gebet um die Geisttaufe?', *ZKT*, 100 (1978), 36–61, which I found rather disappointing; M.-A. Chevallier, *Souffle de Dieu. Le Saint-Esprit dans le Nouveau Testament,* I: *Ancien Testament. Hellénisme et Judaïsme. La tradition synoptique. L'œuvre de Luc (Le Point théologique*, 26) (Paris, 1978). I have not been able to obtain F. D. Bruner, *A Theology of the Holy Spirit. A Pentecostal Experience and the New Testament Witness* (Grand Rapids, 1970), who seems to have dealt especially with baptism in the Spirit.
2. W. Hollenweger, *The Pentecostals* (London, 1972; Minneapolis, 1972, 2nd ed. 1973), pp. 323–341.
3. See H. J. Venetz, ' "Christus anziehen" ', *Freiburger Zeitschrift für Philosophie und Theologie*, 20 (1973), 3–36.

4. This is, according to G. W. H. Lampe, *The Seal of the Spirit*, 2nd ed. (London, 1967), p. 4, baptism in the Spirit.
5. Apart from J. D. G. Dunn, *op. cit.* (note 1), who studies the texts one after the other, with the intention of excluding both a Pentecostal and a 'sacramentalist' interpretation, see J. K. Parratt, 'The Holy Spirit and Baptism. II: The Pauline Evidence', *The Expository Times*, 82 (1971), 266–271.
6. Irenaeus, *Adv. haer.* III, 17, 2 (*SC* 211, p. 332); V, 11, 2 (*SC* 153, p. 138); *Dem.* 41 (*SC* 62, p. 96); see also A. Benoît, *Le baptême chrétien au second siècle. La théologie des Pères* (Paris, 1953), pp. 205–208. Tertullian speaks of sanctification of the water by the Spirit (*De bapt.* IV, 1) and then says: 'non quod in aquis Spiritum sanctum consequamur sed in aqua emundati sub angelo, Spiritui sancto praeparamur': see *De bapt.* IV, 1 and R. F. Refoulé's note in *SC* 35, p. 75, note 1. The water designates baptism and the Spirit (Jn 4:10): see F. M. Braun, *Jean le théologien*, III: *Sa théologie*, 2: *Le Christ, notre Seigneur hier, aujourd'hui, toujours* (Paris, 1972), pp. 139–164.
7. For water as the symbol of the Spirit, see *Dictionnaire de Spiritualité*, VI, cols 13–19. For poetry, see especially Paul Claudel.
8. See Mk 1:8; Jn 1:33; Acts 1:5; 11:16. The statement can be regarded as authentic: see M. Isaacs, *The Concept of Spirit* (London, 1976), pp. 114–115. There is no article in any of the texts; it is only found in Jn 1:32, in the context of Jesus' baptism. J.-P. Dietle's comments will be found in his article, 'Le réveil pentecôtiste dans les Eglises historiques', *Positions luthériennes* (October 1974), 223–287, especially 250.
9. See E. Schweizer, '*pneuma*', *TDNT*, VI, p. 398, note 417. This theme has been preserved in the liturgy: 'qui venturus es iudicare mundum per ignem'. See also Georges de la Vierge, 'Le signe du feu dans la Bible', *Carmel* (1960), 161–171.
10. E. Schweizer, '*pneuma*', *TDNT*, VI, p. 399; M.-A. Chevallier, *op. cit.* (note 1), pp. 99–108, who suggests that the statement should be seen at three levels: what the Baptist in fact said, what the Christian community understood and what the editor or editors of the present text believed.
11. I. de la Potterie, ' "Naître de l'eau et naître de l'Esprit". Le texte baptismal de Jn 3, 5', *Sciences ecclésiastiques*, 14 (1962), 417–443, repr. in *La vie selon l'Esprit, condition du chrétien* (*Unam Sanctam*, 55) (Paris, 1965), pp. 31–63; F. Porsch, *Wort und Pneuma. Ein exegetischer Beitrag zur Pneumatologie des Johannesevangeliums* (Frankfurt, 1974), pp. 90, 98ff., 125ff.
12. This has been accepted not only by de la Potterie and Porsch, but also by F. M. Braun, who has quoted a number of other authors: see *RSPT*, 40 (1956), 15ff.; *NRT*, 86 (1964), 1032, note 21; 'Le Baptême d'après le IVe évangile', *RThom*, 48 (1948), 358–368.
13. Faith: Jn 1:13; 1 Jn 3:9; 5:1. Conversion: Mk 1:15; Mt 18:3 par. (becoming a child: being born).
14. For this datum and its importance in the interpretation of Jn 3:5, see C. H. Dodd, *The Interpretation of the Fourth Gospel*, 5th ed. (Cambridge, 1960), pp. 308–311; X. Léon-Dufour, ' "Et là Jésus baptisait" (Jn 3, 22)', *Mélanges E. Tisserant*, I (*Studi e Testi*, 231) (Rome, 1964), pp. 295–309; F. Porsch, *op. cit.* (note 11), pp. 50, 125–130.
15. References in I. de la Potterie, *op. cit.* (note 11), p. 33.
16. See E. Schweizer, '*pneuma*', *TDNT*, VI, pp. 413–415; J. D. G. Dunn, *op. cit.* (note 1), chapter 9 (1977 edition, from which I quote), pp. 90–102; M.-A. Chevallier, *op. cit.* (note 1), pp. 195ff.; G. Haya-Prats, *L'Esprit force de L'Eglise* (*Lectio divina*, 81) (Paris, 1975), pp. 130–138, notes pp. 267ff.
17. Further on in Acts, in 19:5, the text: 'in the name of the Lord Jesus' is found. A whole movement of faith is expressed here. See the notes in the Jerusalem Bible on Acts 2:38 and in the French *Traduction œcuménique* on Acts 2:38; 3:16; 4:12.
18. It is also not said that there was speaking in tongues when Paul was baptized, although that baptism was accompanied by the gift of the Spirit (see Acts 9:17, 18).
19. In Acts, the term *prostithēmi*, to be added, joined to, to increase, should be noted (see

2:41, 47; 5:14; 11:24). The Church is apostolic and is therefore only an extension of what began in Jerusalem at Pentecost (see Lk 24:47).

20. M.-A. Chevallier, *op. cit.* (note 1), 202: 'In addition to the Pentecost of the Jews in Acts 2 and that of the gentiles in Acts 10, Luke wanted to show how two special groups, the Samaritans and the disciples of John the Baptist, were able to benefit from the same eschatological outpouring and enter the one people of God. It is therefore possible to speak, by extension, of the Pentecost of the Samaritans and of that of the disciples of John, insofar as these episodes were turning-points of great importance in the missionary spread of the Church. It would go against a true exegetical interpretation of these texts to regard them as examples that could be generalized.'
21. A vitally important sequence is present here: *fides*, faith, designates simultaneously the act of faith on the part of the believer, the creed, and baptism, in which that faith is professed; this latter is traditionally the sacrament of faith: see my *Tradition and Traditions* (Eng. tr.; London and New York, 1966), Part Two, pp. 243–249, text and notes.
22. Referring to Acts 2:38, 42; 8:12ff.; 8:37 (D); 16:14ff.; 16:31–33; 18:8, Dunn adds (*op. cit.*, p. 96): 'In the case of the Ephesians [Acts 19], the sequence of Paul's questions indicates that *pisteusai* [to believe] and *baptisthēnai* [to be baptized] are interchangeable ways of describing the act of faith'.
23. Dunn mentions a great many, whose work is held in high esteem: *op. cit.* (note 1), p. 98, note 17. Haya-Prats also names several exegetes: *op. cit.* (note 16), p. 268, note 40. To these, I would add O. Cullmann: 'There is no Christian baptism without the gift of the Spirit': *Le baptême des enfants et la doctrine biblique du baptême* (Neuchâtel and Paris, 1948), p. 35; E. Trocmé: 'According to Luke, the Holy Spirit is given to everyone who receives baptism in the name of Jesus Christ and who thus becomes a member of the Church': *L'Esprit Saint et l'Eglise. L'avenir de l'Eglise et l'Œcuménisme* (Paris, 1969), p. 25.
24. W. Hollenweger, *op. cit.* (note 2), pp. 336ff.; J. D. G. Dunn, *Jesus and the Spirit* (Philadelphia, 1975), pp. 121, 191; M.-A. Chevallier, *op. cit.*, p. 209.
25. M.-A. Chevallier, *op. cit.* (note 1), pp. 213–214; see also H. Küng, *The Church* (London, 1967), pp. 164–165. The Pentecostals could have concluded that water-baptism calls for another 'baptism', that of the Spirit, but this would, of course, separate the Spirit from the baptism given in faith in the name of Jesus Christ and, as we have seen, there is no question of this at least in the New Testament. Simply as an exegete, Dunn is very critical of the Pentecostals. Hollenweger, *op. cit.*, p. 341, quotes a profession of faith used by the German Pentecostal Mülheim Association: 'The attempt to present the baptism of the Spirit as the second spiritual experience, to be fundamentally distinguished from regeneration, has no basis in Scripture'.
26. *Theological and Pastoral Orientations on the Catholic Charismatic Renewal* (Eng. tr. of Malines document; Notre Dame, Indiana, 1974), p. 22.
27. René Jacob, *Unité des chrétiens*, 21 (January 1976), 16. See also L. Fabre, *Lumière et Vie*, 125 (November-December 1975), 12.
28. Lk 3:16; Acts 11:16 have *en*; Gal 4:6 has *eis*; Acts 1:8; 2:3, 17; 8:16, 17; 10:44ff.; 11:15ff.; 19:6 have *epi*. In Acts 8:16; 10:44, the verb *epipiptō*, 'to fall on', occurs; in 19:6, the verb *ēlthe*, 'came' is used.
29. See also E. O'Connor, *The Pentecostal Movement in the Catholic Church* (Notre Dame, Indiana, 1971), pp. 117, 131ff., especially 136, 215–218. I believe that there is even more than this in the laying on of hands—it expresses a desire to communicate, at God's pleasure, a gift that has been received from him. For brotherly mediation, see K. and D. Ranaghan, *Catholic Pentecostals* (New York, 1969), pp. 148ff.
30. The same interpretation will also be found in H. Caffarel, *Faut-il parler d'un Pentecôtisme catholique?* (Paris, 1973), pp. 21ff., 53–58; J.-M. Garrigues, 'L'effusion de l'Esprit', *VS* (January 1974), 73ff.; F. A. Sullivan, 'Baptism in the Spirit: A Catholic Interpretation of the Pentecostal Experience', *Greg*, 55 (1974), 49–68; Cardinal L. J. Suenens, *A New Pentecost* (London, 1975), pp. 83ff.

31. A.-M. de Monléon, *Istina* (1976), 347, note 19, correctly cites Thomas Aquinas in this context: 'An invisible mission takes place in accordance with a growth in virtue or an increase in grace. . . . Still an invisible mission in accordance with the increase of grace is taken to occur in a special way in one who goes on to a new action or a new state of grace, as, for example, when he is raised to the grace of miracles or prophecy or when he reaches the point when he can, by the fervour of charity, expose himself to martyrdom, give up all his possessions or undertake some very difficult work' (*ST* Ia, q. 43, a. 6, ad 2).
32. E. O'Connor, *op. cit.* (note 29), devotes chapter 6, pp. 141–175, to 'The Effects of the Movement'. This chapter is subdivided into the following sections: Knowledge of God, Prayer, Love of Scripture, Transformation and Deepening, Deliverance, Physical Healings, Peace and Joy, Attitudes towards the Institutional Church, No Instant Sanctity and Durability of Effects.

4
THE RENEWAL AND ECUMENISM

The Renewal and the ecumenical movement were clearly meant to come together—not only because the same Spirit gives them to us as two ways of achieving what he wants to do with us, but also because the Renewal is in contact with and has even absorbed some of the elements of Pentecostalism (if only through reading books) and, in shared meetings, Catholics have prayed with Protestants. The leaders of the Renewal have also thought a great deal about this question. I would like to present and discuss some of these reflections and proposals of various kinds that have been made at different levels.

(1) Paul VI gave Léon Joseph Suenens the task of following the progress of the charismatic Renewal, and the Cardinal participated personally in the movement, exercising his special function of *episkopē*, concern or supervision. The result was the valuable 'Malines document', which appeared in 1974. A second publication, in 1978, was a kind of directory, consisting of eight chapters and 85 paragraphs, so that it would be easier for group study.[1] The Cardinal sees ecumenism and the Renewal as two movements brought about by the Holy Spirit, both directed towards the same end, which is the unity of the disciples of Jesus Christ on the basis of one faith and personal self-giving. On the one hand, we recognize that the Holy Spirit is at work in 'others' and in other Christian communities,[2] while, on the other, ecumenism fundamentally calls for conversion and what the Second Vatican Council called a spiritual ecumenism, using the words first employed by Paul Couturier. As Cardinal Willebrands said at the Renewal Congress held at Rome at Pentecost 1975, 'We need ecumenical activities in all sectors—contacts, dialogues and collaboration—based on the spiritual source which is conversion, holiness of life and public and private prayer'. Cardinal Suenens therefore aimed to give practical guidelines so that Catholic members of the Renewal might experience it as Catholic. He outlined all the necessary precautions and stressed that the Church and the functional charism of the bishops were the guarantee that there would be no deviation in the spread and use of the gifts of the Spirit:

> It would be wrong to succumb to a euphoric state of ecumenism and, in the warmth of newly discovered brotherhood, forget the doctrinal problems that have not yet been solved—the definition of the place and the significance of the sacramental structures and the part played by man in those structures when we speak of the

activity of the Spirit; talk of faith without defining what it contains and means; failure to define a common faith in the Eucharist and the function of the one who presides at the Lord's Supper . . . (cf. *op. cit.* (note 1 below), p. 45).

(2) The following directives were, at the suggestion of Heribert Mühlen,[3] adopted in the course of the third European Charismatic Leaders Conference, held at Craheim Castle, near Schweinfurt, in June 1975:

'There are varieties of gifts, but the same Spirit' (1 Cor 12:4). This also applies to the Churches, which are now separated because of man's fault.

1. *Finding (evaluating) oneself*
Each Church has its own established spiritual tradition and not all the gifts of grace are completely realized in each one. Each Church should therefore ask itself what inalienable vocation it has preserved from its historical origin.

2. *Openness*
Each Church should be capable of recognizing with gratitude the gifts of grace of the other Churches and of being enriched by them. Each Church will then be able to ask itself whether it has not made its own gifts of grace absolute, and to what extent it has a responsibility for the present division in the one Church of Christ. Charismatic openness to all the gifts of the Holy Spirit may in this way make the future of the Church fruitful.

3. *Welcome*
Each Church must, on the basis of its own inalienable vocation, ask itself what it can accept of what is offered by the other Churches, and it must do this by evaluating it critically, if necessary. This receptive attitude must be taken to the very limits of what is possible, since all the gifts of grace are there 'for the common good' (1 Cor 12:7).

We pray to the Lord of the Church that the dialogue between the Churches will lead to convergence and agreement. We know that this can be reached, not by human effort or even by good will, but only by an intervention by Christ who will come again (Mk 10:27; Phil 1:6).

It is not for the author of *Chrétiens désunis* to dispute that this programme is, in what it says at least, essentially in accordance with ecumenism. What it says, moreover, is no different in fact from what is already happening. Ecclesiological questions, however, have to be asked about what the text of this statement does not say. It speaks as though there were no ecclesiological truth, as though a Church of the Spirit began with 1 Cor 12. An ecclesiology, or rather a plurality of ecclesiologies, is, however, implied in the words 'what inalienable vocation it has preserved from its historical origin'. This should certainly be lived critically, since history has undoubtedly burdened the inalienable inheritance with much that is very relative, and at times with what is open to question. Ecumenical theologians are bound to undertake, on the basis of an authentic understanding of history and in dialogue with others, a very radical examination of these forms that have developed in the course of history and have, at certain times, played a very important part in dividing Christianity. This critical examination does in fact yield an ecclesiological core of great importance. Is it really possible to apply the theme of the diversity of gifts of the 'Churches', as though a Church that was indeed universal were composed of the divided Churches, in the way that a community of Christians is composed of people who all have their own gifts and who come together to build up the community by serving it in their own way? It has to be recognized that the Craheim document did not have the task of providing the theological foundations of ecumenism, but we should be clear about what is at stake even in the most generous of approaches.

It is therefore worth trying to elaborate this question of the application of the theme of the charisms to the Churches both positively and critically. Cullmann tried to do it, but limited himself to Catholicism and Protestantism.[4] Following the ideas that he had already developed on the structures of the history of salvation, he suggested that the harmony of the gospel keeps two forces or tendencies—concentration and universalism—in a state of balance. The grace of the Catholic Church is that it is in search of universalism, although there is always a danger of syncretism in the Church's openness to the world and its tendency to lose the purity of concentration on Christ. The charism of the Reformation, on the other hand, has been to reaffirm insistently the demands made by this concentration on the Bible, Christ and justification by faith alone.

> The spiritual *charism* of ideal Catholicism is its universal radiation and its ability to surround the gospel with external forms which can preserve it from disintegration. On the other hand, the special *danger* of Catholicism is to be found both in syncretistic identification with the world and in a juridical narrowing down at the doctrinal and institutional level.
>
> The classical *charism* of Protestantism is its concentration on one centre of radiation and the value that it places on the freedom of the Spirit. The *danger* of Protestantism is to be found, on the one hand, in a hardening and isolation of that central doctrine and, on the other, in a subjectivism without limits which has often led modern Protestantism to undermine the central foundation of Christianity and to accept in a way that is much too wide purely temporal norms that can only be partly assimilated.
>
> The ecumenical task should not be a hurried merging of the Churches, but a confronting of each Church with the duty to become fully conscious of its own charismatic character and then to purify that character and take it to a deeper level. This process of purification will inevitably go against any tendency to be exclusive. The encounter will then take place, not on the periphery, but at the centre—the ideal universalism of Catholicism must be concentrated on the central truth of the gospel and the ideal concentration of Protestantism must therefore become radiation.
>
> Each Church must live in a state of co-existence and close and peaceful collaboration with the other. At the same time, it must deepen and purify its own special charism in such a way that it feels itself obliged to recognize the other's charism, but that it also regards the distortion of the other Church's charism as a serious warning.

(3) Jean-Miguel Garrigues has approached the question from within the Renewal.[5] He expresses, perhaps not a criticism, but at least a certain dissatisfaction with the theological agreements that have been reached, especially those of the mixed commissions and even more those of 'Faith and Order'. They are, he believes, intellectual conclusions which were not based on a community of prayer and express too little hope of a gift of God that moves towards fullness. Although it is doubtful whether this criticism can really be applied to the work of the Dombes group in France, it certainly pinpoints a very real question. The Renewal is a way of experiencing the same mystery of Christ that is experienced at the same time by other Christians and of experiencing it with the brethren, while receiving from it the substance of a living tradition. Many other elements, which are nevertheless connected with the authentic substance of the experience of the same mystery, have been included within this experience, and these have to be purified and so subjected to criticism. What has above all to be done is to take what is valuable in this experience to a deeper level. It is clearly sinful to accuse the other by considering only his purely human aspect and thus failing to be aware of his experience of the fullness towards which we all ought to be moving.

An echo of an experience that is, at its own level and in its more positive aspect, quite beyond dispute can be clearly heard in this approach to the question. As Mgr Pézeril has pointed out, 'God can surely have no stronger way of repudiating our disunity than by this grace, which is poured out on all of us by his Spirit and by which we invoke him, love him, sing his praises and lose ourselves in him'[6] and, I would add, by which we do all this together. Confronted with this experience, a responsible theologian who is speaking in the name of the truth that he is trying to serve nevertheless feels constrained to ask a number of questions. He feels, intervening in this way, rather like a lexicographer in the presence of an inspired poet. But what is he to do if grammar and dictionaries are his profession?

(4) Several Christians who have shared this experience have spoken of the danger of being overcome by the language and therefore by the theology of Pentecostalism.[7] The stories published by the movement were widely read and have in this way exerted a strong influence on the Catholic Renewal, although it is true, as the Ranaghans have observed, that Pentecostalism played hardly any part at all in the origins and early development of the Catholic Renewal. Whether the Renewal shares directly in this way with other Christians or not, however, its fundamental experience of the Spirit is certainly not in itself tied to the forms of the Catholic Church. On the contrary, to use an image that has been suggested, the Renewal covers all the different lakes of the divided Churches with an immense expanse of water that is common to all and is filled by the irresistible rain of the Spirit.[8]

For many members of the Renewal whom I know, there is no special problem—the Church is where they experience the Spirit. This fact is part of a much wider framework: a unity among Christians—or rather, a unity of Christians without any corresponding unity of the Churches—is happening just about everywhere. This is because the level at which the unity of the Renewal exists and the type of unity to which the Renewal points are different from those of the unity sought by ecumenism. The Renewal claims to have gone beyond the latter and in fact speaks of 'post-ecumenism'. But, like the so-called 'secular post-ecumenism', the post-ecumenism of the Renewal has not been able to overcome the problems of Church unity except by simply ignoring them and going either above or around them. I readily accept that this contains a positive aspect at the providential level of reintegration in unity, but I would hasten to add that what is needed is not only spiritual, but also visible unity. It is not possible to give a kind of autonomy to the pneumatological element without at the same time being concerned with the implications of the very necessary Christological reference.[9] If we were to use different theological categories, we would speak of a search for the *res* at the expense of the *sacramentum*—this is closely related to the question of immediacy—and of an attempt to achieve unity in grace without being concerned with the instituted means of grace.[10,11]

There is a classical procedure in theology of making a distinction between two levels, known in Latin as the *res* and the *sacramentum*. God in fact calls us to communion in his life by the mediation of visible and tangible means. These include the history of the patriarchs of Israel, the words of the inspired prophets and psalms, the incarnation—the Word of revelation does not come about simply as a human word, but also becomes flesh—and, on the basis of that incarnation, the ministry of the Twelve and those appointed to succeed them, words, baptism, the Eucharist and other messianic signs. All these have entered human history and have assumed concrete forms. These are, of course, relative, but they are the forms in which the gift of God is offered to us. In this history too, the disciples have become a people, as Israel became a people, beginning with the twelve sons of Jacob. We ourselves can only become fully disciples of Jesus if we become part of that people that is the Church, in solidarity with the apostles and the brethren. 'They devoted themselves to the apostles' teaching and fellowship, to the breaking of bread and the prayers' (Acts 2:42).

All this points to spiritual fruit. The Word is there for our faith. The gospel is there for love and the sacraments are there for grace, that is, our life as sons of God by being incorporated into Jesus Christ. The ministries of the Church are intended to further the spiritual life, our communion with God and our brethren and our offering of our lives in union with the sacrifice of Jesus himself. Existing between these two levels or dispensations, we find once more the dialectical tension between what is 'already' present (the *res*) and what is 'not yet' there (the *sacramentum*). Following J. D. G. Dunn, we have already seen that this forms part of the condition of the Spirit here below.

This is the normal situation and is part of God's plan. It is clear from a survey of history, however, that it is possible for each of these two levels—the spiritual level and that of the visible and tangible means—to develop autonomously. There have been ecclesiologies that have been dominated by a persistent affirmation of the means and have therefore become juridical and clerical in the extreme. There have also been ecclesiologies with an almost exclusive emphasis on the inner life and the immediacy of the spiritual fruit, more or less completely overlooking the visible and tangible means. It is well known, for example, that Luther waged war on both fronts, against those who cried '*Geist! Geist!*', 'Spirit! Spirit!' and those who could only call '*Kirche! Kirche!*', 'Church! Church!' Since his time, there have been, on the one hand, the Quakers and similar groups and, on the other, an entirely juridical and external form of ecclesiology, clearly favouring a uniform and almost monolithic Church society. The opposite tendency, emphasizing the inner life and an immediate relationship with God, is always in danger of leading to an intimate form of individualism and of forgetting the shared demands made by the people of God, the Body of Christ.

The classical theological analysis that I have summarized above may help to throw light on the relationship between the Renewal and the sort of ecumenism that aspires towards the embodiment of all Christ's disciples in a visible unity of one Church. There may clearly be a unity at the level of spiritual fruits and realities in a meeting of prayer, openness and devotion to Jesus and the Spirit, since, in such a meeting, the same Lord and the same Spirit are communicated with great intensity. A unity is therefore reached which goes beyond confessional membership and Church divisions. We have seen that, in the creed, the article in which we confess faith in the Church is connected with that on the Spirit. This means, then, that a certain Church unity is also reached in these meetings. This is already a very great deal, and we thank God fervently for it.

At the same time, however, unity has not been reached. This was sadly obvious at the Pentecost meeting between Christians of different Churches at Lyons in 1977. The Church and its particular unity consists of different elements and exists at a different level. The ultimate level may have been encountered, but the penultimate has been missed out. The Church is, we know, the beginning of the Kingdom, but it is so in the sense of being its vestibule. The Temple contains an altar of sacrifices and a holy place of incense and showbreads before the Holy of Holies is reached. The Church is not simply communion in and through the Spirit—it is also a sacrament. It is also the word and the confession of faith. It is the celebration of the Eucharist and the other sacraments. It is a community and it is ministries. It is a personal and communal discipline. In all these respects, we are not yet united. We may therefore conclude that, as such, the Renewal is not *the* solution of the monumental ecumenical problem. This problem calls for other attempts as well and, thank God, they are being made today.

It is, however, legitimate also to put the question whether unity in the spiritual realities that can be achieved by the Renewal will leave those differences and divisions that exist at the level of the 'sacrament' untouched. Here we need to let those who are active in the Renewal and at the same time belong to different Churches bear witness. My own contribution must be more modest. Each of us can only sing the song that he has been given to sing. My song is that of a theologian and I am neither proud nor ashamed of it. In this particular case, it consists of four verses:

(1) Praying together, meditating together about the Word of God and observing that those who belong to different Churches obviously have gifts of the Spirit, those who take part in ecumenical meetings and even more particularly those who are members of the Renewal are able to recognize each other as authentic Christians and as possible brothers, because they are already real brothers. They cannot dispute that there are difficulties which have not yet been resolved, but they feel that they will be transcended one day. What unites them is stronger than what separates them.

(2) The present emphasis on pneumatology is one of the factors that is currently changing the face of the Church and the significance of our membership of it as a living reality. This applies above all to the present importance given to the charisms in the sense in which Paul speaks of them, especially in Rom 12:6 and 1 Cor 12:4ff., that is, in the sense of gifts or talents which are given to each one of us and which the Holy Spirit wants to be used by us for the building up of the Body of Christ or of the communities of disciples. In the conditions that I have discussed elsewhere in this work, these charisms are used as *ministries*. The Church is, in this sense, no longer defined in terms of its priesthood, consisting of priests carrying out their task with lay people as their 'clients'. Instead, it is seen as a community that is being built up by the brotherly contributions made by all its members. This does not mean that the ordained ministry is no longer required. That ministry is still indispensable. It does, however, mean that the Church can be and is being declericalized. It also commits us in principle to a fully Trinitarian view, in contrast to the pre-Trinitarian monotheism or what A. Manaranche called the 'Jesuanism' of the past, both of which were inadequate.

(3) It is possible to transfer to the Churches and to the great traditions or spiritual families this fundamentally pneumatological and Trinitarian theology of the charisms. I would not wish to accept O. Cullmann's suggestion (see below, note 4) or the theme of a 'conciliar community' that is so favoured at present by the World Council of Churches without asking a number of questions, but I would agree with what Brother Roger Schutz said on 1 February 1977 at Zürich: 'If two people who are separated are trying to

be reconciled with each other, they have first of all to discover the specific gifts that are present in the encounter. If each one claims to have all the gifts and believes that he can contribute everything without receiving anything, there will never be any reconciliation. The same applies to reconciliation between the Churches.'

This means that the great Christian communities, which often represent distinct cultural settings, have also incorporated equally distinctive gifts of the Spirit and these have to be respected in a unity of faith, the Eucharist, ministry and mission, the bond of which is the same Spirit. In the last of the Malines Conversations held during the nineteen-twenties, Cardinal Mercier read, it may be remembered, a report by Dom Lambert Beauduin, in which the latter insisted that the 'Anglican Church should be united with Rome, but not absorbed'. Pope Paul VI more recently took up the same idea. Ecumenism has the task of trying to apply this principle by respecting at once the demands made by the true unity of the Church and the originality of the gifts of the One who distributes them 'as he wills'. The experience and the reflection that are required in the Renewal movement will, if they are deepened in a climate of humility and patience, perhaps help us to search for unity in a way that goes far beyond our human means.

(4) My deeply spiritual friend Dom Clément Lialine, towards the end of his life, attacked the heresy which he called ecclesiolatry or ecclesiocentricism. By this he meant making the Church absolute and giving a supreme value to the Church and all that concerns it, rather than to God, the Word, God's initiative and the gospel. This is a very delicate matter. Rather like prayer in relation to the perfection of the sons of God, the Church is a means consubstantial to the end in view. It is therefore not possible to oppose or separate the two. Irenaeus expressed this idea perfectly in a formula which is so balanced that it proclaims a very difficult programme: 'Ubi enim ecclesia, ibi est Spiritus Dei; et ubi Spiritus Dei, illic ecclesia et omnis gratia'—'Where the Church is, there is also the Spirit of God and where the Spirit of God is, there is the Church and all grace'.[12] Is the presence of the Spirit conditioned by the Church or does the Church have to be defined by the presence and the manifest action of the Spirit? Reformed Christians would be very happy with the second of these statements, whereas Christians of the Counter-Reformation would prefer the first. A truly Catholic synthesis calls for both. Would the Renewal not perhaps be a favourable place in which to conduct the search for this synthesis?

There are, however, certain conditions. The first is that those who belong to the Renewal should recognize that they have no monopoly of the Spirit and also that the Renewal and its activities do not form a Church for them. It is quite right that they should love the Renewal and that it should make them happy, but it would be unsound if they made it into their Church. They should above all form part of the great Catholic community with its sacraments, its pastors, its activities, its mission and its service to the world. They should fully accept its history and its life, in solidarity with their brethren who do not belong to the Renewal, but who are also animated by the Spirit and in whom the Spirit also dwells. All this is very obvious and hardly needs to be said, but there is some value in repeating it. A sound and critical rejection of any form of ecclesiolatry should find its place within an immense, deep and warm love of the Church, and experience has shown that such a love is very favourable to a life of prayer and praise.

The second condition is, as it were, the basis for the first. It is concerned with the soundness of all life in and through the Spirit. I have already criticized what my Orthodox friends call Christomonism in an article published some years ago.[13] This name is given to a theological construction that is so firmly linked to Christ that the Spirit is in danger of being forgotten. As long ago as 1934, Pastor Charles Westphal told me: 'You Catholics often give me the impression that you want to economize on the Holy Spirit'. We ought to take this comment seriously and give the Holy Spirit his rightful place. The soundness of any pneumatology, however, is dependent on its reference to Christ. The Spirit is the object of a special 'mission'. Pentecost followed the incarnation and Easter. The eucharistic consecration is brought about by the account of the institution *and* by the epiclesis. The Spirit, however, does not do any work other than that of Christ. There is only one economy of salvation and only one baptism, which is both in the paschal event of Christ and in the Spirit. Both Paul and John make the reference to Christ a criterion for the action of the Spirit:

> No one speaking by the Spirit of God ever says 'Jesus be cursed!' and no one can say 'Jesus is Lord' except by the Holy Spirit (1 Cor 12:3).

> 'The Paraclete, the Holy Spirit, whom the Father will send in my name, he will teach you all things and bring to your remembrance all that I have said to you' (Jn 14:26).

> 'When the Spirit of truth comes, he will guide you into all the truth; for he will not speak on his own authority, but whatever he hears he will speak. . . . He will glorify me, for he will take what is mine and declare it to you' (Jn 16:13–14).

> By this you know the Spirit of God: every spirit which confesses that Jesus Christ has come in the flesh is of God and every spirit which does not confess Jesus is not of God (1 Jn 4:2–3).

To accept a Christological criterion for the authenticity of a pneumatology is fundamentally to look for the way in which the actions and the fruits that are attributed to the Holy Spirit are of a piece with or at least in accordance with the work of the incarnate Word, Jesus Christ the Lord. The Spirit is the breath and he is the dynamism; he is both the inner life and the power. He makes the gift of God that comes to us in Jesus Christ personal and inward—he is 'sent into our hearts' (Gal 4:6). At the same time, he also urges the gospel forward, within the unknown context of the 'things that are to come' (Jn 16:13). The Word is the form and the face given to the communication of God's gift: the word, the teaching; the visible signs of our communion, baptism, the Eucharist and the other sacraments; the ministry of the Twelve who were appointed to undertake a universal mission (Mt 28:19–20), and the function of Peter within the apostolic college. The Spirit, together with the Word, has entered man's history and in that history they have together brought about the Church, its Tradition and the testimony of its saints. Accepting a Christological criterion for the genuineness of a pneumatology is to recognize the freedom of the Spirit to 'blow where he wills' (Jn 3:8; 2 Cor 3:17), but it is also to affirm that that freedom is at the same time the freedom of truth (Jn 8:31; the 'Spirit of truth': 16:13) and that the 'mission' or the coming of the Spirit is related and in agreement with that of the Word. It is the Spirit who makes us members of the Body of Christ (1 Cor 12:13; Rom 8:2ff.), but that Body is not the Body of the Holy Spirit—it is the Body of Christ.

To return now to the question of what the Renewal—in the Spirit—can contribute to ecumenism, we can now see that it does not leave the difficult question untouched. It experiences the truth that the Church is built up from within and that communion in love is higher than any external organization or mediation. But at the same time, it would be wrong to regard itself as achieving unity beyond and in spite of all the differences that continue to exist. The ecclesiological problem continues in the form of a Christological reference to the institution of the Lord, the *sacramentum* of the Church that he founded. This cannot simply be erased in the name of an immediate experience of the Spirit and his fruits.

The Spirit and Christ, the Word, condition each other. The Spirit is referred to the Word. He does not do away with the demands made by the Word. He makes the way open to them, so that the Word becomes present, inward and dynamically active. In a biblical meditation of great depth, Etienne Garin, a Catholic member of the Renewal, has said: 'Without the Spirit, the Word is barren, like a seed without water. Without the Word, the Spirit is blindly wandering in search of water without the seed.'[14] O great, holy and enthralling Church—you are the Body of Christ and the Temple of the Holy Spirit, the City built on the Lord's apostles and the place where the Spirit 'who has spoken through the prophets' is active!

NOTES

1. Cardinal L. J. Suenens, *Ecumenism and Charismatic Renewal: Theological and Pastoral Orientations* (Eng. tr.; Ann Arbor and London, 1978).
2. A quotation from Vladimir Soloviev appears on p. 108 of the document, *op. cit.*: 'In order to come closer to one another, we have to do two things: the first is to ensure and intensify our own intimate union with Christ; the second is to venerate, in the soul of our brother, the active life of the Holy Spirit who dwells in him'.
3. H. Mühlen has developed this programme in *Morgen wird Einheit sein. Das kommende Konzil aller Christen: Zeil der getrennten Kirchen* (Paderborn, 1974). My critical review of this book was published in *RSPT*, 59 (1975), 517–519.
4. O. Cullmann, *Vrai et faux Œcuménisme* (*Cahiers théologiques*, 62) (Neuchâtel, 1971).
5. J. M. Garrigues, 'L'Œcuménisme', *Il est vivant*, 18 (Spring, 1978), 3–6, 13–15.
6. Daniel Pézeril, in his preface to John V. Taylor, *Puissance et patience de l'Esprit* (1977), p. 12 (Fr. tr. of *The Go-Between God* (London, 1972)).
7. Not only J.-R. Bouchet, *Le Renouveau charismatique interpellé* (*Collection Renouveau*, 5) (Paris, 1976), p. 188, but also W. Storey, *ibid.*, pp. 99, 119, have pointed to this danger. Others who have referred to it are the Protestant pastor L. Dallière and the contributors to *Pro Mundi Vita*, 60 (1976). See above, pp. 147–148.
8. See Jim Brown's parable, reported by A. Wohlfahrt in *Foi et Vie* (July-October 1973), 11, and before this by G. Appia in *Réforme* (11 November 1972). See also, in the same number of *Réforme*, 67, J.-P. Gabus: 'The present movement brought about by the Holy Spirit is creating in the West *an entirely new Church* which will be neither Catholic nor Protestant, but simply evangelical or, if you like, Catholic-Orthodox-Evangelical'.
9. By 'Christological reference' I mean not only the person of the Lord Jesus, his teaching, his cross and his demanding programme, but also the introduction of these into the Church and the means of grace that come from the incarnate Word. The danger that a 'Church' will be formed from the experience of warmth and security that is shared in meetings, is by no means imaginary.
10. Paul VI pointed several times to a tendency to overestimate the charismatic aspect of the Church at the expense of its hierarchical and sacramental structures: see the references in E. O'Connor, 'Charisme et institution', *NRT*, 96 (1974), 3–19, especially 4, note 4.
11. What follows is based on my article, 'Propos sur l'Œcuménisme et Renouveau par l'Esprit', *Tychique*, 13–14 (January 1978), 81–86.
12. Irenaeus, *Adv. haer.* III, 24 (*SC* 211 (1974), p. 474).
13. See my study, 'Pneumatologie et "christomonisme" dans la tradition latine', *Ecclesia a Spiritu Sancto edocta. Mélanges théologiques. Hommage à Mgr Gérard Philips* (Gembloux, 1970), pp. 41–46.
14. E. Garin, 'Construire l'unité bien sûr, mais quelle unité?', *Tychique*, 13–14 (January 1978), 89–95, especially 91.

CONCLUSION

'IN THE UNITY OF THE HOLY SPIRIT, ALL HONOUR AND GLORY'

The two 'missions' of the Son and of the Holy Spirit, proceeding from the Father and taking place in favour of creatures, return to the Father in cosmic, universal and total praise.

A. IN JESUS, GOD GAVE HIMSELF A HUMAN HEART, PERFECTLY THE HEART OF A SON

The Father said: 'You are my beloved Son, with whom I am well pleased' and again and again Jesus said: 'You are my Father; I have come to do your will'.

Did this dialogue begin in the eternity of the life within the Trinity? Is it possible to detect in it the formula of what is known in theology as the active and the passive begetting? We can only do this on condition that we do not distinguish a duality or a trinity of consciousnesses.[1] It is, of course, true that the temporal 'missions' of the second and the third Persons are the term of the eternal processions in creatures, but the divine begetting of the Word, the Son, ends in a conscious and free humanity which has something to say to the Father, and that is: 'You are my Father; you have prepared a body for me; I have come to do your will' (see Ps 40:7; Heb 10:5–9). The Son's words can only be transferred to the Father in the 'essential' or immanent Trinity if we see the 'You are my Father' as the fruit *constituted* by the 'You are my Son', in other words, as an expression of passive begetting.[2]

We shall therefore examine only the dialogue between the Father and the holy but human consciousness of Jesus. When the Holy Spirit made Mary's capacity as a woman to be a mother active in her, what he did was to bring about in her a humanity which the Father was truthfully to address with the words: 'You are my beloved Son' (see Heb 1:5ff.). The hypostatic union that took place at that time was the personal act of the Word-Son, but the Spirit (perhaps by appropriation?) brought about the sanctification of that first human beginning, causing a son's soul and a son's love to arise in him. In the language of classical theology, this would be called the operation of sanctifying grace, the absolute fullness of which was given to Jesus as the Head and the first of many brethren ('capital grace').

Ought we—and is it possible—to attribute, from that moment onwards, to the first seed of man in Mary the response 'You are my Father', the principle of which in him would be the sanctifying Spirit? The author of the Epistle to the Hebrews says: 'When Christ came into the world, he said, "Sacrifices and offerings thou hast not desired, but a body hast thou prepared for me. . . . Then I said, 'I have come to do thy will, O God' " ' (10:5ff.). This is a global proclamation about the disposition of the soul of Christ, who 'through the eternal Spirit offered himself without blemish to God' (Heb 9:14; cf. Phil 2:8). What is certain is that God aroused in Jesus a human heart that was perfectly the heart of a son and an absolute adorer. I have already discussed this to some extent above, when I spoke of Jesus' soul as Son.[3] And what should we say about his life of prayer and the nights that he spent praying in solitude?[4] At the same time, however, we have, for our own inspiration, to recall the great moments of the relationship 'You are my Son' and 'You are my Father'.

When he was twelve years old, Jesus remained behind in Jerusalem after the feast was over and the pilgrims had left. After three days of searching, his parents found him again in the Temple. He asked: 'How is it that you sought me? Did you not know that I must be in my Father's house?' (Lk 2:49). What consciousness did Jesus have of his relationship with his Father at the level of his human knowledge? As we have already seen, the substantial union that existed between his humanity and the Person of the Word, the Son, left to his human nature the normal use of his faculties. He had also to enter into his Father's plan for him on the basis not of clarity, but of obedience. This episode in Luke's gospel shows, however, that, in his understanding of his relationship with his Father, he was at that time already more advanced than his parents, despite the fact that they had some evidence of a supernatural mystery.

When he was baptized by John the Baptist, Jesus was anointed by the Spirit for his messianic work: 'When he came up out of the water, immediately he saw the heavens opened and the Spirit descending upon him like a dove; and a voice came down from heaven, "Thou art my beloved Son; with thee I am well pleased" ' (Mk 1:10–11). According to Luke, Jesus was at prayer—'Thou art my Father; I have come to do thy will'—and the Spirit descended on him and a voice from heaven said: 'Thou art my Son; today I have begotten thee' (Lk 3:22, referring to Ps 2:7). In the dispensation with the Trinity, 'the Father begets his Son incessantly, in a perpetual today'.[5] He begets him in Jesus the man in accordance with the stages of the 'economy': conception, baptism–messianic anointing (see Acts 10:38), resurrection and glorification, until the *humanity* of Jesus is invested with the sovereign condition of a humanity of the Son of God, that humanity mentioned in 1 Cor 15:45 and Phil 2:9–11.

In his prayer, through the Spirit which descended on him and the voice which applied to him the words referring to the Servants: 'My servant whom I uphold, my chosen, in whom my soul delights' (Is 42:1), Jesus quite consciously accepted obedience as a son which would impose on him the way of the Servant. He cleaved in advance to the will of his Father as expressed in the gospels by such formulae as 'It was necessary that . . .' or 'so that the Scriptures might be fulfilled'.[6] Very soon, moreover, Jesus was put to the test with regard to his obedience to the way of the Servant, and the demon contrasted that way with his condition as the 'Son of God': 'If you are the Son of God . . .'. Jesus, however, was led into the wilderness by the Spirit, with whom he was filled (Lk 4:1), with the result that his reply to the demon points to his own submission: 'You shall worship the Lord your God and him only shall you serve' (4:8).

Augustine said: 'Just as being born was, for the Son, being from the Father, so too was being sent, for the Son, knowing that he was from him'.[7] In other words, it is saying to him: 'You are my Father'. That is precisely what Jesus confessed throughout the whole of his public life:

> In that same hour he rejoiced in the Holy Spirit and said, 'I thank thee, Father, Lord of heaven and earth, that thou hast hidden these things from the wise and the understanding and revealed them to babes; yea, Father, for such was thy gracious will' (Lk 10:21).
>
> 'My food is to do the will of him who sent me and to accomplish his work' (Jn 4:34; cf. Mt 7:21).
>
> 'As the living Father sent me and I live because of the Father . . .' (Jn 6:57).
>
> 'My teaching is not mine, but his who sent me' (Jn 7:16)
>
> 'I do nothing on my own authority, but speak thus as the Father taught me' (8:28; 12:49–50; 14:10).
>
> 'I always do what is pleasing to him' (8:29).
>
> 'I do as the Father has commanded me, so that the world may know that I love the Father' (14:31).

This last statement ends with the words: 'Rise, let us go hence'. Jesus was, in other words, leaving the upper room to go to Gethsemane. Those who witnessed his agony were the same men who witnessed the transfiguration, at which the same words that were spoken at the theophany of the Father at Jesus' baptism were pronounced: 'This is my beloved Son, with whom I am well pleased; listen to him' (Mt 17:5; Mk 9:7; Lk 9:34–35).[8]

The agony in the garden was the dramatic occasion of Jesus' cry to the Father: 'Abba, Father, all things are possible to thee; remove this cup from me; yet not what I will, but what thou wilt' (Mk 14:36). This is another way of saying: 'You are my Father; I have come to do your will'. Did the Father reply to this cry? In Lk 22:42, an angel comforts Jesus, and John goes even further: ' "Now my soul is troubled. And what shall I say? 'Father, save me from this hour'? No, for this purpose I have come to this hour. Father, glorify thy name". Then a voice came from heaven, "I have glorified it and I will glorify it again" ' (Jn 12:27–28).

This brings us to Jesus' crucifixion. According to Heb 9:14, he offered himself through an eternal spirit and this text has been included in the prayer before communion in the Roman rite of the Mass: 'cooperante Spiritu Sancto'. Jesus began with the opening words of Ps 22: 'My God, my God, why hast thou forsaken me?' when he was dying (Mt 27:46; Mk 15:34), his 'You are my Father' becoming an appeal to the absent one: 'O Son without a Father! O God without God!'[9] I am personally convinced, however, that he continued this psalm or at least said some of the later verses, expressing the hope of 'You are my Father' in his heart:

> In thee our fathers trusted;
> they trusted and thou didst deliver them.
> To thee they cried and were saved;
> in thee they trusted and were not disappointed. . .
> Since my mother bore me, thou hast been my God
> (Ps 22:4–5, 10).

In Luke 23:46, Jesus' last words are taken from another psalm (31:5): 'Father, into thy hands I commit my spirit'.[10]

The Father's response came a day and a half later and consisted of the words: 'You are my Son' said in absolutely new conditions: 'The good news that what God promised to the fathers, this he has fulfilled to us his children by raising Jesus; as also it is written in the second psalm: "Thou art my Son, today I have begotten thee" ' (Acts 13:32–33). Paul makes it clear in what way the Son was begotten on that day: 'The gospel concerning his Son, who was descended from David according to the flesh and designated Son of God in power according to the Spirit of holiness by his resurrection from the dead, Jesus Christ our Lord' (Rom 1:2–4). The same Son of God, the same Christ, after having assumed the condition of a servant and after having obeyed to the point of death on the cross—'You are my Father; I have come to do your will'—received from God, his Father, the sovereign condition of *a humanity of the Son of God* and the title of Lord (Phil 2:6–11; Acts 2:36; Rom 14:9). The same Holy Spirit, by whose power a shoot from the line of David had been brought forth, a descendant who was to be called Son of God, enabled Jesus to be born, as an eschatological gift, to the glory that was appropriate for the Son of God. Jesus was therefore able to give the same Spirit himself (1 Cor 15:45; Jn 7:37–39).

B. IN JESUS, WE ARE DESTINED TO BE SONS OF GOD; HE COMMUNICATES FILIAL LIFE TO US THROUGH HIS SPIRIT

We are called to be sons in the Son:

> Those whom he foreknew he also predestined to be conformed to the image of his Son, in order that he might be the first-born among many brethren (Rom 8:29).

> He chose us in him before the foundation of the world, that we should be holy and blameless before him. He destined us in love to be his sons through Jesus Christ. ... In him you ... were sealed with the promised Holy Spirit, which is the guarantee of our inheritance (Eph 1:4–5, 13–14).

> Because you are sons, God has sent the Spirit of his Son into our hearts, crying: 'Abba! Father!' So through God you are no longer a slave, but a son and, if a son, then an heir (Gal 4:6–7).

> If the Spirit of him who raised Jesus from the dead dwells in you. ... You have received the Spirit of sonship. When we cry, 'Abba! Father!' it is the Spirit himself bearing witness with our spirit that we are children of God and, if children, then heirs, heirs of God and fellow-heirs with Christ (Rom 8:11, 15–17).

These passages are enormously rich and we can draw certain propositions from them which it is easy and delightful to illustrate with comments made by the Church Fathers.

We are predestined in Christ. This means that God (the Father) has included us in the plan of grace that he has brought about and is still bringing about through the one to whom he said: 'You are my Son' when Jesus was conceived, baptized, resurrected and glorified.[11] We, then, are loved by the same love with which the Father loved his Son.[12]

God's effective love constitutes us as sons. There is a difference, of course, between being a Son by nature and a son by adoption[13] and Jesus in fact made this difference explicit.[14] John points to it in his gospel and epistles by using *huios* for the first and *tekna* for the second.[15] Despite this, however, we are really sons of God by adoption and by grace. We form with the Son one single being as sons.[16] He is the only Son (*Monogenēs*), but he is also the first-born of many brethren. That is why the Father is able to say, in Jesus and thanks to him, to us: 'You are my son'.

We are sons by the Holy Spirit, that is, by a communication of the Spirit of the Son (see Gal 4:6; Rom 8:14ff.). That Spirit enables us to pray: 'Abba! Father!' and he is in us like water which whispers 'Come to the Father!'[17] Thanks to Christ, 'we both have access in the one Spirit to the Father' (Eph 2:18).

If it is true, then, that the Father says to us: 'You are my son' through and in the two missions of the Son and the Spirit, how are we to respond to him and say: 'You are my Father; I have come to do your will'? We can do this by praying: 'Our Father, . . . hallowed be thy name. Thy kingdom come, thy will be done, on earth as it is in heaven . . .' (Mt 6:9ff.). We can also respond to him by directing the whole of our life towards him. Life led in this way is a 'spiritual sacrifice' of the kind described by Paul in Rom 12:1, or it may be a life lived according to the Spirit, in a struggle against the 'flesh', as described in a previous chapter. Finally, it is also possible to orientate our life towards God in the same direction as the Servant who sacrificed himself and thus became a source of life for others. This applies to all believers, but more particularly, of course, to the ministers of the gospel.

Paul was conscious of the fact that this quality of sons of God, the earnest-money or guarantee of which has been placed in us by the Spirit, also has a cosmic dimension. The destiny of the world was, he believed, closely connected with ours and it too was waiting for an Easter through which it would come to share in the glory and freedom of the children of God (see Rom 8:18–25; cf. Eph 1:3–14).

This is and will be possible because the same Spirit exists in Christ, our Head, and in all his members or his Body. He is present in fullness in our Head and he has existed as such in him from the very beginning as the principle of holiness, and since Christ's 'sitting at the right hand of the Father' as the power of the Lord, who received that power from his messianic anointing (Acts 10:38), but not in the way he received the Spirit when he had been exalted to the right hand of God, as Lord, and as such able to pour it out (Acts 2:33–36; Jn 7:39). Corresponding to our own predestination to be sons in the Son who is the first-born of many brethren is the fact that it is by the same, identically the same, Spirit, *idem numero*, that we are such sons.[18] He is, however, in our Head in absolute fullness, whereas he is in us according to the measure of God's gift and according to the degree of welcome that we give him.

C. THE SPIRIT OF GOD FILLS THE UNIVERSE HE GATHERS EVERYTHING THAT EXISTS IN IT FOR THE GLORY OF THE FATHER

'The Spirit of the Lord has filled the world and that which holds all things together knows what is said' (Wis 1:7)—'Thy immortal breath is in all things' (12:1). There is clearly an echo of Stoicism in these statements, but the theme has been completely theologized. What we have here is the breath of *Yahweh*.[19] As C. Larcher has pointed out,[20] this theme has clear antecedents: the breath of God was not simply extended to man (Gen 2:7; 6:3; Job 21:3; 33:4; Ezek 37; Eccles 12:7)—it was also given to all living creatures (Ps 104:28–30; Job 34:14–15). What is more, the 'Breath of God' is also the creative Breath (Jdt 16:14; Ps 33:6; 104:30). Like Wisdom, the Spirit of God is at work everywhere.

1. *The Spirit is at work everywhere*

The Fathers were certainly convinced of this. Following the apologists, what they developed was rather the theme of the Logos who was present and active in every true thought and who made the world rational.[21] But Irenaeus believed that the gift of the heavenly Spirit was sent *in omnem terram*—'into the whole of the earth',[22] that he had been 'poured out in these latter days on the whole of mankind'[23] and that 'he descended on the Son of God who had become the Son of man and that, with him, he was therefore able to dwell in the human race, rest on men and live in the work fashioned by God'.[24]

The Christian authors living and writing before the Scholastic period agreed that the Holy Spirit was the principle of all true knowledge.[25] The mediaeval theologians were fond of quoting and commenting on a maxim first used by Ambrosiaster, which they attributed to Ambrose of Milan: 'Omne verum, a quocumque dicitur, a Spiritu Sancto est'—'All truth, no matter where it comes from, is from the Holy Spirit'.[26] Some of them believed that this was the truth about God, while others spoke of judgements involving the will. Thomas Aquinas sometimes cited the principle without any further explanation,[27] but he also made a distinction between the natural light that came from God and the light that came from the gifts of grace,[28] or else between simple present movements of the Holy Spirit *movente, sed non habito* and lights given to living faith.[29] Albert the Great accepted a much wider concept of 'grace' and, in reply to the question as to whether all truth that is the object of knowledge was inspired by the Holy Spirit, he said: yes, so long as every gift that is gratuitously given by God is called grace.[30] This was, he thought, the case with existence itself.

Today, Christians are inclined to revive this Ambrosian theme and even to extend it. There is evidence of this, for example, in the Pastoral Constitution *Gaudium et Spes*, promulgated at the end of the Second Vatican Council.[31] The Orthodox theologian Georges Fedotov believes that the Spirit is active in the dynamism of the cosmos and in the inspiration of everyone who creates beauty and is convinced that the Church should try to overcome the ambiguity in this situation by applying the criterion of the cross.[32] There is open recognition in *Gaudium et Spes*, 44, of the Church's debt to man's efforts in society and culture in the task of proclaiming the message of Christ. Although he does not explicitly refer to this text, the Protestant theologian Langdon Gilkey has expressed his conviction that the dialogue between the Church and its theologians on the one hand and the world and its cultural representatives on the other is of benefit to both and that this presupposes the presence of the Spirit in both.[33] The same principles, he believes, should also be applied with increasing urgency to our dialogue with other religions. I would certainly agree with him and in this I would also be supported even by such a firm and classically Catholic man of the Church as the nineteenth-century Cardinal Manning.[34] It would not be at all difficult to find many texts on the presence of the Spirit and his work in the life of men.[35]

An Anglican theologian, John V. Taylor, the Bishop of Winchester, has made a connection between what I have said about the active presence of the Spirit everywhere and the special character of the third Person. He calls the Spirit, understood in this sense, the 'go-between God', that is, the God who acts as a kind of broker and who penetrates subtly everywhere in order to create true relationships. The Holy Spirit, he says, is 'that unceasing, dynamic communicator and Go-Between operating upon every element and every process of the material universe, the immanent and anonymous presence of God. . . . the true ground of all mission is this creative-redemptive action at the heart of everything. . . . The Bible is consistent from beginning to end in its understanding that God works always through the moments of recognition when mutual awareness is born. It is a history of encounters.'[36]

2. *The Spirit secretly guides God's work in the world*

History is like a huge play that is not enacted on the public stage alone. Irenaeus compared the Holy Spirit to a theatrical producer, directing the drama of salvation on the stage of history in such a way that the actors, men, know him and allow themselves to be seized by him and his work. This is the fundamental meaning of this text, the original Greek of which has survived:[37]

> Everything in him (the spiritual man) is consolidated: in relation to the one almighty God, 'from whom are all things' (1 Cor 8:6), an integral faith; in relation to the Son of God, Jesus Christ our Lord, 'through whom are all things', and to his 'economies', by which he was made man—he, the Son of God—a firm adherence; and in relation to the Spirit of God, who enables us to know the truth, who *produces the 'economies' of the Father and the Son, according to each generation*, with men in view, as in the Father's will.

The Spirit is able to reveal 'the economies of the Father' to each successive generation because he is Love and because he puts into all creatures a beginning of love and hope (see Rom 5:5). One of the leading concepts of Neoplatonic thought is that Love moves the world, and Aristotle put forward the idea of the Prime Mover who was himself unmoved, but who moved all things *hōs erōmenon*, 'as loved'.[38] Spiritual men have understood that idea deeply, but differently. The Persian mystic Rūmi (†1273) described the ascending movement of all things in the following way:

> Know that it is waves of Love that make the wheel of the heavens turn. Without Love, the world would not be animated.
>
> How can an inorganic thing be transformed into a plant? How can vegetable things sacrifice themselves so as to be endowed with spirit?

How could the spirit sacrifice itself for that Breath, an expiration of whom made Mary pregnant? . . .

Every atom is seized by that Perfection and hastens towards it. . . .

That haste says implicitly: 'Glory be to God'.[39]

A generation later, the European poet Dante ended his *Paradiso* with the following vision:

In the depths I saw everything that is scattered in the universe, united, bound by love into a single book. . . .
I believe that I saw the universal form of that unity, because while saying it, I feel my joy opening out more fully. . . .
My spirit, suspended, looked fixedly, unmoving and with great attention, becoming more and more enflamed by the ardour of contemplation.
That light so moves one that it is impossible ever to consent to turn away from it to a different view,
because the good, which is the object of desire, gathers everything into it, and what is perfect in it seems deficient outside it. . . .
Here, my strength was not enough for the sublime vision, but already, like a wheel moving steadily round, my desire and my will were directed by the Love that moves the sun and the other stars.[40]

After these incomparable verses, dare I quote those of a canticle sung in our assemblies and coming from the sons of St Bernard? I think I may, because the words are inspired by the Bible and they express the same sublime doctrine:

Sun of justice—
he makes the universe ripe
and in our desert his Spirit
is a source of living water!

3. *The Spirit combines in a Doxology everything that is for God in the world*

'Jesus said, "Woman, the hour is coming when neither on this mountain nor in Jerusalem will you worship the Father. . . . The hour is coming, and now is, when the true worshippers will worship the Father in spirit and truth, for such the Father seeks to worship him' (Jn 4:21, 23). We are called to be true worshippers (see below, section 4), but I felt the need to write, in my book *Le mystère du Temple*, a section on the 'dimensions of the spiritual temple . . . the breadth and the depth'.[41] God in fact has worshippers everywhere. The prophets proclaimed that the peoples would go up to Jerusalem to worship him.[42] Even in their case, it was less a geographical and a material question and much more a spiritual one. It was fundamentally a proclamation of an extension of man's knowledge of God. At Pentecost, however, Jerusalem, as it were, burst out on the whole world and God knew his own (see 2 Tim 2:15). 'Can a man hide himself in secret places so that I cannot see him? says the Lord. Do I not fill heaven and earth? says the Lord' (Jer 23:24). Are we not therefore entitled to join those who have heard and expressed the secret harmonies of creation and grace—the spiritual men and the poets?

> The Word of God
> has left the lyre and the cithara,
> instruments without a soul,
> to tune the whole world, gathered into man,
> in to himself through the Holy Spirit.
> He makes use of him
> as an instrument with many voices
> and, accompanying his song,
> he plays to God
> on that instrument that is man![43]

> 'Well, it says in the New Testament that man and all creation "*are subject to vanity, not willingly*" [Rom 8:19–22], and sigh with efforts and desire to enter into the liberty of the children of God. The mysterious sighing of creation, the innate aspiration of every soul towards God, that is exactly what interior prayer is. There is no need to learn it, it is innate in every one of us!'[44]

This is not simply a 'groaning'—it is also a hymn of praise. The Bible bears witness to this cosmic hymn of praise, which the elements and those living beings that have no consciousness sing, but which man interprets. There are many well-known scriptural and other Christian texts[45] and for this reason it is interesting to look at two which are not Christian, but which nonetheless point in a very profound way to this truth:

> Have you not seen that it is before God that everything bows down—everything in the heavens and everything on earth and the sun and the moon and the stars and the mountains and the trees and the animals? (*Quran*, XIII, 13).

> Have you not seen that God—everything in the heavens and on earth proclaims his praises and also the birds while stretching out their wings? Everyone knows his prayer and his praise and God knows what they are doing (*ibid.*, XXIV, 41).[46]

4. *The Church expresses the Doxology of the Universe*

It is possible to speak to a 'kenosis' of the Spirit, who acts without revealing himself except in the acts that he secretly inspires. For we may ask where the kingdom of God is now. Where is it realized? Walter Kasper has asked this question and suggests that, according to Jesus' own words, it is not possible to point to it and say: It is here or it is there. It is rather in the midst of us in an inexpressible way (see Lk 17:21). It is found everywhere where men trust in God and in his love, even if they do not explicitly speak of God or Jesus (see

Mt 25:35ff.). That is why, he concludes, the kingdom of God is a hidden reality of which it is only possible to speak in parables.[47]

God has, however, also revealed himself. He constituted a people who, under the new dispensation of the Word, the sacraments and the gift of the Spirit, were to be called the Church.[48] Within the great domain of everything that belongs to God and is for God in this world, the Church is the illuminated zone consisting of the people who know and confess him, and who form what Peter Berger and other sociologists have called a 'cognitive minority'. This is true, so long as this is not an attempt to define a reality that is above all a sacramental and doxological communion. Because it is such a reality, the Church not only experiences its own obedience in faith and its own praise, but also gathers into that praise 'all the prayers that are not even said'[49] and all the 'undeciphered' and 'unrevealed' comings of the Spirit[50] together with all those 'sacred points' which, unknown even to most souls, say *Pater noster* in themselves.[51]

The Church gathers all this together and offers it up. But it is hardly possible to say that it is extraneous to the Church. It already belongs to the Church—as Paul Evdimokov has insisted, 'we know where the Church is, but it is not for us to judge and to say where it is not'.[52] The Church is more than their ideal space. It is their real homeland and it is in a mysterious sense their mother. How I love Psalm 87, which sings of the City of God:

Among those who know me I mention Rahab and Babylon;
  behold, Philistia and Tyre, with Ethiopia—
  'This one was born there', they say.
And of Zion it shall be said,
  'This one and that one were born in her'.

The Church, who knows God and seeks his glory, wants to share that knowledge in order that God's glory may be increased. The many reasons leading to the Church's missionary activity and above all the intention to gather the whole human race into one people of God, one Body of Christ and one Temple of the Holy Spirit were all discussed at the Second Vatican Council and the conclusion was reached, in the document on the Church's mission, that 'the plan of the Creator, who formed man to his own image and likeness, will be realized at last when all who share one human nature, regenerated in Christ through the Holy Spirit and beholding together the glory of God (see 2 Cor 3:18), will be able to say "Our Father" '.[53]

This is clearly an eschatological perspective. Does the Church not ask God for itself: 'As this broken bread, once dispersed over the hills, was brought together and became one loaf, may your Church be brought together from the ends of the earth into your kingdom'?[54] Even now, however, we are gathering together all that, in the world, is for God. Or rather, we offer that sheaf that has been bound together invisibly by the Holy Spirit. All the Eucharistic Prayers end with this doxology:

Through him,
with him,
in him,
in the unity of the Holy Spirit,
all glory and honour is yours,
almighty Father,
for ever and ever. Amen.

And in French the priest may continue: 'Unis *dans le même Esprit*, nous pouvons dire avec confiance: Notre Père . . .', 'United *in the same Spirit*, we can say with confidence: Our Father . . .'.

Two specialists in the liturgy have suggested their own interpretations of the doxology. J. A. Jungmann believed that 'in the Holy Spirit' was the equivalent of Hippolytus' 'in the holy Church'.[55] Dom B. Botte, however, traced the history of this formula, which first appeared in 420, and has concluded that it is an essentially Trinitarian formula, expressing the unity of the divine Persons and their common glorification.[56] I do not intend to go into this debate here, but would simply say that, as a Christian and a priest, I say the words of this doxology every day with great intensity and I personally interpret it in this way: The Holy Spirit, who fills the universe and who holds all things in unity, knows everything that is said and gathers together everything that, in this world, is for and tending towards God (*pros ton Patera*). He ties the sheaf together in a hymn of cosmic praise through with and in Christ, in whom everything is firmly established (Col 1:15–20).

After this doxology, we believers, who know the Father and the one whom he has sent, together with Christ make once again present among us the invocation that he taught us and that the Spirit enables us to pray: 'Abba! Father! You are my Father!' In this way, the Eucharist, which is a great thanksgiving, is made fully present. That, at least, is my own daily Mass over the world.

God brings about for himself in the world sons—in a mysterious way and by the grace of his Spirit. The same grace of the same Spirit enables those sons to reply—often in a language without words, but he knows everything that is said: 'You are my Father! Glory to you!'

NOTES

1. K. Rahner, *The Trinity* (Eng. tr.; London and New York, 1970), p. 76, note 30: 'Hence within the Trinity there is no reciprocal "Thou". The Son is the Father's self-utterance which should not in its turn be conceived as "uttering".'
2. This is not everything that is to be said about the divine life within the Trinity; see the Note following this chapter for an insight into that life.
3. See above, pp. 104–105, and for what follows on Jesus' consciousness and knowledge, see Volume I, pp. 17–18.

4. It is hardly possible to understand Jesus without taking his prayer into consideration; see my *Jesus Christ* (Eng. tr.; New York and London, 1966), pp. 86–106.
5. Origen, *Comm. in Ioan*. I, 39, 204, (ed. E. Preuschen, *Orig. W.*, IV, p. 37), following a quotation of Ps 2:7, this is also quoted by Clement of Rome (*1 Cor* XXXVI, 4), Justin Martyr, Methodius and others.
6. See my book, *op. cit*. (note 4), p. 78, text and notes 17, 18. These formulae occur mainly in connection with the passion.
7. Augustine, *De Trin*. IV, 20, 29: 'Sicut natum esse est Filio a Patre esse, ita mitti est Filio cognosci quod ab illo sit'.
8. John combines an equivalent of the agony with an evocation of Jesus' glorification by the Father (12:27–28). For the parallel between the baptism scene and the transfiguration, see L. Legrand, 'L'arrière-plan néotestamentaire de Lc 1, 35', *RB*, 70 (1963), 162–192.
9. L. Chardon, *La Croix de Jésus* (Paris, 1937), p. 158.
10. J. Guillet said of this text: 'Committing one's spirit into God's hands does not mean, for the one praying in Ps 31, dying; on the contrary, as the following couplet shows, it means: "You will deliver me, O Lord, faithful God" and help me to find life and peace again': see his *Thèmes bibliques* (*Théologie*, 18) (Paris, 1951), p. 227.
11. One of the great patristic insights is that Christ does not go without Christians. This is, of course, a biblical theme: see especially the verbs with *sun-* in Paul's letters and the dynamism of the mystery of Christ in John. For the Fathers, see Cyprian, *Ep*. LX, 13 and LXVIII, 5 (ed. W. von Hartel, pp. 711, 754); Athanasius, *Contra Arian*. I, 50; II, 69–70; Gregory of Nyssa, *Contra Eunom*. II (*PG* 45, 533). See also T. J. van Bavel, *Recherches sur la Christologie de S. Augustin* (Fribourg, 1954), pp. 74–102; R. Bernard, 'La prédestination du Christ total', *Recherches Augustiniennes*, III (1965), pp. 1–58.
12. See Rom 8:28–30, 39; 2 Cor 5:19; Eph 4:32; Jn 17:23: 'thou hast loved them even as thou hast loved me', and 26: 'that the love with which thou hast loved me may be in them, and I in them'.
13. By adoption: Gal 4:5; Rom 8:15, 23; Eph 1:5. See also E. Schweizer, '*huiothesia*', *TDNT*, VIII, p. 399.
14. 'My Father and your Father': Jn 20:17. Augustine: 'Dicimur filii Dei, sed ille aliter Filius Dei'; *Enarr. in Ps*. 88, 7 (*PL* 37, 1124).
15. *Huios*: see the various concordances; *tekna*: Jn 1:12; 11:52; 1 Jn 3:1, 2; 5:2.
16. 1 Cor 1:9: *eis koinōnian tou huiou*; Gal 3:25–29; Athanasius, *Contra Arian*. II, 59: 'The Father is really only the Father of the Son and nothing created is really his Son. It is therefore clear that we do not in ourselves become sons, but the Son in us. . . . Therefore the Father, before those in whom he sees his Son, declares that they are his sons and says: I have begotten you and this verb "beget" refers to the Son, while the verb "make" refers to creatures' (*PG* 26,273; based on Fr. tr. by E. Mersch; Cyril of Alexandria, *De recta fide ad Theod*.: 'Christ is both the only Son and the first-born son. He is the only Son as God; he is the first-born son by the saving union that he has established between us and him when he became man. By this, we, in and through him, have been made sons of God, both by nature and by grace. We are sons by nature in him and only in him; we are sons by participation and grace through him in the Spirit' (*PG* 76, 1177; based on Fr. tr. by E. Mersch); Augustine, *De div. quaest*. LXXXIII, q. 69 (*PL* 40, 79); *In Ioan. ev*. XLI (*PL* 35, 1696); *In ep. ad Parth*. X (*PL* 35, 2055). See also E. Mersch, *Le Corps mystique du Christ*, 2nd ed. (Brussels and Paris, 1936), II, pp. 86ff.
17. Ignatius of Antioch, *Ad Rom*. VII, 2 (and 116) (ed. F. X. Funk, I, p. 260). Is this an echo of Jn 4:14? See also Athanasius, *Ad Ser*. I, 25: the Son, through his incarnation, 'ennobles the whole of creation in the Spirit by making it divine, by making it son, and he takes it to the Father' (*PG* 26, 589).
18. 'Idem numero Spiritus', Encyclical *Mystici Corporis, AAS* 35 (1943), 219. See also above, p. 23, note 19.

19. See M. E. Isaacs, *The Concept of Spirit. A Study of Pneuma in Hellenistic Judaism and its Bearing on the New Testament* (*Heythrop Monographs*) (London, 1976).
20. C. Larcher, *Etudes sur le Livre de la Sagesse (Etudes bibliques)* (Paris, 1969), p. 362, note 1.
21. See Irenaeus, *Adv. haer*. III, 18, 1 (*PG* 7, 932; *SC* 211/2, p. 342: 'semper aderat generi humano'); *Dem*. 34 (*SC* 62, p. 87: 'according to his invisible state, is poured out among us in the whole of this universe'); Clement of Alexandria, *Protrept*. 112, 1 (*GCS* Clem. I, p. 79); *Strom*. VI, 6, 44, 1 (II, p. 453); 13, 106, 3 and 4 (II, p. 485). See also W. Bierbaum, 'Geschichte als Paidogogia Theou: Die Heilsgeschichtslehre des Klemens', *Münchener Theologische Zeitschrift*, 5 (1954), 246–272. For the *Semina Verbi*, see also A. Luneau, *L'histoire du salut chez les Pères de l'Eglise. La doctrine des âges du monde* (Paris, 1964), pp. 89 (Justin Martyr), 113ff. (Clement). Later the Fathers were more critical: pp. 148–149 (Basil the Great), 157 (Gregory Nazianzen), 240 (Hilary of Poitiers), 281. The same teaching was taken up again by Pius XII in his encyclical *Evangelii praecones* of 2 April 1951, 58 and 62; broadcast message of 31 December 1952; address of 29 November 1957: *AAS*, 49 (1957), 906–922; and by John XXIII in his encyclical *Mater et Magistra*: *AAS*, 53 (1961), 444; see also the Dogmatic Constitution on the Church, *Lumen Gentium*, 16, and the Pastoral Constitution on the Church in the Modern World, *Gaudium et Spes*, 57, 4.
22. *Adv. haer*. III, 11, 8 (*SC* 211, pp. 168, 169); 17, 3 (pp. 330, 331).
23. *ibid*., III, 11, 9 (pp. 171, 172).
24. *ibid*., 17, 1 (pp. 330, 331).
25. See Isidore of Seville, *Sent*. I, 15, 4 (*PL* 83, 569); Beatus, *In Apoc*. I, ed. H. A. Sanders (Rome, 1930), p. 44; Walafrid Strabo, *De exordiis*, pr. (*PL* 144, 919; *MGH*, Cap. II, p. 475); Pope Zacharias, in 743 (Jaffé, 2270); Pope Zosimus, quoted by Prosper of Aquitaine, *Contra Collatorem*, 5 (*PL* 51, 228A); Peter Abelard, *Theologia* (*PL* 178, 1221C). A cosmic view of the part played by the Spirit was sometimes suggested—Abelard thought, for example, that the soul of the world to which the philosophers referred might point to the life-giving activity of the Spirit in the universe, at least *per involucrum* or 'by envelopment': see M.-T. d'Alverny, 'Abélard et l'astrologie', *Pierre Abélard. Pierre le Vénérable (Cluny 2–9 juillet 1972)* (Paris, 1975), pp. 611–628. This was why Abelard was accused, at the Council of Sens in 1140, of making the Holy Spirit into the 'soul of the world': see *DS* 722.
26. *PL* 17, 245. Z. Alszeghy, *Nova Creatura—La nozione della grazia nei commentari medievali di S. Paolo* (Rome, 1956). p. 196, refers to Hervetus of Bourg-Dieu (*PL* 181, 939ff.); Peter Lombard (*PL* 191, 1650); Peter the Chanter, John of La Rochelle and Peter of Tarantaise, *Dilucidatio* (Antwerp ed., (1617), 215a).
27. Thomas Aquinas, *Comm. in Tit*. c. 1, lect. 3, end; *Comm. in ev. Ioan*, c. 8, lect. 6.
28. *ST* Ia IIae, q. 109, a. 1, ad 1.
29. *Comm. in 2 Tim*. c. 3, lect. 3.
30. Albert the Great, *In I Sent*. 2, 5 (ed. A. Borgnet, XXV, 39); II, d. 25, c. 6 (Borgnet, XXVII, 433). For Albert, the Holy Spirit was *in omnibus*: see *De grat. Cap*., ed. I. Backes, *Florilegium Patristicum*, XL (Bonn, 1935), p. 20. In other words, no man is without some grace.
31. *Gaudium et Spes*, 41, 1 speaks of the Spirit's task in helping men in their religious need; in 38, 5, the document refers to the gifts of the Spirit leading men to salvation; and finally, in 26, 4 and 42, 4, every movement towards justice and unity in the world is attributed to the activity of the same Spirit.
32. G. Fedotov, 'De l'Esprit Saint dans la nature et dans la culture', *Contacts*, 28 (No. 95: 1976), 212–228.
33. Langdon Gilkey, 'L'Esprit et la découverte de la vérité dans le dialogue', *L'expérience de l'Esprit. Mélanges Schillebeeckx (Le Point théologique*, 18) (Paris, 1976), pp. 225–240, especially pp. 231–232.

34. In the Dedication of *The Internal Mission of the Holy Ghost* (London, 1875), Manning says: 'It is true to say with S. Irenaeus, *Ubi Ecclesia ibi Spiritus*,—Where the Church is there is the Spirit, but it would not be true to say, Where the Church is not, neither is the Spirit there. The operations of the Holy Ghost have always pervaded the whole race of men from the beginning and they are now in full activity even among those who are without the Church.'
35. Two contributors to *Concilium* have, for example, spoken about this: Y. Raguin, 'Evangelization and World Religious', *Concilium*, 114 (1978), 47–53; W. Dwyer, 'The Theologian in the Ashram', *ibid*., 115 (1978), 92–101, whose article deals with Kabīr, a mystical poet of the fifteenth century.
36. John V. Taylor, *The Go-Between God* (London, 1972), p. 64.
37. *Adv. haer*. IV, 33, 7ff. (*SC* 100, pp. 818 and 819, which contain the Fr. tr. on which the above rendering is based). I have followed the explanation of the expression: *tas oikonomias . . . skēnobatoun* given by H. J. Jaschke, *Der Heilige Geist im Bekenntnis der Kirche. Eine Studie zur Pneumatologie des Irenäus von Lyon im Ausgang vom altchristlichen Glaubensbekenntnis* (Münster, 1976), p. 51. The precise meaning of the verb translated as 'produces' is 'to produce on the stage'.
38. Aristotle, *Physics*, VIII.
39. Rūmi, *Mathnawi*, V, 39ff.: see Eva de Vitray Meyerovitch, *Mystique et Poésie en Islam. Djalâl-ud-Din Rûmi et l'Ordre des Derviches Tourneurs*, 2nd ed. (Paris, 1972), p. 184, note 5.
40. Dante, *The Divine Comedy: Paradise,* XXXIII.
41. Y. Congar, *The Mystery of the Temple, or the Manner of God's Presence to his Creatures from Genesis to the Apocalypse* (Eng. tr.; London, 1962), pp. 188ff.
42. See Is 2:2–3 (= Mic 4:1–3); 56:6–8; 60:11–14; Zech 8:20ff.; 14:16. See also *The Mystery of the Temple, op. cit.* (note 41), esp. pp. 77ff.
43. Clement of Alexandria (†c. 211–216), quoted by M.-D. Chenu, *Peuple de Dieu dans le monde* (Paris, 1966), p. 34.
44. *The Way of a Pilgrim* (Eng. tr.; paperback ed., London, 1972), p. 47. R. Laurentin's statement may perhaps be too optimistic, since the world always presents us with an ambiguous image: 'The Spirit changes the tragic, hopeless groaning of creation (Rom 8:19–23) into the ineffable groaning of hope (8:26). It is not the Spirit who groans but he brings to a new stage of awareness both man and his human environment in their anxious yearning for salvation': *Catholic Pentecostalism* (London, 1977), p. 158.
45. They can also be found in the liturgy; for example: 'Father, you are holy indeed, and all creation rightly gives you praise' (Eucharistic Prayer No. 3).
46. See also Eva de Vitray Meyerovitch, *op. cit.* (note 39), p. 192.
47. W. Kasper, *Jesus the Christ* (London and New York, 1976), p. 100.
48. See the Dogmatic Constitution on the Church, *Lumen Gentium*, 9.
49. Charles Péguy, *Le mystère des saints innocents* (NRF duodecimo ed., p. 51):
'I can see the fourth fleet. I see the invisible fleet.
And it is all the prayers that are not even said, the words that are not even pronounced,
But I can hear them. Those obscure movements of the heart, the obscure good movements, the secret good movements
Which rise unconsciously, are born and unconsciously ascend to me.
The one in whom they have their seat may not even be aware of them. He knows nothing—he is only their seat,
But I gather them up, says God, I count them and weigh them,
Because I am the secret judge.'
50. Maurice Clavel, *Ce que je crois* (Paris, 1975), p. 234: 'A young Christian whom I met, a member of the Charismatic Renewal who had been a ringleader in the riots of May 1968, told me, shrugging his shoulders: "May? A Pentecost without the Spirit at the most!" I replied, still faithful to my doctrine and thinking of the passage, which was also a doctrine:

"With an undeciphered Spirit, from whom they suffered". He said: "If you like, but in that case really unrevealed!".'

51. Paul Claudel, 'Cantique de Palmyre', *Conversations dans le Loir-et-Cher* (Paris, 1935), p. 731: 'There are many souls, but there is not one with whom I am not in communion by that sacred point in it which says *Pater noster*'.
52. P. Evdokimov, *L'Orthodoxie* (Paris, 1959), p. 343.
53. Conciliar Decree on the Church's Missionary Activity, *Ad Gentes divinitus*, 7, 3.
54. *Didache* IX, 4; see also X, 5: 'Gather it (the Church) from the four winds, sanctified, into your kingdom'.
55. J. A. Jungmann, 'In der Einheit des Heiligen Geistes', *Gewordene Liturgie* (Innsbruck, 1941), pp. 190–205; *Missarum Sollemnia* (Freiburg, 1948), II, p. 321; 4th ed., pp. 329–330 and *Nachtrag*, pp. 592–594; *The Mass of the Roman Rite* (abridged Eng. tr.; New York, 1959), pp. 457–458; 'In unitate Spiritus Sancti', *ZKT*, 72 (1950), 481–486.
56. B. Botte, *M-D*, 23 (1950), 49–53; *idem, L'Ordinaire de la Messe* (Paris, 1953), pp. 133–139. Certain additional references can be found in P. Smulders, *Dictionnaire de Spiritualité*, IV, col. 1275.

A NOTE ON 'YOU ARE MY FATHER' IN THE ETERNITY OF THE INTRA-DIVINE LIFE

It would be wrong to postulate a reciprocity between the divine Persons of the Trinity that might lead to our acknowledging a plurality of consciousnesses and might be tainted with tritheism. This wrong interpretation is sometimes suggested, at least in forms of expression, when psychological findings with regard to intersubjectivity are applied to God. But this does not close the discussion. For, without separating them and even without making a distinction between them, the New Testament, for example, speaks of Jesus the man and Saviour because of his death on the cross and of Jesus existing 'in the form of God'.[1] If Christ is present in this way in the eternity of the Trinity, he must also, in these conditions, be the image of 'God' (that is, of the Father) and return to him the reflection of his own similarity. The least that can be said is that it was part of the eternal plan of God that Jesus the man should be his image, that is, God revealed as man: Christ the 'lamb without blemish or spot' who was 'destined before the foundation of the world, but made manifest at the end of times for our sake' (1 Pet 1:19–20).

If, however, this was God's eternal plan, does it not imply that the Son, the perfect uncreated image of the Father, was conceived eternally by that Father as due to be the perfect created image of God in a created world? Does it not mean that the Son, the Word, was conceived and begotten eternally as *incarnandus* and *immolandus*, due to be made flesh and sacrificed? It is in *that* Son, the Word, that the adventure of the world can be understood and that 'all things hold together' (Col 1:17). If this is really the situation, is the perfect human response of Jesus Christ: 'You are my Father; I have come to do your will' not to some extent at least present in the eternally begotten Word?

Let us stay a little longer with the life of God within the Trinity. What is the part played by the Spirit in a possible reciprocity between the Father and the Son, the Word? In Volume III of this work, we shall see that certain Orthodox theologians, such as Paul Evdimokov, say that the Word was begotten *a Patre Spirituque*. The order of the processions which makes the Spirit the third Person (without making God three, since the Persons are consubstantial) makes it, I feel, impossible to speak as Evdimokov does. In the Augustinian view of the Spirit as the bond of love between Father and Son, which has had very little influence of Eastern theology, 'the Father directs a fatherly love towards the Son and takes delight in the one whom he begets as his equal, and he does so in the way that is appropriate, that is to say by spirating that love [the Spirit]. The Son also takes delight in the Father, but as a son, in being born of him.' This way of putting it runs the risk of slipping from an essential love that is common to all three Persons to a so-called 'notional' love that is characteristic of the third Person, the Spirit. The author who made the above statement, E. Bailleux, however, goes on to say: 'Whereas the Father desires [but is this by his essential will?] to be the principle of the Son, the reciprocal opposite cannot be true, nor is this necessary for a real reciprocity of love. It is by spirating the Spirit as a son that the Son turns towards his principle and takes delight in the Father, by wishing to be what he in fact is personally, the principle without principle and the unbegotten.'[2] It is therefore by this spiration of the Spirit—by the Father as the first and absolute source, that is, *principaliter*, and by the Son, the Word, depending on the Father—that a reciprocity of love between the first two Persons of the Trinity occurs, and that reciprocity is the Spirit, within the firm consubstantiality of the three Persons. This means that there is a reciprocity of love between the absolute principle, the Father (who loves the Son: see Jn 3:35; 5:20), and the one who proceeds from him by pure begetting, both in dependence as a son and in equality of being, let alone in reality of substance.

NOTES

1. Jesus Christ was 'in the form of God' (Phil 2:6); he plays a part in creation (1 Cor 8:6; Col 1:15); he is the image of God (2 Cor 4:6; Col 1:15; Heb 1:3); he is 'before Abraham' (Jn 8:58); he had the glory with the Father 'before the world was made' (17:5, 24). See P. Benoît, 'Préexistence et Incarnation', *RB*, 77 (1970), 5–29. According to some readings, the Lamb in Rev 13:8 was sacrificed 'before the foundation of the world', though the Jerusalem Bible and the French *Traduction Œcuménique* translate this verse differently [as does RSV].
2. See E. Bailleux, 'L'Esprit du Père et du Fils selon S. Augustin', *RThom*, 77 (1977), 5–29, especially 20.